Baroque Modernity

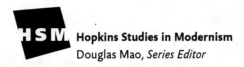

Baroque Modernity

An Aesthetics of Theater

Joseph Cermatori

Johns Hopkins University Press
Baltimore

This book has been brought to publication in part through the generous funding of the American Comparative Literature Association's Helen Tartar First Book Award.

© 2021 Johns Hopkins University Press
All rights reserved. Published 2021
Printed in the United States of America on acid-free paper
9 8 7 6 5 4 3 2 1

Johns Hopkins University Press
2715 North Charles Street
Baltimore, Maryland 21218-4363
www.press.jhu.edu

Library of Congress Cataloging-in-Publication Data is available.

ISBN-13: 978-1-4214-4152-8 (hardcover)
ISBN-13: 978-1-4214-4153-5 (paperback)
ISBN-13: 978-1-4214-4154-2 (electronic)

A catalog record for this book is available from the British Library.

Frontispiece: Opera house of the Margraves (1744), view from the stage. Bayreuth, Germany. Courtesy Erich Lessing/Art Resource, NY.

Special discounts are available for bulk purchases of this book. For more information, please contact Special Sales at specialsales@jh.edu.

In memory of my
grandmother Antonia,
who crossed oceans
and loved books

Boredom is a warm gray fabric lined on the inside with the most lustrous and colorful of silks. In this fabric we wrap ourselves when we dream. We are at home then in the arabesques of its lining. But the sleeper looks bored and gray within his sheath. And when he later wakes and wants to tell of what he dreamed, he communicates by and large only this boredom. For who would be able at one stroke to turn the lining of time to the outside? Yet to narrate dreams signifies nothing else.

—Walter Benjamin, *The Arcades Project* (D2a,1)

"On the day when I know all the emblems," he asked Marco, "shall I be able to possess my empire, at last?" And the Venetian answered, "Sire, do not believe it. On that day you will be an emblem among emblems."

—Italo Calvino, *Invisible Cities*

Contents

Illustrations xi
Preface xiii
Acknowledgments xvii
On "Baroque" xxii

Introduction: Envisioning an Orphic Modernism 1

1 **Overcoming Ascetic Style: Nietzsche and the
   Transvaluation of the Baroque** 27
   Against Classical Rhetoric and Drama 31
   Nietzschean and Wagnerian Theatricalities 41
   Resentful and Affirmative Baroques 50
   De Te Fabula Narratur 58

2 **The Matter of Spectacle: Mallarmé and the Futures
   of Theatrical Ostentation** 64
   The Drama of Silence 68
   Hérodiade, "A Horrible Birth" 75
   Becoming Ornamental 83
   The Theater of the Book 99

3 **Landscapes of Melancholy: Benjamin, Trauerspiel,
   and the Pathways of Tradition** 102
   "History Passes into the Setting"—Baroque
   Spatialization 106
   Baroque Allegory as Nonmimetic Theatricality 118

The Catastrophe in Permanence 130
"Enter, fleeing" 142

4   The Citability of Baroque Gesture: Unsettling Stein 146
"To Mount It Up"—Baroque Citationality on
   Stage 149
Allegorical Temporality 159
Functional Baroque Forms in Performance 165
Last Act./Which is a fact? 178

Epilogue: Glancing Back, Reaching Forward 182

Note on Translations 193
Notes 197
Bibliography 261
Index 289

Illustrations

Opera house of the Margraves (1744), view from the stage. Bayreuth, Germany. *frontispiece*

1. Richard Wagner conducting Ludwig van Beethoven's Ninth Symphony in the old Margrave's Opera House in Bayreuth, May 22, 1872 28

2. Gustave Moreau, *The Apparition*, 1874 88

3. Samuel Joshua Beckett, [Loie Fuller Dancing], ca. 1900 91

4. Franciscus Lang, gesture illustrations I-III from *Dissertatio de actione scenica* 117

5. Teatro Olimpico in Vicenza, designed by Andrea Palladio (1508-80) 131

6. *Four Saints in Three Acts* theatrical program book (1927) 150

7. Production photograph from *Four Saints in Three Acts'* premiere 154

8. Production photograph from *Four Saints in Three Acts'* premiere 177

9. Jack Smith, "Interns Become Baroque Apprentices," advertisement flyer 188

Preface

This book had its beginnings in a simple observation, namely, that many of the most prominent artists of the late twentieth century were creating work described, either by themselves or by others, as "baroque." This was true despite vast differences in their methods and sensibilities. My initial list began with a few entries, jotted each time I encountered this odd interpellation, and grew from there with what seemed like logarithmic speed.[1] On closer investigation, it became apparent that the first fifteen years of the twenty-first century had seen this pattern continue and perhaps even intensify. Instead of changing course from the direction charted by their predecessors, a younger cohort of advanced contemporary artists was making work under this same designation with what seemed like renewed vigor.[2] It was hard to discern whether there were substantive connections between these figures that could lend credibility to their grouping under the same aesthetic category. Was it something more than a Procrustean Bed or "family resemblance" that united them? Or was the word "baroque" operating simply as a placeholder, a name to be called upon whenever a critic or artist needed to articulate some sense of the new not easily assimilable to their immediate experience?

One explanation I encountered fairly quickly had to do with something named "postmodernism," which had been hailed by various parties as a species of the "neobaroque." For reasons that will become clear in the following pages, this solution did not strike me as fully persuasive. For one, it depended on a clean division between modern and postmodern, suggesting the former as given to austerity and classicism, and the latter as exuberant and ostentatious, with no possibility for any overlap. Surely that way of dividing things up was too easy. Numerous influential thinkers have shown that the historical and philosophical problems attributed to "postmodern-ism" were already contained and anticipated within the historical frame-works of early-twentieth-century modernism itself.[3] Likewise, an obvious concern in aesthetic theory with the subject of "baroque" dated back to the 1880s, when the word itself first gained currency as a term of art. A Google Ngram Viewer graph of the word's appearance in printed books over the past 150 years reveals it gaining gradually, then swiftly, in popularity over the 1910s and 1920s. I was uneager to traffic in large-scale conceptual mappings (from the Cartesians to the Kardashians, say), but it was difficult to deny the presence in recent cultural production of something like a ba-roque *orientation*, greater than a trend but rarely rising to the status of a self-identified movement. This orientation predated the rise of "postmod-ernism" in the 1960s and '70s by a long shot. Far from anomalous, it looked to be constitutive of some of the most pressing developments in art and theory between the 1870s and the 1930s. Gradually, those contempo-rary makers of performance and art began looking like part of a longer history.

The book that grew from these observations seeks to deal with two sets of questions.[4] First, given the modernist emphasis on novelty and the rejec-tion of tradition, why did conventions recognizable as "baroque" become increasingly significant around the turn of the twentieth century, when they could have faded into historical obsolescence? I suspected that our under-standing of modernism had grown too narrow and that certain historico-philosophical conditions underpinning modernism could help account for its anachronic convergences with the baroque past. My studies proceeded as a search for what those conditions were.

More broadly, I was restless with the ways in which we humanists con-ventionally frame our historical objects. We have often considered Western "modernity" as being initiated amid a spirit of revolt (e.g., "the Protestant Reformation") or in some halcyon time of classical rebirth ("the Renais-sance") or in some set of sociological conditions (the emergence of the bour-geois public sphere or of industrialization). And, recently, we have come to consider the initiatory period of modernity, more simply but less descrip-tively, as "early modern." But if, for the sake of argument, we regarded the modern world as having its origins in an aesthetic framework ("the ba-roque"), one that is, for many, still a largely exotic one at that, how might our historiographies look different? The thinkers I analyze here raised this

Preface

xv

question in their time, sometimes with delight, sometimes with a mixture of sympathy and revulsion, but always with concern for the precipitousness of their present moment.

Second, what is the theater's role in preserving the cultural memory of the past against its threatened destruction? In Europe during the heyday of Gian Lorenzo Bernini, the theater was viewed as the summit and glorification of all the arts. Since then, how has it participated in the modernization of what may still be regarded, however tendentiously, as the Western world? This second set of questions stemmed from my frequent travels between academic literary and performance studies, on one hand, and practical criticism and dramaturgy, on the other. Among the various arts, the stage has long been a suspicious medium, as Jonas Barish demonstrated in his 1981 study, *The Anti-theatrical Prejudice*. What is more, within certain modernist circles, theater has been held in distinctly low regard. With the rise of the bourgeois novel, film, and new media, it has become an almost endangered species among art practices, a fact that no doubt fuels the contempt with which it is often held. All the more remarkable, then, that many twentieth-century writers concerned themselves demonstrably with conceptualizing the baroque era, an age whose significance for Western playwriting, performance, and stage design is unparalleled. Why did baroque *theatricality* become urgent during the lifetimes of Nietzsche, Mallarmé, Benjamin, and Stein at a time when the stage was being rapidly eclipsed by newer media forms? What is it that connects these authors (and us) to the early modern past? Could it be that the theater—that machine par excellence of rehearsals, repetitions, doubles, revenants, ghosts, and hauntings—can shed unique light upon the "afterlives" of cultural forms?[5]

The wide-ranging twentieth-century movement known as modernism arose in response to a crisis of historical progress narratives and norms of representation in the arts and sciences alike. The theater has functioned across time to remediate the groundlessness resulting from violent breaks of this kind. For some, it has even formed a constant motor for the production of "ever *new* modernisms" in response to an experience of modernity as *terra infirma*.[6] Modernism's baroque is thus a matter of crisis and critique. As I write this preface, I am mindful that this book's development spanned the 2010s, a period whose tumult, written into the margins below, only continues to reverberate in the new decade. Today, when certain emancipatory visions based in the project of the European Enlightenment are coming under increasing pressure, it has seemed ever more important to return to basic terms and dialectical principles. In what follows, although I have mostly restricted my analyses to an early-twentieth-century context, I hope to have delineated an archaeology of the contemporary in the histories of literature, philosophy, and performance.

Chelsea, New York

Acknowledgments

My research for this book took place over many years, and while the book's status was "still unpublished" (*toujours inedité*, to borrow Mallarmé's phrase, which I once considered adapting into a subtitle), I amassed many debts of gratitude. My first thanks go to those professors who oversaw this book's early life as a PhD thesis: my supervisor, Julie Stone Peters, together with Judith Butler and Jean Howard. I cannot praise these advisors enough for their insights, dedication, and extraordinary generosity of mind. Were it not for their mentorship throughout the entire dissertation process, I could never have developed the argument that appears in the chapters that follow. Just as important, I must thank Douglas Mao, Catherine Goldstead, and the staff of Johns Hopkins University Press for their keen and professional stewardship of my work, along with the two anonymous reviewers whose enthusiasm cleared its path to publication.

This project received wonderful input during my graduate school years at Columbia University from scholars across a wide range of specializations, including Arnold Aronson, Katherine Biers, Lydia Goehr, and Bruce Robbins and, farther afield, from Richard Halpern at New York University. Tracy Davis and Martin Puchner sponsored my writing at crucial stages by inviting me to summer research institutes at Northwestern and Harvard, respectively. In those programs I had the good fortune to enter into dialogue with Kate Bredeson, Andrés Henao Castro, Ryan Anthony Hatch, Katherine Hollander, Lindsay Brandon Hunter, Kareem Khubchandani, and David Kornhaber, and I'm honored these fellow travelers have since become friends. In addition, Elinor Fuchs has been an intellectual guide for me at many decisive steps along my journey: she was the first to cultivate my love of "theory" and also the first to suggest that I read Walter Benjamin's *Origin of the German Trauerspiel*. Joseph Roach, my tutor in all things Orphic for many

xviii Acknowledgments

years, provided crucial feedback as my dissertation developed into a book. As editor of *PAJ*, Bonnie Marranca has supported, challenged, and nourished my thinking since I was an undergraduate. For all these dear ones and interlocutors, I am ever thankful.

The earliest idea for this project took root during my dramaturgy studies at Yale University with Hilton Als, Jonathan Kalb, Jim Leverett, Marc Robinson, Gordon Rogoff, Tom Sellar, and Catherine Sheehy. Even earlier, Paul Binnerts, Michael Cadden, Nancy Gabor, Hilde Harper, and Tamsen Wolff steered me to theater studies with great care and encouragement. Each has left an enduring stamp on my writing. Among my graduate school peers, I must especially thank, for their fierce intelligence and sustaining cheer, Minou Arjomand, Matthew Cornish, Amanda Culp, Nijah Cunningham, Julia Fawcett, Jason Fitzgerald, Miriam Felton-Dansky, Jacob Gallagher-Ross, Christopher Grobe, John Kuhn, John Muse, Noémie Ndiaye, Vasiliki Touhouliotis, and Seth Williams. In the larger profession, I am grateful for my friendships with Christian DuComb, Lindsay Goss, Kyle Meng, Emily Woodman Maynard, Patrick McKelvey, Ernie Mitchell, Elise Morrison, Nick Salvato, and Aaron Thomas, among many others. Exchanges with these colleagues challenged and enriched my work at every turn. Their wisdom and comradeship have been my good fortune over the years.

This book's fourth chapter originally appeared in an earlier version as an article in *Modern Drama* (58, no. 4 [2015]: 347-69) and I thank that journal's editors for permission to reuse it here. For the financial support that buoyed me throughout the writing and publication process, I gratefully acknowledge Yale University's Beinecke Rare Book and Manuscript Library, the US Department of Education's Jacob K. Javits Fellowship Foundation, the Marion Posner Fellowship Fund, the Skidmore College Faculty Development Grant program, and the American Comparative Literature Association's Helen Tartar Subvention fund.

For opening their doors to me and for their invaluable research assistance, I wish to recognize the staff librarians of Yale's Beinecke Library; the Akademie der Künste's Walter Benjamin and Bertolt Brecht Archives in Berlin; the Moravian Church Archives in Bethlehem, Pennsylvania; New York University's Fales Library; the Salzburg Festival; the Goethe-Schiller Archive in Weimar, Germany; and the Vienna Theatermuseum. Special thanks go to Howard Eiland for sending me his new translation of Benjamin's *Origin of the German Trauerspiel* while it was still in page proof so that I could consult the most up-to-date English version; to Janifer Stackhouse for her mag-

Acknowledgments

xix

nificent translations of Andreas Gryphius's plays; and to Tappan Wilder for making accessible Thornton Wilder's papers and for his consistent warm-heartedness.

The ideas presented here had early audiences at the American Society for Theater Research, the Association for Theater in Higher Education, and the American Comparative Literature Association. I extend my thanks to those conference organizations for providing me space to debut material and receive constructive criticism on it in nurturing environments. My thoughts on baroque performance aesthetics also took shape in and through my early teaching work, including in my courses "Theater and Performance Theory" and "Baroque Forms of Excitement" at The New School in New York City. I wish to thank Ivan Raykoff, Cecilia Rubino, Zisan Urgulu, and the students in those seminars for the superb intellectual opportunity that appointment presented me.

My English department colleagues at Skidmore College provided the context in which this book could reach fruition. I am privileged to work alongside them, and I especially thank Barbara Black, Susannah Mintz, and Mason Stokes for their guidance as department chairs, and Catherine Golden, Robert Boyers, and Peg Boyers for encouraging my writing in ways great and small. My heartfelt appreciation to Theresa Knickerbocker for her unflagging administrative support and good spirits over the years. Outside the department, many Skidmore colleagues have helped promote my development, especially Michael Arnush, John Cosgrove, John Michael DiResta, Lisa Jackson-Schebetta, Jason Ohlberg, and Joseph Underwood. My students at the college spurred my thinking the entire time I was finishing this book and never cease to amaze me. In particular, I need to thank my two stellar research assistants, Salvatore Juliano and Miriam Harrow, for all their help in this book's final phases of production.

Beyond academia, I am indebted to Andrew Ondrejczak, Zane Pihlstrom, and Tommy Russell for our ongoing friendships and many conversations on performance and art. Zachary Woolfe deserves thanks on these counts as well; he generously created opportunities for me to write about theater, music, art, and baroque style in more journalistic arenas. I reserve unique gratitude for Daisy Alter for her wise counsel over the entire period of this book's formation.

Dialogues with artists working in the field of baroque opera lie at the bedrock of this volume. Thank you to Anthony Roth Costanzo, Bejun Mehta, and R. B. Schlather for your friendship and our many plunges into the depths of baroque reflection together. Your brilliance and passion have been my inspiration.

My parents, Paul and Maria, and my siblings, Gina and Francis, have spurred me to excellence in all my endeavors since childhood. I am thankful for their love, patience, and good humor over the years.

Above all, my husband, Ryan, partnered this book throughout every stage of its evolution. I never could have started nor finished it without him. I have no words to describe how he animates all that I love and write. "And so they sat in silence, on a park bench . . ."

On "Baroque"

From the *Oxford English Dictionary*:
baroque, *adj. and n.*

Pronunciation: /bəˈrəʊk/
Etymology: French *baroque* adjective, Portuguese *barroco*, Spanish *barrueco*, rough or imperfect pearl; of uncertain origin. [. . .]
A. *adj.*
Irregularly shaped; whimsical, grotesque, odd. ('Originally a jeweller's term, soon much extended in sense.' Brachet.) Applied *spec.* to a florid style of architectural decoration which arose in Italy in the late Renaissance and became prevalent in Europe during the 18th century. Also *absol.* as *n.* and *transf.* in reference to other arts.

This term and *rococo* are not infrequently used without distinction for styles of ornament characterized by profusion, oddity of combinations, or abnormal features generally.

1765   H. Fuseli tr. J. J. Winckelmann *Refl. on Painting & Sculpt. Greeks* 122   This style in decorations got the epithet of *Barroque* taste, derived from a word signifying pearls and teeth of unequal size.

1846   *Athenaeum* 17 Jan. 58/2   Sometimes *baroque*, Mr. Browning is never ignoble: pushing versification to the extremity of all rational allowances, and sometimes beyond it, with a hardihood of rhythm and cadence little short of Hudibrastic. [. . .]

1867   W. D. Howells *Ital. Journeys* 77   The building . . . coldly classic or frantically baroque.

1877   *Baedeker's Central Italy & Rome* (ed. 5) p. lix   The authors of the degenerated Renaissance known as Baroque were really Vignola

xxii On "Baroque"

(1507-73) and Fontana's nephew Carlo Maderna (1556-1639). . . . An undoubted vigour in the disposition of detail, a feeling for vastness and pomp, together with an internal decoration which spared neither colour nor costly material to secure an effect of dazzling splendour: such are the distinguishing attributes of the Baroque style.

1882 A. Beresford-Hope *Brandreths* I. i. 3 Studded with baroque pearls.

1921 B. F. Fletcher *Hist. Archit.* (ed. 6) i. 546 In the fullness of time the Renaissance . . . passed into the Baroque, which at the beginning of the seventeenth century gave expression once again to the human side in architecture, for it was a spontaneous breaking away from orthodoxy in plan, design, and treatment.

1928 *Times Lit. Suppl.* 15 Mar. 188/2 French-Canadian art . . . is being recognized . . . as a baroque style which is other than the European baroques.

1938 W. S. Maugham *Summing Up* 28 The sonorous periods and the baroque massiveness of Jacobean language.

1938 *Mod. Lang. Notes* Oct. 547 The period of literature . . . described as 'baroque' ends about 1690, when German baroque architecture . . . is beginning to develop.

B. *n.*
Grotesque or whimsical ornamentation.

1879 S. Baring-Gould *Germany* II. 358 French baroque was too much under Palladian influence to be other than formal.

Baroque Modernity

Introduction

Envisioning an Orphic Modernism

> It may turn out, then, that going back can be a way to go
> forward.
>
> —Marshall Berman, *All That Is Solid Melts into Air*

Baroque is one of those consuming subjects of modernity for which it is difficult to develop only a casual interest. Within the broader framework of that subject, the repertoire of baroque theater exerts uniquely vertiginous powers of attraction. Sometime around 1935, for example, the American playwright and novelist Thornton Wilder became obsessed with it. The idea of the baroque had already intrigued him since the time of his earliest writings and would continue exercising a strong appeal to him throughout the rest of his life.[1] There appears in one of his journals from this period an undated essay or lecture entitled "The Barock, or how to recognize a miracle in the daily life," spanning more than twenty handwritten pages. It was never published in his lifetime and has been long forgotten by his critics and biographers, a remarkable omission since it appears in his notebook alongside the first drafted scene for his most famous play, *Our Town* (1938), sketched in July 1935.[2] Although the document's philological background is still murky, it was likely composed around the time Wilder was staging and performing in a production of Handel's opera *Xerxes* at the University of Chicago, in honor of the composer's 250th birthday.[3] For an author writing in the vein of modernism, Wilder's interest in baroque performance and art may strike readers today, at least initially, as fanciful or merely anachronistic. For many, being modern has meant emphasizing novelty and absolute originality, the need to "make it new," as Ezra Pound demanded in 1934. Wilder's interest in the baroque, then, might seem to some of his readers like the sign of a retrograde artistic temperament. Perhaps it is little surprise that this writing never appeared in print before his death.

The document's reappearance now casts Wilder's writing and modernity into an unfamiliar new light. As his essay ranges over Shakespeare, Calderón de la Barca, and seventeenth-century Catholic theater, Wilder claims that baroque style finds the miraculous within the realm of the mundane. He particularly praises the Jesuit theater's command of onstage special effects, writing learnedly on what was then, and is still today, a little-studied subject. "There were saints riding by on clouds; there were showers and floods; there were ascensions and there was hell-fire. It was a great theatre epoch, now lost to us, because the greatness did not rely on the text, but on the effect of the parts relating to the whole and the psychological appropriateness of the symbols seen as spectacle."[4] Decades before Roland Barthes defined theatricality as "theater-minus-text," Wilder realized that the artists of the baroque stage envisioned a theater beyond the primacy of dramatic litera-ture.[5] In the manuscript, this vision holds out an enduring allure. The heyday of the baroque theater ended with the suppression of the Jesuit orders in 1773, he asserts, but, "an energy from it survives floating on in the minds of men under various guises." In the works of Mozart, the German Romantics, and their Bavarian and Austrian successors can be found vestiges of the baroque capacity for glimpsing miracles within the daily life. As Wilder explains:

> The Austrian soul could not forgo the representation of the superhuman and when the veto was placed on the religious aspect [i.e., with the closure of the Society of Jesus in 1773], the need reappeared under another form: the extrava-ganza. Vienna knew a long theatre of wizards, fairies, talking animals, wishes and curses fulfilled. Religion wore the masque of magic. The best-known example of this is Mozart's *The Magic Flute*. . . . The Jesuit theatre lives on in the plays of Raimund, a very great dramatist. . . . (When the English-speaking world finally tires of looking at French literature, it will find great nourishing masterpieces waiting for it in Kleist and Raimund and Nestroy and Hölderlin; and entirely new facets of Goethe and Lessing.) It was no accident that Bayreuth was founded in the Bavarian hills: *Parsifal* is the last Jesuit play—there are both magicians and miraculous swans and there is the apotheosis of the Mass. And it is no accident that the Baroque genius of Max Reinhardt should come to its completion in the Baroque jewel that is Salzburg.

In these lines, Wilder advances something like a dialectical history of taste and modern secularism, organized around a consequential moment of sub-

Introduction 3

lation (*Aufhebung*): "the marvelous," it turns out, can never be fully eliminated from art, but can only ever be *partly canceled, partly preserved*, and *transformed at a higher level*. The rupture with the baroque past is also a repetition and a reinscription, which transmits the baroque theater as something more than a dead inheritance. Moving swiftly from Shakespeare and Calderón's era to modern impresarios like Richard Wagner and Max Reinhardt, Wilder claims baroque style instead as an ongoing cultural patrimony. "The Baroque," he suggests, continues to evolve in his own lifetime, ever traditional and yet ever new.[6]

Within this idiosyncratic history of the stage, Wilder uncovers an idea of theater wholly different from the one familiar to twentieth-century playgoers. "The sense of the marvelous finally left daily life and left its theatre," he observes with some mild derision. "Now we have Hedda Gabler burning Lövborg's book in the stove; we have three sisters longing to go to Moscow; we have Fröken Julie seducing her footman. In the first scenes of *St. Joan*, Bernard Shaw reveals so inept a sense of the supernatural that he exhibits Jeanne d'Arc as making hens lay eggs and changing the direction of the wind." So much for Ibsen, Chekhov, Strindberg, and Shaw, and for realistic drama as a modern movement. By the 1930s, modern realism and the "boxset stage" conventions of the bourgeois theater had become tiresome to Wilder: the baroque manuscript announces flatly, "[A] realistic novel or play is impossible to a great hand."[7] The manuscript does not entertain the possibility that realism itself, even when practiced by its most faithful adherents, might possess certain qualities of baroque style, or that there might be more and less baroque forms of realistic representation in the arts. Instead it casts realism and baroque as oppositional terms, making clear that Wilder desired a different genealogy of modernism in dramatic literature and performance than the one that culminated, triumphally, in the bourgeois theater of his lifetime. The baroque genealogy he traced through Jesuit Austria was a minor theater tradition, perhaps, but it was one with which he could claim special kinship. He saw in baroque style what today we might consider an "alternative modernity," one organized not around disenchantment and the austere representational economies of modern drama but, rather, around excessive expenditure and the truth and life of myth.[8]

For the theater historian, Wilder's example raises many questions. What does it mean that he felt drawn to baroque style in this way and identified his own modernism with it? Is there more to this identification than an embrace of what was already being called "magic realism" in the literary debates of those years, debates with which Wilder surely was familiar?[9] Rosalind Krauss has noted that members of the artistic vanguard have worn many "guises" over the decades: "revolutionary, dandy, anarchist, aesthete, technologist, mystic."[10] Wilder's example suggests that another such guise, and a privileged one as I will argue, was that of the baroque theatricalist. The avant-garde's claim of originality has always functioned as a "modernist myth," as Krauss has made clear, but a new vision of modernity can emerge when modernism's aesthetic origins are tracked to the early modern past. Perhaps above all, Wilder's manuscript might force us to ask: How could we reimagine modernism by expanding its typical chronological boundaries past the window of 1890-1945 to introduce a frame of longer duration, stretching back to the early seventeenth century?[11] And how would we understand baroque differently if we found its traces lingering in the early twentieth century?

This book's primary goal is to pursue that expansive tracework. It documents a fascination with baroque style among modernists connected to the theater and exhibits "the baroque" as a set of artistic and performative antecedents that constitutively persisted into the early twentieth century. For some readers, this will seem a counterintuitive project. Since the early 1910s, the discourse of modern style in the arts has espoused at key points the virtues of functionalism, futurism, minimalism, and purity of medium. The baroque theater that Wilder describes—lavish, anachronistic, decorative, and multimedial—runs afoul of all these modernist expectations. If baroque style names a kind of modernism, some critics might immediately retort, it could only be a failed or abject one, a "bad modernism" akin to those Douglas Mao and Rebecca Walkowitz have highlighted in recent years. (It would be, in other words, only a species of kitsch.[12]) Even the onstage life of modern drama would seem to bear the skeptics' hesitancy out. Superficially, a play like *Our Town* could not be more different from the rich spectacles of the early modern church and court theater. One need only compare the former's famously empty stage with Wilder's description of fully visualized "ascensions and hellfire" to recognize the dissimilarity. But Wilder was not interested in calling for a simple baroque revival of any kind. In his writings on the seventeenth-century theater, he described what is better called the baroque *survival*, the long persistence of early modern forms into the time and space of the 1930s.[13] Borrowing a distinction once proposed by the architect Frank Gehry, one sees that Wilder understood his work to

Introduction 5

be less *neo*baroque than "the *new* baroque," the latest iteration of an ever-renewing inheritance.[14]

This new baroque theater need not bear any obvious resemblance to the aims or outward appearances of the historical baroque theater at all, which flourished in Europe and its colonies during the century and a half between 1600 and 1750.[15] Wilder was not describing a historicist recycling of cultural materials, and he understood intuitively that his modernist baroque would require more than a simple pastiche of the ancien régime's stylistic paradigms. His notion of baroque suggests something like a *tradition* in T. S. Eliot's dialectical sense of that word.[16] Such a "tradition" comprises a complex of style given more to historical repurposement than to unchanging self-preservation. From Shakespeare's theater to Raimund's to Reinhardt's, baroque style seems only to "go viral," replicating, repeating, and transforming itself across vast expanses of time.

Strikingly, Wilder also asserts the metaphysical rudiments of baroque style by emphasizing the qualities of *difference* and *repetition* essential to Counter-Reformation liturgy. Describing "the life of the Catholic in a great Catholic age," he writes: "[T]he day opened with the miracle of Transubstantiation in the Mass. Now, when the universal society in which one lives believes that God in person becomes literally present in every one of the myriad churches of one's world, then one has introduced the supernatural into daily life and immediately a thousand consequences follow it." Divinity re-presents itself, punctually, every day at the hour of the Mass throughout all the Catholic churches of the baroque world in the fetish form of the consummated Eucharist. In light of this divine dissemination, extraordinary phenomena like miracles come to appear ordinary, diffuse, and repeatable.[17] This metaphysics of repetition produces the effect of the marvelous in the Jesuit theater and in baroque visual art, but also renders problematic any simple realism in Wilder's own playwriting. When, in the last act of *Our Town*, Emily Webb returns, Eurydice-like, to the shadowy realms of death after reliving her twelfth birthday, she is overwhelmed by the miracle that was her daily existence, asking "Do any human beings ever realize life while they live it?—every, every minute?"[18] Even if the stage of *Our Town* does not brim over with the special effects of live hellfire and heavenly ascensions, its third act is a baroque apotheosis, cloaked in the supposed "minimalism" of the empty stage. In this way, as it lays bare the "miracle in the daily life," *Our Town* enacts a modernist kind of baroque drama.

The chapters that compose this book provide an account of the historical, artistic, and philosophical circumstances that made Wilder's vision of baroque modernism possible in the 1930s. Together, these case studies reconstruct the epistemic preconditions under which twentieth-century ideas about performance could come to be regarded as elaborating aesthetic and epistemological concerns originally implicit in the theaters of early modern Europe. While each chapter adopts a different approach to this overarching question, each pursues the subject of the baroque as a discursive formation with a density all its own. Tracking the term's conceptual historiography from 1875 to 1935, I show how the very idea of baroque style gained traction and appeal for writers in both the theater and aesthetic theory of this period, contemporaneously and with varying degrees of consciousness on those writers' part. The cultural legacy of the early modern theater, I argue, exerted a powerful shaping force over artists writing for the modernist stage. In turn, their artistic work proved formative for philosophical debates surrounding the subject of baroque style during this same period. That is, philosophers and theater artists effectively joined together, despite their vaunted hostility toward each other, to construct an idea of the baroque in modernist art and aesthetic theory. This orientation, like Walter Benjamin's Angel of History, dared to look backward while also being pressed forward precariously at the same time. The figure of Orpheus, the founding myth of the earliest baroque operas, can be said to preside over this fabulous double movement. From within an Orphic two-step, the modernist preoccupation with the baroque forms a movement of restoration *and* originality. For, as Reginald Shepherd once wrote, describing his poetry in terms of an aesthetics of partial redemption, "the word *original* . . . means both 'of the first instance' and 'of the origin, of the source.' To be original is at once to do what has not previously been done, to produce something which did not exist before, and to draw on the beginnings of one's practice, to move forward by casting back."[19] Through this dialectical shuttling between an unprecedented future and an unacknowledged past, these baroque modernists went in pursuit of the new, while finding in their early modern predecessors a set of stylistic and philosophical antecedents.

Modernism arose during this period in response to an increasingly turbulent experience of historical life, the feeling of modernity as "a maelstrom," to use Marshall Berman's eloquent metaphor.[20] Amid a moment of rapid scientific and artistic innovation, a network of experimental "little theaters" sprang up across the Global North where European and North

Introduction 7

American dramatic modernism had its earliest flowering. It is not coincidental that a new way to recognize the artistic output of early modern Europe
became possible during this period as well. This baroque turn in modernism
functioned at its historical outset as a deferred, collective recognition of the
earlier traumas of European modernity, and a moment when the modernisms of the dawning twentieth century answered to what Berman calls "the
modernisms of the past," those of the dawning seventeenth.[21]

As the art historian and theorist Stephen Melville has written, "[I]f 'the
modern' is an event, that event is primarily grammatical and not—not easily
—chronological. 'Modernism' seems almost to invade history, transforming
that field in such a way that every point within it is able to bear the weight
both of radical rupture with the past and of resolution of continuity with
it."[22] Melville's insight accords with Charles Baudelaire's famous aphorism in
The Painter of Modern Life: "[F]or any 'modernity' to be worthy of one day
taking its place as 'antiquity,' it is necessary for the mysterious beauty which
human life accidentally puts into it to be distilled from it."[23] These authors
understand modernism/modernity in a critically expanded sense, as persistent historical configurations that recur in ever-original circumstances. At
any historical juncture, modernism is always a Janus-faced phenomenon,
something named into being. The point, for Baudelaire, is not that modernity and antiquity are interchangeable, but that even the ancient world
knew its own processes and experiences of modernization. This view was
not unfamiliar to Wilder, who knew how to see the ruined past and the
modern present together, in an almost stereoscopic focus.[24] This doubleness of perspective amounts to an allegorical way of seeing in which the
visible reality of the historical present obscures a hidden and residual past.
Through this way of seeing, baroque theater became for Wilder and his
contemporaries an archaeology of the modern.[25]

Deferred recognition, for all its belatedness, brings with it the advanta-
geous power of *naming*. As early as 1946, René Wellek was able to demonstrate that the word "baroque" was not in use as a term of art during the
period it now typically describes, from 1600 through 1750. The term
emerged only later, during the mid-eighteenth century, as a colloquial label
of abuse synonymous with "bizarre" or "extravagant."[26] At its most colloquial, the term can be said to nominate anything that seems irregular in the
extreme, against the grain or the norm. With the publication of such works
as A. W. Ambros's *History of Music* (1878), Heinrich Wölfflin's *Renaissance
and Baroque* (1888) and *Principles of Art History* (1915), Alois Riegl's *Origin of*

Baroque Art in Rome (1908), and Morris Croll's "Baroque Style in Prose" (1929), the term acquired the meaning it retains today, designating a unified and pervasive style for what could otherwise be called the long seventeenth century. (This transformation can be seen as part of a more widespread movement toward historical periodization in academic studies of literary and artistic culture, with roots in the 1840s.[27]) Even prior to Wölfflin's *Renaissance and Baroque*, and well through the time of Wellek's writings in 1946, this term was regularly conscripted as one half of the binary opposition "baroque/classical." In light of what queer theorist Eve Sedgwick once described as the "epistemology of the closet" in the late nineteenth century, this "baroque-classical" dyad—so congruent to the "homo-hetero" binary that emerged contemporaneously alongside it—appears as one of the master terms for the twentieth century.[28]

I will return to the question of queer epistemologies momentarily. For now, it suffices to say that "baroque" has only continued to provoke methodological uncertainty to this day. The term is especially contested in the Anglophone field of English literary studies, where "Renaissance" continues to enjoy prominence, however tenuously, as a catchall name for early modern cultural production.[29] In France, disputes over the word's usage even prompted Gilles Deleuze to remark in 1988 that, while "the best commentators [on the subject of the baroque] have had their doubts about the consistency of the notion, and have been bewildered by the arbitrary extension that, despite themselves, the notion risked taking . . . it is nonetheless strange to deny the existence of the Baroque in the way we speak of unicorns or herds of pink elephants."[30] In his view, elaborating on Leibniz's *Monadology* (1714), the baroque forms a philosophical concept or invention that designates an infinite (meta)physical operation, namely, the endless production of folds within and between the domains of matter and soul.[31] Accordingly, there is no baroque essence as such, only a continual perturbation in the order of essences. In this regard, to speak of "the baroque" is inevitably to employ a rhetorical catachresis or philosophical misnomer.[32] The phrase "the baroque" denotes no existing being, thing, or form; still less is "the baroque" a coherent *Zeitgeist* or *Weltanschauung*. What is called "the baroque" is performed into being only through repeated speech acts that attempt to pinpoint this perturbing movement (or "operation") through historiographic language. As Deleuze writes: "Irregular pearls exist, but the Baroque has no reason for existing without a concept that forms this very reason. It is easy to call the Baroque inexistent; it suffices not to propose its concept."[33]

Introduction 9

While it has become necessary to put the term itself under erasure in this way, or (at another level) to question its status as a conceptual abstraction or reification in its own right, "baroque" still functions as a useful descriptor for European cultural production "from the last decades of the sixteenth century to the middle of the eighteenth century," as Wellek claimed.[34] In the theater specifically, this era is defined by an assemblage of formal and institutional factors that together consolidated the stage as a distinct medium unto itself for the first time in modern European history. These include, primarily, the migration of the theater space indoors and the emergence of illusionistic scenery (as in Vicenza's Teatro Olimpico, ca. 1585), along with the invention and decoration of the proscenium arch (as in Parma's Teatro Farnese, ca. 1618). In an era defined largely by courtly and ecclesiastical patronage, this indoor, framed stage was increasingly sought as a tool and ornament of monarchical power. At its outset, the baroque coincides with these developments in the theater as a new means for the administration of spatiality, interiority, and spectacle. The Renaissance stage had been defined by the recovery of ancient literary works, primarily Seneca's tragedies, furthering a notion of the theater as a primarily logocentric, textual art. By contrast, the baroque period corresponds with the emergence of the theater as a medium grounded even more resolutely in architectural, visual, performative, and mechanical support systems. It thus coincides with that moment when—to adapt the terms that Lessing would later develop in his *Laocoön*—the modern theater became not just an art of time, as is dramatic poetry, but *also* an art of space.

Yet even while early modern stages were becoming increasingly contained within the discrete, architectonic boundary of the proscenium arch, experiments were already under way to subvert that boundary's stability, combining other media or reflecting the stage back upon itself in order to augment the theater's rhetorical power. These transformations date to the rise of French court ballet in the 1580s, the first experiments in Italian opera around 1590, and the circulation of manuals for perspective scenery, special effects, and gestural acting in the early *seicento*.[35] The rise of a modern practice of "metatheater" has been traced to this period as well, in England, for example, with the theatricalist plays of Kyd and Shakespeare.[36] With all these transitions, the physical theater became a domain in which architecture, music, dance, painting, sculpture, light, clothing, engineering technology ("special effects" machines), and the self-reflexive capacities of the stage itself could be combined into the service of an overarching rhetorical effect. Characteristically, these effects aimed at violating or collapsing the visual boundaries of the proscenium frame with an overwhelming appeal to the embodied pathos of the spectator. The baroque thus names not just an emergent era of technical mediation in early modern Europe but a new affective regime, a novel way of using the stage as a multimedia experimentation site for engaging the spectator's passions. The theatrical *as such*—and here I mean the term to designate that emphatic tendency to hail or address the spectator directly in this way—amounts to a necessary and constitutive condition for baroque style, its sine qua non. Friedrich Nietzsche was the first to have recognized the necessary importance of theater for the stylistic operations of the baroque, as I argue in chapter 1. And Thornton Wilder, in his description of "saints riding by on clouds," was far from the last.[37]

The baroque will to theatricalize has been most visible in the work of Gian Lorenzo Bernini, the famed sculptor and architect who is less widely known as the primary theater impresario and playwright for the Roman Barberini court. (For many commentators, Bernini's name has become virtually synecdochic for baroque art in general.[38]) After visiting Rome in 1644, the English diarist John Evelyn reports he attended a "public opera" in which Bernini "painted the Scenes, cut the Statues, invented the Engines, composed the Musique, writ the Comedy, and built the Theater all himself."[39] If Evelyn is not exaggerating his report, the total control of the stage mechanism he attributes to Bernini was unprecedented at the time and unsurpassed until the construction of Richard Wagner's festival theater at Bayreuth in 1876. Where "the marvelous" is concerned, the 1630s and 1640s supplied Bernini with opportunities to perfect several breathtaking *coups de théâtre* via machinic means. His own Orphic stagecraft looked back to a world of sacred myth and forward to contemporary engineering all at once, caught in the double bind that Horst Bredekamp has described, in an evocative phrase, as "the lure of antiquity and the cult of the machine."[40] Bernini's fame rested on his ability to unite these divergent elements, interweaving the most advanced artistic techniques and scientific learning of his time into an impressive synthesis. And, where the baroque criterion of *meraviglia* (marvel, wonder, shock, astonishment) is concerned, Bernini's abilities in the theater are evident from several eyewitness accounts that survive from this period.[41] As the historian Pamela Smith has recorded:

In the *Inundation of the Tiber* performed in 1638, Bernini set boats out to sail on a flooded stage. Suddenly, the retainers holding back the water collapsed under

Introduction   11

the pressure and the water flooded toward the audience. The audience panicking and rising to flee before the onrushing waters were amazed to see barriers go up and the water drain before their eyes. All the audience had experienced the flood, but not a single onlooker had got wet. Not long after this spectacle of deception, Bernini staged *The Fair* in which a torch bearer apparently accidentally lit the scenery ablaze, but before the audience could quite trample each other to the doors, a rain storm began on stage and extinguished the flames.[42]

In the art of producing stupefaction, Bernini knew no equal. His example is indicative of the specific powers with which the baroque period endowed its notion of the theater. With each of these descriptions, the spectacle refuses to stay safely on the stage or behind the proscenium frame as a delimited object of viewing and knowing. Abhorring a vacuum, it instead invades and pervades the space of the auditorium. As the renowned Bernini scholar Irving Lavin observed, the technologies Bernini utilized were not new or uniquely his own, but he made use of them in unprecedented and astounding ways. "When Francesco Guitti flooded the Farnese theater, it was for a marine performance in the middle of the arena; when Bernini did his trick, the water was on stage and threatened to spill out over the spectators. . . . Bernini's fire was not presented as part of the play in a scene of hell; in a feigned accident with the torch held by the actor, it threatened to burn down the theater itself."[43] What Bernini described as "inundation," *l'inondazione*, today would be considered a new experience of *immersiveness*. With spectacles such as these, he effectively overwhelmed the spectator into a fully theatricalized relation. His aim was to generate a situation of sensual excitement and phenomenological derangement in which what is real and what is artifice, referent and sign, become dizzyingly interchangeable. Shakespeare and Calderón had already given expression to the baroque feeling that "all the world's a stage" and that "life is a dream," but Bernini sought to manufacture this feeling of derealization as a spatial experience within the actual theater itself.

Given his proximity to papal authority, some readers might assume Bernini's theater was wholeheartedly in the service of what Stephen Orgel once described as "the illusion of power." A closer look at the surviving records of Bernini's involvement with the stage, however, reveals a different picture. Beyond the lavish spectacles at court, he also staged smaller plays at his home and professional workshop, sometimes casting himself in leading roles.[44] One such play, his only surviving drama, is an unnamed *commedia erudita*, not rediscovered until 1963. Its protagonist is a stage designer in the mold of Bernini himself, one Graziano, whom Bernini likely played in performance, who has been commanded to produce a comedy for the prince. For the occasion, Graziano intends to compose a drama about an impresario like himself, opening up a metatheatrical game of mirrors. The play's second act takes place in Graziano's workshop, likely set in Bernini's own workroom (in what today would be deemed a "site-specific" maneuver), with Bernini's famed stage machines lying about idly before the audience's gaze. From among these inoperative devices, there appears a clownish servant, or *zanni*, who cracks jokes to the audience. As a schemer who plots comic subterfuges as skillfully as the impresario plots entrancing stage effects, he amounts in the play to Graziano's double and foil, contributing an additional level of metatheatrical instability to the drama.

Although a minor role in the overall scheme of Bernini's play, the clown is endowed with a significant gestic function, one that will helpfully complicate the scenes from Bernini's theater I have exhibited thus far. As the *zanni* imagines the illusion Bernini's machines will create onstage, he remarks ironically to the audience: "I can already see a sky full of beautiful clouds. *When a thing looks truly natural, there's got to be some craft behind it.*" ("Dov'è naturalezza è artifizio"; literally: "where there is naturalness, there is artifice.")[45] For the Orphic historian, this comment—which finds the extraordinary within the mundane in a sense other than Wilder intended—can be read in two directions at once. Looking back to the seventeenth-century context of its inscription, it forms a *buffo*, *aparté*, or parabasis that ruptures the mimetic fiction of the play, a moment of direct address with the onlooker. (The stage rhetoric of the baroque emphatically does not require an *illusionistic* appeal to the spectator.) But looking forward to Wilder's era, it can be said that Bernini offers a foretaste of the dawning hermeneutics of suspicion that would come to characterize European modernity over the nineteenth century and into the twentieth. If *The Inundation of the Tiber* and *The Fair* left Bernini's audiences astonished, carried away by the excitement of the illusion and unable to think clearly, in Graziano's metacomedy, readers and viewers are wonderstruck in another way. They are invited to lift the veil of illusion the theater can cast and to glimpse the undisguised means of spectacle production. In this moment, Bernini demonstrates a distanced form of viewing that twentieth-century formalists would later call *ostranenie* or defamiliarization, reading history into whatever seems apparently natural. Although it is an anti-illusionistic gesture, it cannot be simply de-

Introduction 13

scribed as an anti-theatrical one, since Bernini here uses the very mechanisms of the theater itself to make his point, and so augments the glory of the medium even as he undercuts it. (Still, "When a thing looks truly natural, there's got to be some craft behind it" could be deemed a kind of baroque slogan for the protocols of paranoid reading that today still govern much of the work of critique.) With Bernini, it is clear that baroque theatricality demanded not only the creation of overpowering scenes of emotional excitement but also opportunities for crucial, critical detachment.

This idea of theatricality—as being forced to recognize the truth of illusion, of spatially involving or distancing the spectator, of violating or proliferating frames—is not only a key aesthetic aspect of the baroque.[46] It has become a central concept in the discourse of modernism thanks to the critical writings of Michael Fried. In "Art and Objecthood" (1967), Fried criticized the minimalist sculptures of Donald Judd and Robert Morris as "theatrical" for appearing to address their beholders as an onstage actor might address a spectator in an auditorium. Fried perceived that the minimalist (or, as he called it dismissively, *literalist*) sensibility in sculpture approached the condition of theater by becoming too conspicuously concerned with the circumstances of the object's beholding. Praising modern artworks whose interest resided autonomously within the work itself, he disdained those that demanded to be experienced as "an object in a situation—one that, virtually by definition, *includes the beholder*" (emphasis in original).[47] Art of this kind effectively determines and activates the entire spatiotemporal environment of its beholding, making the viewer aware (uncomfortably, he thought) of their presence as an embodied audience.

In this context, Bernini's manipulations of the proscenium arch take on new meaning. His eagerness for the theater to spill into, burn down, or take over the space of the auditorium thus appears as a forerunner to Judd and Morris's advancements in the sculptural field. In Fried's account, "[B]y the 1630s, theatricality of an obvious sort did become a conspicuous strain in what we have come to call baroque art—not only in painting but also, more importantly, in sculpture and architecture, beginning in the early seventeenth century (the great exemplar is of course Gian Lorenzo Bernini)."[48] Fried here notably says nothing of Bernini's theater works. Only with Diderot's art criticism of the 1750s would a new emphasis on "absorption" arise as an antithesis to "the theatrical," the former term now designating the artwork's ability to refuse any apparent "consciousness of being beheld."[49] From those decisive debates forward, in Fried's account, modern French painting has had repeatedly to invent new solutions for the problem of the beholder's presence. The continual project of modern art, in this view, is how best to maintain art's own autonomy from the viewer, along with the "supreme fiction" that the beholder does not exist before the artwork being beheld.[50]

Taken altogether, Fried's writings compose an entire narrative of modernity from the 1590s to the 1960s in which dissident forms of theatricality that emerged for the first time within the historical baroque period needed repeatedly to be overcome or suppressed. But the theater is ineradicable, every bit as much as the "primordial convention" that paintings are meant to be viewed. Even so, where modernism is concerned, Fried's arguments have defined an era of critical judgment in the visual arts in opposition to theater as a very medium. At his most polemical moments in "Art and Objecthood," it comes to function as the antithesis both to modernism and to art *tout court*: "Theatre and theatricality are at war today, not simply with modernist painting (or modernist painting and sculpture), but with art as such—and to the extent that the different arts can be described as modernist, with modernist sensibility as such."[51] Fried's Greenbergian definition of modernity—as the project of each art medium seeking out its own specificity to the exclusion of all other disciplines—allots no proper place to an inherently multidisciplinary art such as the theater. The theater is, in this view, not only premodern in the sense of being obsolete, but perhaps even primordial in the sense of being *archaic*.

In theater studies, Fried's view has been adopted most emphatically by Martin Puchner, who has argued that anxieties about the theater itself form a constitutive basis of modernism in general and modern drama more specifically. In Puchner's view, early-twentieth-century modernism required "an irreversible dissociation of the value of theatricality from the realities of the actual theater," so that the theatrical, as such, could emerge as the negation to modernism in the arts.[52] While anti-theatricalism has a long and generative history in European thought dating back to Platonic Athens, and while Puchner makes clear that anti-theatricality is not a simple enemy to the actual theater but a necessary part of its functioning dynamics, what appears in Thornton Wilder's notes on the baroque is, instead, a modernist *pro*-theatricalism—both furtive and fervent at once. Michael Fried's view of modernism as essentially opposed to theater cannot fully account for a modernist like Wilder's fascination with the spectacular ingenuity of the baroque stage, or for Wilder's suggestion that the baroque might furnish a

Introduction 15

countergenealogy for the twentieth-century theater.[53] Rather, these must be taken as a sign that something more complicated is afoot than a negation of the theater as such. Wilder's example indicates—as Phoebe von Held has more recently shown, in a convincing rereading of Puchner's argument—that theatricality "needs to be considered as a lead concept rather than as an aesthetic failure or antidote to modernism."[54]

The great usefulness of Fried's argument to theater studies is its revelation that a certain anxiety about theater coincides with the entire duration of Western modernity since the time of its onset in the seventeenth-century European baroque. With Bernini's gifts for manufacturing wonder in view, it is clear that the theater effectively mediated a newfound sense of groundlessness in the domain of early modern thought. If "the baroque" names anything, it is a period-historical complex of style, original to Bernini's lifetime, that registers the loss of stable foundations with which audiences could orient themselves in respect to their lived experience of historical reality. In Europe, it arises from within the wake of the Counter-Reformation, that crisis moment when the hegemony of the medieval Catholic Church was called into question, asserted programmatically through the ecclesiastical arts, disputed in a series of continental wars, and finally delegitimated. The emergence of baroque forms in early modern Europe (the undulating line in architecture and sculpture, for example) attests to this crisis in belief, during which the traditional supports for thinking were shaken to their core.[55] In such a moment of radical disenchantment—the famous *desengaño* of Spanish Golden Age literature—the most fundamental philosophical questions are thrown again into radical doubt, such as whether or not it is possible to know anything, whether other minds or an ultimate domain of truth exists, and whether and how words mean anything. Bernini's cult of the theater amounts to just one expression of the same cultural disorientation that produced the widespread philosophical skepticism and anti-foundationalism of the European sixteenth and seventeenth centuries.[56] When the familiar grounds of truth are seen to decay in this context, what remains behind is rhetoric and persuasion, that which produces the *feeling* of truth. (Nietzsche will say the *pathos* of truth.) In such a moment, the theater as a veritable machine for the manipulation of affects achieves a new and unprecedented power.

For this reason, it is also suggestive that, early on, the word "baroque" described not just an asymmetrical pearl, its standard definition among Iberian jewelers, but also a form of philosophical argument thought to be sophistical and elaborate.[57] This relationship of philosophical Sophism to baroque style runs deep, flowing through Nietzsche's concerns with the baroque arts, a subject to be discussed in chapter 1. For the Sophist, fully truthful forms of knowledge are impossible once all perspectives upon truth are seen as relative, and particularly so with respect to one's cultural and linguistic positions (as the anonymous author of the Sophistic treatise *Dissoi Logoi* argued). This relativistic view requires the Sophist, with keen awareness of the kairotic needs of the situation, to use the arts of seduction in persuading his audience of the rightfulness of his view. The Sophist is concerned not with what is truthful but with what is *convincing* and with the accrual of power (as anyone attuned to the abuses of public speech and media in recent years is well aware). Bernini's age saw the arts pressed increasingly into the service of repressive state institutions: the absolute monarchy, the Counter-Reformation church, and the settler-colonial state as it engaged in primitive accumulation. As these institutions' claims to legitimacy grew increasingly ideological, there arose within them a corresponding need for increasingly sophisticated rhetorical effects in art like the ones that had made Bernini's name. The baroque as an apparatus of tyranny and propaganda thus amounts to one widely held view of baroque style.[58]

A turn toward Sophistic rhetoric is the outer sign of an inner crisis in epistemological confidence. The widely observed excessiveness of baroque style is born from *an essential emptiness*. Its invasive spatial morphology, its surplus of sensuous matter, its accretion of physical signs, the extremity of its appeal to the viewer as an embodied and affective beholder—all these betray what Guy Debord once called a "gilded poverty."[59] Although the baroque has sometimes been thought of as a conservative or reactionary movement within the arts, its anarchic energies pursue rhythms all their own. Like the empty Presidential theater box at the end of Kafka's *Der Verschollene*, which reminds Karl Roßmann of nothing less than a proscenium archway, the baroque is an ornamental framework of fractalesque flourishes, opening onto a shimmering void. Baroque style involves a movement that careens between disproportionate or absurd extremes—between fullness and emptiness, presence and absence—as if along a Möbius strip. "Baroque," then, amounts to something more troubling than a simple historical style. It goes beyond sheer ornamentalism to discover what Bolívar Echeverría has suggestively called a kind of "absolute theatricality."[60] Here, it is worth restating Echeverría's adaptation of Theodor Adorno's definition of baroque: "To point out that the baroque is decorative does not say every-

Introduction 17

thing about it. It is *messinscena assoluta* [absolute staging], as if it had emancipated itself from every theatrical purpose (that of imitating the world) and created an autonomous world. It ceases to set anything on stage (as an imitation of the world); on the contrary, it is nothing but staging."[61]

In recent years, an abundant critical literature has arisen around an awareness of this troubling fact.[62] As the philosopher and literary critic William Egginton has argued, "[T]he Baroque must be understood as the aesthetic counterpart to a problem of thought that is coterminous with that time in the West we have learned to call modernity, stretching from the sixteenth century to the present. . . . [one] that affects or unsettles an entire culture in the largest possible sense."[63] In Egginton's argument, "baroque" corresponds to the problem that "truth can only ever be an effect of the appearances from which we seek to free it," and that the gap or difference between "appearances and the world as it is" is ultimately irreducible.[64] The invention of the proscenium as a clear and distinct framing device, used to differentiate between subjects and objects of vision, would appear as just one of many early attempts to remedy that irresoluble gap. It is a problem that Egginton, like Fried, names as theatrical, in so far as it reveals the absence of any stable ground on which an unassailable and transcendent knowledge could be built.[65] When modernists like Wilder expressed dawning interest in baroque drama and performance, together with a shaken faith in bourgeois realism, those developments signal only "the exhaustion of all previous attempts to solve, undo, or otherwise remove this problem."[66] (Fried would say "to neutralize" this problem.[67]) In these terms, "baroque" amounts to what has been called "the aesthetics of modernity."[68] This is why it makes little sense to speak of an initial, seventeenth-century baroque and its subsequent, nineteenth-century "return" or "neobaroque," except in a purely metaphoric way.[69] The baroque does not come and go; it does not get lost and reappear. As an aesthetic framework, the term instead names something like a stubborn, underlying *condition* of modernity, one whose "latency" runs in theater from the time of Denis Diderot's absorption to that of Henrik Ibsen's realism.[70]

In the chapters that follow, I sometimes transpose Fried's agon between the *absorptive* and *theatrical* qualities of artworks into another set of terms. As the conventions of the historical baroque theater diminished in popularity over the eighteenth century, Aristotle's notion of drama as poetic *mimesis* came to take renewed priority over all other nontextual elements of the stage, including direct address, music, and spectacle (*parabasis*, *melos*, and *opsis*, respectively).[71] During a period when ornamentation in the arts, architecture, and clothing was increasingly renounced, this turn also involved the attempted subordination of theater's allegorical impulses to its mimetic ones, if not the attempted elimination of allegory entirely.[72] These attempts coincide with the long-standing modern effort to reduce the gap between "appearances and the world as it is" described in Egginton's work. For these reasons, the later, twentieth-century modernist interest in baroque style expresses a new attunement in the theater to the power of allegory over that of drama as realistic mimesis. Baroque modernism made available, with far-reaching consequences, a new understanding of allegory as (literally, etymologically) a means of *speaking otherwise* and (as Sigrid Weigel has put it) the "speech of the Other."[73] I explore these dynamics at length in chapter 3, which takes up Walter Benjamin's *Origin of the German Trauerspiel* and the significance of allegory in that study as the central trope of baroque rhetoric. My larger purpose is to show that modern attempts to renounce the unruly force of allegory and theater have never proven fully successful. Rather, in light of the evidence I advance, these civilizing projects appear to have undermined themselves from within.[74]

Apart from its privileged place in the domain of baroque art history, allegory has formed a signal concept in the philosophical history of modernism as well, particularly within deconstruction, since the time of Paul de Man's *Allegories of Reading* (1979). This fact is germane to the modernist reappropriation of baroque form in that the twentieth century translated early modern allegorism into an awareness of the impossibility of structural linguistics. De Man's work makes clear that allegory's renewed cultural force at the turn of the twentieth century answered to a growing philosophical skepticism about the power of language to correspond truthfully with the world as an object of knowing.[75] When modernists around the turn of the century embraced increasingly baroque strategies and conventions within the theater, they did so as part of a broader cultural reactivation of allegory's long residual energies. In this sense of the word, "allegory" designates one of representation's discontents. As Stephen Greenblatt has observed: "Insofar as the project of mimesis is the direct representation of a stable, objective reality, allegory, in attempting and always failing to represent Reality, inevitably reveals the impossibility of this project. This impossibility is precisely the foundation upon which all representation, indeed all discourse, is constructed."[76]

Introduction

In this way, the emergence of a conspicuous baroque strain of modernism in the late nineteenth century functioned as a kind of Freudian "belated recognition" (*Nachträglichkeit*) in which an earlier traumatic situation is understood only in retrospect and in light of its subsequent, symptomatic recurrence.[77] From the early seventeenth century to the twentieth, the persistence of allegory evinces a troubled faith in existing metaphysical and epistemological support systems, an enduring crisis of both religious and scientific knowledge. This crisis can be renounced, or its aesthetic forms repressed, but it cannot be fully eliminated. It precipitates both the linguistic turn of the nineteenth century's last two decades and Nietzsche's declaration of God's death as conceptual dynamics with which modernist thinkers would have to contend.[78] Just as the dramatists of the baroque drew little influence from Aristotle, allegory's reemergence in the late-nineteenth-century modernist theater coincides with the deconstruction of Aristotelian mimesis and the assertion of the theater's material specificity. In this regard, the modernist turn to the baroque anticipates the rise of what Hans-Thies Lehmann has recently called the postdramatic regime of theater.

In the theater, allegory always involves those material dimensions of the stage that Roland Barthes considered irreducible to the literal text of the drama: "sensual artifice, gestures, sounds, tones, distances, substances, lights," and so on.[79] In the seventeenth century, as in the time of modernism, baroque style demands an unavoidably physical—even *sensual*—deployment of forms. Quite unlike the tradition of closet drama, the baroque impulse in theater necessitates staging, bodies, gazes, gestures, spectatorial affects and desires. The material and visual excessiveness of the early modern stage itself testifies to a dialectics of lack and superabundance: there, *eros* is displaced into scenography.[80] The queer theorist Leo Bersani already observed as much in detecting that one could draw a line of intensification, of increasing psychic desublimation, connecting Racine's *Andromache* in the 1660s to Robert Wilson's "theater of desire" in the 1970s.[81] In this respect, it is remarkable that the words "baroque" and "queer" appear to derive from a shared etymological root, the proto-Indo-European -*terkw*, which describes a twisting or off-centered movement, a form of torque or distortion, like that seen in the nonspheroid form of the baroque pearl. Even the spelling of the word "baroque"—like that of "queer," both flirtatiously conjoining the letters *q* and *u*—has the perfume of prohibited desires surrounding it.[82] The frequent suspicion and polarization that baroque style routinely engenders are not unrelated to this secretive, queer aura. Between the extremes of uncritical baroccophilia and reflexive baroccophobia it can be a difficult task to navigate.

In this sense, it is useful to revisit one of the earlier uses of "baroque," designating an irregularity of form in art and a resistance to universal formal norms. ("Baroque," like "queer," shares the peculiar historical trajectory of having started its life as a pejorative, only to be reclaimed and radicalized as historical conditions have changed.) Baroque style only *seems* strange or irregular. In reality, it simply conforms to formulae of infinite complexity whose logics are not fully discernible to a normative, classical gaze. Notwithstanding the professed heterosexuality of the male figures I survey in this volume, one of my inquiry's stakes is to propose that modernist discourses of baroque style are forerunners of debates on queer formalisms in our own time.[83] Recent scholarship by Jennifer Doyle, David Getsy, and Jonathan Flatley has sought to ascertain the queer resonances of abstract contemporary art, even subjecting Judd and Morris's minimalism and Fried's anti-theatricalism to a queer rereading.[84] The legacy of baroque style in the theater intersects contemporary queer formalism at this juncture. My own view is that—whether one is speaking of sculpture by Judd and Morris, or *Our Town*'s blank stage, or Samuel Beckett's dramaturgy of radical subtraction, or the music of Philip Glass, to name just a few examples—the rhetoric of "minimalism" in twentieth-century art has been largely misleading. Recent scholarship in the field of critical theory has sought both to underline and dislodge the minimalist-maximalist binary, even subjecting it to allegorical scrutiny.[85] But the final and best judgement on minimalism is likely to have been rendered by Deleuze, who folds minimalism into the aesthetics of the baroque by noting that "*minimal* art is appropriately named following a law of extremum."[86]

Furthermore, the recurrent temporality that follows the coherence of baroque conventions across the *longue durée* of the modern era is surely a queer one.[87] Traversing the time and space of the seventeenth and twentieth centuries, the legacy of baroque style has not persisted according to a straightforward pattern of linear development. Rather, it proceeds by fits and starts, as part of a precarious effort to affirm rather than negate the theater in a modern context hostile to the more radical consequences of the theater's flourishing. Flashing up at crucial moments, this process has taken shape through what performance theorist Joseph Roach calls "uneven developments and periodic returns"—*percolation* in time rather than *flow*.[88] I

Introduction   21

explore the queer appeal of baroque style most directly in chapter 4, on Stein, which also addresses the relationship of baroque to camp sensibility. Still, because I do not seek to minoritize Stein and do not think the queerness of baroque style can so easily be confined to queer-identifying cultural producers, the reader will find that this subject forms a motivic pattern across all four chapters that follow.

To offer an initial summary overview, each chapter below focuses on a modern author whose writing takes place in the spaces *between* theory and theater—a liminal terrain that, at least since the time of Gotthold Ephraim Lessing, has been demarcated as the traditional field of dramaturgy. In this, my work extends a movement in recent theater studies to conduct research at the crossroads of performance and philosophy.[89] Each chapter is organized around a series of close readings, and in this way, my project has benefited from the recent methodological return in literary studies to formalist methods, sometimes called the "new formalism."[90] In each, I sift through the textual remains of dramatic and philosophical modernism to find the residua of performances past, an approach inspired by recent writings in performance studies on the enduring afterlives of performance.[91] Each chapter isolates those exemplary baroque theater forms that most excited their modernist interpreters: opera for Friedrich Nietzsche, French tragedy for Stéphane Mallarmé, German mourning plays for Walter Benjamin, and the saintly miracle play for Gertrude Stein. I do not seek to overemphasize the demonstrable networks of material influence that conjoin each of these examples (Nietzsche's abundant impact on Mallarmé, for instance, or Mallarmé's on Benjamin), but prefer instead to depict an intertextual constellation of shared aesthetic concern.

Chapter 1 examines baroque style in the writing of the first thinker to make it a subject of coherent philosophical interest. Over the course of the 1880s, Nietzsche would repeatedly insinuate that his sometime friend the composer and opera impresario Richard Wagner represented a turn toward baroque strategies in art. In his analysis, the reemergence of baroque tendencies in nineteenth-century performance signals a transformation within the sphere of the linguistic, one that necessarily ensnares philosophy itself, as well as theater and the other arts. Nietzsche thus initiates a theoretical discourse on the baroque that unites early modern and fin de siècle theater practices under the sign of a shared baroque aesthetics, and he invokes the baroque to characterize the performativity of philosophy itself. In the final analysis, there emerges within Nietzsche's thought a key internal contradiction that his work identifies in baroque style, between resentful and affirmative deployments of artistic media.

The book's second chapter takes up the writings of Stéphane Mallarmé, long recognized by critics and theorists as a modern writer with affinities for baroque poetics. I examine Mallarmé's theater-theoretical fragment "Mimique" (1886), which envisions a theatrical stage, a linguistics, and a poetics beyond classical representation. I then turn to Mallarmé's fragmentary Salome drama, entitled *Hérodiade* (begun 1864, left incomplete at his death in 1898), as a modernist rewriting of Jean Racine's *Phèdre* (1677). Here I show that *Hérodiade* rejects the ideology of *drama as representation* while embracing a *theatrical play* of spectacular, material forms: prismatic repetitions, incantatory syllables, emotional and haptic excitations, operatic but nonreferential language, and statuesque gestures. *Hérodiade* laid the groundwork for a nonmimetic theater of the future and led to Mallarmé's final, most enigmatic and experimental project, the so-called Book, which links the ambition of Wagner's Total Artwork to the rise of performance art as a distinct generic category in the twentieth century. In Mallarmé's vision of a modern, nonrepresentational theater ritual—something akin to a secular Catholic Mass—*Hérodiade* was to play a key role, transmitting the baroque trace to inheritors of Mallarmé's project such as F. T. Marinetti, John Cage, and Dick Higgins. Here, I close by arguing that Mallarmé's feeling for a "Crisis of Verse" during the Belle Époque cannot be separated from a crisis of faith in economic institutions, and that Mallarmé's baroque style mounts a resistance to the hegemony of late-nineteenth-century capital.

From Mallarmé's poetic dramaturgies, I move next to examine Walter Benjamin's 1928 postdoctoral dissertation (or *Habilitationsschrift*), the *Origin of the German Trauerspiel*, both as an idiosyncratic work of theater history and as a theory of baroque theatricality. The rise of German Expressionist theater in the 1910s animated his interest in the baroque *Trauerspiel*, or mournful stage play. In this light, I demonstrate that Benjamin's Trauerspiel study characterizes the baroque as a necessarily spatial and medial phenomenon of style, one incompatible with humanist notions of sovereign subjecthood. Trauerspiel in Benjamin's description anticipates the rise of twentieth- and twenty-first-century "landscape" theaters as described by numerous contemporary critics (Elinor Fuchs, Una Chaudhuri, Hans-Thies Lehmann). Hence the emphasis in baroque theater generally on spectacle and choreography, on *staging* as such, subjects on which Benjamin develops crucial insights

Introduction

that have regularly been overlooked by Benjamin scholars. With reference to German baroque mourning plays like Andreas Gryphius's *Leo Armenius* (1650) and *Catharine of Georgia* (1657), I put Benjamin's concept of allegory into conversation with the idea of theatricality that Michael Fried developed in his writings on painting. As I show, this theoretical dialogue allows for a new appreciation of the baroque qualities of many modernist theater movements and makers, not least of all Bertolt Brecht, whose practice of Epic Theater Benjamin invests with a baroque historical legacy all its own.

In the book's final chapter, I consider how Gertrude Stein's dramaturgy makes possible a baroque paradigm not only in avant-garde playwriting but also in theatrical performance onstage. Focusing on her opera *Four Saints in Three Acts* (written 1927-28 and premiered in collaboration with the composer Virgil Thomson in 1934), this chapter reveals that discussions of baroque style permeated the opera's development from its planning and composition to its staging and critical reception. In the decades since its premiere, Stein's *Four Saints* and overall body of work have become foundational touchstones for generations of the avant-garde in theater and performance, inspiring such artists as Cage, Robert Wilson, and Mark Morris. Reading the textual and performance history of *Four Saints* alongside Stein's theoretical writings on drama, I argue that she claimed affinity with baroque theater in order to unsettle norms of representation across an array of registers—in language, writing, historiography, and identity.

To be clear, this book is meant more as a descriptive aesthetics than a normative one. Although certain passages of it may acquire the character of a manifesto, I do not intend it as such, for the most part. Rather, I have largely sought to describe a situation I see reflected empirically across a constellation of cultural materials. Moreover, the baroque genealogy of modernity I track in the following chapters is not meant to be exclusive of different narratives. Numerous other figures from the domain of theater history can easily be seen to have important places in a baroque history of modernism. Recent studies have sought in various ways to emphasize the baroque characteristics of figures as disparate as Luigi Pirandello, Edward Gordon Craig, Isadora Duncan, Wyndham Lewis, Djuna Barnes, Federico García Lorca, Jean Genet, Tom Stoppard, and Tony Kushner.[92] In this context, it is also possible to remember Susan Sontag's essay on Antonin Artaud, which claims that Artaud's imagination was fired by the legacy of Shakespeare, Tourneur, Webster, and "the Dark Elizabethans."[93] Elsewhere, in the field of German philology, Barbara Nagel has traced a significant baroque influence over early-nineteenth-century writers crucial to the later emergence of German modernism, such as Heinrich von Kleist and Georg Büchner.[94] Her argument gives further credence to Thornton Wilder's instinct to search as far back as the generation of Hölderlin for a baroque lineage.[95]

It is likewise true that the modernisms of certain national literatures could be brought productively to bear on this argument. For example, a uniquely baroque resonance can be detected in Austrian modernism from the late Biedermeier period onward, not only in Raimund and Reinhardt's work, as Wilder's essay alleges, but also in Hugo von Hofmannsthal, Stefan Zweig, and perhaps in Karl Kraus as well. (Walter Benjamin would be especially attentive to Hofmannsthal's interest in baroque literature and love of Calderón de la Barca.) Thoroughly overdetermined by the country's Catholic history, Austrian modernism in particular raises still other questions about the role baroque style might play in negotiating persistent distinctions between the elite and popular arts, between "highbrow" and "midcult" artistic production, as Hofmannsthal and Zweig have sometimes been regarded as emblems of bourgeois "middlebrow" literature. Pivoting to an American context, the *Partisan Review* literary critic Dwight Macdonald was swift to dismiss Wilder's *Our Town* along exactly these lines.[96] It is perhaps no surprise that Theodor Adorno and Walter Benjamin can also be seen to disagree on these very grounds. The former ultimately came to suspect the modern renewal of interest in "baroque" as a symptom of the culture industry's operations, whereas the latter found it a matrix of radical, antiestablishment forces. Such debates are especially applicable to the late-twentieth-century emergence of "postmodernism," with its supposedly unprecedented leveling of artistic hierarchies, as they are to the dawn of queer "camp" sensibilities and to what historian Steven Watson has called the "mainstreaming" or "defanging" of modernism.[97]

Where the rationale behind my study's selection is concerned, the four case studies of my analysis have been chosen for the specific way they illustrate a constant dialogue between the fields of philosophy and dramaturgy. The four chapters aim *not only* to show how the baroque stage formed a significant historical forerunner to practices in the contemporary theater (with its emphases on "postdramatic" performance, defocalized landscape, and the destabilization of the autonomous subject or character); they *also* demonstrate the baroque as a precursor to the practice of deconstruction

Introduction

as a contemporary form of modernist theory. From a chronological standpoint, others have shown how it is possible to trace a persistent fascination with baroque style across every decade of the entire twentieth century: in this regard, the design historian Stephen Calloway's book *Baroque Baroque: The Culture of Excess* has been most comprehensive. For my part, I focus exclusively on the period between 1875 and 1935, starting from when "baroque" first entered philosophical aesthetics as an explicitly named conceptual framework, until the time it acquired a more common usage in modernist theater. A later work like W. H. Auden's Pulitzer Prize–winning dramatic poem *The Age of Anxiety: A Baroque Eclogue* (1947) has been excluded, for wearing its baroque debts too openly on its sleeve.

Geographically speaking, I have just as deliberately restricted my focus not only to the Global North but to the context of northern Europe (France and Germany especially) and, by way of Stein's Paris, to the northeastern United States. In short, the present study offers just *one* baroque modernity, but does not seek to discount others. This geographical mapping endeavors to destabilize certain received ideas, namely, that as an aesthetic phenomenon the baroque is somehow primarily suited to descriptions of Mediterranean cultures and the colonies of Mediterranean states. An aversion to acknowledging the possibility of baroque styles in French- and English-language literature in particular has been a feature of the term's conceptual history since its very beginning.[98] Meanwhile, a robust critical discussion of baroque aesthetics has grown up among Hispanists, Italianists, and scholars of Latinx literatures and culture. Bolívar Echeverría has gone so far as to theorize the existence of a wide-ranging baroque "ethos" significant to the cultures of southern Europe, Latin America, and the Jewish diaspora that can powerfully contest the hegemony of both capitalist modernity and whiteness as a pair of repressive, civilizational projects.[99] Perhaps even more influentially, the poet, philosopher, and critic Édouard Glissant has spoken of "a baroque abroad in the world" that transcends any European locus, precipitates *métissage* or *mestizaje*, and produces a global "being-in-the-world": "We can sum this up: the Baroque has undergone a naturalization, not just as art and style but as a way of living the unity-diversity of the world. This process of naturalization prolongs the Baroque and re-creates it, beyond the flamboyant realms of a unique Counter-Reformation, to extend it into the unstable mode of Relation; and, once again, in this full-sense, the 'historical' Baroque prefigured, in an astonishingly prophetic manner, present-day upheavals of the world."[100]

If I focus, then, on the way baroque style seems an urgent concern for thinkers active in northern Europe, it is to demonstrate that this style poses a set of problems for these thinkers that cannot effectively be quarantined to faraway territories or peoples with racially marked skin.[101] And so, while it may seem a contradiction that I articulate the baroque as a "bad modernism" of sorts while tracing its legacy through a uniquely "high" road of modernist thinkers (Nietzsche, the Symbolists, the Frankfurt School, Brecht, Gertrude Stein, and in the book's coda, the postwar American avant-garde), I do this with a deliberate goal in mind. I posit the baroque theater as an arena in which the normatively white, (northern) European subject, at some of the "highest" moments of its own theoretical self-articulation, came to glimpse something of its own decentering, its own self-deconstruction. What follows is a moment of high noon, and also an eclipse.

From the generation of Wagner to that of Wilder, Benjamin, Brecht, and beyond, each succeeding group of vanguardists in theater and theory alike has rediscovered the appeal of baroque style anew and tried, with varying degrees of cognizance, to reinvent it. In what has become a pervasively reified world, the idea of this style has formed an ever-replenishing source of inspiration in the modernist quest not only for new forms of art but also for new models of aesthetic and political consciousness. For those modernists included in the present study, the notion of baroque held out a liberatory promise, one to be read against the grain of the frequently reactionary program of seventeenth-century baroque art. If what some have called a "baroque of the revolution" can be mentioned in this context, each of these thinkers played a vital role in helping conceive it as a possibility.[102] Like theater in general, and like epistemological skepticism, baroque formalism in both its early modern and modernist contexts cannot be described as uniformly subversive or hegemonic, and the chapters that follow attest to the difficulty of disentangling those two potentials. Just as the physical stage can be used as an apparatus for reinforcing ideologies, so can theatricality function to help dismantle them or illuminate their limitations.[103] With each new era, the baroque tradition has needed to be recognized anew. And with each new enemy, its emancipatory potential has needed to be contested again and again amid always precarious circumstances. In my own limited way, with the Orphic meditations that follow, I wish to fan a spark of hope in the past.

1 Overcoming Ascetic Style
Nietzsche and the Transvaluation of the Baroque

> His book resembles a play within a play, an audience
> observed by another audience.
>
> —Friedrich Nietzsche, *Assorted Opinions and Maxims* 113
> (239)

On May 22, 1872, his fifty-ninth birthday, Richard Wagner visited the Bavarian town of Bayreuth to witness the foundation stone of his future festival theater being laid, and the young philosopher Friedrich Nietzsche, then twenty-seven, joined him for the proceedings. A concert performance of Beethoven's Ninth Symphony had been planned in honor of the new construction, but rain forced the ceremonies into the nearby Margravial Opera House, the town's already-existing theater. When Wagner visited a year earlier to assess the town's potential as a site for his future artistic home, the Margravial had struck him as inadequate for the *Ring* cycle, too small, ostentatious, and antiquated. A theater in the old Italian style, it was built in the 1740s for the court of Princess Wilhelmine of Prussia and boasts to this day ornate furnishings by the stage designer Giuseppe Galli Bibiena, one of the greatest scenographers of the late baroque period. It was a curious scene, then, that Nietzsche witnessed from the parterre as Wagner conducted Beethoven's masterwork: gesticulating magnetically before a crowd of amazed admirers, the mastermind of opera's future inaugurating that future from within the architectural confines of the baroque past, literally framed by the historical scenography of the Margravial's proscenium arch. Within a year, Wagner would instruct Otto Brückwald, architect of the Bayreuth Festspielhaus, to do away with all neobaroque ostentation in the project's designs. Prefiguring modernist architect Adolf Loos's general proscription of all surface decoration by more than thirty years, Wagner would write on the

The groundbreaking ceremonies of the Festspielhaus in the old Margrave's Opera House in Bayreuth on May 22, 1872. Richard Wagner conducting Ludwig van Beethoven's Ninth Symphony on Wagner's fifty-ninth birthday. Courtesy bpk Bildagentur/Art Resource, NY.

draft plans for the future theater: *"Die Ornamente fort!"*—"Away with the ornaments!"[1]

One need not adopt a psychoanalytic outlook to suspect that anything banished with such an imperious command (*"fort"*) can reappear by some mysterious procedure and be suddenly there (*"da"*) again. As if to fulfill this insight, by the close of the 1870s Nietzsche would end his friendship with Wagner and begin describing him explicitly as a modern representative of baroque style in the arts. One can only speculate as to how and when this idea first occurred to him, but Nietzsche clearly began entertaining it during his years as a professor at the University of Basel. As early as 1873, he was using the term "baroque" in his *Untimely Meditations* to disparage the complexity of David Strauss's labyrinthine writings, which he likened to "theological catacombs" full of obscure and convoluted "baroque ornamentation" (*UM* I 5 [23]; *UM* I 9 [44]). As the decade wore on, however, Nietzsche would

Overcoming Ascetic Style

exchange ideas with Jacob Burckhardt—his Basel faculty colleague, the era's leading specialist on early modern art—and, while poring over Burckhardt's writings on baroque style in *Der Cicerone*, his thinking would undergo a metamorphosis.[2] What might it mean for aesthetics and theater historiography that he made this claim of Wagner as baroque so repeatedly? Few scholars have questioned what he thought of the baroque in general, and even fewer have asked what he intended by assigning Wagner to this category.[3] These are queer lacunas in an otherwise abundant critical discussion. They are especially stark considering that Nietzsche is the first philosopher to treat the baroque substantively, as a topic of serious aesthetic concern, rather than dismissively, as a species of artistic ugliness. This landmark historical shift, a wholesale transvaluing of artistic values, now deserves greater attention, as does Nietzsche's place at its outset.

The story of Nietzsche's role in constructing the baroque as a modern concept raises questions for many disciplines, but especially for theater studies. Wagner's vision of a new and modern form of theater, one that would paradoxically be a rebirth of Aeschylean tragedy, required him to make an effective break with opera's past. For him this vision meant the conscious rejection of French grand opera, operetta, the culture of Giacomo Meyerbeer, the ideology of theater as entertainment, and so on. In his disdain for the Margravial theater, he also sought, whether consciously or not, to break with the theater's baroque past as well. Still, repressed cultural materials find ways of returning. What is more, the history of the modern theater and the history of the baroque as a modern concept cannot fully be disentangled from each other, for at least two reasons. On one level, this is because baroque style necessitates theatricality, as Nietzsche was the first philosophical commentator to suggest.[4] On another level, in their efforts to theorize baroque style, Nietzsche's writings also reflect a theater critic and patron's attitudes, one whose thinking grew up in dialogue with the modern stage's developing conventions. At both levels, Nietzsche's writings on the baroque invite new interpretations as documents of theater and aesthetic theory. In these writings and in his doomed intimacy with Wagner, the concept of baroque style has a largely unnoticed conceptual origin, important both for the development of modern philosophical thought and for modernism in artistic practice.

Curiously, Anglophone theater and literature scholars have paid scant attention to the subject of the baroque, allowing art historians to dominate conversations on it since the time of Heinrich Wölfflin's major works. With

Renaissance and Baroque and *Principles of Art History*, Wölfflin came to over-shadow Nietzsche's earlier, more fragmentary writings on the subject. But in Wölfflin's classic-baroque binary—itself a repurposed version of Nietzsche's Apollo-Dionysus dialectic from *The Birth of Tragedy* (1872)—one finds significant, if allusive, debts to Nietzsche's thought.[5] The baroque as it has become conventionally understood in art-historical discussions thus carries with it traces of a covert Nietzscheanism that are still too little understood. This is remarkable because Nietzsche's primary critical arena for investigating baroque style is not art history, as Wölfflin might prefer, but rather the fields of theater and rhetoric. For this reason, I have oriented my inquiry into Nietzsche's understanding of the baroque by focusing on his explicit statements on theater and baroque style, rather than proceeding by other potentially productive research avenues (for example, by analyzing his philosophical sympathies with Baruch Spinoza). Though relatively miniscule, these statements illuminate the significance of theater not only to baroque style but also to Nietzsche's own philosophical self-conception.

To make this significance clear requires the risky business of exposing Nietzsche, a philosopher uniquely vexing for philological interpreters, to a series of close readings. Doing so reveals Nietzsche's baroque as an unsettling phenomenon of "style," one necessarily theatrical in its orientation and effects. A detailed, historical reconstruction of Nietzsche's notion of theatricality is therefore presented in the pages to follow. Although he is sometimes considered an outright enemy of the theater on the basis of his late writings, my analysis of his lifelong interest in baroque style depicts a more equivocal posture. Nietzsche recognizes in baroque style a form of theatricality dependent on rhetorical direct address to an audience (or parabasis), a theatricality fundamentally at odds with the classical concept of drama as representation (or mimesis).[6] Seeing theatrical address as an indication of baroque style, Nietzsche claims that the baroque privileges rhetorical passions and gestures over the Aristotelian criterion of represented action (*mimesis praxeos*). Gesture, the kinesthetic mode of rhetorical ornament, here functions as a tell-tale signifier of baroque style in performance, one analogous to physical ornament in architecture. By prioritizing gesture and passion, these writings suggest an understanding of theatricality as powerfully informed by Nietzsche's early career lecturing on Greek oratory as it was by any concrete experience in the actually existing theater of his lifetime.[7] I am thus particularly interested in Nietzsche's body, both his body of writings in its ability to perform a philosophical conception of the baroque, and his

Overcoming Ascetic Style

physical body as an irreducible "site" for encountering and reflecting materially on that concept, as spectator, speaker, and author.[8]

The new currency of baroque forms during Nietzsche's lifetime signaled for him a widespread crisis of thought and belief, one with roots stretching back to the early modern past. In his dispersed comments on rhetorical Sophism, Bernini, Counter-Reformation Christianity, early opera, and ultimately on Wagner, Nietzsche weaves together the image of a pervasive semiotic and theological shift: the secularization of the world and of the word. (Walter Benjamin later traced this process to a "crisis of the aura" with origins in the Counter-Reformation wars of religion, expressed in the emergence of baroque allegory.) These concerns feed into a complex of paradigmatically Nietzschean preoccupations, with nihilism, instrumental reason, the "irrational," and the functioning of power. The nineteenth century's baroque crisis signaled to Nietzsche that a certain Enlightenment project—organized around naturalism in the arts and sciences—had run its course. Amid this crisis, Nietzsche saw baroque style as a symptom that the distinctions between philosophy and performance had become tenuous and, furthermore, that new modes of art and immanent critique were needed for the future. Where the last of these consequences are concerned, Nietzsche's baroque modernism clears the way for the later modernisms of Mallarmé, Benjamin, Stein, and others. To be sure, Nietzsche's insights into the baroque are tendentious and delimited by his historical context, and they may even strike some readers as altogether erroneous. Even so, his vast influence behooves us to take note and entertain performance theorist Rebecca Schneider's recognizably Nietzschean injunction "to ask what mistake gets right."[9] Doing so reveals, despite any idiosyncrasies on Nietzsche's part, his initiatory role in fashioning baroque style into a modernist inheritance.

Against Classical Rhetoric and Drama

Nietzsche's direct analyses of the baroque stem from his transitional work *Human, All Too Human* (1878-79), a text whose style departs noticeably from that of all his previous publications. Here he abandoned the systematic, teleological argumentation and strident German nationalism of *The Birth of Tragedy* in favor of an aphoristic style closer to the writings of French ancien régime moralists like La Bruyère, Rochefoucauld, and Pascal. He would later describe this book as "the monument to a crisis"—a personal one, surely, but a historical and philosophical one as well (*EH* "Human" 1 [115]; cf. *EH* "Destiny" 1 [143]). In the most personal realm, the book marks the moment of his famed break with Wagner. He had previously (in *The Birth of Tragedy*) hailed Wagner as a harbinger of tragic culture's Dionysian return, but his faith in the composer collapsed at the inaugural Bayreuth Festival's opening night in 1876. In the words of American philosopher Arthur Danto, Nietzsche had hoped to find there "one grand chorus of dancing, singing satyrs," but instead the spectators at Bayreuth "were simply people out for a good time. Anyone with 900 marks could gain admission; the audience was opulent, made up in at least as high a proportion of paunchy businessmen from the nearby Marienbad, and their wives in diadems and lavalieres, as it was of noble spirits."[10] Wagner found himself delighted to be at the center of what Danto describes as "a circus."[11] The town of Bayreuth swarmed with preening bourgeoises and members of the ruling class, all seeming to reek of German beer, as Nietzsche vividly describes in *Ecce Homo* (*EH Human* 3 [117]). These included numerous imperial oligarchs and even the new emperor, Wilhelm, himself. The scene repulsed Nietzsche. Long racked with illness, his migraines and nausea gave him an alibi to flee Bayreuth after the first act of *Das Rheingold*.

Bayreuth was initially intended as a ritual site for the consecration of a new German culture, one conceived from the spirit of Feuerbach and the 1848 Dresden revolutions, in which Wagner had been a participant. The drama of the *Ring* had been conceived as an allegorical narrative of the collapse of religion, state, and capitalism alike, as numerous commentators have discussed.[12] Yet, in its transition from concept to fully realized creation in 1876, *Der Ring des Nibelungen* transformed from a revolutionary drama celebrating the overthrow of the existing order into a document of Schopenhauerian resignation, from which Nietzsche sought to distance himself. Over the following two years, his relationship with Wagner unraveled further, giving rise to much critical speculation. It cannot go without mentioning here that their complicated relationship depended on a homosocial intimacy bordering, unconsciously perhaps, on a kind of classical psychological and pedagogical erotics between men. This intimacy proved consequential in a famous episode when, in 1877, Wagner wrote the physician Otto Eiser intimating that the young philosopher, whom Eiser had once examined, harbored unseemly desires that only marriage could resolve. This insinuation quickly entered into the Bayreuth gossip, where Nietzsche was soon rumored to be a sexual deviant.[13] I wish neither to overstate nor to overlook the uncertain queerness that attends the Nietzsche-Wagner friendship from the beginning, but pause on it briefly here because it forms an illuminating backdrop

Overcoming Ascetic Style

to their rift, with consequences unspoken (perhaps unspeakable by Nietzsche) for the concept of baroque style. With *Human, All Too Human*, his first attempts to approach the baroque philosophically occur in close proximity to this momentous turning point.

Nietzsche's reflections on baroque do not yield a traditional concept—a schema fully capable of seizing and subordinating diverse examples or notional particulars under a uniform category. Instead the Nietzschean baroque amounts to a phenomenon that resists the stability of a concept. It entails a perpetual *breaking out* of forms, including the controlling logic of conceptual form. This breakage is apparent in *Human, All Too Human*'s two most explicit passages on the baroque, both of which express opposition to Aristotle's rules on oratory and theater. Where Aristotle's *Rhetoric* discourages young speakers from overly histrionic gesture, Nietzsche offers a more ambiguous perspective.[14] Passage 131 of *Human, All Too Human*'s second volume (the *Assorted Opinions and Maxims* of 1879) offers an initial, sidelong inquiry into the metaphysics of baroque style by focusing *"[o]n excitement in the history of art."*[15] Through a genealogy of rhetoric in Hellenistic Athens, Nietzsche describes the emergence of what he deems an ancient form of baroque style in public speech:

> If we follow the history of an art, that of Greek rhetoric for instance, as we proceed from master to master and behold the ever increasing care expended on obedience to all the ancient rules and self-limitations and to those added subsequently, we are aware of a painful tension in ourselves: we grasp that the bow *has* to break and that the so-called inorganic composition, bedecked and masked with the most marvelous means of expression—the baroque style of Asia [*der Barockstil des Asianismus*] that is to say—was sooner or later a necessity and almost *an act of charity."* (243; emphases in original)

Here Nietzsche reprises the traditional development of Greek oratory in the third century B.C.E. from a plainspoken "Attic" style to a more florid one, designated in orientalist terms as "Asianist" by Roman teachers of rhetoric. The *stylus asiaticus* flourished in Athens in and after Demosthenes's lifetime as a late outgrowth of the Sophistic tradition.[16] There is more to this note than first meets the eye, beyond its obvious philological or antiquarian concerns. This classic-baroque, Attic-Asian binary recalls immediately the dialectics of Nietzsche's *Birth of Tragedy*, with Attic speech obeying the formal restraint of Apollo while its Asianist counterpart pursues the expressive release of Dionysus. From this early moment in Nietzsche's career, baroque style and the Dionysian drive implicate each other mutually. (Remarkably, both Asianism in rhetoric and Dionysus in myth reflect an anxiety about the foreign-born Other. Both were reputed to have infiltrated Greece from the East.) This more Dionysian mode of oratory was reputed for breaking with classical prohibitions against flagrant *hypokrisis*, the Greek term for both rhetorical delivery and acting. Against the decorousness of the Attic school, the Asianist opted for oratorical flamboyance.

And then there is the image of the bow breaking, the central figure for excitement bursting forth after generations of time-worn "rules and self-limitations." Clearly the explosive appearance of this new, exciting style was a relief from the tediousness of ancient orthodoxy. But if the excitement of the baroque *stylus asiaticus* attracts the author of this passage, something about it also seems to repulse him. In a double gesture of embrace and repudiation, one that recurs whenever Nietzsche writes subsequently on Wagner or theater, he praises the iconoclasm and stylishness of this so-called "inorganic style" while also insinuating—in a moment of trepidation—that its arrival was "*almost*" an act of charity, *not quite* the relief it first seemed. Since Plato's time, the Sophists were renowned for their complex syntax, witty inventions, sonorousness, and emotionality. Their grandiose style brimmed with gestural and figural embellishment, envisioning oratory as a form of magical spellbinding. In maxim 131, when "the bow *has* to break," both the metaphor of the snapping bow and the seemingly gestural emphasis added typographically to "*has*" (in German, an italicized "*muss*") function in a conspicuous and self-referential manner. Within *Human, All Too Human*'s mosaic of maxims, passage 131 suggests Nietzsche himself as the one breaking with standard rhetorical conventions.

But Sophism is no mere game. As baroque style, it raises the unsettling question of what place *style itself* can have in a responsible truth-seeking discourse.[17] Against Aristotelian orthodoxy, Sophism elevates style to the same plane as substance, allowing oratorical showmanship to rival argumentative diction and thinking. In its "baroque style," Sophism licenses rhetoric to approach the condition of theater. In his 1872-73 teaching notes at Basel, Nietzsche warns his rhetoric students against dismissing the *stylus asiaticus* as a relic of the distant past. "Never, down to the present moment, has the Asianism of style ceased. . . . So let us beware of scoffing: *de te fabula narratur*" (*LR* "Eloquence" [233-34]). Maxim 131 is more than a lapidary history of discourse in some far-off time and place. *De te fabula narratur: this story concerns you*. When Nietzsche invokes Asianist rhetoric in 1872 and

Overcoming Ascetic Style

baroque style in 1879, he is describing an ancient problem that persists into his contemporary moment, implicating his students, his readers, and himself. Sophistry amounts to a kind of stylish nihilism, as in the Sophist Gorgias's claim that "[n]othing exists; or if it does, we cannot know it; or if we can know it, we cannot communicate it."[18] The Sophist starts from a tragic insight, namely, that accessible and transcendent truth is lacking, and proceeds from this lack to an excessive, luxuriating mode of speech. Such luxury plays a strategic function in the "marketplace" of ideas, where just the right convincing gesture or well-spun turn of phrase can persuade a listener to "buy" what the orator is "selling." When the Sophist pronounces that no truth is fully truthful, he declares a situation in which truths have become commodities, vying within an epistemological market for supremacy. In fact, Nietzsche's contemporaneous essay "On Truth and Lying in an Extra-moral Sense" (1873) frames the way truth disintegrates into rhetoric using a metaphor of deteriorating currencies: truths are "coins, which having lost their stamp, are now regarded as metal and no longer as coins" (*TL* 1 [146]). Instead of prior, communicable truths, the Sophist expresses faith only in competing rhetorical perspectives doing *battle* or *competition* in a chaotic void. Seeking a buyer, the Sophist correspondingly pursues power through persuasion.

Far from using economic terms, however, Nietzsche's linguistic theory couches his attitude toward Sophistic rhetoric within a more (post-)Kantian vocabulary. In his private teaching notes, which echo claims Nietzsche made influentially in "On Truth and Lying," he parts ways with all linguistic naturalism, arguing that one's relation to the truth is always mediated by the conventions of one's language. In a multilingual world, each word for any given thing expresses etymologically only a part or an association of that thing; the full object (as a thing-in-itself) always escapes the total grasp of meaning.[19] Here Nietzsche expresses something of a historical and materialist understanding of language practice. A word has no natural or organic connection to the thing it signifies, but is secretly a rhetorical figure—a synecdoche, metonym, and so on—offering a flawed but functional designation for its ultimately ineffable referent. In their inability to speak truthfully about the world of things, words function "as illusions of which we have forgotten that they are illusions" (*TL* 1 [146]). This defamiliarized relation to language, which remembers the sensuous and material power of the word, creates a shock of recognition in which the ordinary, unconscious approach to language becomes a scene of deception at every point. Once sign and thing no longer cohere in the familiar way but instead yawn apart to a sublime distance, a powerful symbolic derangement comes to afflict the apparent continuity of language. In a reversal of Aristotle's subordination of rhetoric to just one kind of language use, Nietzsche claims that, "in sum, with respect to their meanings, all words are tropes in themselves, and from the beginning, . . . [that] language never expresses something completely but displays only a characteristic which appears to be prominent to it" (*LR* III [23]), and ultimately, that "tropes are not just occasionally added to words but constitute their most proper nature."[20]

In all these reversals, Nietzsche appears as a harbinger of the later, twentieth-century linguistic turn, cutting a path for the theories of Gottlob Frege, Ferdinand de Saussure, J. L. Austin, Jacques Derrida, and Paul de Man.[21] He also creates a theoretical space for the further, queer development of speech-act theory in the work of Judith Butler and Eve Sedgwick.[22] If "language never expresses something completely," because a word's relation to its object is just conventional and performative, and if words can never fully name their objects, this means that at the level of the nominative signifier, language as a system of speech acts regularly deviates from its goals. Butler and Sedgwick have argued that queerness names precisely this possibility of "deviation" by which speech acts go astray of their aims: "something 'queer' is at work at the heart of gender performativity," claims Butler.[23] If so, then something queer is also similarly at work in Nietzsche's linguistic theories of Sophistry and Asianism; and something queer works away at the heart of baroque style, as Nietzsche allegorizes it. These linguistic considerations are above all most consequential in the domain of theater. If all language is secretly rhetoric, this banal fact imparts a theatrical aspect to linguistic and lived experience alike. A Kantian or a Schopenhauerian might describe this situation as one in which an impenetrable curtain of tropes now covers over and obscures the objective, "real" world. A more Nietzschean formulation would deny that this hidden "real" world exists as such, and would instead posit the world of material and linguistic forces as an immanent, ultimate reality unto itself—a weave of words and things neither at one with themselves nor at rest. Suddenly "every word is also a mask";[24] but no metaphysical substance hides behind these masks, only more and more masquerading. Endlessly aestheticized by rhetoric, Nietzsche's world comes to seem a distorted *theatrum mundi*, where waking life is a dream.[25]

From the baroque view of language as figural, denying of all linguistic naturalism, several consequences follow involving the practice of theater

Overcoming Ascetic Style

and rhetoric in performance. Baroque ostentation fulfills not only a stylistic function but an epistemological one. It becomes incumbent upon the baroque stylist to demonstrate and affirm the world's infinite play of difference and theatricality through his style. Here I argue that, for Nietzsche, the use of *gesture* to elicit feelings of *excitement* forms a crucial component of this task. Involving more than just metaphors and other forms of ornamental language, baroque style also implicates bodies: limbs and hands, nimble fingers, expressive faces, piercing eyes, declaiming voices. It unfolds a displacement of semantic content from the domain of language into the supplementary and nonverbal field of kinesthetic action.[26] With these material elements, the baroque mounts an indulgent opposition to ascetic style.[27] Its gestures are not intended for the eye alone, but relay the corporeal intensity of flesh in motion, communicating haptic impulses from an embodied performer to an embodied observer. It appeals to *pathos* and the excitation of feelings, and those of the rhetorician are not excluded. In performance, the orator experiences the many autoaffective pleasures of speaking and gesticulating. Through the enjoyment of a highly decorated speech, his artistic body seems to dilate, increasing its rhetorical capacity to vie for advantage and glory.[28] With the baroque, the point is not to summon passions solely to purify them as in a typical catharsis, but rather to celebrate and play with them, ultimately even to let the passions "enjoy" themselves.

In all this, baroque style contradicts more than Aristotle's mimetic aesthetics; it also opposes any mimetic or representational view of truth as correspondence. For the Sophist, the truth cannot be divorced from one's perspective, kairos, or "place of seeing" (*theatron*). Neither can knowledge of the truth be separated from the feeling or *pathos* of truth. Baroque style thus entails a triumph for the theater and a catastrophe for the purposive intellect, rejoicing in what Simon Critchley and Jamieson Webster have described as the "Gorgiastic paradox" of the theater medium. According to Critchley and Webster, the theater is always Sophistic in its ability to manipulate the feelings of its audience, to make the false *feel like* the true. It is a space where "the deceiver is more honest than the nondeceiver, and the deceived is wiser than the nondeceived."[29] Like rhetorical Sophism and theater, baroque style employs histrionic maneuvers to generate the *feeling* of a plentiful truth's presence, thus taking rhetorical advantage of its absence.

Nietzsche elaborates these connections further in the 144th passage of *Assorted Opinions and Maxims*. There again the baroque amounts to a matter of *style*, not just in oratory but in thinking and writing primarily and all the

38 Baroque Modernity

other arts consequently, one that functions by amassing force through the manipulation of passionate emotions. Not content to treat the baroque in brief or passing terms, here Nietzsche offers a fuller definition:

> *On baroque style* [*Vom Barockstile*; literally, "on baroque styles"].—He who knows that, as a thinker or writer, he was not born or educated for dialectics or the analysis of ideas will involuntarily reach for the *rhetorical* and *dramatic*: for in the long run what he is concerned with is to make himself *understood* and thereby to acquire force [*Gewalt*], its being a matter of indifference to him whether he conducts sensibilities towards him along a level path or overtakes them unawares— either as a shepherd or a brigand. This applies to the plastic as much as to the poetic arts; where the feeling of a lack of dialectics or inadequacy in expressive or narrative ability, combined with an over-abundant pressing formal impulsion, gives rise to that stylistic genre [*Gattung des Stiles*] called the *baroque*. . . . The baroque style originates whenever any great art starts to fade, whenever the demands in the art of classic expression grow too great, as a natural event which one may well behold with sorrow—for it means night is coming—but at the same time with admiration for the substitute arts of expression and narration peculiar to it. To these belong the choice of material and themes of the highest dramatic tension of a kind that make the heart tremble even without the assistance of art because they bring Heaven and Hell all too close: then the eloquence of strong emotions and gestures, of the sublime and ugly, of great masses, of quantity as such . . . all these qualities in which this style possesses its greatness are not possible, not permitted, in the earlier, pre-classical and classical epochs of a species of art: such delicacies hang long on the tree as forbidden fruit. (245-46; emphases in original)

As with the emergence of Asianist rhetoric from the Attic school described in maxim 131, here one finds again a narrative of baroque style emerging belatedly, "whenever the demands in the art of classic expression grow too great," embracing all that was previously "not permitted" for expression. Since the style appears "whenever" classic authority falters, it corresponds to a repeated historical event. This suggests a *cultural* incapacity for dialectics or analysis rather than any individual writer's personal insufficiency. If, as the Sophistic position insinuates, referential language cannot attain to truth, then neither can dialectical or analytical thinking attain to knowledge. With thought and language alike entering a critical stage, artistic means are needed to shore up the deteriorating sphere of communication. Nietzsche had already made precisely this claim in his 1876 meditations on *Richard*

Wagner in Bayreuth, describing Wagner as one who sensed the pervasive sickness of language and the need for art to remedy it.[30] Against the disappearance of traditional pathways to truth, the baroque stylist offers artistic supplements: "the *rhetorical* and *dramatic*." He can communicate only what feels like truth either subtly or forcefully, as "a shepherd or as a brigand."[31] Concerned only to grown in forcefulness, this baroque stylist needs to "make himself *understood*"—writes Nietzsche with conspicuous emphasis conveyed with stylistic (here typographic, grammatologic) means, as though such gestures would guarantee his intelligibility.

In these reflections, the relationship of drama to the practice of gesture plays a decisive part. First, in lieu of philosophical reason, the baroque thinker "will involuntarily reach for the *rhetorical* and *dramatic*." (The reaching itself describes a gesture.) In this grasping movement, he pursues "material and themes of the highest dramatic tension [*höchster dramatischer Spannung*] of a kind that make the heart tremble," tension evoked by "the eloquence of strong emotions and gestures." When mentioning *drama* here, Nietzsche's opposition to Aristotle is once again in evidence. From 1870 until 1888, he repeatedly defined drama against the Aristotelian paradigm widespread in Europe since Racine's time. Where Aristotle influentially conceived drama as *mimesis praxeos*, the imitation of action through a logically causal, anthropocentric narrative, Nietzsche rejects this view as a bad translation and, as he put it in 1888, "a real misfortune for aesthetics" (*CW* 9 [249]). On the contrary, he claims the ancients understood *drama* to mean "*scenes of great pathos*. . . . [Drama] specifically excluded the plot (which it placed *before* the beginning or *behind* the scenes). The word drama is of Doric origin: and following Doric linguistic usage it means the 'event,' 'story,' both words in the hieratic sense" (249). The original idea of drama involved sacred or mythic tales—"not a doing but rather a happening [*Geschehen*]: in Doric, *dran* has absolutely no connotations of 'doing.'"[32] Rather than heroic actions, this untraditional concept of drama privileges a sacred passion— the death and rebirth of the Dionysian god—ritually mimed through scenic images and priestly gestures. It necessitates spectacle: music and dance, dithyramb and gesticulation. Discarding Aristotle's idea of drama as a transcendent representation, Nietzsche opts instead for drama as an immanent form of *presentation*.[33]

This preference for drama as presentation is of utmost importance to Nietzsche's baroque, which deploys theatrical effects that cannot be reduced to "drama" more normatively conceived.[34] By yoking together the *rhetorical* with this sense of the *dramatic*, the baroque artist channels a non-mimetic theatricality already prefigured in ancient forms of speech (rhetorical Sophism) and dance (dithyramb). Theatricality as such amounts to the primary and necessary condition of baroque style. Supplanting dramatic mimesis with the immanence of staging, this style functions above all to address an impressionable audience. The baroque stylist wants "to make himself understood . . . to conduct sensibilities towards him . . . to make the heart tremble": all these needs demand a spectator as their destiny. They depend upon a form of theatrical relation typical in the baroque visual arts, in which, as Michael Fried has shown, the art object refuses to maintain "the supreme fiction of the beholder's nonexistence."[35] The baroque embraces just this form of theatricality, unabashedly and directly addressing beholders with a proliferation of material effects, striving whether overtly or covertly to set hearts ablaze. It organizes all the appurtenances of the theater in a nonmimetic (Fried would say anti-absorptive) manner—reveling in the joy of mise-en-scène and affective persuasion—all for the purposes of magnifying the theater's own power.

But why should Nietzsche worry himself at all with the subject of the baroque? Why should it be anything more than a matter of antiquarian concern? As it turns out—*De te fabula narratur*—baroque style is a historical problem of thinking and writing that specially implicates his own present moment. Although he posits baroque style as a phenomenon specific to early modern Europe, claiming Michelangelo as "the father or grandfather of the artists of the Italian baroque," he simultaneously argues that baroque styles also circulate repeatedly through history. "For a baroque style has already existed many times from the age of the Greeks onwards—in poetry, rhetoric, in prose style, in sculpture, as well as in architecture."[36] In this light, his description of Hellenistic Asianism as a "baroque style" in maxim 131 involves more than an unconsidered application of that phrase. There is a nascent thought of eternal recurrence here, of history as a baroque cycle. Yet a curious shift occurs in the last sentences of maxim 144, when Nietzsche suddenly shifts his focus to contemporary music. "It is precisely now, when *music* is entering this last epoch, that we can get to know the phenomenon of the baroque style in a particularly splendid form and learn a great deal about earlier ages through comparison with it" (*AOM* 144 [246]). All signs point to Wagner, on whom Nietzsche was souring, as the unspoken referent of this remark. The passage concludes on a note of continued ambivalence, stating only that baroque style "has always lacked the highest

Overcoming Ascetic Style

nobility" and that "he whose receptivity for the purer and greater style is not blunted by it may count himself lucky" (ibid.). It remains unclear from this remark whether Nietzsche includes himself fully among "the lucky," those able to resist any baroque enticements. Only in his later writings on Wagner does there emerge a clearer picture of the baroque as a modern complex of forces and conditions impossible for anyone to escape, Nietzsche or Wagner alike.

Nietzschean and Wagnerian Theatricalities

More than a casual sideswipe, the insinuation of Wagner as a baroque stylist in *Human, All Too Human* echoes a claim Nietzsche made throughout the rest of his sane life. Several other passages in the volume (e.g., *HH* 219; *AOM* 171) attest to this view sub rosa, while Nietzsche's private letters are even more explicit. He wrote to the musician Carl Fuchs (on 29 July 1877) comparing Wagner explicitly with Bernini; to the writer Reinhart von Seydlitz (on 4 January 1878) decrying *Parsifal* as the "spirit of the Counter-Reformation"; to Wagner's friend Mathilde Maier (on 15 July 1878) describing the composer's "baroque art of overexcitement and glorified extravagance"; and again to Maier (on 6 August 1878) urging her to rethink her admiration for Wagner and "For God's sake, read about baroque style [in] J. Burckhardt's *Cicerone*!!!"[37] Several unpublished diary fragments from the summer of 1878 assess Wagner in similar terms (*KGW/NF*-1878, 30 [26, 107, 138, 140]). Letters to Fuchs a full decade later (26 August and 9 September 1888) continue to restate the Bernini connection explicitly. Still another message to the critic Carl Spittler (11 December 1888) indicates that Nietzsche originally intended to publish *Nietzsche contra Wagner* with a special section entitled "Barocco."[38] The view of Wagner as a baroque figure was one he thus held consistently to the end of his working life.

Advanced musicological training is not needed for one to notice that Wagner's music sounds nothing like the output of Europe's historical baroque period (conventionally dated 1600-1750). Nevertheless, in a diachronic sense if not a strictly historicist or synchronic one, the many correspondences Nietzsche perceives between Wagner and the baroque in maxim 144 are striking. Nietzsche's words bear repeating: baroque art necessitates "the choice of material and themes of the highest dramatic tension of a kind that make the heart tremble even without the assistance of art because they bring Heaven and Hell all too close: then the eloquence of strong emotions and gestures, of the sublime and ugly, of great masses, of quantity as such."

To varying degrees these descriptions could apply, say, to the sculpture of Bernini, the painting of Caravaggio, or Bach's *Saint Matthew Passion*, but at another level they are equally plausible as descriptions of the *Ring* cycle or *Parsifal*. Each of these artists exhibits, however differently, a stylistic will to theatricality through artistic media used to sensual, exciting effect. The 1876 Bayreuth Festival was a tipping point for Nietzsche in recognizing this connection, as it was there he witnessed Wagner's theory of the *Gesamtkunstwerk*—the total work of art, a synthesis of all art forms into a higher vision—translated to theater practice.[39] The Wagnerian *Gesamtkunstwerk* was prefigured by the idea of total theater that stirred artistic imaginations during the time of the historical baroque, from Bernini's spectacles in Rome to the Jesuits' sacred theater in Bavaria. At Bayreuth, Nietzsche drew this connection intuitively.

Numerous commentators—from modernists like Hugo von Hofmannsthal, Thornton Wilder, and Walter Benjamin to contemporary theater scholars like Kristiaan Aercke and Matthew Wilson Smith—have remarked on the complicated debts of Wagner's "Total Artwork" idea to baroque theater practice.[40] The Jesuit theater of the Counter-Reformation, for example, pursued the goal of this totalization after the manner of an Ignatian spiritual exercise. By appealing to the spectator's separate senses through the coordinated use of multiple artistic media—spectacle, poetry, music, and so forth—these theaters created onstage scenes of overwhelming sensory excitement for the spectator to contemplate spiritually—even to "enter" so to speak, as one might enter imaginatively through one of St. Ignatius's meditations on a vivid scene from the life of Christ. The Catholic effort to combat the spread of iconoclastic Protestantism authorized this form of multimedial combination in baroque architecture, sculpture, and painting similarly. Wagner's own Bavarian theater at Bayreuth built upon these various techniques, depicting allegorical narratives through the help of heavy, phantasmagorical machines. Combining the arts into an overwhelming spectacle, it aimed to entice viewers to project themselves into the mythic onstage fiction, to immerse themselves in feeling, a goal that Nietzsche recognized as ideologically strategic.[41] The Bayreuth stage formed a space where the arts could intermingle in the pursuit of this magical goal, a medium or technology that sought paradoxically to heal an overly mediated or technologized modernity.[42] In its darkened auditorium, images of ancient myths appeared like luminous dreams while metaphysical song flooded the spectators' ears from an invisible source. With Wagner, the modern theater—both despite

Overcoming Ascetic Style

and by virtue of its technological modernity—embraced sorcery and religious ritual. What spectator could resist such powerful appeals to passionate feeling, such persuasive stage rhetoric?[43]

Apparently, Nietzsche could. In the context of *Human, All Too Human*, Wagner's talent for stagecraft now seems little more than the spellbinding sophistry of the *stylus asiaticus*, with the theater functioning as a rhetorical medium for enchanting a mass audience.[44] Wagner's theater, dramatic not so much in the Aristotelian sense as in Nietzsche's sense, indexes the disintegration of theater's representational capacities into a more purely presentational relation to the audience: a relation of hailing that cuts through the otherwise closed framework of the proscenium arch. To borrow a theater metaphor developed in Wagner's lifetime by the stage director André Antoine, but harkening back to the Enlightenment *drame* of Diderot, Wagner's theater shows signs of a deteriorating "fourth wall," that stable boundary enshrined in theater architecture by the proscenium frame, separating the spectator from the delimited and fictional play-world.[45] An increasing porousness between theater and auditorium, viewing subject and onstage objects, "art" and "life," is evident at Bayreuth in several ways. It consists in the stage image's "extension" into the auditorium through Bayreuth's famous double proscenium and recessive transverse walls; and also in the obscuring of the orchestra pit (or "mystical abyss"), allowing music to permeate the darkened auditorium from an invisible source.[46] Both of these innovations permit the audiovisual spectacle to *bleed* across the proscenium boundary into the space of the audience. Furthermore, Wagner's innovation of "endless melody" deserves to be mentioned here—his esteemed "art of transition," which abolished the distinction between dialogue and aria for a higher metaphysical synthesis, but ultimately struck Nietzsche as little more than a kind of soupy baroque recitative (*CW* 8 [248]). Wagner's insistence on endless, unresolving melody threatened to transform opera into a kind of "half-sung declamation."[47] As Theodor Adorno would later observe, the basic musical structuring unit for Wagner, the leitmotiv, pursues a gestural function in its own right.[48] Key leitmotivs exist to underscore and intensify the physical actions of the singers onstage. In this respect, even the more purely musical elements of Wagner's compositional practice can be understood as emphatically gestural. Thus, in its architectural and musical aspects alike, the total spectacle of Bayreuth can be seen as a practice of rhetorical address to the onlooker.

But, if Nietzsche came to view Bayreuth as a baroque enterprise of sorts, and this insight struck him as lamentable, helping fuel his schism with Wagner, how then to interpret his ambivalent posture toward baroque style in *Human, All Too Human*? What to make of the fact that, despite his reservations, he seems in some ways to *identify* with the baroque orator of maxim 131, the stylist who has broken with plainspoken style once and for all? Is it possible that Nietzsche recognized an inclination toward baroque style in his own work "as a thinker and writer"?

At this point, the tendency toward theatricalization manifest in Nietzsche's own writing demands examination. Because Nietzsche has already suggested that all language involves an inherent performative functioning for its intelligibility, I do not wish to conscript him to the idea of "performative writing" that others have persuasively detailed elsewhere.[49] Rather, Nietzsche's writing can regularly be seen to display and reflect on itself, making language's performativity conspicuous in the manner of a simultaneous staging and unmasking. Whereas Jonas Barish once described Nietzsche in terms of his opposition to theater as such, more recent scholarship has detected and analyzed this theatrical quality of Nietzsche's work in greater detail.[50] It is not only that his writing entails a perpetual game of masks and characters that serve as philosophical mouthpieces, as Martin Puchner rightly observes.[51] Nor is it only that his discourse sometimes has recourse to the narrative structures of traditional dramatic literature, as Paul de Man once observed by noting that *The Birth of Tragedy* proceeds according to a dramaturgy all its own—one similar to the baroque genres of Florentine opera and German Trauerspiel, at that.[52] Nietzsche does not require *literal* (i.e., physical) masks and (visual) scenic devices to animate his texts; his own theatrical aim, not unlike Wagner's, is to cultivate a certain space of excitation between material and respondent, even if his theatrical style demands a kind of mental or imaginative tension that Wagner's mythic pageants, by their very spectacular nature, are designed to elide. All the more reason that Nietzsche's rhetorical style should be considered for its frequent recourse to just that sort of theatricality described in *Human, All Too Human* as baroque: that is, a nonmimetic form of theatricality aimed at the arousal of powerful, persuasive effects in an external audience.

Doing so, we are bound to notice Nietzsche's frequent figural and gestural solicitations to his reader, his way of transforming direct address into something like a stylistic principle. "Yes, my friends, believe as I do in the Dionysiac life and in the rebirth of tragedy. The time of Socratic man is past," writes the author of *The Birth of Tragedy*, sounding more like an evan-

Overcoming Ascetic Style

gelist than a philologist (*BT* 20 [98]). Here and elsewhere, his discourse refuses to proceed mimetically, refuses to remain absorbed in representing its analytical objects, and instead becomes a form of direct-address appeal. This fact invites us to borrow and extend Antoine's metaphor to the realm of philosophical rhetoric: with Nietzsche, the "fourth wall" between author and reader has become remarkably permeable, so to speak. Paul de Man notes this quality when he examines *The Birth of Tragedy* "in terms of its own theatricality" and ends up describing it as "a harangue" and almost "a sermon" to a congregation.[53] One such sermonizing example can be found at the end of the book when Nietzsche personifies and ventriloquizes ancient tragedy, writing that it "says to us 'Take a look! Take a close look! This is your life! This is the hour-hand on the clock of your existence!'" (*BT* 24 [113]). There is a kind of pulpit oratory happening here, similar (in Anglophone ears) to the sermons of a John Donne or a Jonathan Edwards, the "sound" of the text working to cultivate complicity between its speaker function and its reader. The effect is not always so obvious: in his later works, Nietzsche is just as likely to nurture this complicity with a more ironic, even sarcastic posture. Still, a consciousness of an external reader or listener as the necessary condition for discourse saturates Nietzsche's writings from *The Birth of Tragedy* (1872) to *Ecce Homo* (1888) in both explicit and implicit forms.[54] Wherever a reader encounters such moments, there is hardly any avoiding the text's stylistic devices. When telling his reader to "Take a look! Take a close look!" Nietzsche's deictic pointing and punctuation overflow into exclamatory furor, aiming to provoke the *pathos* of a Dionysian shock. If baroque rhetoricians seek to persuade by hook or by crook, in this example the reader is being beaten with a club.

Of course, the histrionic, quasi-Wagnerian emotionality of an early work like *The Birth of Tragedy* at times recalls the tradition of pathetic gesture developed in the romantic and melodramatic theaters of the mid-nineteenth century, which gradually ceded ground to more naturalistic forms of dramatic performance.[55] It also bespeaks a rhetorician's approach to drama, a will to (melo)dramatize from behind a lectern, so to speak. Nietzsche's treatment of the written word so radically opens a deconstructive slippage between the practices of speech and writing, *phonè* and *grammé*, that it comes as no surprise to find that he believed strongly in the ancient Greek practice of declaiming his own writings aloud to himself while in the solitary act of composing them. This factoid all on its own suggests a view of writing as one kind of performance.[56] Neither does it come as a surprise to learn that his high admiration for certain pre-Socratic philosophers consisted in his theatrical sense of their use of gesture. Of Anaximander, for example, he writes, in terms that cannot fail to strike the reader as self-referential: "We can easily credit the tradition that he walked the earth clad in an especially dignified garment and displayed a truly tragic pride in his gestures and customs of daily living. He lived as he wrote; he spoke as solemnly as he dressed; he lifted his hands and placed his feet as though this existence were a tragic drama into which he had been born to play a hero" (*PTAG* 4 [49]). It is a challenge to read these lines without imagining Nietzsche, alone at his desk or speaking before a group of listeners, coordinating his hand and feet movements with those of his ancient subject. It is Nietzsche here, far more demonstrably than Anaximander, who understands his own existence as tragic drama. It is Nietzsche who sees philosophy as a rhetorical and dramatic endeavor.

In its most hortatory, grandiloquent moments, then, Nietzsche's closet rhetorical practice serves at least two functions. The first is pedagogical: to instruct and engage the reader or student by dramatizing the delivery. The second is more compositional: to listen for the musicality of the writing, to find the proper gesture in the text, and to borrow Hamlet's advice for the theater, to "[s]uit the action to the word, the word to the action." "This is the hour-hand on the clock of your existence!" is every bit as much a gesture, an *actio*, as it is a philosopheme. The danger with gestural action of this sort is that it can get easily overblown, with the prose style careening from resplendent and passionate to shrill and pompous. Derrida claims that Nietzsche's style takes place "between histrionics and hysterics," but, if this is so, it is precisely because his tragic outlook, again, perceives both the ontological world and the languages that seek to capture it as having, in turn, grown "hysteric" and "histrionic," so to speak.[57] Philosophy must not only describe or represent this situation but also enact or mime it before an audience, as a necessary proof of its reality. For Nietzsche, that is, when ritualized gestures are gradually disappearing from both the theater and public life, the emphatic philosophical gesture becomes everything.[58] It aims at calling into question the autonomous sphere of truth from its very foundations.

There is evidence that Nietzsche cultivated this gestural style of writing with extreme deliberateness. His correspondence with his friend (and would-be lover) Lou Andreas-Salomé, for example, includes a list of ten suggestions "toward the teaching of style."[59] They conceive writing style in terms of public rhetoric, based on the direct-address relation between orator and auditor. Note 2 describes the space between writer and reader precisely in terms of this relation, framing it as a rhetorical feedback loop of sorts: "Style should be suited to the specific person with whom you wish to communicate. (The law of *mutual* relation)." Note 4 revisits the familiar bond between communicative lack and compensatory excess: "Since the writer *lacks* many of the speaker's *means*, he must have in general for his model a *very expressive* kind of presentation of necessity, the written copy will appeal much paler." Note 5 makes writing into a play of gesticulation and feeling: "The richness of life reveals itself through a *richness of gestures*. One must *learn* to feel everything—the length and retarding of sentences, interpunctuations, the choice of words, the pausing, the sequence of arguments—like gestures." Here one gets a sense of how Nietzsche, himself a talented amateur musician, found ways to put his musical sense of expressivity, phrasing, cadence, rhythm, and so forth, into the service of an exceptionally dramatic rhetoric. Notes 7 and 8 highlight the role of feeling in written and oral communication. Note 7 reads: "Style ought to prove that one *believes* in an idea; not only that one thinks it but also *feels* it"; and note 8 states: "The more abstract a truth which one wishes to teach, the more one must first *entice* the senses." Given all these prescriptions for stylish, gestural writing, Nietzsche comes to resemble the various baroque stylists he describes in *Assorted Opinions and Maxims'* passages 131 and 144.

Nietzsche's foremost concern across his late, anti-Wagnerian writings, however, is with the theater—with the modern stage's becoming baroque. It may surprise some readers to learn that he was reasonably knowledgeable about baroque opera, particularly its musical dimensions, even though he lived more than two centuries after its heyday. His *Nachlass* displays a breadth of research on the musical conventions of that period and their relationship to ancient Greek tragedy. Though no specialist in early modern musicology, while writing *The Birth of Tragedy*, he studied the debates in late-sixteenth-century Florence over the relative primacy of music and poetry in the new *dramma per musica*. He had a working knowledge of the main participants in these debates who were responsible for the earliest "operas"—the composers Jacopo Peri and Claudio Monteverdi and the librettists Ottavio Rinuccini and Giulio Caccini.[60] The early operas of those collaborators were being reconsidered during the 1870s—by authors whom Nietzsche consulted and cited such as August Wilhelm Ambros—as evidence of a shift from the music of the Renaissance to that of the baroque. The early operatic tradition even forms the subject of the nineteenth chapter of *The Birth of*

Tragedy, which compares it negatively to Wagner's innovations. Early opera was born, the chapter alleges, out of the "amusement-hungry luxury of certain circles in Florence and the vanity of their dramatic singers."[61] It was a product of "Socratic" or "Alexandrian culture" (*BT* 19 [89, 91]), an artistic offspring of Renaissance "theoretical man," one that subsumed Dionysian music to words and "the reason-governed rhetoric of passion."[62] In every respect, *The Birth of Tragedy* figures Wagner as a Dionysian solution to Socratic problems with origins in the historical baroque. Even so, just a few years later, in *Human, All Too Human*, Nietzsche reverses course, claiming Wagner's work as itself a problem with baroque origins.

Likewise, while he was no orthodox historian of early modern theater, Nietzsche's concept of baroque theatricality reflects extraordinary insight into early modern performance practices. The stage history of the period often revolves around asides, soliloquys, prologues, epilogues, choral interludes, intermezzi, songs and arias, emblematic figurations, and other moments that interrupt the closed circuit of mimetic representation, requiring the performer to gaze outward at his beholders. These moments of address function as allegories of spectatorship, reminding the audience that they are witnessing a work of theater, of stage pretense. They would be systematically purged from the stage beginning in the late eighteenth century, the time of Diderot (as I have claimed elsewhere in an argument indebted to Péter Szondi's work).[63] Prior to the Enlightenment, however, as Joseph Roach has demonstrated, stage performance during the early baroque was in most cases a species of direct-address oratory, delivered outwardly to the audience and focused almost exclusively on the criterion of *actio* or pathetic gesture received from ancient authorities (from Cicero and Quintilian, mostly, whose views were adapted and disseminated by modern gesture theorists like Bulwer). As Roach writes of early-seventeenth-century stage practice, "Oratorical delivery, by definition, orients the speaker face to face with his audience, whose continuous presence he must at least implicitly acknowledge."[64] The outward-facing gaze accompanying the orator's vocal and manual delivery served effectively as a form of gesture all its own, creating a rift in the closed fictive world of the play, a hole in the fabric of representation.

Such delivery sought to set hearts trembling and to conduct sensibilities with an almost electromagnetic force, as Nietzsche clearly observed.[65] Roach has further shown that gesture was understood in the early modern theater as a means of commanding animal spirits, manipulating the humoral body in both physiological and psychological ways; and, in all this, passionate

Overcoming Ascetic Style

histrionics were celebrated and feared as a magical summoning of chthonic forces.[66] Demonic powers attached to the passions—a Nietzschean might call them Dionysiac powers. It was the rhetorician's job to use sound and gesture to conduct these passions from the lower depths of the listener's body. In maxim 144, the task recalls that of the modern orchestral conductor, who coordinates the energies of musicians in performance for the sake of enforcing a musico-emotional impact on the audience. With fulminating *hypokrisis* and *pathos* the baroque actor (like a Wagnerian conductor) directs sensibilities toward himself, out of the audience, as a metal pole conducts lightning. Especially in the later Wagner of *Tristan und Isolde*, the *Ring* cycle, and *Parsifal*, this outward and parabatic orientation is consistently notable on the part of the singers onstage, necessitated by the material's mythic and allegorical orientation, which sets limits to any possibility for realism or absorption. At the climactic end of *Tristan* for example, an opera Nietzsche considered "the real *opus metaphysicum* of all art" (*UM* IV 8 [232]), as Isolde exhales her transfiguring *Liebestod* ("Love Death") song over the corpse of her lover, she becomes a stationary onstage emblem of redemption through love. Conventionally facing the auditorium of onlookers directly, she permits Wagner's music to hail them directly through an extended scene of mesmerizing gestures. As with Bernini's Saint Theresa, Isolde's ecstasies guarantee the theatrical medium its surest moment of triumph.

This technique has origins in baroque mise-en-scène, as scholars of Nietzsche's lifetime knew well—including Ambros, whose work Nietzsche admired. Stage realism from Diderot's time on primarily used scenes of absorptive action to transfix its audience, as Michael Fried has shown.[67] Instead, the authors and composers of the baroque stage characteristically inverted this tendency. In baroque opera, as in baroque theater more generally, the theatricality of direct address functions as a primary means to captivate attention. Since Ambros hailed Wagner as a "modern Monteverdi," an example from Monteverdi's 1607 *favola in musica* (musical fable) *L'Orfeo*, the oldest surviving baroque opera still regularly performed, will help demonstrate the similarity.[68] Based on the Orpheus myth, it opens with a prologue sung by Music, allegorically personified, who addresses the assembled audience directly to command their attention. She instructs the pastoral landscape onstage to cease its sound and movement, just as Orpheus's music will work its own hypnotic effects on the natural world, and just as Monteverdi seeks to hush the crowd of Florentine nobles. The allegory of Music chants: "Now, as I vary my songs from joy to sorrow, / May no small bird move in these plants, / May no sounding wave be heard on these banks, / And may every little breeze be stopped still in its path."[69] With a look, a gesture, a moment of address, time comes to a standstill. Everything freezes in its place for a moment, suspended as if at high noon. On the baroque stage, frame-breaking moments of this kind often privileged operatic passion over heroic action and were the source of the theater's most powerful enchantments. In the onstage, outward-facing figure of Isolde, in whom all musical and metaphysical motion finds a similar ultimate stillness, Wagner reveals himself an inheritor to the cultural weight of this baroque history. Nietzsche was the one to take note.

But, if Nietzsche counted himself "lucky" to detect Wagner's baroque debts, this noticing was a mixed blessing to say the least, given his own ambiguous closeness to baroque style. It is not accidental that those baroque characteristics Nietzsche finds in Wagner's musical aesthetics ("the eloquence of strong emotions and gestures, of the sublime and ugly," etc.) cut equally in the direction of his own theatrical rhetoric. Nietzsche's writing also sets the heart trembling; its materials and themes are likewise of the highest dramatic tension; it too trades in powerful emotions, striking gestures and figures, in its own furious, sometimes ugly sublimity. Not only does Nietzsche often resemble the baroque orators of maxim 131, but he would also claim in his private notes of summer 1878 that "the Dionysian dithyramb is the baroque style of poetry"; and by the late 1880s he would even take to writing his own dithyrambic poetry, at the very same time he was preparing to denounce the baroque charlatan Wagner in the most vitriolic terms.[70] Nietzsche apparently felt drawn to the baroque as to a dangerous but ineluctable force. In *The Case of Wagner*, baroque style would finally prove for him a desired, if ambiguous, means of self-overcoming.

Resentful and Affirmative Baroques

In his public account, Nietzsche's decision to end his friendship with Wagner came in 1878, when Wagner mailed him a copy of *Parsifal*'s libretto, a gift that Nietzsche esteemed a mortal insult. He sent the composer in return a copy of *Human, All Too Human*, later describing the exchange in *Ecce Homo* as a crossing of swords (*EH* "Human" 5 [119]). The two men never saw each other again. From then until 1882, when *Parsifal*'s premiere consecrated the Bayreuth Festspielhaus as a shrine to Wagner's religion of art, Nietzsche kept his distance and studied the new work's musical score. Then, in 1886, three years after Wagner's death, Nietzsche began voicing public

Overcoming Ascetic Style

disgust with *Parsifal*'s overt religiosity, even without having ever heard it performed professionally. With this last work, he claimed, "Richard Wagner, seemingly the all-conquering, actually a decaying, despairing romantic, suddenly sank down helpless and shattered before the Christian cross" (*HH* "Preface" 3 [210-11]). Wagner had not only abused the young Nietzsche's friendship and love, it turned out, but betrayed the ancient tragic values that had initially drawn them together, and fled in the end back to the Christian faith and the Catholic "spirit of the Counter-Reformation."[71] Far from a modern, emancipatory metaphysics of art, *Parsifal* was just the old, decaying metaphysics in a new disguise. But Nietzsche's public denunciation of *Parsifal* masked a more ambivalent opinion, one he had secretly held toward Wagner's music since his first encounter with it.[72] In 1887, when he finally had the chance to hear the opera's overture performed orchestrally, he wrote to his friend Peter Gast of his admiration for the work (27 January 1887), comparing it favorably to Dante's poetry: "[D]id Wagner ever compose anything better?"[73]

One year later, Nietzsche's *Case of Wagner* (1888) made yet another about-face and put the late composer on trial for the crime of histrionics. Rather than a great musician, *The Case* describes Wagner as "an actor" (*CW* 7 [245]). It alleges that Wagner made music into a kind of "theatrical rhetoric, a means of expression, of intensifying gestures, of suggestion, of psychological picturesque" (*CW* 8 [247]) and that "as a musician [Wagner] is still a rhetorician" (*CW* 10 [251]).[74] The later *Nietzsche contra Wagner*—assembled from fragments of Nietzsche's previous writings but only published after his mental collapse—reiterates these charges:

> You will guess that I am essentially anti-theatrical, that I regard the theatre, this art of the masses *par excellence*, with the same deep contempt from the bottom of my soul that every artist today will feel. . . . But Wagner, apart from the Wagner who created the loneliest music in existence, was, conversely, essentially a man of the theatre and an actor, perhaps the most enthusiastic mimomaniac that ever existed, *even as a musician*. And, incidentally, if it was Wagner's theory that 'the drama is the end; the music is always merely the means'—, his practice was always from beginning to end, 'the attitude is the end; the drama, and the music, too, is always merely *its* means.' Music as a means of clarification, strengthening, internalization of the dramatic gesture and the actor's appeal to the senses; and the Wagnerian drama a mere occasion for many dramatic attitudes! (*NCW* "Objections" [267])

These indictments are summed up with a term that Nietzsche borrows (and adapts) from Plato's *Laws*: "*Theatrocracy*—, the sheer idiocy of believing in the priority of the theatre, that theatre has the right to dominate over the arts, over art" (*CW* "Postscript" [256]). Not only does Wagner render music secondary to drama in the Aristotelian sense of representational poetry and plot, but he instinctually renders music and poetry both secondary to statuesque poses, gestures, attitudes, all to gain a sensuous control over his audience. Music and poetry are here both dominated by the tendency to grasp for "the rhetorical and the dramatic." In these last condemnatory writings, the composer again appears as a baroque figure, his name a sign for "*the downfall of music*, as Bernini is for the downfall of sculpture" (*CW* "Second Postscript" [259]).

Several critics have taken these late anti-Wagnerian pronouncements as evidence of an unambiguous anti-theatrical posture on Nietzsche's part.[75] *The Case of Wagner*, however, complicates this view by asserting effectively that there is no outside to Wagnerism, no point of pure or transcendent critique uncontaminated by the pervasive will-to-theatricality Wagner represents. Leaning heavily on a rhetoric of cultural decadence borrowed from Paul Bourget's writings, Nietzsche confesses: "I am just as much a child of my age as Wagner, which is to say a *decadent*: it is just that I have understood this, I have resisted it. The philosopher in me resisted it. . . . Wagner sums up modernity. It's no use, we must first be Wagnerians."[76] Wagner is given to histrionics, but what modern subject is not? Nietzsche's efforts to name Wagner's baroque style now appear as part of a vision of European modernity, writ large, as a baroque process of ruination. Eve Sedgwick has argued that Nietzsche's recognition of Wagner's decadence follows the format of homosexual attribution within the late-nineteenth-century epistemological context established by the closet. The "interminable logic" of recognizing another person as a fellow decadent is always: "*it takes one to know one.*"[77] The same goes for baroque style, whose description in *Human, All Too Human* cuts toward both Wagner and Nietzsche alike. A deeper sympathy and a covert self-referentiality motivates Nietzsche's comments on baroque style and Wagner—*it takes one to know one*. This self-referential quality becomes most explicit with Nietzsche's late confession in *Ecce Homo* (1888) that he previously used Wagner's name in his own writings as one of his many rhetorical disguises. "Unmasking" himself, he reveals: "[A]t every psychologically decisive spot I am only talking about myself,—you can put

Overcoming Ascetic Style

my name or the word 'Zarathustra' without hesitation wherever the text has the word 'Wagner'" (*EH* "Books" BT: 4 [111]).

This is an admission of great consequence for all of Nietzsche's writings —a psychoanalyst might designate it an almost schizoid instance of depersonalization, or an intensely narcissistic conflation of the self and the other —and it makes clear that the polemic against Wagner cannot be understood as a purely anti-theatrical screed in any simple sense. If the name "Wagner" functions at times rhetorically to disguise Nietzsche's name in the earlier works, Nietzsche's allegations of Wagner's theatricality suddenly throw his own metatheatrical histrionics into high relief. For, if "[i]t's no use, we must first be Wagnerians," then any attempt to criticize Wagner's predisposition to theatricality from a purely external, innocent position would be subject to a kind of performative "backfiring." Rather, Nietzsche's late writings do more than condemn his external adversary. They must be understood instead as attempts at *self*-overcoming, *self*-disidentification. *The Case of Wagner* can easily be read as *The Case of Nietzsche*, or else, borrowing Nietzsche's subtitle for *The Birth of Tragedy*'s 1886 preface, as "An Attempt at Self-Criticism." In recognizing Wagner as a representative of baroque style in the arts, Nietzsche came to understand his own susceptibility to forms of baroque style in thinking and writing. The concept of the baroque then functions in a dual way in Nietzsche's work, both prosecuting Wagner and indicting the prosecutor Nietzsche at once, an ironic and immanent critique. Hence Nietzsche's thoroughgoing ambivalence, equal parts sympathy and revulsion, toward baroque style. *De te fabula narratur*. He knows that this story is about him.

And about us too. Often hailed as the first diagnostician and initiator of what is sometimes still called "postmodernity," Nietzsche found the concept of the baroque useful for naming a widespread cultural condition that the twentieth and twenty-first centuries would only continue to intensify. With Nietzsche it can be said that if there is no outside to Wagnerism, then there can be no outside to the baroque either, no normative and ascetic classicism to which one might successfully appeal: there is now only baroque and counterbaroque. The baroque thus entails a crucial, internal division between competing tendencies, variously Wagnerian and Nietzschean in orientation. The difference between the two—complicated by the fact the Nietzsche clearly perceived similarities to Wagner within himself— cannot be reduced to a simple opposition between baroque romanticisms and modernisms, or between unwitting deployments of baroque style and more calculated ones. Clearly, neither tendency involves either a simple embrace or a disavowal of theater as a value; each exploits forms of theatricality differently. How, then, to tease apart these two competing visions of baroque style?

In the case of Nietzsche, the difference pertains ultimately to the figure of Dionysus, in that Nietzsche recognized the ancient Dionysian dithyramb as "the baroque style of poetry." At a basic level, baroque style can be characterized as a Dionysian phenomenon, a counterweight to the tendency in "classic expression" toward Apollonian restraint. But a distinction *internal* to the baroque also clearly exists, one that divides its own immanent Apollonian and Dionysian orientations against each other. This is clear because, at yet another level, Wagner's baroque style appears in some respects more Apollonian in its approach, if not in its final effects. Nietzsche's 1888 writings criticize the composer on grounds that have a decidedly Apollonian resonance: "Was Wagner even a musician? In any case he was something more: an incomparable histrio, the greatest mime, the most astonishing genius of the theatre that Germany has ever seen, our *scenic artist par excellence*."[78] Wagner puts Dionysian music to the Apollonian ends of formal images (*Bilder*) and appearance (*Schein*): mimetic-dramatic poetry, visible and sculptural gesture, visual scenic effects, the psychologically "picturesque," and so forth (*CW* 8 [247]). Nietzsche further argues that "Wagner's whole struggle was to find every means of procuring clarity" (*UM* IV 9 [242]), recalling the baroque stylist's need "to make himself *understood* and thereby to acquire force."[79] All these aims bespeak an Apollonian desire to separate eye and rational mind from ear and intuitive feeling, elevating the former over the latter. For Nietzsche, Wagner seeks a form of melody that suits tone to word, allowing the dramatic libretto to become intelligible, putting Dionysian sound under the dominion of Apollonian word, all for the purposes of maximum persuasiveness.

It would be one thing if these clearly defined gestures and poses were somehow *stylized*—in the ritualistic sense Nietzsche demands of drama in his rejoinders to Aristotle, or even in the highly formal nature of gesture on the baroque stage (a subject to explored later in my analysis of Walter Benjamin). Instead, Nietzsche sees Wagnerian performers as too "naturalistic" in their gestural and attitudinal deportment—hence not plastic, sculptural, or Apollonian *enough* (*NCW* "Danger" 1 [269]). In reproducing the empirical habits of everyday gesture, they behave in ways that are more scientific or

Overcoming Ascetic Style

observational. To continue using the lexicon of *The Birth of Tragedy*, they are more Euripidean or Socratic than Dionysian.

Rather than creating a true sacred ritual appropriate for a post-Christian world, Wagner's dramas were simply human, all too human, focusing on bourgeois, naturalistic, psychological characters parading around in fancy mythological dress. The heroines, in particular, reminded Nietzsche of Flaubert's Madame Bovary (*CW* 9 [250]). Far from reanimating the spirit of ancient tragedy, Wagner had only managed to create a modern pastiche of tragic drama: closer in structure, as Samuel Weber has argued, to the allegorical plays of the baroque theater than to Aeschylus.[80] These collisions—of antiquity and modernity, myth and scientific naturalism, tragedy and Christianity, Greek and baroque—produce what Nietzsche deemed an affected quality. Although *The Birth of Tragedy* suggests Wagner's music holds out certain Dionysian promise, when this music is translated into total spectacle, this promise gives way to forces of *ressentiment* which reject the phenomenal world as a Dionysian becoming. As such, Wagner's theater ends up becoming baroque, and in the worst of all possible ways.

This reading conforms to the fact that, in 1886, Nietzsche refers on two separate occasions to prevailing norms of Christian morality—that greatest expression, in his estimation, of resentful world disavowal—as "baroque" and "unreasonable" ("barock . . . unvernünftig"; *BGE* 198 [85]; 261 [157]). Modern Christianity in this view has become a force of philosophically irrational, baroque complexity and, by suggestion, has never fully escaped its Counter-Reformation moment. Against this usage one must also juxtapose Nietzsche's belief that "the Dionysian dithyramb is the baroque style of poetry." From this claim, it is clear he also understood baroque style to contain another set of possibilities altogether, for better rather than for worse. With Nietzsche's late writings, the baroque appears divided between its *life-affirming* (hence Dionysian) and *life-denying* tendencies, between an impulse to celebrate the world as a ceaseless becoming and an impulse to negate it, resentfully, in favor of some supposedly more real, just, or perfect reality. In short, there is a baroque style of Dionysus, and a baroque style of ressentiment, and the former must continually contend with the latter.[81]

On this count, *Parsifal*'s baroque style is most explicitly offensive, regardless of what Wagner's "original intentions" for it might have been. Whether *Parsifal*'s late Christianity was genuinely evangelical or was a strategic metaphor for the future of art, or bad faith, or just cynical pandering to whatever seemed to be in popular demand—all these explanations are beside the point. In Wagner's traditional love of mimesis, and in *Parsifal*'s dramaturgical preference for Christian redemption, Nietzsche detects a reactive and melancholy metaphysics, one that despises the innocent *fluxus* of the world. Whether consciously or not, Wagner promotes baroque forms of excitement in *Parsifal* in order to assert this revanchist metaphysics. Nietzsche's baroque style unfolds as theater to an opposing set of ends. It demystifies every life-negating metaphysics, encourages active and independent thinking in the most vigorous sense, and affirms the physical world in all its Dionysian dynamism.

In *The Case of Wagner*'s last full-length chapter, Wagner's reactionary baroque metaphysics extends beyond the realm of art and into politics, with catastrophic consequences. At Bayreuth, Wagner the theater director becomes a transcendent force organizing the total spectacle from outside, like a divine sovereign or chief executive. This was a marked departure from the prior tradition of actor-managers who organized the process of theatrical collaboration from within. Such role play holds a wide potential for political regression, as Nietzsche suggests: "Wagner the actor is a tyrant," a craven one who is eager to dominate the passions of an audience but also depends slavishly on that audience in return (*CW* 8 [247]). On both sides of the equation, only contemptible, secondhand, reactive affects are at stake, *merely theatrical* passions rather than Dionysian ecstasies. This tyrannical emotional manipulation, far from seeking to overthrow existing conditions, wants to retrench the now-disenchanted metaphysics of the past, a metaphysics already evaporated in a world whose perpetual secularization Nietzsche would allegorize in his narrative of the death of God. Amid this crisis of theological values, Wagner's baroque rhetoric functions to manipulate a "guided culture," shepherding his audience through a crisis moment to an even more dangerous and retrograde destination.[82] As Nietzsche sees it, Wagner desires a herd of followers whose capacity for critical judgment is violently overthrown amid an experience of ravishing sublimity (*CW* 5, 6, 9). More accurately, the crowd *thinks* it experiences the sublime but is really able only to wonder vaguely in response to the narcotic stupefactions Wagner has to offer.[83]

Nietzsche is not only expressing concern here about the political dangers of a new kind of theater: his criticisms of Wagner target an entirely new kind of personality or social subjectivity, organized around the notion of spectacular display, an extreme extroversion predicated on understanding social life as suffused everywhere by performance before the eyes of others.

Overcoming Ascetic Style

As Nietzsche predicts, the specifically political effects of this new theatrical culture will prove dire. As he writes in an often-overlooked passage: "It is of profound significance that Wagner emerged at the same time as the *Reich*: both facts prove the same thing—obedience and long legs.—There has never been more obedience—or better orders. Wagnerian music directors in particular are worthy of an age that posterity will one day refer to, with a sort of timid respect, as *the classical age of war*. Wagner knew how to command; he was the great teacher of this as well" (*CW* 11 [254]; emphasis in original). In the end, Nietzsche sees Wagner's rise as heralding a new era of human unfreedom and violence. With Wagner's baroque style only making matters worse, a baroque counterforce is needed to stop Europe from sleepwalking into the abyss. There is no need to underline the sense, as so many have already done, that these claims carry the ring of prophecy when faced with the dawning century that Nietzsche never lived to see. He had clearly enough memory, of his own historical experience in the Franco-Prussian War and, in the more distant historical rear view, the seventeenth-century wars of religion in the age of baroque absolutism. Wagner's life-denying metaphysics, Nietzsche suggests, will produce not sublimity but actual, world-destroying horrors. From the initial seed of Dionysian promise that Nietzsche first detected in Wagner, there springs a poisoned fruit of resentment, which will in turn unleash actual violence upon the world.[84]

These criticisms tell us much about Nietzsche's preferred vision of baroque style by contrast. Against the Dionysian shapelessness, as it were, of Wagner's extended musical phrases—which Nietzsche claims plunge the listener into a groundless, oceanic depth of sound or a bath of Genovese broth[85]—Nietzsche now appears in his final writings to pause in dread. If baroque style can be thought a Dionysian phenomenon, Nietzsche would rather temper it with the pagan or tragic force of Apollo than with Christian resentfulness. In the final analysis, a recrudescent Apollonianism marks Nietzsche's thoughts on baroque, one with clear connections to his much-vaunted spiritual and artistic "elitism." The baroque is not only a mode of Dionysian expressiveness; it also possesses its own Apollonian radiance: Nietzsche admires the grandeur of the baroque age for its "aristocratism" and embraces baroque style for its noble strength, its valuing of distinction, and its resplendent, aesthetic morality.[86] As *The Case of Wagner* implies, such aristocratism need not favor the literal, violent exercise of force, tyranny, imperialism, or warfare. Neither does it authorize aristocracy in the literal sense of the word as the enforced rule of a ruthless economic elite: Nietzsche's disdain for the wealthiest members of his own bourgeois society is manifest throughout his body of work.[87] Still, considering *The Case of Wagner*'s comments about the manipulation of theater audiences, Nietzsche's aristocratic embrace of baroque style reflects an anxiety about the dangers of mass culture and rapid democratization. Within certain conditions, Nietzschean aristocratism could paradoxically become the necessary antidemocratic homeopath required for any authentically democratic project to succeed, as Wendy Brown has suggested.[88] If so, with *The Case of Wagner*, the baroque of church, bourgeoisie, empire, and the eternal law now appears to belong to the past. What Nietzsche clamors for instead is a properly Zarathustrian vision of baroque style, a noble, active, and life-affirming force, full of multiplicity, variation, and perpetual difference. It was a style of the greatest antiquity that his own writings fought against Wagner to prepare, a dissident theatricality if ever there were one. Call it *Zukunftsbarock*, the baroque of the future.

De Te Fabula Narratur

Once Nietzsche can be recognized as a baroque theorist, his body of writings transforms. This insight extends to *The Birth of Tragedy*, which Paul de Man recognized as possessing a baroque dramaturgy all its own, filled with the operatic-mythologic stage machinery of gods, intriguers, and mythic heroes. It enfolds Nietzsche's claim that the Übermensch greets the thought of eternal recurrence by "insatiably calling out *da capo*" (*BGE* 56 [51]), giving it the name of baroque opera's paradigmatic aria structure, popularized by Handel.[89] The musicologist Martin Lorenz has even argued recently that Nietzsche's 1883 Dionysian dithyramb entitled "Ariadne's Lament" ("Klage der Ariadne") is best understood as an "opera scene" in response to the aria "Lamento d'Arianna" by Monteverdi, a fragment of a forgotten baroque opera (*L'Arianna*, 1608) rediscovered in Paris in 1868.[90] Nietzsche's poem takes shape as a solo dramatic soliloquy in direct address, spoken or sung by Ariadne at the climax of a Dionysian ravishment, a scenario like that depicted in Bernini's *Ecstasy of Saint Theresa*. In a moment of textual theatricality, the poem concludes with a stage direction and a magical event of the sort typically seen in baroque opera, the "onstage" appearance of the god whom Ariadne had previously been addressing ("A flash of lightning. Dionysus becomes visible in emerald beauty"). Dionysus concludes the poem by telling Ariadne: "I am thy labyrinth" (*DD* "Ariadne's Complaint" [59]). Nietzsche authorized the poem's publication in 1888 among his other Dionysian

Overcoming Ascetic Style 59

dithyrambs as one of his final literary acts before succumbing to madness. This fact suggests that his fascination and identification with baroque theatricality continued unabated until the very end.

The mythic topos of Ariadne's labyrinth offers a final insight into Nietzsche's baroque. The philosopher Karsten Harries has traced a persistent fascination with labyrinth figures in Nietzsche's rhetoric and has found in them evidence of consistent connection to the baroque "world-picture."[91] Whereas early modern Christian thinkers (such as Comenius) saw the world as a labyrinth or theater created by the fall of man, Harries observes that the new scientific rationality (of Bacon and Descartes) had claimed the authority to lead mankind out of this fallen state, thus constituting "modernity . . . in opposition to Christian Mannerism and the Baroque, in opposition to their key metaphors of theater and labyrinth."[92] For Harries, Nietzsche's preoccupation with labyrinths calls into question whether modern scientific rationality can guide humanity out of the great labyrinth or theater of the world of appearance toward some external domain of Truth. Harries writes that for Nietzsche, the labyrinth amounts to

> a *mysterium tremendum et fascinans* that Nietzsche longs to enter, even if this should mean death. . . . Nietzsche—having refuted Descartes's claim to the discovery of Ariadne's thread—is often invoked today as a kind of antipode, a thinker who mocks all suitors of truth and shows us the way back into the labyrinth. From this perspective modernity seems encircled by a postmodern labyrinth that answers to the labyrinth of Mannerism and the Baroque. . . . [I]t is precisely because our attempts to secure our existence have so effectively left the Mannerist or Baroque labyrinth behind that Nietzsche dreams of the labyrinth and seeks "an Ariadne's thread" leading into it.[93]

The baroque as *a style of reasoning* involves a conceptual wandering within labyrinths without the guarantee that instrumental reason (*Vernunft*) will deliver one from the Minotaur's clutches into some redemptive Truth outside. Cultivating his philosophical baroque style through the medium of the printed word—which addresses its audience in the form of the solitary reader, rather than as a mass public—Nietzsche need not make any assurances that his works will communicate to his reader a full and final truth. What he offers is not a Cartesian way out but an Ariadne's thread back into the labyrinth of the world, even with all its terrifying complexities and catacombs. Once again, this intention has important ramifications not only for Nietzsche as a producer of philosophical content (questions, methods, claims, etc.) but for his form as well, in terms of his writing style and chosen medium. In Wagner's theater, one can easily fall prey to the Gorgiastic feeling of a truth's plentiful presence. With Nietzsche's baroque rhetoric, however, the reader is always addressed directly and asked to interpret the author's complicated, ironic, theatrical style. It is no overstatement to say that the history of Nietzsche's reception is a history of the very literal dangers that attend this injunction to interpretation.

Where theater is concerned, Nietzsche's dialectics of the baroque also involves a set of positions regarding the use and meaning of gesture. In the still-Christian ideology of Wagner's baroque, the gesturer onstage (or in the orchestra pit) is understood in metaphysical terms as a cause, and the resulting gestures are consequent effects whose physical conduct and communicative meaning remain fully under his control. This metaphysics of stage gesture shores up a consoling, identitarian notion of the self as a stable and centered subject. Nietzsche's Zarathustrian baroque dispenses with these possibilities altogether. In his writing, the "gestures" of the text become "hysteric," losing control of themselves and their significations in a drive toward Dionysian self-abandonment. These gestures point, as it were, to no single stable referent, but in a multiplicity of directions at once. They open up an abyssal game of reflections, a space of infinite play. Where Wagnerian gesture was overly naturalistic, reflecting the near-total identification of actor and represented character, Nietzsche's gestures are essentially enigmatic in their functioning. They resemble less the sort of gestures we expect from actors in the modern realist or naturalist theater than those from the history of oratory, from the Sophists to Bulwer. They do not spring from an internal self as a transcendent source. They instead come to the gesturer (as is always the case with conventional, rhetorical *gestus*) from the outside in. They are thus nonmatrixed, nonunified, enfolding a distance between the gesturer and the gestured that can never fully be bridged.

Unraveling the performer's sovereignty with every movement, such enigmatic gestures become opportunities for a different mode of address. If Wagner's theater hails its audience directly to enthrall them before the mystery of that address's "source," Nietzsche's theatricality directly opposes this maneuver. His texts invite the dispersal of religious mysteries precisely through their theatricality, by asking the reader to participate in the active, interpretive construction of their meanings.[94] This attitude on his part presupposes a different understanding of baroque wonder. With Wagner's the-

Overcoming Ascetic Style

61

ater, the gesture's wonder-producing power is directed toward overthrowing the spectator's capacity for independent thought amid intensely elevated feeling and vague, unthinking anticipation. Ventriloquizing Wagner, Nietzsche writes, "Our notion of 'style' takes this as its point of departure. Above all, not thinking! Nothing is more compromising than a thought!" (CW 6 [243]). With Wagnerian wonder, thinking is held in abeyance while the audience is suspended amidst an overwhelming, passionate chaos (*CW* 6). It is, in other words, a kind of metaphysical awe that Wagner's baroque demands, akin to that demanded by the God of monotheism in *Ecce Homo*'s description: "God is a ridiculously crude answer, an *undelicatesse* against us thinkers—, basically even a ridiculously crude *ban* on us: thou shall not think!" (*EH* "Clever" 1 [85]). Such baroque awe serves subtly to entrench the status quo, to reinforce a "reified" view of the world's current order as full of metaphysical inevitability.[95]

By contrast, the form of baroque wonder embraced by Nietzsche proceeds toward the horizon of defamiliarization. It deploys theatrical effects and their attendant excitements to produce not theological awe but philosophical wonder as the necessary prior condition for the beginnings of critical thought. Wagner's baroque style still evinces faith in the old metaphysics —a credulous, dogmatic faith in truth, representation, action, teleology, and so forth. In peering obscurely through the "fourth wall," Nietzsche's baroque casts this entire regime into doubt. Once this fourth wall is effectively broken, the Nietzschean baroque comes to see theater everywhere. It torques the old theocentric metaphor of the *theatrum mundi*, or the world as a stage— with a fixed spectator-creator, together with stable roles and actors—into a vision of the world as a theater with no center at all—a *mysterium tremendum et fascinans*, and a labyrinthine field of immanent play.

Some commentators may take fault with Nietzsche's critique of Wagner as baroque, arguing that it is unfair to charge the composer with the crime of theatricality when all art and performance require the presence of an audience. There can be no denying this requirement as an inescapable condition of all art-making practices. Nietzsche's critique amounts less to an assault on a single artist's histrionic predilections than to a widespread diagnosis: that denying the presence of the audience is no longer possible or believable; that naturalism in representation as such has entered the realm of the incredible. Stage realism, in its mimetic depiction of the world as a fixed ensemble of facts or conditions, becomes suspicious in this framework as a kind of life-denying anti-reality. What Nietzsche desires and models instead is a mode of anti-realistic theatrical staging that puts the world into vital play as much as possible.

With the emergence of this "Nietzschean baroque," the conditions are set for the later development of modernist defamiliarization effects on the stage, most notably by Bertolt Brecht, himself a devout Nietzschean as a young man. (Walter Benjamin will offer his own account of the historical roots of such defamiliarizing techniques in his concept of baroque allegory.) Nietzsche's *Untimely Meditation* "Richard Wagner in Bayreuth" expresses these aims in terms that most radically seem to anticipate Brecht's later work. That which is "untimely," as this meditation professes, is precisely the capacity "to regard the commonplace and everyday as something very uncommon and complex" (*UM* IV 4 [210]); or, as Giorgio Agamben has argued, the capacity for feeling disconnected, anachronistic, or out-of-joint with one's present time.[96] Against the myth of progressive history whereby the past is repeatedly repressed (or oppressed) in favor of an advancing triumphal civilization, the *Untimely Meditations* asserts the genealogist's need to stand apart from the flow of time, outside the optimism that views the historical present as necessary and unchangeable. In a passage that resonates vividly with Marx's "Theses on Feuerbach" and Brecht's "Short Organum for the Theater," Nietzsche writes disdainfully of German historians:

> Most of them involuntarily believe that the way things have turned out [in history] is very good. If history were not still a disguised Christian Theodicy, if it were written with more justice and warmth of feeling, it would truly be of no use whatever for the purpose to which it is now put: to serve as an opiate for everything revolutionary and innovative. Philosophy is in a similar situation: all most people want to learn from it is a rough—very rough!—understanding of the world, so they can accommodate themselves to the world. . . . To me, on the other hand, the most vital of questions for philosophy appears to be to what extent the character of the world is unalterable: so as, once this question has been answered, to set about *improving that part of it recognized as alterable* with the most ruthless courage. (*UM* IV 3 [207-8]; emphasis original)

Against the illusion of a given reality that must be accepted as a necessary fate, against what Wagner's Christian baroque posits as the "apparently invincible necessity [of] power, law, tradition, compact, and the whole prevailing order of things" (*UM* IV 4 [212]), Nietzsche proposes untimeliness as the means to an attenuated but still liberatory variability. Through this anach-

Overcoming Ascetic Style

ronic posture, the untimely reader or spectator attains to an astonishing defamiliarization of everyday "reality." This attainment accounts for Nietzsche's untimely embrace of baroque style as a means to critical thought.

While Nietzsche's transvaluation of the baroque helped inspire Wölfflin's later interest in the subject, his debate with Wagner stretches far beyond the academic study of baroque art history and into the larger emergence of modernism.[97] Nietzsche would go on to influence generations of European and American playwrights, as David Kornhaber has shown with respect to the plays of August Strindberg, George Bernard Shaw, and Eugene O'Neill.[98] These authors largely drew on Nietzsche's theory of tragedy for the sake of creating new, renovated versions of that form, in the case of Strindberg and O'Neill, or of creating the philosophical dialogue play or "Drama of Ideas," in the case of Shaw. All three playwrights also contributed to the development of stage naturalism and realism (for example, Strindberg's *Miss Julie* and O'Neill's *Long Day's Journey into Night*). Beyond these figures, Nietzsche also exerted a widespread influence over new generations of playwrights and theorists who found themselves in an even more conflictual relation with the classical demand for mimesis, as the ensuing chapters show. In addition to the Nietzsche whose visions of ancient tragedy and critiques of Christian morality inspired new representational dramas on social themes, there was also a Nietzsche who became influential as a theorist of style, of the baroque, and of a future anti-representational theatricality.

Even where Nietzsche's influence cannot be traced directly, the constitutively modern condition of crisis his writing diagnoses would only continue to crescendo over the twentieth century. The problem of theatricality in the field of modernist (and "postmodern") art would continue to trouble thinkers well into the late 1960s, as Michael Fried's writing makes clear, and beyond that time into our present day. Likewise, the convulsions of the modern world with which Nietzsche associates the baroque—stemming from modern secularization, nihilism, commodity circulation, identitarianism, and tyranny—have only become more urgent since Nietzsche's lifetime. It is therefore little surprise that the question of the baroque should become a subject of vibrant concern for thinkers such as Stéphane Mallarmé, Walter Benjamin, Gertrude Stein, and others. These twentieth-century Nietzscheans developed his baroque vision into a theory and praxis for modernist performance, one that still holds out a promise for twenty-first-century readers as well.

2 The Matter of Spectacle
Mallarmé and the Futures
of Theatrical Ostentation

> an image marked by the mysterious seal of modernity, at
> once baroque and beautiful . . .
>
> —Stéphane Mallarmé, "The Ecclesiastic"

Amid the many pleated fans and bleating fauns found in Mallarmé's poetry, amid the saints and angels painted in gilt, the vicars in cassocks that undulate with lust, the art nouveau plumage, the ornate room interiors, the elaborate reliquaries, the diction as fine as Sèvres porcelain, the yearning to wear female masks and noms de plume . . . Amid so many tortuous phrases and clauses, amid the paroxysms of metaphysical uncertainty, the mounting feelings of crisis in economy and language—what does Mallarmé have to say of baroque style? Moreover, what might baroque style make Mallarmé's theater *mean*, and what does his theater mean for the baroque? At a basic level, the sheer *difficulty* of his poetry, notorious among his critics, brings these questions at least initially into focus and recalls the connotation of "baroque" as a species of extreme complexity.[1] Perhaps Mallarmé's connection to baroque style simply begins and ends there, with mere sophistication, the value of being difficult in art. Certainly his verse resists the principle that Charles Bernstein calls poetic "absorption," aiming instead for an "impermeability" that foregrounds both the artificiality of poetic writing and the reader's "self-consciousness about the reading process."[2] Mallarmé's writings defamiliarize the act of reading itself, casting the reader into what can be called (following Bernstein and Michael Fried) a "theatrical" and an interactive relation. This instinct in Mallarmé makes for laborious reading, especially if one expects a more plainspoken or journalistic approach from a modern poet. Be that as it may, Mallarmé's poems are not just a repertory of Brechtian defamiliarization effects aimed at exposing the labor of literary

The Matter of Spectacle

production. They are also difficult in that they teem with rich imagery (monstrances, tapestries, goldsmithery, rivulets of shimmering hair) self-consciously invoked through lavish but semantically unstable linguistic material. Mallarmé may be difficult, but there is a marked sensuality to all this difficulty. This luxurious playfulness is the outward sign of a much deeper erotics of art. His poetic corpus unfurls as a kind of excitement, a teasing game of signification that systematically withholds the reader's satisfaction or exceeds its thresholds. Is this flamboyant and sensual difficulty the sign of an orientation specifically toward baroque style in Mallarmé's work? If so, what importance might theater have in his modernist and baroque aesthetics?

In a dialogue with Maurice Guillemot in which he deflected the charge of obscurity by calling himself instead a *syntaxer*, Mallarmé offers an initial hint. "At Versailles, there is a kind of florid, spiraling foliage ornamentation, lovely enough to make one weep; shells, coils, curvatures, repeated motifs —that is how the phrase I throw out onto the paper appears to me at first, a summary outline, one that I then revise, purify, reduce, synthesize."[3] Here, of course, it may seem to some that Mallarmé wishes, like Wagner at Bayreuth, to do away with the ornaments altogether. Upon a closer look, Mallarmé's approach to syntax embodies a somewhat different instinct. Unlike Adolf Loos, who would desire to purify modernist architecture of its ornaments and thus reveal the pure undecorated structure, Mallarmé both flees *and follows* the outlined curvatures of baroque decor. Ornament functions not as an embellishment upon some prior structure, something easily extricated, but as a source of a foundational structure in itself. In Mallarmé the ornament has become fugitive, has gone into hiding, so to speak. Nevertheless, the scrollwork of thought is primary and inevitable, the necessary starting point.[4] A thought casts itself like a dice throw upon a page, and its initial shape is elaborate, full of linguistic turns and detours. The poet may try to purge these divagations through a "synthetic" process, but they will remain largely irreducible. For Mallarmé, elaborateness of style can only be sublated: partly canceled, but also preserved, carried forward, ultimately to be disseminated throughout his writing.

It is therefore not surprising to find that numerous prominent critics— including Albert Thibaudet, Jorge Luis Borges, René Wellek, Umberto Eco, and Octavio Paz—have sought various ways to interpret Mallarmé under the sign of baroque aesthetics.[5] This tendency is especially pronounced in French critical and aesthetic theory, where Mallarmé has compelled the attention of almost every major philosophical writer from Jean-Paul Sartre to Jacques Rancière. In this field, the poet's baroque qualities have been most apparent to critics working in the expanded field of "poststructuralist" thought. To name just the most eminent examples, beginning in the 1960s, after the structuralist Jean-Pierre Richard noted recurring images of folds in Mallarmé's work, Jacques Derrida reformulated the Mallarmé fold into a grammatologic figure through his own reading of Mallarmé in *Dissemination* (1972).[6] In turn, Gilles Deleuze adapted Mallarmé and Derrida's figure of the fold into the central, dominating concept for his analysis of Leibniz and baroque philosophy in *The Fold: Leibniz and the Baroque* (1988). Through Deleuze's reading especially, Mallarmé has become both a touchstone for the philosophical concept of the baroque and a particularly baroque modernist in turn. As Deleuze writes, "The fold is probably Mallarmé's most important notion and not only the notion but rather, the operation, the operative act that makes him a great Baroque poet."[7] Likewise, in another incisive reading of Derrida's *Dissemination*, the American critic Samuel Weber has claimed that Mallarmé's poetry enacts a deconstructive theatricality through its very grammar.[8] In Mallarmé's writing, Weber finds the "grammatical hallmark" of this theatricality "in the fold of the present participle." Through these poststructuralist rereadings of the fold as topos in Mallarmé, the poet's expressly theatrical qualities and his debts to baroque style come into focus together.

For Mallarmé, then, as for Nietzsche in *Human, All Too Human*, the question of baroque style is best posed as one of theatricality. It is thus no surprise that Mallarmé's exemplary baroque modernism emerges most notably in his theater writings. To date, however, his work continues to be undervalued or misconstrued in academic theater scholarship, where he seems a poetic outlier to the mainstream of theater history. Of course, there are exceptions to this general tendency: some scholars have seen Mallarmé as a prophet of theater's future who felt theatricality to pervade everyday life.[9] All too often, however, he is still depicted as an anti-theatricalist, a writer of a "virtual" or mental drama, an author of plays that are unstageworthy because they violate the most basic conditions of stage performance.[10] These negative descriptions are not wholly inaccurate. Mallarmé exhibited unmistakable scorn toward the bourgeois, commercial theater of his time and clear interest in theater as a philosophical metaphor for consciousness. Yet questions of stageworthiness and what is possible as theater—the matter of spectacle as such—were always at the forefront of his critical intelligence. Even if he retreated from the stage in the 1860s when his writing was re-

The Matter of Spectacle

jected from the Théâtre-Français, it does not necessarily follow (pace Martin Puchner) that he then opposed theater altogether.[11] Rather than simply reject theater, Mallarmé's poetry develops a theatricalist impulse to reform or reinvent theater conditions at their most foundational level. If his works "fail" as drama in the traditional sense of (classical or neoclassical, well made, realist, or naturalist) mimesis, they nevertheless demonstrate a widening gap between mimetic *drama* and a nonmimetic *theater*.[12] This gap is not just an important feature of modernist theater history; its roots lie in the allegorical theater of the baroque past, as Walter Benjamin argued decades after Mallarmé's death.

In this chapter, I claim that Mallarmé's work enfolds a sensuous, materialist, ultimately allegorical form of theatricality that both sets the terms for the new avant-gardism in performance (such as would be explored by Maurice Maeterlinck, F. T. Marinetti, John Cage, and many others) and carries within itself historical traces of baroque style. Mallarmé's writing is often credited with initiating the movement of modernist vanguardism altogether, and so the historiographic importance of his place in the long history of baroque style can hardly be overstated.[13] In his theater writing, and particularly in the *Hérodiade*, his great, perhaps impossible work for the theater and the main subject of this chapter, there emerges a vision of the baroque that provided an originary impetus for modernism at its very outset. Regardless of Mallarmé's conscious intentions, wherever his writings exert their greatest dialectical pressure upon prevailing norms of representation or mimesis, they conspicuously cite and reiterate seventeenth-century theatrical practices, including commedia dell'arte, pantomime and dumbshow, early forms of opera and ballet, and above all the tragic plays of Jean Racine. As the subject of this chapter, *Hérodiade* is the definitive example of this citationality, a text that mediates for Mallarmé the transition away from mimesis and toward a new vision of theater inspired by the materially sumptuous spectacles of the baroque past. Although *Hérodiade* abolishes the typical rules governing the relation of dramatic texts to performance, it is not, for that reason, reducible to the category of closet drama. Rather, in this chapter, I demonstrate how Mallarmé's lifelong vision of a single and totalizing poetic work—the so-called Book or *Livre*, which was left unfinished (or perhaps never started) at the time of his death—imagines the theatricality of a public ceremonial, one that could specifically recuperate the ritual gestures of the baroque Mass. For Mallarmé, it was less urgent to continue the conventions of the naturalist and realist stage, which had already found

68   Baroque Modernity

expression in the French theater of Émile Zola and André Antoine, than it was to lay the ground for a new "religion of art" of the sort that Hegel had described in his lectures on aesthetics, one with revolutionary potential not only in the realm of art but in politics as well.[14] As this chapter shows, the theater of the baroque served Mallarmé as the medium with which to envision this radical new aesthetic and spiritual practice.

The Drama of Silence

Mallarmé's affinity for baroque styles can be traced to an extended period of medical, psychological, and spiritual crisis he endured during his early twenties, the contours of which are sketched most vividly in his correspondence. During the spring of 1866 particularly, the young Stéphane suffered a general bout of ill health, with pangs of terror at the thought of his own mortality and anxious conviction of his own personal nonexistence disturbing enough to require a mirror constantly beside his writing desk.[15] He complains of feeling a terrible emptiness within his chest, but to his friend Cazalis he writes of having gained insight into a more profound and metaphysical emptiness, "the Void." In terms that anticipate what Existentialist philosophers would later term "the absurd," he describes this metaphysical abyss: "Yes, *I know*, we are merely empty forms of matter, but we are indeed sublime enough in having invented God and our soul. So sublime, my friend, that I want to gaze upon the spectacle of matter, having consciousness that it exists, and yet launching madly into Dream, despite knowing that Dream has no existence, extolling the Soul and all the divine impressions of that kind which have collected within us from the beginning of time and proclaiming, in the face of the Void which is truth, these glorious lies!"[16] These melancholy reflections on "the spectacle of matter" have much in common with the dialectics of truth and lies, nature and myth, waking and dreaming, found some years later in Nietzsche's *Birth of Tragedy*. As Henry Weinfield has noted, they reflect outward to "a general religious crisis occurring in Europe during the nineteenth century, with roots that stretch back much earlier."[17] Such roots sprout from the prior secularizations of early European modernity during the Reformation and Counter-Reformation, as Walter Benjamin later argues, and they cut through Mallarmé's life and aesthetic program from beginning to end.

If the Void is truth—if "God is dead" as Nietzsche later declares—such a truth imposes a state of "exquisite, fundamental crisis" upon not only metaphysical belief but also poetry, literature, and language in the broadest sense.[18]

The Matter of Spectacle

It is not just that the French alexandrine has fallen into historical obsolescence, increasingly replaced in Mallarmé's lifetime by vers libre, as he later observes in his essay "Crisis of Verse," though that shift can in itself be accounted a particularly obvious sign of the larger historical transformation. Rather, the knowledge that "we are merely empty forms of matter" and that "Dream has no existence" places strict formal demands upon modern poetry, for which an entirely new aesthetics, utterly disarmed of theological presuppositions, is necessary.

It took Mallarmé's entire adult life to envision, plan, and begin implementing this new aesthetics, culminating with his final, experimental work, *A Throw of the Dice Will Never Abolish Chance* (1897).[19] In a celebrated passage in the late "Crisis of Verse" essay, Mallarmé explains that no linguistic signifier can convey the full significance of its reference because, inevitably, many languages exist upon the Earth. "Languages imperfect insofar as they are many; the absolute one is lacking: thought considered as writing without accessories, not even whispers, still *stills* immortal speech; the diversity, on earth, of idioms prevents anyone from proffering words that would otherwise be, when made uniquely, the material truth."[20] As in the letter to Cazalis cited above, here Mallarmé is at his most Sophistic, in the sense of the word I detail in my comments on Nietzsche's refusal of linguistic naturalism in chapter 1.[21] In the writing of verse, Mallarmé finds only what Leo Bersani has rightly called a sense of "language's emptiness, of the lack of correspondence, between verbal fictions and being."[22] (Psychoanalytically speaking, if the death drive is to be located anywhere, it is perhaps most at home within the signifier itself.) In Mallarmé's cosmos, the Void is an ultimate reality in both an ontological and linguistic sense: the immortal Word is stilled or silent, and human language cannot hope to represent the pure truth in itself. In yet another turn that links Mallarmé's linguistic theory with Nietzsche's, the essay "Crisis of Verse" alleges that poetry springs directly from this general lack of an absolute language and compensates for it. Were a supreme, perfect, Adamic language available for human articulation, there would be no need for poetry at all. That is, from the time of his youthful crisis in 1866, Mallarmé's radical modernity can be attributed to the thought that modern poetry must affirm and perform its self-consciousness of language's incapacity for representational truth.

In light of such consciousness, the classical tradition of mimesis in literature—whether in poetry or in drama—necessarily becomes problematic. As Philippe Lacoue-Labarthe remarks of Mallarmé's dramaturgy: "It is not an Aristotelian theater: neither *mimesis* nor, consequently, *katharsis* is essential to it."[23] In this respect does Mallarmé's place in a larger baroque aesthetics of modernity become clearest. It would become his credo from this early period onward to pursue an explicit strategy of linguistic indirection, detouring away from direct depictions of the objective world—away from practices of linguistic correspondence and from what J. L. Austin terms the constative speech act. Increasingly from the mid-1860s onward, his writing enacts elaborate syntactic deviations, simulating and exciting the flux of phenomena in all their complex interdeterminacy. In October 1864, having begun a new work for the theater, he announces to Cazalis: "I have finally commenced work on my *Hérodiade*. With terror, for I am inventing a language which must necessarily erupt from a very new poetics, which I could define briefly thus: *Paint, not the thing, but the effect that it produces*" (*C* 206; translation mine, emphasis original).

More is at stake in this dictum than a simple shift from ontology to phenomenology, from existent things to the cognitive and perceptual processes that apprehend them. In Mallarmé's poetics, the object or referent experiences what he terms a "vibratory near-disappearance" into "the play of language" (*D* 210). It may be that the truth of things is the Void, that a transcendent truth can no longer be cognized through language, and that poetry cannot represent things directly in themselves. Even so, poetry might still summon a spectral impression of presence through processes of circumlocution and suggestion, which for Mallarmé will take a highly complex, self-referential, and luxurious form. The new poetics would require a shift away from authorial intentions and toward sensations (*C* 127), away from writing with the head and toward writing with the nerves and body (*C* 249), away from the *askesis* of speaking directly of things and toward a greater *eros* of language. It would entail, in short, a practice of *speaking otherwise*, or allegory.[24]

Allegory is one major facet of Mallarmé's baroque inheritance: it will require Walter Benjamin's later intervention to make clear its significance to Mallarmé's aesthetic project as a form of baroque modernism. Even so, the slogan "not the thing, but the effect" enfolds a still more necessary connection to baroque aesthetics. It bears obvious similarities to the emerging visual program of Impressionist painting, a movement whose practitioners Mallarmé knew well, influenced, and took as the subject of his later essay "The Impressionists and Édouard Manet" (1876). Through the Impressionists, this dictum had a deep significance for the historiography of the baroque shortly after the period of Mallarmé's lifetime. It has not generally

The Matter of Spectacle

been acknowledged that the demand to paint *not the thing, but the effect* became in modified form a central component of Heinrich Wölfflin's foundational definition of baroque style shortly after Mallarmé's death. As part of Wölfflin's effort to distinguish classical (linear) from baroque (painterly) style in art, he asserted in his landmark 1915 study, *Principles of Art History*, that "*the former* [classicism] *represents things as they are, the latter* [baroque] *as they seem to be.*"[25] Wölfflin argued influentially that baroque style takes for its founding principle the depiction not of stable objects but of fleeting appearances, impressions, aftereffects. If so, the baroque impulse in the arts prefigured the visual strategies of Impressionist painting or, perhaps, amounted to an earlier historical instance of those same strategies. In making this influential claim, Wölfflin implicitly adduced Mallarmé's 1864 aesthetic program as a central theoretical device for the baroque as a larger concept of style. *Principles of Art History* thus not only authorized and disseminated Mallarmé's schema for later efforts at understanding the baroque but also helps cast Mallarmé, tacitly, further into a baroque light.

Because the injunction to paint *not the thing, but the effect* inaugurates an assault on the traditional notion of mimesis, and because mimesis has been foundational to the classical notion of drama since Aristotle's *Poetics*, it is not inconsequential that Mallarmé developed this aesthetic program while preparing a new work of theater. At the time of his youthful spiritual crisis, he was engrossed in work on *Hérodiade*, his only dramatic text, still unfinished at the end of his life. Before turning to those elements of baroque style discernible within the *Hérodiade*, however, it is necessary to consider certain fundamental aspects of Mallarmé's general theory of drama. While Mallarmé maintained a lifelong interest in theater, his hostility to the bourgeois theatrical institutions and conventions of his time evinces a strongly anti-mimetic bent, as numerous critics have observed.[26] His most concentrated challenge to these conventions would come only later, some decades after his early spiritual crisis, with the publication in *La Revue Indépendante* of "Mimique" (1886)—his most succinct theoretical statement on drama and on what can be called the emblematic function of theatrical gesture. This text takes the form of an extended reflection on "Pierrot, Assassin of His Wife," a one-act pantomime written and performed by the poet's cousin Paul Margueritte at the Théâtre de Valvins, an amateur summer theater where Mallarmé sometimes served as a stage director and prompter. Mallarmé may never have seen Margueritte perform the role of Pierrot live in 1881—he may have simply read the script, printed only subsequently in

72 Baroque Modernity

1886. From his comments on the play, however, Mallarmé clearly envisions Margueritte's performance as a dynamic text in itself—a kind of postdramatic "performance text."[27] In his description of "Pierrot," Margueritte's play comes to sound like a distant memory of some forgotten theater of the past, or a manifesto for a dreamed-of theater not yet existing:[28]

> Silence! sole luxury after rhymes, an orchestra only marking with its gold, its brushings with thought and dusk, the detail of its signification on par with a stilled ode and which it is up to the poet, roused by a dare, to translate! the silence of an afternoon of music; I find it, with contentment before the ever-original reappearance of Pierrot or the epitome of poignancy and elegance, Paul Margueritte. Such is this *Pierrot Assassin de sa Femme*, composed and set down by himself, a mute soliloquy that the phantom, white as a yet unwritten page, holds in both face and gesture at full length to his soul. . . . The stage illustrates the idea, not any actual action, in a Hymen (out of which flows Dream), tainted with vice yet sacred, between desire and fulfillment, perpetration and remembrance; here anticipating, there recalling, in the future, in the past, *under a false appearance of the present* [italics original]. That is how the mime operates, whose act is confined to a perpetual allusion without breaking the ice or the mirror: he thus sets up a medium, a pure medium, of fiction.[29]

Margueritte's play provides Mallarmé an opportunity both to contemplate performance as a series of hieroglyphic components and to affirm it precisely as nonmimetic theater. On the surface Mallarmé is describing a pantomime, while at another level he is describing his own process of poetic composition, *poetry-as-mime*. His comments in "Mimique" also demonstrably helped program the future development of avant-garde theater into the 1890s with Lugné-Poe's Symbolist Théâtre d'Art. The mood set by "Mimique" became central to the Symbolists' stage aesthetics, the scenography of which often reflected the thematically connected images Mallarmé sketches here: hints of gold (as in an illuminated manuscript, baroque tracery, or a painting by Moreau or Klimt); inscrutable, dreamlike situations and atmospheres; and glacial or enigmatic onstage business, echoing a more metaphysical or cosmic event.[30] Whereas theatrical Symbolists like Maurice Maeterlinck would later make use of static stage tableaux, devoid of action in the Aristotelian sense, Mallarmé here calls for a nonmimetic theater that shows only "a succession of exteriors of an act without any moment's having any reality, and what happens is, finally, nothing at all" (*D* 120-21).

In Mallarmé's ghostly theater, the stage is to be marked by the blank

The Matter of Spectacle 73

pallor of Pierrot's face and costume, "white as yet unwritten page." Significantly, for Mallarmé, the stage is also a page, and its mise-en-page is also a mise-en-scène. We enter here into a domain where theatricality and textuality, Theater and the Book, traverse each other at every point. Whether in performance or in poiesis, Mallarmé's mime is not so much an impersonator of a fictional persona as an *operator* ("That is how the mime operates"; "*Tel opère le Mime*"), an officiator at an esoteric ritual, unfolding hieratic gesticulations that install a medium of "fiction" and of "Dream." Against the backdrop of this "yet unwritten page," the theater spectator reads the onstage figure or figures, along with their mimic gestures, as if they were so many printed, typeset characters, spaced apart from one another by a compositor. Their gestures result, as Walter Benjamin later says of Brecht's Epic Theater, from the process of repeatedly interrupting action. That is, the mime presents the viewer with what might be called, borrowing the title of one of Mallarmé's prose poems—*un spectacle interrompu*.[31] Amid their various arcane gestures, these figures recall the personages that populate a baroque book of emblems or acting techniques, in that they illustrate some abstract Idea, or set of Ideas, rather than traditionally Aristotelian characters and human acts.

That is, the theatricality envisioned in "Mimique" takes place as a form of "gestures drama"—drama not in the Aristotelian sense of imitated action but in Nietzsche's baroque sense of exciting, ritualistic gesture. The theater of "Mimique" is nearer to drama as a sacred *actio* or gesture than to drama as *mimesis praxeos*. With Mallarmé, the "mimetic" functions of theater are short-circuited in favor of its more "mimic" functions. This means that in performance, the performer cannot be a Stanislavskian actor who identifies with some character furnished to him by some prior script. Rather, the dramatic events remain alienated, kept "in both face and gesture at full length to his soul," and the gestural actions *produce* the text *in* or *as a result* of their execution. Derrida's canonical reading of "Mimique" names this process of gestural citation and inscription "corporeal writing."[32] It amounts to a kind of performance closer to allegorical dance (specifically, the masque dance forms France knew best in the seventeenth-century *ballet de cour*) than to the acting one expects from a performer in the realistic theater. Where mimetic actors produce what might be called (following Roland Barthes's famous formulation) "reality effects," Mallarmé's miming produces only what should be considered *emblem effects*, the suggestion of enigmatic significations that must be read or contemplated by a spectator.[33] In "Mimique," Mallarmé valorizes pantomimic allusiveness over mimetic illusionism. Rather than imitating something "external" to itself, his mime only "mimes imitation" itself (as Derrida puts it), thus opening up a referential *mise-en-abîme*.[34]

This gestural inscription gives rise to a peculiar series of aesthetic effects. In the first place, it generates an unusually syncopated and liminal temporality. In Mallarmé's description of "the ever-original reappearance of Pierrot," the onstage mime seems repeatedly to re-present himself with each gesture as in an ongoing series of temporal punctuations. Metaphorically speaking, a kind of constant stroboscopic flashing captures and anatomizes each of Pierrot's movements. He (re)appears anew at each turn, is repeatedly original, and this repeated appearance establishes an uncanny rhythm, a queasy sort of temporal flux. Mallarmé's mime moves back and forth through the spatiotemporal registers of a certain betweenness, a "Hymen," in the spaces separating one gestural iteration from the next. The illustration takes place "between desire and fulfillment, perpetration and remembrance; here anticipating, there recalling, in the future, in the past, *under a false appearance of the present.*" Fredric Jameson notably sees this passage as a prefiguration of Gertrude Stein's later anxieties about temporal syncopation, and her sense of being always either behind or ahead of the plays she would attend as a spectator, a subject I discuss further in chapter 4. Jameson claims in *The Modernist Papers* that both Stein and Mallarmé stage a situation in which "[i]t is the very existence of the present which is in doubt . . . and which it is the most august function of spectacle to convey."[35] One should go further and assert that Mallarmé's theater can ever hope to communicate only a *sense* of the present, and a ghostly one at that. Pantomime does not rely upon the actual presence of onstage objects to support its gestures, but rather communicates a simulacral presence to such properties only by tracing their absences through gestured movement. (One may think of even the most stereotypical figure of the mime, say, of the Marcel Marceau variety, who demonstrates the stock game of being "trapped in a box" by exploring the absent boundaries of his confinement with precise, gestural indications of the hands and fingers.) And so, with the figure of the mime, Mallarmé establishes a game of presences and absences, eliciting less securely present things or the present moment than a haunting, implacable doubt about their actual existence.

If there is no immediate access to any sense of presence in Mallarmé's

The Matter of Spectacle

theater, there is nevertheless an erotic play of presence and absence within an irreducible medium or "Hymen." The mime's medial theater is not, or not only, melancholic in the face of the absent signified; rather, it eroticizes this absence by its material suggestiveness and its capacity for distanciation. Samuel Weber regards this medium as *theatricality*, and in this sense, Mallarmé can be seen as an eminent forerunner of Georg Fuchs; that is, Fuchs's call for "re-theatricalizing the theater" is just one horizon toward which Mallarmé's influence extends.[36] Theatricality in Mallarmé, the result of the mime's inscriptive and indeterminate gestures, results in a hymen-like texture, a highly textile medium. It generates a *distancing* effect that mediates between performance and spectator (or reader and poem), resisting any naturalizing gaze. In this way, it has an analogue in the gauze curtain the Symbolists would later extend along the edge of their proscenium stage at the Théâtre d'Art, whose translucency would enhance the dreamlike quality of their theater works (a visual analogue to Wagner's "mystic gulf," the hidden orchestra pit at Bayreuth).[37] For all the absence that plagues Mallarmé's ghostly stage, there is a material lushness to this theater that must not go overlooked. In Derrida's reading of "Mimique," this "pure medium of fiction" forms a kind of textile that embraces "all the veils, gauzes, canvases, fabrics, moirés, wings, feathers, all the curtains and fans that hold *within their folds* all—almost—of the Mallarméan text."[38] Cloaked amid a curtain of rippling fabrics, Mallarmé envisions a form of theatricality that takes place, like dumbshow, in and through the splendid baroque space of the fold.

Hérodiade, "A Horrible Birth"

Mallarmé's one surviving text composed in the form of dramatic dialogue, *Hérodiade*, transposes the theoretical sketches that appear in "Mimique" into a baroque dramaturgical practice that envisions new spatiotemporal relations, affects, and gestures in the theater. It can rightly be considered *the* major dramatic project of Mallarmé's lifetime. He worked on it continuously from 1864 until his death in 1898 without ever completing it, and the surviving text furnished to readers in the Pléiade edition of the poet's complete works retains an unfinished, fragmentary quality.[39] He appears to have considered *Hérodiade* by turns both as a tragedy to be performed on stage and as a text to be read.[40] In reality, the matter of his intentions for the piece are complicated by the ways his writing effectively undoes neat binary distinctions between reading and theatrical experience, as we have already begun

76   Baroque Modernity

to note. In Deleuze's description, the play amounts to Mallarmé's vision of a "theater of reading," a baroque intermediation between the theater and the book.[41]

This is not to say that the work takes up a necessarily hostile attitude toward theater or theatricality across the board, as some have argued.[42] Far from it. Not all reader's theater can be reduced to closet drama; as Walter Benjamin later argues, the German baroque theater, especially, knew forms of hieroglyphic theater that demanded both to be read allegorically and to be performed before spectators. Like his dramatic pastoral interlude, *The Afternoon of a Faun*, which he began in 1865 during a pause from his work on *Hérodiade*, Mallarmé conceived the latter project by way of a central ambivalence: this was a work that was "absolutely scenic, not possible as theater, but requiring the theater" (*C* 242).[43] A play like the *Hérodiade*, written under the command to depict *not the object, but its effect*, would be impossible for any theater still organized around the central, dominating principle of Aristotelian *mimesis*. In lieu of dynamic action, *Hérodiade* sees the flow of time drawn to tense standstill, where drama resides instead in a play of sensuous forms: prismatic repetitions, incantatory syllables, otherworldly images, emotional and haptic excitations, expressive but nonmimetic language, movements, and gestures. Parting ways with the Aristotelian notion of drama, Mallarmé's theater makes space instead for a play of sensory effects, for the bodies that register them, and for space itself.[44] Writing of this kind demands a new and "retheatricalized" form of theater—a theater no longer mimetic in Aristotle's sense, but closer to Lehmann's postdramatic theater of the twentieth century.[45] In *Hérodiade*, typical Aristotelian considerations of represented action and textual primacy are subordinated to the autonomy of more grossly material, theatrical values. Even if the object that traditionally grounds representation is no longer secure or available, the need to depict its effects is still pressing, which is why *Hérodiade*, while unmoored from traditional norms of mimesis, still sets up a medium for the presentation of these effects, that is, still *requires the theater*. One cannot effectively depict the Void with nothing.

In Deleuze's description, *Hérodiade* is "already the poem of the fold."[46] It is a work in which a set of particularly baroque rhetorical resources and theatricalizing effects converge in an extravagant manner. In a letter to fellow Symbolist Villiers de L'Isle-Adam (dated December 1865), Mallarmé introduces the properly allegorical distinction between the *ostensible* subject of *Hérodiade*—namely, the Biblical myth of Salome, Herodias, Herod, and

The Matter of Spectacle

John the Baptist—and its *actual* subject, which he designates simply as "Beauty."[47] But Mallarmé's is never the traditional beauty of mimesis. His poetry attends instead to the beauty of nonexistent dream, the glorious lie, the void that is truth—in short, to the deathly and unthinkable beauty of the abyss, a subject that can be approached in language only by way of its effects. Appropriately enough given the principle of painting not things but their impressions, in the course of the poem the ostensible subject of Beauty becomes, in Henry Weinfield's evocative phrase, "a vehicle for its own transcendence."[48] What comes to the fore while the ostensible matter of Beauty recedes in this way is a struggle enacted within the text over Mallarmé's own process of aesthetic development. *Hérodiade* represents no central action, only a constellation of fragmentary images emerging from the Biblical Salome story, abstracted to the point of unrecognizability. It neither mentions nor dramatizes the fundamental events of the narrative: the lust of Herod, the decapitation of the Baptist, the severed head displayed upon a silver trencher. Most starkly absent of all is Salome's legendary dance, the Biblical mytheme that would best emblematize the poet's quest to glimpse a beautiful, mutable truth—a truth that refuses to unveil itself fully, even to the point of death. (If the famous dance does not appear in dramatized form in the final, published edition of the work, experimental efforts at depicting it in concrete poetry do appear among Mallarmé's literary remains in a set of experimental notes, where they would provide germs for his later experiments with free verse.[49]) Ultimately, all these central narrative elements of the Salome myth are abandoned or refused in pursuit of a more self-referentially performative reflection on the creative act itself.

In this reflection, Hérodiade, Mallarmé's fatal protagonist, fuses the Biblical persona of Salome with the name of her mother, Herodias. She serves as Mallarmé's attempt to personify an unapproachably ideal artistic perfection. At the same time, *Hérodiade*, the broader poem in which that character "finds herself," dramatizes the doomed attempt to conceive and depict such perfection in poetic language. (Notably, not only is Hérodiade's name the poem's eponym, but it also *declares itself* to be the title of a poem, as in *Iliade, Dunciade, Henriade*.) The choice to adapt the Salome myth in this impossible and unexpected way, as an emblem for the modern poet or artist's process, bespeaks a formal arbitrariness that verges on figural violence. But if the *Hérodiade*'s mythic narrative and the modern purpose to which Mallarmé puts it seem at odds, this mismatch is echoed at another level by the marked lack of onstage incidents when coupled with the extraordinary violence of its mythic substrate. The *Hérodiade* thus takes the form of a *discordia concors*, in which violence becomes a necessary component of the allegorical process.[50] In describing the extraordinary popularity of orientalist Herod-themed dramas of martyrdom in the baroque theater, Walter Benjamin remarks upon the violence of allegory in terms that are consonant with the Salome myth as a source of material for modern adaptation. Personifying allegorical signification in terms of "a gloomy sultan in the harem of things," he writes: "It is, indeed, characteristic of the sadist to humiliate his object and thereupon—or thereby—to satisfy it. That, then, is what the allegorist does too in this age drunk with cruelties both real and imagined" (*OGT* 197). The myth of Salome embodies the lustful drive of death, the jouissance of desire and violence, and in Mallarmé's treatment, its sadism is matched only by the violent arbitrariness of allegorical figuration. As the allegory of Salome, Mallarmé's *Hérodiade* becomes one of the first and most preeminent works of modernism to attempt a restaging of baroque style in theater.[51]

The poem is divided into three disconnected episodes or movements, stations in a modern mystery play.[52] Preceding them, there appears in the Pléiade edition of Mallarmé's complete works a dedicatory sonnet entitled "Don du Poëme" (Gift of the Poem, 1865) that functions as a prologue of sorts for the ensuing drama. In its rhymed anapestic alexandrines, this brief work summons a tragic mood that instantaneously recalls for a French listener the poetic sound world of Racinian tragedy. As the sonnet's octave builds up an interior scene, its sestet heralds an "*horrible naissance*": this is at once the terrible birth of Hérodiade the character, the birth of her tragedy, and the birth of a new and tragic poetics.[53]

> Je t'apporte l'enfant d'une nuit d'Idumée!
> Noire, à l'aile saignante et pale, déplumée,
> Par le verre brûlé d'aromates et d'or,
> Par les carreaux glacés, hélas! mornes encore,
> L'aurore se jeta sur la lampe angelique.
> Palmes! Et quand elle a montré cette relique
> A ce père essayant un sourire ennemi,
> La solitude bleue et stérile a frémi.
> O la berceuse, avec ta fille et l'innocence
> De vos pieds froids, accueille une horrible naissance (*OC* 40)

> I bring you the child of an Idumeaen night,
> Black and with featherless wings bled white:

The Matter of Spectacle

> Through the windows burnished with incense and gold,
> The rimed panes mournful, alas, from the cold,
> The Dawn spread her fingers upon the angelic
> Lamp, and when she had offered this relic
> To the father smiling in spite of his qualms,
> The sterile, blue silence was wafted by palms!
> O mother cradling your infant daughter,
> Welcome the birth of this untimely monster! (*CP* 24)

Some thing is coming into being with these words, "only under the species of the non-species," as Jacques Derrida might say, "in the formless, mute, infant, and terrifying form of monstrosity."[54] Whatever baroque monster, as yet unnamable, is coming to light in the process of this invocation, it can only be something bizarre, grotesque, unrecognizable. An ominous prodigy, the newborn appears something like a pale and deplumed raven with bleeding wings, as unusual in its shape as the tumorous baroque pearl. This offspring of Edom presents an almost apocalyptic vision of the new in all its promise and horror, rising up with the morning sun like Yeats's "rough beast, its hour come at last, / slouching toward Bethlehem to be born." The "Don du Poëme" "takes place" in a mournful room populated with various physical accoutrements familiar from the iconographic repertory of medieval Catholicism but presented in only passing glints—incense, gilt tracery, tiled windows, palm leaves, a lamp in the form of an angel, a relic or monstrance. All the while, the blue, sterile solitude of the empty heavens produces a shudder. By contrast, the sonnet's last two couplets take an ambiguously hopeful turn as the poem's speaker calls for a lullaby ("*berceuse*"), evoking echoes of a strange, ancestral music:

> Et ta voix rappelant viole et clavecin
> Avec le doigt fané presseras-tu le sein
> Par qui coule en blancheur sibylline la femme
> Pour les lèvres que l'air du vierge azur affame? (*OC* 40)

> And with your voice like viol and harpsichord, O singer,
> Will you press upon your breast a faded finger,
> Through which in sibylline whiteness woman flows
> For lips starved from the air the virginal azure blows? (*CP* 24)

Whose Sibylline voice is it that sounds in these final lines? (Weinfield's choice to address them to a "mother" finds no explicit correlative in Mallarmé's text: the final lines' addressee is "*la berceuse,*" the lullaby itself, gendered feminine in the French.) Within the space of the anonymous, prophetic voice opened up in this final quatrain, an unexpected and strangely *operatic* instrumentation is heard to resound—not the thunderous brass of the Bayreuth orchestra pit but the viol and harpsichord of the baroque past. Although the poem on the page is mute, a silent music haunts it from an obscure and half-forgotten era. Following this prelude, *Hérodiade* passes through a series of three movements, at least two more of which are given musical titles. Beginning with an initial "Ouverture Ancienne" (Ancient Overture) sung by Hérodiade's Nurse, there follows a "Scène" in dialogue between this nurse and Hérodiade herself, before the triptych concludes with a "Cantique" (Canticle) sung by Saint John the Baptist. If we read the whole of *Hérodiade* alongside the viol and harpsichord that serve as its prelude, how might the poem appear anew in light of its baroque orchestration?

The Nurse's ancient overture is explicitly termed an "Incantation." Somewhere between ritual chanting and a mystical enchantment, this incantation follows the precedent of Shakespeare and Racine in summoning the drama's setting into being through words and images rather than through literal scenery. The chant opens with a nearly impenetrable mass of language that illuminates no clear situation or event, even as it generates scintillating flashes of sensation:

> Abolie, et son aile affreuse dans les larmes
> Du bassin, aboli, qui mire les alarmes,
> Des ors nus fustigeant l'espace cramoisi
> Une Aurore a, plumage héraldique, choisi
> Notre tour cinéraire et sacrificatrice,
> Lourde tombe qu'a fuie un bel oiseau, caprice
> Solitaire d'aurore au vain plumage noir (*OC* 41)

> Abolished, and her frightful wing in the tears
> Of the basin, abolished, that mirrors forth our fears,
> The naked golds, lashing the crimson space,
> An Aurora—heraldic plumage—has chosen to embrace
> Our cinerary tower of sacrifice,
> Heavy tomb that a songbird has fled, long caprice
> Of a dawn vainly decked out in ebony plumes (*CP* 25)

The briefest of "plot summaries" for the *Hérodiade* would note that the poem seems to "take place" within a fairy-tale tower of the sort familiar from

The Matter of Spectacle

Tennyson's "Lady of Shallot," where a princess must wait under mysterious circumstances, her gaze fixed upon a mirror.[55] In fewer than one hundred lines, the Nurse's opening monologue depicts both a physical space and a landscape of melancholy, seen, once again, only in lavish glimpses: a basin (already abolished), a tomblike tower chamber in golds and crimsons, plumage of the darkest black, a songbird (already fled), a distant dawn. As the incantation continues, further scenic details are evoked: the vista of a tearful lake and a garden, tarnished silver, the aroma of roses, spent candles, a bed abandoned by its inhabitant, another distant dawn glimpsed through a window, and yet another avian emblem of poetry, this time a lamentable swan (*"cygne/lamentable"*) whose homophone is a lamentable sign (*signe lamentable*). Baroque folds can be found rippling throughout the Nurse's depiction of this space, and as Leo Bersani has shown, the repeated word *pli* (fold) serves rhetorically in this overture to initiate an unstable play of words and things in which identities between discrete objects of representation can be seen to slide, distressingly. Baroque folds undulate in the decorative tapestries adorning this tower's inner chamber, unsettling a cloth covering a confused mass of discarded monstrances. They roil through a funereal shroud, over Hérodiade's abandoned bedsheets, and in the pages of a book (or "grimoire") of ancient spells. Even thought and dreams themselves are also said to accrue in yellowed folds in this chamber.[56]

Against the critical interpretation of Mallarmé's supposed anti-theatrical bias, this overture suggests a different interpretation. Numerous critics have remarked upon Mallarmé's interest in interior spaces, typically filled with enigmatic objects, whose recurring appearances throughout his poetry suggest a theater stage or a curiosity cabinet.[57] As *Hérodiade* transpires entirely indoors (in Hérodiade's chamber, at her toilette, and finally in the prison where Saint John is executed), the drama should be considered alongside certain comments Mallarmé offered about the placement of female figures within interior locations in the visual arts. Writing on the subject of Édouard Manet and Impressionist painting in 1876, he remarks on Manet's canvases depicting female bodies in sunny, open-air settings as opposed to interiors illuminated artificially with candles or gas. If the outdoor, noonday setting lends artistry to Manet's female figures, it also stands in stark contrast to the interior setting of the *Hérodiade*: "Those persons much accustomed . . . to fix on a mental canvass the beautiful remembrance of woman, even when thus seen amid the glare of night in the world or at the theatre, must have remarked that some mysterious process despoils the noble phantom of the artificial prestige cast by the candelabra or footlights, before she is admitted fresh and simple to the number of everyday haunters of the imagination."[58] Sunlight ruins the "artificial" glow of prestige that only lustrous stage lighting can produce. The plein air tradition "despoils" the female body of an aura it might otherwise acquire on a stage.

In the curious light of this description, the female body as depicted in *Hérodiade* acquires a necessarily theatrical quality. Mallarmé's imagined female figure finds herself in a space not unlike Plato's cave. She is fixed upon the "mental canvass" within an interior space, one that reflects a sense of strangeness and mystery, a "noble phantom" that emanates from the scintillations of candelabra and footlights. For Mallarmé, it is this theatricality that Manet's paintings aim to resist by transferring the female figure to a midday, outdoor setting (as, for example, in *Le Déjeuner sur l'herbe* of 1862-63). By contrast, the first two movements of *Hérodiade* evoke images of women in claustral indoor spaces, at the crimson hour of sunrise, when light is at its most distorting. Manet may be seeking to defeat the theater, but Mallarmé's *Hérodiade* is succumbing to it, luxuriating in it.

As the "Ancient Overture" drives toward its conclusion, the "unstable designation" Bersani detects produces a form of thought that is, in his argument, both ontologically "distressing" and also manifestly erotic.[59] Where, at the level of content or imagery, the overture obsesses over lavish materials and textures, building a tragic mood with quasi-operatic intensity, its highly complex syntax initiates a game of internal allusions and redirections reflecting inwardly within the text itself, without respect to any external referent. In the Nurse's opening lines, for example, the reader confronts immediately the baffling participle *"Abolie,"* "abolished," which attaches in typical Mallarméan fashion to no obvious subject or object. *Some thing* has been ordered out of existence, annihilated by *some thing* else, but any clear sense of identity for either the obliterated thing or the obliterating force is quickly dissolved into a cloud of language, shot through with internal rhymes, repeated vowel sounds, and images revealed in flashes. Although the loss of the thing is mournful, and its further inability to be named can be deemed a source of melancholy, what results from this double loss is a certain sensuousness, which for Bersani raises the question: "What can it mean to transcribe a sensation which no one has had, a sensation without a human subject?"[60] Here sensations and passions enjoy only themselves within the space of the void, in the absence of a subject.

It is characteristic of Mallarmé's preoccupations that this scene, so re-

The Matter of Spectacle

plete with sensual imagery, is also a scene of violence and death. Where Mallarmé's poem aims at allegorizing poetry's efforts to approach Beauty and the Void, this effort, for all its "terror," attains a conspicuous sensuality. The Nurse, Cassandra-like, pronounces visions of doom that soon approach a pitch of terror:

> "Crime! bûcher! aurore ancienne! supplice!
> Pourpre d'un ciel! Étang de la pourpre complice!
> Et sur les incarnats, grand ouvert, ce vitrail" (*OC* 41)

> Crime! torture! ancient dawn! bright pyre!
> Empurpled sky, complicit in the mire,
> And stained-glass windows opening red on carnage" (*CP* 25)

No incident is directly represented or reported, but clues, as if from a crime scene, are strewn about in a bloody aftermath. From the tower window in the overture's final stanza, the nurse glimpses an "enigmatic" heap of corpses beneath an infernal dawn. She awaits the return of a king: "Will he ever come back from the Cisalpines?/Soon enough! For all is bad dream and foreboding!"[61] This tragic return, recalling both the beginnings of Aeschylus's *Agamemnon* and the ramparts of Elsinore in *Hamlet*, is also a "second coming" that brings on the apocalypse. A dawn that is also possibly a sunset seems to herald the end of time. Nevertheless, infinitely small shards of hope glint from within this general atmosphere of despair. In the overture's final lines—which, full of prismatic ornament, bring together mournfulness and ostentation—the old swan glimpsed in the poem's opening stanza is carried away, mysteriously, by no clearly designated agent, "from the plumage of grief to the eternal highway/of its hopes, where it looks on the diamonds divine/of a moribund star, which never more shall shine!" (*CP* 28).[62]

Becoming Ornamental

Under Mallarmé's allegorical vision, the eternal hides within a jewel, a universal mystery within a gemstone: the entirety of the *kosmos* is reflected within *kosmoi*—cosmetics, adornments, and accessories.[63] In this sense, it is natural that Hérodiade's entrance into the "Scène" of her tragedy plays out as an operatic struggle over baroque jewelry. In this, her arrival into the drama reprises one of the most iconic entrances of French theater history dating back to the baroque time of Jean Racine. Into the strange space delimited by the Nurse's overture, the princess "presents" herself, in a highly attenuated way. Already spectral, her lively presence is called immediately into question at the moment of the Nurse's first remark to her: "Tu vis! Ou vois-je ici l'ombre d'une princesse?" (*OC* 44; "Are you a living princess or her shadow?" [*CP* 29]). The question resonates across many levels: Is the nurse exclaiming that Hérodiade has a deathly look to her? Is her remark meant to call into question the character's ontological stability? Or is it an indication that Hérodiade is but the intertextual simulacrum of another, yet more vivid princess?

In just the barely 150 lines following the Nurse's enigmatic question, Mallarmé stages a brief scene between Hérodiade and her nurse, one that plays out according to the recognizable Racinian convention of dialogue between a tragic protagonist and her confidante.[64] The "Scène" effectively rewrites the famous entrance of Racine's Phèdre into her own tragedy (*Phèdre*, 1677). When Racine's doomed queen makes her first appearance in that drama, in a short scene with her own nurse, she is already undergoing an extreme psychological crisis and buckling with exhaustion under the weight of her ornaments, clothes, and hair. Phèdre tears these baroque adornments from her person, violently undoing the nurse Oenone's handiwork as she succumbs to a fiery passion of the blood.[65] Mallarmé's Hérodiade likewise undresses herself, and similarly refuses her Nurse's efforts to assist with her toilette, but keeps all her ornamental decorations on her person. In keeping with the vision of theater outlined in "Mimique," no overarching action is depicted here. Mallarmé's Hérodiade is not ensnared within a tragic plot, as Racine's Phèdre is. Still, as others have noted, the "Scène" revolves around three gestures of aid or supplication on the Nurse's part—attempts to approach the princess's person, hair, and jewelry—and three countergestures of refusal or negation on the part of Hérodiade. While Martin Puchner and Patrick McGuinness have argued that these three gestures function as metaphors for Mallarmé's refusal of stage performance, they can better be understood to signify his refusal of traditional forms of mimesis altogether, and his preference instead for a nonmimetic theater of striking and enigmatic poses, a modern baroque form of gestures drama.[66]

At first, the Nurse seeks to kiss Hérodiade's fingers and rings, but the princess spurns her with the icy and laconic command "Reculez" (*OC* 44; "Forebear" [*CP* 29]). The Nurse then offers Hérodiade a perfume, the funereal essence of withered roses, which Hérodiade likewise rejects: "Laisse là ces parfums!" (*OC* 45; "Away with those perfumes!" [*CP* 30]). Finally, the

The Matter of Spectacle

Nurse tries to adjust a lock fallen out of place in Hérodiade's hair, and Hérodiade repulses this advance as well: "Arrête dans ton crime" (*OC* 45; "Cease and desist from your crime" [*CP* 31]). Unlike Oscar Wilde's Salomé, who is nearly consumed with desire for Jokanaan to desire her in return, Mallarmé's splenetic Hérodiade refuses all human contact, in favor of a desired, absolute self-sufficiency. This Beauty will not be touched or represented but wishes only to repose inviolably in itself and for itself, an ideal image whose self-sufficiency is itself a form of cruelty. Such a poetic "object" cannot be depicted, even if its effects *demand* depiction.

Although it transpires in dialogue, an unearthly inertia persists throughout this scene, one that was to become a favored dramaturgical motif among later Symbolist playwrights.[67] The young princess repeatedly interrupts her Nurse's advancing hand, freezing it in its motion before it can reach its goal, and as the scene becomes increasingly gestic, it likewise becomes increasingly cold. Racine's Phèdre seethes in a hot-blooded lust that demands all her queenly jewels be ripped away within the first eight lines of her appearance onstage. By contrast, the icy Hérodiade: though denuding herself of her royal garments to the point of nakedness, she not only keeps all her ornaments upon her but—in a process of supremely unstable designation in which properties between subjects and objects become disoriented and transferred—seems almost to *become an ornament in herself*. At each of the Nurse's three advances, the dark princess exclaims her desire to become more and more frigid and gemlike, in language of rich physical sensation. In her first lines alone, after the Nurse's first approach, Hérodiade withdraws and declares: "Le blond torrent de mes cheveux immaculés / Quand il baigne mon corps solitaire le glace / D'horreur" (*OC* 44; "The blond torrent of immaculate hair / Bathing my lonely body, freezes it / With horror" [*CP* 29]). At the Nurse's second supplication, Hérodiade proclaims something like a desire to revert to a state of inorganic matter, declaiming the wish that her tresses should attain "la froideur stérile du métal / Vous ayant reflétés, joyaux du mur natal" (*OC* 33; "the cold sterility of metal, / Reflecting the jewels of my walls ancestral" [*CP* 30]). Hérodiade greets the Nurse's third and final attempt to touch her as an impious "crime / Qui refroidit mon sang vers sa source" (*OC* 44; "crime / Which chills my blood unto its source" [*CP* 31]). In each of these rejoinders, it is as if the folding coils and rivulets of Hérodiade's torrential hair are frozen in the midst of their restless, torrential cascading, while Hérodiade's flesh seems to petrify, her form becoming statuesque: "Du reste, je ne veux rien d'humain et, sculptée, / Si tu me vois les yeux perdus au paradis,/C'est quand je me souviens de ton lait bu jadis" (*OC* 47; "I want nothing human; and if some day, a stone Statue you find me, my eyes lost in bliss,/It's when I remember the milk of your breasts" [*CP* 33]).

The "Scène" culminates in an emphatic monologue for Hérodiade of extraordinary linguistic richness, a flourishing declamation that on its face recalls the *tirades* of Racine's tragic protagonists. Before spurning her Nurse's third advance, she calls for a mirror in which to fix her gaze, as though such a sight could assure her of her own ontological self-identity. In this moment, the poem comes dangerously near to accomplishing Mallarmé's stated aim for it, namely, to enact a self-reflexive, poetic quest into an absolute or self-sufficient realm of Beauty. Such self-identity is ultimately not on offer in the Void of Mallarmé's universe, and the desire for it seems almost a retrograde, theological wish.[68] The Nurse continues to badger Hérodiade with questions pertinent only to the background situation at hand, in which an unnamed king is on the verge of a long-awaited return. For Hérodiade, the specifics of this heroic arrival seem hardly to matter—any clear sense of a mythic action might as well be abolished in Mallarmé's staging. Her regard is narcissistically absorbed within the frame of her mirror. Asked by her Nurse, "Pour qui . . . gardez-vous la splendeur ignorée/Et le mystère vain de votre être?" (*OC* 46; "For whom . . . do you keep the unknown/Splendor and mystery of your being?" [*CP* 32]), Hérodiade's extended, passionate reply unfurls like a narcotic, bejeweled blossom:

> Oui, c'est pour moi, pour moi, que je fleuris, déserte!
> Vous le savez, jardins d'améthyste, enfouis
> Sans fin dans vos savants abîmes éblouis,
> Ors ignorés, gardant votre antique lumière
> Sous le sombre sommeil d'une terre première,
> Vous, pierres où mes yeux comme de purs bijoux
> Empruntent leur clarté mélodieuse, et vous
> Métaux qui donnez à ma jeune chevelure
> Une splendeur fatale et sa massive allure! (*OC* 47)

> Yes, it's for me, myself, that deserted I bloom!
> You know this, gardens of amethyst, deep
> In the dazzling, unfathomable caves where you sleep;
> Hidden gold hoarding your antique light
> Beneath the dark slumbers of primordial night;

The Matter of Spectacle

> You stones, like the purest of gems, whence my eyes
> Borrow melodious clarities;
> And metals that give to my youthful hair
> Its fatal splendor and massive allure. (*CP* 33)

This moment defies a literal or realist staging of any kind. Ablaze amid a horrific, deathly euphoria, Hérodiade becomes something like what Mallarmé elsewhere describes as a kind of "living allegory" (*CP* 107).[69] The text's language is densely, heavily material, and yet the luster of gems and precious metals seems to travel upward from the subterranean world, as a peculiar movement shivers and convulses Hérodiade's body all the way to her flaming hair. In this exquisite rush, only "dead," mineral substances—the treasures of the earth, buried deep in darkened caves—can know the abyssal truth of Mallarmé's beauty, a truth that defies any human intentionality. In theatrical terms, an outburst like this one succeeds more as a kind of operatic aria than as a moment of dramatic dialogue. It amounts to a powerful overflow of *pathos* to the point of death or self-shattering, similar to Isolde's *Liebestod* at the end of Wagner's *Tristan*. As with Wagner's dramaturgy, an "aria" of this sort also demands to be understood only as an attempt to commence a sacred gesture that could enshrine a secular religion of art. In these lines, Hérodiade suffers a breathless intoxication. Gazing at her own nude body in a mirror, while viol and harpsichord throb beneath her, she appears caught up in a sudden surge of euphoria, carried away by the shattering of a feminine jouissance.[70] In her ecstasies—in which Hérodiade's body is shot through with rippling shimmers and seems to transform before her Nurse's eyes into a gem-encrusted sculpture—the baroque tendencies of Mallarmé's tragic masque achieve their most resplendent elaboration.

Albert Thibaudet rightly draws attention to the bejeweled quality of the "Scène" in claiming that the poem "takes on the aspect of a Byzantine mosaic, recalling the *Theodora* of Ravenna."[71] The figure of Hérodiade could also productively be compared to the mosaic-like depiction of Salome in Gustave Moreau's 1874 painting *The Apparition*. In the "Scène," Mallarmé's baroque dramaturgy finds its fullest, most luxuriating treatment: the language overbrims with mention of rich jewels and metals and with even richer sensations and pulsations of movement, particularly in the exquisite drama of Hérodiade's blood running cold as wave upon wave of congealing horror courses through her petrifying body, all in a white shudder, a "*frisson blanc*" (*OC* 47). "In a clear sense," writes Charles Lyons, "the language of this

Gustave Moreau. *The Apparition*, 1874. Musée Gustave Moreau, Paris, France. Courtesy Erich Lessing/Art Resource, NY.

The Matter of Spectacle   89

piece is emphatically visual, moving from image to image as the body of Hérodiade herself becomes a dazzling scene within her imagination."[72] But for all the spectacular visuality of Mallarmé's language here, Lyons understates the stirring physical and haptic resonances of the scene. The ostensible object or referent of this allegory, Beauty, may be in danger of being lost irretrievably, but the sensual effects being depicted here nevertheless proliferate in a dazzling ripple of impressions: the softness of shuddering flesh, the flight of flaming hair, and the flashing stoniness of accessories. It is not enough to say that she appears as a dehumanized figure, an affront to the possibility of being represented by an actor in a theater. She instead becomes a princess of the ancien régime, crusted over with gems and baroque finery, a futile signifier under the weight of her own ostentation, an image to be beheld. Hérodiade's reply refuses her intersubjective encounter with the Nurse, becoming instead an extended parabasis to an audience. Caught up in her own reflected image, she becomes a theatrical emblem of absorption. Although *Hérodiade* rejects the Aristotelian principle of drama as mimesis, it does so only by becoming real allegory, both ornamental and theatrical.

In her ravishing movement between the early modern past and Mallarmé's fin de siècle present, Hérodiade's body pulsates with hidden pleasures. Her image recalls the poet's fascination during the 1890s with the American dancer Loie Fuller, whose shimmering, fluttering gowns would communicate to him something of the "virginity of undreamt-of places."[73] Though nude, Hérodiade's body is caught up in a surge of feminine erotic enjoyment that looks backward to the glowing and fluttering robes of Bernini's *Saint Theresa* and forward to the luminescent folds of Fuller's veiled performances. Even if *Hérodiade* is rarely or never performed, I wish to emphasize that there is an implicit queerness to all this dazzling hypertheatricality, an erotics to what I am tempted to call this Mallarméan drag act, which resonates at the two registers of highest significance for Mallarmé: "Everything is summed up in Aesthetics and in Political Economy."[74] First, where aesthetics is concerned, in the context of the *Hérodiade*'s interior setting and Mallarmé's comments on Impressionism, Hérodiade becomes theatrical, as if by footlight glare, in precisely the sense delimited by Michael Fried. For Charles Lyons, who has extended Fried's conceptual framework into an analysis of Mallarmé and Manet, "[t]he impetus toward realism displays human figures absorbed in their activity, and their action and language is confined to the space represented. The behavior suppresses their awareness of the presence of the viewer. . . . In the theatrical painting, the subject of the painting—like [Georg] Fuchs's actor—directs her or his gaze out to the spectator."[75] In anti-realistic or operatic moments like this manic aria before Hérodiade's mirror, which possess what Bersani calls a "seductive unread-ability," the spectator does not so much attend to any *thing* directly *repre-sented* as register the sensual and phenomenological act of spectatorship itself.[76] Like the new actors called for in Fuchs's 1909 essay *Revolution in the Theater*, and against the tendencies of the realistic stage perfected in the fourth wall of André Antoine, Hérodiade seems "to thrust forward toward the audience in an overt theatricality, . . . [so as to] break loose and confront the space of the audience."[77] In this she takes on a certain quality of flatness or facingness, which Thibaudet identifies with Byzantine iconography (the Theodora mosaic of Ravenna) and which Nijinsky would famously model in his bas-relief choreographic adaptation of Mallarmé's other major dramatic work, *The Afternoon of a Faun*. Put differently, as an object for contempla-tion in Mallarmé's mystery religion of art, Hérodiade becomes not only erotic but auratic. Taking on all the flatness and two-dimensionality of a sacred icon, she evokes in the reader's mind an image on an illustrated page, arrested into a pose, almost a fashion plate. One might say today, almost a Vogue cover.

Where political economy is concerned, Mallarmé's sumptuous ideal of beauty in *Hérodiade* is noticeably, even *heavily* material. As he abjures the roundedness of psychological character common to realist or naturalist the-ater, Hérodiade's flatness seems akin to a coin's impressed face. As an alle-gorical personage, she appears internally divided between two possibilities —the ornament as quintessence of beautiful, decorative uselessness and the commodity as the supposed epitome of utility and use-value. In this regard, the *Hérodiade* reflects not only the poet's dawning captivation with Fuller or with questions of performance, but also, in elaborately divagated form, his mounting concern with the material conditions of economic value in con-temporary France. He would register a critical anxiety with the phantasma-goric power of currency in a pair of essays ("Grand Fait Divers," on the Panama scandal in 1893, and the highly edited prose-poetic version of that text entitled "Gold," included in *Divagations* in 1897) that warn of the arbitrari-ness of economic valuation in an age marked by extreme market fluctuations, colonial liberalism, rampant imperial investment, and financial corruption. Following the spectacular breakdown of the French efforts to construct the Panama Canal in 1892, in which nearly a half billion francs from hundreds

Samuel Joshua Beckett. [Loie Fuller Dancing], ca. 1900. Gelatin silver print, 10.3 × 13.3 cm (4 × 5 ¼ in.), irregularly trimmed. Gilman Collection, Purchase, Mrs. Walter Annenberg and The Annenberg Foundation Gift, 2005 (2005.100.950). The Metropolitan Museum of Art, New York, NY, U.S.A. Image copyright © The Metropolitan Museum of Art. Courtesy Art Resource, NY.

of thousands of investors were lost, Mallarmé noted, "At the crash of a Bank, vague, mediocre, gray./Currency, that terrible precision instrument, clean to the conscience, loses any meaning. . . ./[O]ne searches, with this hint that, if a number increases and backs up toward the improbable, it inscribes more and more zeroes: signifying that its total is spiritually equal to nothing, almost./Mere smoke and mirrors, those billions, outside the moment to grab some."[78] As the baroque syllogism has it, "All that glisters is not gold."[79]

As the supreme token by which monetary value can be conferred, even gold loses its luster in this context of catastrophic devaluations. Wasted investments grow so astronomical, they seem only a mass of zeroes lined up end to end, "equal to nothing, almost."[80] In the light of the Panama affair, when unheard-of sums vanished as if in a theatrical disappearing act, the auratic power of currency and the precious metals that ground its economic value seems to disperse. (All this is to say nothing of the many workers who died senselessly in Panama of malaria, yellow fever, floods—or of the miners who labored in "unfathomable caves" to extract gold for the wealth of European nations.) It is the task of the poet to alchemize these brute historical events into a valuable and critical artistic form. To return to *Hérodiade*, in this obscured historical context, it is full of poetic and political significance that the protagonist's "body" seems to become a statuesque assemblage of precious stones and rare metals. As an ideal of beauty, this "body" is evoked through an obscure process of objectification that Walter Benjamin will name "petrifaction," which, as discussed in chapter 3, mimes both the work of allegory and that of commodification. With both allegories and commodities, dynamic historical processes have been brought to a standstill and frozen (Lukács would say *reified*) into fetishes. The commodity form and the form of allegory will amount in Benjamin's analysis to the two emblematic faces of a single historical phenomenon: two sides of one coin, so to speak.

Beyond presenting the reader with an ideal and impossible beauty, the *Hérodiade* also dramatizes the allegorical work of commodification and the commodifying power of allegory. Over the course of the play's central "Scène," the commodity emerges as a ruinous translation of the no-longer-accessible form of a formerly transcendent *logos*. In Mallarmé's nihilistic, noisy era of journalism and Gilded Age capitalism, what once was thought to be Truth has become a commodity: what remains now are so many circulating, transactional coins, passing from one hand to another (*OC* 368) and doomed eventually to lose their stamp (as Nietzsche's "On Truth and Lying" puts it). While the figure of Hérodiade was intended as a personification of Beauty in itself, the moment when Hérodiade glimpses her petrifying image in a mirror at the midpoint of the "Scène" reveals the dream of this ideal in all its monstrous nudity, as a spectacular but sterile token of currency, the ultimate, inhuman basis of capitalist economics. *Hérodiade* thus stages an uncertainty about the ontological status of ideas as such, raising questions about the form these ideas can take under Mallarmé's contemporary situation of metaphysical and politico-economic crisis. Without directly representing the violence of class warfare or the depredations of the capitalist economy (as a realist work like Gerhart Hauptmann's *The Weavers*

The Matter of Spectacle   93

might, for example), it stages the effects of commodity fetishism through an elaborate strategy of indirection in which the relationship between poiesis and aesthesis has become indeterminate, requiring allegorical reading. To detect and make manifest this politico-economic staging in the text requires, as Fredric Jameson suggests, "new representational strategies and therefore new reading processes."[81] As Mallarmé's most enduring experiment in the theater, *Hérodiade* trains its readers and its spectators in these new processes of representation and interpretation. It addresses a truly modern reader, preparing that reader to interpret the phantasmagorias of capitalist production on critical terms.

The third and final movement of *Hérodiade* builds upon the iconographic qualities of the second. It draws on much the same imagery of brilliance and hardness as does the "Scène" but pulls the drama closer to a form of saintly pageant or martyrdom tragedy. The closing "Cantique," sung by Saint John the Baptist either *at* or just *after* the moment of his beheading—the exact setting is indeterminate—depicts an image of decapitation favored by painters of the historical baroque period, Caravaggio most notable among them. Just as the "Scène" unfolds in an eerie stasis, this "Cantique" takes place in what appears to be a moment of solar or sidereal standstill, its lines advancing in rhyming couplets of funereal trimeter: "Le soleil que sa halte/Surnaturelle exalte" (*OC* 49; "The sun as it's halted/Miraculously exalted" [*CP* 36]). The drama occurs at the moment of the shortest possible shadow, just before this sun "Aussitôt redescend/Incandescent" ("Resumes its descent/Incandescent"). Just as the Feast of Saint John, which aligns with the summer solstice, celebrates the sun at its zenith and optimal splendor, the solar drama's peripeteia, this "Cantique" transpires during an uncanny calm amid a scene of violence. The Baptist speaks or sings this canticle, but the poem does not specify a hearer within the scene of his execution. The addressee is, again, none other than the drama's reader or spectator, whom the poem hails implicitly. As shadows grip the shuddering corpse, the head rises up in the third of the poem's seven stanzas ("ma tête surgie"), whether miraculously, as in an onstage *machina* effect or, more simply, in the executioner's grip. As the speaker details in the final stanza how the defunct body's pure gaze ("son pur regard") reaches upward to meet the glacial, azure sky, this disenchanted firmament extends to the martyr an enigmatic "salut." A greeting, toast, or perhaps a salvation; the ambiguous word is significant in Mallarmé's oeuvre, as it forms the last word of the *Hérodiade*'s three parts but also names the title of the poem he selected to appear first in his collected

Poésies. This end is a beginning, this slaughter is also a baptism by blood, this baroque martyrdom is also a drama of redemption. The poetic sequence ends by opening to some unknown but, it seems, messianic futurity. John the Baptist allegorizes the figure of the poet as author who must die so that a purer poetry founded in autonomous writing and reading can be born. But if so, "the Death of the Author" or "the Death of Stéphane Mallarmé" appears here in the perverse form of an inscrutable and comfortless redemption.

Taken together, the three musical "scenes" of the *Hérodiade* have an ambiguous role in Mallarmé's larger oeuvre. On one hand, the *Hérodiade* appears as a transitional work between the poet's earlier, representational aesthetics, which it seeks to overcome, and his later, more fully self-referential work, which strives to abandon any extratextual referent whatsoever to give the performative autonomy of language more priority. Mallarmé began glimpsing this absolute poetics only in the late 1860s—immediately after he first abandoned the *Hérodiade*—with the so-called "Sonnet allegorical of itself," in which the poem no longer describes any action or event whatever and instead *becomes* one self-reflexively through the ritual of its composition and reading.[82] In this way, the baroque dramaturgy of the *Hérodiade* performed special work for the poet in his larger quest to transform the domain of modern writing. The *Hérodiade* was not only the first modernist drama to stage itself as a replaying of baroque theater—a tradition that would be taken up later by Gertrude Stein in *Four Saints and Three Acts*. It also made possible the concrete dramaturgy of language, sound, space, and situation one finds in Mallarmé's final, most radical works, including the monumental and seemingly aleatoric concrete poem *A Throw of the Dice Will Never Abolish Chance*. In sum, with *Hérodiade*, baroque style becomes Mallarmé's vehicle for traveling between the mimesis of poetry's past and a more deconstructive écriture.[83]

On the other hand, even if the *Hérodiade* initiated a transitional process in Mallarmé's poetic development, this process appears to have been ultimately interminable. He continued to make changes to *Hérodiade* over the course of his life, leaving it unfinished at his death in 1898. He even imagined a privileged place for it as "one of the twisted, splendid, and Solomonic columns" (*C* 200; translation mine) to the temple that would be his *grand oeuvre*, the legendary Book or *Livre* that would effect an Orphic explication of the earth. Although Mallarmé clearly gave up his hopes that his allegorical, modernist-baroque, tyrant-and-martyr drama would ever be performed

The Matter of Spectacle

at the Théâtre-Français, it persisted among his private obsessions. All the while his later poetry continued to strive resolutely toward what Weinfield calls "a baroque elaboration of syntax that strains almost to the breaking point" (*CP* 256). With respect to Mallarmé's baroque style, then, *Hérodiade* instructed the poet in a continued program of writing ever more divorced from mimesis and bound to allegory. The poet's language, regardless of whatever syntactical purifications and refinements he would aim to introduce, would ultimately fail to escape the complexity, luxury, and self-reference of baroque form. It was *Hérodiade*, baroque drama of salvific death, that taught Mallarmé how such a failure for the artist could be a form of achievement in the domain of modern art.

In his abandonment of *Hérodiade* and his conception of the total *Livre* over the 1860s, Mallarmé's interest shifts from a drama still rooted in mimesis to a baroque mode of nonmimetic theater that could unfold on a more fully immanent plane. The *Livre* that Mallarmé planned, the great and impossible Book to come, never materialized beyond the existence of several hundred pages of preparatory notes, which as Mary Lewis Shaw argues, "should not be equated with the text of Mallarmé's Book."[84] Still, these left-behind sheets and jottings provide a glimpse into Mallarmé's vision of the performance artwork of the future. With the *Livre*, Mallarmé dreamed of a new form of text that could approach the condition of theater, fusing all media of the performing arts and literature into a total artwork altogether different from the one Wagner had imagined. While the *Livre* would be Mallarmé's ultimate poetic opus and not any typical dramatic script, it would nevertheless require ritual enactment for its fulfillment. Mallarmé imagined readings from the Book stretched out over a period of five years, all held in his private library before small, carefully chosen audiences of fellow aesthetes. For these readings, he sought an absolute, obsessive control over all the details of enactment and spectatorship. A set of abstruse mathematical calculations would determine the number of acolytes in attendance at the ritual, the organization of furniture pieces in his library, the arrangements of seating, the cost of tickets, the passages chosen from his writings to be read aloud, the means for determining (by chance) their order and combination, and other performance details. Through these computations, the interior space of Mallarmé's library was to become a peculiar, immersive theater space. Here, Mallarmé can be seen to prefigure the rise of the Futurist *serate*, John Cage's aleatoric composition, Fluxus, Happenings, Intermedia, "solo performance," "loft performance," and what has generally traveled under the name of performance art since the 1960s and '70s.[85]

For Mallarmé, performance of this kind was conceivable only in terms of a specifically baroque theatricality patterned after the manner of a Tridentine Mass.[86] His reading desk, illuminated by lamplight, was to take center stage at one end of his library, facing an arrangement of seats split evenly into two sections by a central aisle, and would be positioned alongside a "diagonally placed piece of lacquered furniture equipped with a specific number of pigeonholes," a Platonic dovecote, of sorts, "to hold the loose sheets that constitute the performance edition of the *Livre*."[87] At the appointed time, an utterly anonymous figure whom Mallarmé called an *operator* would appear at the desk to read aloud fragmentary passages from the *Livre* inscribed on these sheets. The selections would be chosen randomly, allowing aleatoric procedures to dictate the juxtapositions of textual material. (As one of the *Livre*'s Solomonic columns, *Hérodiade* likely would have appeared in randomized and fragmentary form amid the texts available for reading in the *Livre*'s performances.) Following a brief intermission, the operator would reread the same texts again in a different order, allowing different meanings to emerge through new combinations. Along the way, these readings were to be accompanied with a quasi-religious ceremonial of hieratic movements and ritualistic gestures.[88] With the performer's focus absorbed in the act of reading, his place at the reading desk demanded that he at least occasionally return the gaze of his spectators, refusing any semblance of an illusionistic partition. More than just a typical poetry reading, this was to be a quasi-oratorical theater for initiates, a form of closet rhetoric on par with what Nietzsche had accomplished in his quest for an emphatically rhetorical style in philosophy. As Martin Puchner has shown, the fragmentary notes for the *Livre* abound with moments in which the text on the page takes on the graphic quality of gesture itself, and with allusions to "the non-signifying, nonreferential, or to be more precise, decorative elements of the theater, such as chandeliers, curtains, and flies."[89] The theater that the *Livre* evokes is one of pure ornament, rich in luxurious folds, deeply interior, almost a séance with Mallarmé presiding as its chief medium. It was to be an allegorical rite, absconded from mimesis, far removed from the modern, bourgeois stage that Mallarmé viewed as devoid of "majesty and ecstasy" (*D* 144; *OC* 314). These were gestures that could raise the dead, reanimating a defunct corpus of baroque performance practice, through a ceremonial filled with splendor and spiritual elevation.

The Matter of Spectacle   97

For all its closeness to the Catholic mass, however, Mallarmé's *Livre* maintains a crucial difference attributable to the dialectics of secularization, far more ubiquitous in the late nineteenth century than it had been in the seventeenth. The priestly gestures of Tridentine Catholicism are meant to display, to the faithful at least, a series of theological symbols in which divine word and worldly thing enjoy unbroken unity in the transubstantiated Eucharist. By comparison, the operator's physical gestures, along with those described in and enacted by Mallarmé's text, amount to seemingly arbitrary movements of the body with no obvious relation to one another or to the text being read.[90] If Mallarmé had conceived of some necessary connection between word and *gestus*, signifier and signified, that connection has been lost irrevocably amid the apparent incompleteness of the *Livre* notes. As with the theory of theatrical movement sketched in *Mimique*, Mallarmé's *Livre* imagines a form of emblematic gesture, one that demands the beholder's active and interpretive involvement for signifying processes to occur.

As Stephen Orgel has claimed of the hieroglyphic form of the baroque masque in Ben Jonson's England, there is "a pleasure to be derived from mysteries and enigmas, . . . [from symbols] left unexplained to emphasize the occult aspects of poetic wisdom. But in all such cases, to all except the most iconographically sophisticated, they remained enigmatic."[91] The obscure, quasi-sacred gestures of Mallarmé's metatheatrical masque function in precisely this way, as devices of secular enchantment. Framed within the four walls of Mallarmé's monad-like library, this miming transforms the space of the *Livre*'s performances into nineteenth-century homologues for the *Kunstkammern*, libraries, indoor stages, and church interiors of the baroque period, with the *Livre* as a modern surrogate for the Bible. In Mallarmé's description, the great Book was to effect a total (re)theatricalization of things: his oft-cited aphorism "that everything in the world exists to end up as a book" sets the horizon for this pervasive theatricalization (*D 226; OC* 378). His great work was to be a Book of the World, an impossible, culminating totality, the one book sought after by every writer. While this dream of a World-Book is decidedly modernist in character, it too has origins in the time of the historical baroque period. Just as the enclosed space of the *theatrum* proliferates within baroque discourse to encompass not only the allegorical vision of the *theatrum mundi* (theater of the world) but also the *theatrum orbis terrarum, theatrum belli, theatrum Europeum*, and *theatrum naturae*, among so many others, so too did the figure of the "the book of nature" become a commonplace during the seventeenth century.[92] The characteristically baroque sense of the world as a theater is mirrored in its sense of the world as a book, in which all of physical nature can be seen as enclosed within, or coextensive with, a pervasive textuality and theatricality.[93] Advancing this conceit toward its logical, Borgesian extremes, the world comes to be seen as a library, an archive and repository of writings, and the setting for the ritual readings of Mallarmé's Book takes on an even more suggestive character.[94] Summoned or cited as if by Mallarmé's enigmatic gestures, these microcosmic spaces of enclosure—theater, library, book—reemerge from the baroque past, available for poetry to reconfigure according to new, modern needs.

It was Mallarmé's hope that these spaces could provide the setting for a new form of collective ritual, one that would be, in Quentin Meillassoux's assessment of Mallarmé's aims, "capable of founding a civic religion and engendering a profound adhesion of individuals to the ends of their community." The goal of Mallarmé's *Livre* was a kind of aesthetic education, its dream the production of a new spiritual community of humankind. Such a community would necessarily be revolutionary in orientation, an anatheistic sequel to those new quasi-religious systems set up after the French Revolution, whose centennial coincided with the time when Mallarmé was actively at work on the *Livre*.[95] Although the poet's meaning for modern politics has generated extensive debate, particularly in the field of contemporary French aesthetic theory, it is nevertheless clear that Mallarmé conceived the political dimension of his oeuvre in response to Wagner's theatrical project at Bayreuth.[96] Like Wagner's *Gesamtkunstwerk*, Mallarmé's *Livre* aims to put theater into the service of a modern, revolutionary religion of art, one that can rescue the social organism from its alienation and disenchantment by synthesizing all the artistic media (dance, mime, gesture, tone, poetry) into an utterly totalizing ambition. For Mallarmé, the same crowd that Wagner's theater seeks to address, far from being uniquely the product of modern industrialization, is always already what Mallarmé's essay "Stages and Pages" describes as "la foule baroque" (*OC* 328; "the baroque crowd" [*D* 161]).[97] Although Mallarmé largely admired Wagner, he was also critical of Wagnerian music-drama insofar as it continued to depend upon the very forms of mimesis Mallarmé's poetics sought to escape. Like Nietzsche, Mallarmé based his critique of Wagner on visions of an immanent theater beyond mimesis. Nietzsche, of course, saw Wagner's all too "naturalistic" mimomania as evidence of a persistent and melancholy faith in the theological presuppositions of representation. By contrast, to address the manifold crises of nineteenth-century Europe, Mallarmé's writing proposes *mime*, a not strictly

The Matter of Spectacle

mimetic use of gesture. In doing so, the baroque theater of Racine and the baroque theatricality of the mass were his original aesthetic matrices.

The Theater of the Book

Unlikely though it may seem, Mallarmé's vision of baroque theatricalism promises a new politics of reading and spectatorship. As his great, unfinished theatrical endeavor, the *Livre* would establish conditions for a modern, potentially utopian form of community *precisely because* of the interpretive difficulty of its poetry. Like Charles Bernstein, Fredric Jameson argues that Mallarmé's syntax generates "an interactive situation" that Jameson labels *reconstruction*, "in which the reader reassembles a new totality on the basis of hints and directions, and out of the isolated parts, 'significantly' positioned and on tactical offer from the poet."[98] (Bernstein calls this same phenomenon a poem's artifice or *theatricality*, while Jameson, following Benjamin, describes it in Mallarmé's work as a form of *allegory*.) When *Hérodiade* or any of Mallarmé's other texts appears in performance, its interpreters on and off stage must undertake this "reconstruction" to create meanings out of its isolated components, as if through bricolage, a process that Jameson calls "constellation."[99] Mallarmé's writings force their readers and spectators to search for the constituent parts of these constellations and to find ways of bringing them together meaningfully, even in the absence of a final interpretive solution. In doing so, they promote capacities for literacy and constructive thinking that are the necessary condition for a viably democratic politics.

It is also noteworthy that Mallarmé's aesthetics evidently involves a necessary reinterpretation of the "individual" body as a subject or ground for action, in both a theatrical and political sense. His essay "Restricted Action," which he composed amid his preparations for the Book and included in *Divagations*, raises the question of "action" as an explicitly philosophical problem. The essay takes shape as a letter to a young comrade, written in poetic prose, meditating on the question of what it means "to act" and correspondingly "to write." The addressee wonders whether it is better to write poetry or take up political activism. Mallarmé's narrator offers the following predication: to act is "to produce on many a movement that gives you the impression that *you* originated it, and therefore exist: something no one can be sure of."[100] For Mallarmé, one significantly cannot move from "I act" to "therefore I am." His theory of performance inverts the classical Cartesian formula *cogito ergo sum*, putting the ontological security and self-identity of the subject into radical doubt. Insofar as his aesthetics stems from his early spiritual crisis and entails an injunction to *"paint, not the thing, but the effect it produces,"* it evinces uncertainty about transcendent positions or causes, all of which are survived only by their remaining *effects*, which it is the poet's role impersonally to depict or translate. The ultimate horizon of this aesthetics is the elocutionary disappearance of the poet as "author" into the very same anonymity that marks the operator of Mallarmé's ritual of the Book.[101]

As such, Mallarmé's advice in "Restricted Action" suggestively proposes the transformation of the political agent from a secure and autonomous source of action (an integral "I" or transcendent subject) into a more multifarious force field of politically intersecting energies whose actions' consequences can never be foreseen.[102] Involving oneself in the political field as an "individual" who is also part of a larger collective system of life thus means exercising a specifically weak kind of power. (The important thing, Mallarmé also advises his young friend, is to keep writing.) Likewise, I propose that this letter to a young poet also suggests a new vision of theater actors onstage. If previously an actor was thought to have been a physical source of their gestures, in light of Mallarmé they now become an ongoing play of movement and miming that only retrospectively evokes the *impression* of a presence. In theatrical terms, it means that the onstage performer will ultimately cease to represent a stable, self-identical "character" (a "self" who "acts" upon the world) and will instead become a series of extrinsic gestures like the ones prescribed in Mallarmé's notes for the *Livre*. This Mallarméan actor does not produce the gestures but is merely a medium for their communication.[103] In this vision, the stage emerges not as a stable ground for intersubjective exchanges between normatively psychological characters, but as a dynamic scene of effects and forces at play without causal essences grounding them.

Ultimately, Mallarmé's aesthetics effectively destabilizes the categories of identity and action alike, and in this way, it has consequences in the domain of politics far outside the scope of this chapter. In Mallarmé, as in Nietzsche, the self becomes something protean, a blank space capable of trading in a host of character "masks" that can be traced throughout the various writings (Pierrot, John the Baptist, the Faun). If we view Hérodiade herself as one of the greatest and most enduring of Mallarmé's masks, and consider also the fact that Mallarmé published a number of essays on the subject of fashion in *La Dernière Mode* from behind an assortment of female pseu-

The Matter of Spectacle

donyms (Miss Satin, Madame Marguerite de Ponty, and so forth), it becomes clear that Mallarmé's theatrical, baroque vision of modern poetry and language also corresponded to a queer space of play where the author could experiment with a variety of other identity configurations, imaginatively crossing boundaries, not just of genre but of gender.[104] If the world is destined to end up in a book, it is also destined to end up becoming a stage of sorts: not the *theatrum mundi* of Christian theocentric doctrine but a new and immanent *theatrum*, where all social life is increasingly understood under the concept of performance, fated to be perceived by the beholding gaze of others. This shift can also be registered in the ways Mallarmé's poetry resists the plainness of normative modes of representation—in its manner of embracing exuberance, fanciness, and ostentation, thus inaugurating the cultural dynamics of modernism by hearkening back to the baroque past. In this double, dialectical session of moving forward and backward at once, founding a modern poetics while also calling into question the very possibility of *foundation* itself as an act, are Mallarmé's contributions to his emerging baroque modernity most deeply consequential.

3 Landscapes of Melancholy
Benjamin, Trauerspiel, and the
Pathways of Tradition

> to blast a specific era out of the homogeneous course of
> history . . .
>
> —Walter Benjamin, "On the Concept of History" (*SW* 4:396)

During their summer conversations in exile at Skovsbostrand, Denmark, Walter Benjamin and Bertolt Brecht discovered an unexpected convergence in their ideas about theater. On 29 June 1938, as recorded in Benjamin's diary, Brecht turned their dialogue to the subject of accidents in performance that can operate as epic defamiliarization effects. This spurred an involuntary memory in Benjamin, flashing up from twenty-three years before: "I mention[ed] the Geneva production of *Le Cid* where the sight of the king's crown worn crookedly on his head gave me the first inkling of the ideas I eventually developed in the *Trauerspiel* book nine years later."[1] Benjamin had seen a production of Pierre Corneille's 1637 tragicomedy, paragon of French baroque dramaturgy, while visiting the city as a student in 1915. For both Benjamin and Brecht, this lopsided crown could function as an image to help the viewer discover the scene's political meanings, revealing that wherever power seems to rest secure, some decomposing force of nature can unsettle it from within.[2] Brecht used devices of this sort in his own directing practice, as he suggested by turning their conversation next to his Munich production of *Edward II*, to help the spectator sense distances between actor and character, contingency and necessity, distances in which revolutionary potential could inhere. But for the young Benjamin, the sloping crown amounted to an emblem like those that Corneille's age produced in plentiful editions, a *pictura* of disordered sovereignty. That is, where Brecht sees an epic image like one of his own innovations, Benjamin sees instead a form of allegory, original to the age of the baroque. How to interpret this

Landscapes of Melancholy

four-way intersection of baroque and modern, epic and allegory? What meaning might the collision of these terms suggest for the centuries spanning 1637 and 1938, for the period of capitalist modernity itself? Or, to put these questions another way: what might Benjamin reveal if he is read not just as an explicator of Brecht's writing but as a theorist of theater in his own right and, specifically, a theorist of baroque theater and performance?

As a study of seventeenth-century German-language theater, Benjamin's *Origin of the German Trauerspiel* offers us pathways into these questions, while it also stands as the pinnacle of baroque modernism's achievements in critical theory. But, if the Trauerspiel study is a crowning accomplishment, it is also a lopsided one. The book's reputation for inscrutability has persisted since the University of Frankfurt rejected it in 1928, when Benjamin submitted it there as his postdoctoral habilitation thesis seeking faculty employment. (According to Gershom Scholem, Benjamin claimed, perhaps jokingly, that the book could be understood only by a student of the Kabbalah.[3]) While American scholars of performance have conscripted Benjamin's ideas to several notable projects over the decades, the *Origin of the German Trauerspiel* continues to receive neglect in the field.[4] Yet Benjamin's conversations with Brecht reveal that the *Origin* (which Benjamin sometimes called the *Trauerspielbuch* or *Barockbuch*, the "Trauerspiel-book" or "Baroque-book") has roots in the space of the literal theater and in Benjamin's experiences of spectatorship, and they suggest that the book has much to reveal about stage performance in both the seventeenth and twentieth centuries. Modernity, ruin, melancholy, origin, constellation—these concepts rank among the book's signal contributions to Benjamin's critical vocabulary. On a closer look, the book also describes allegory as a distinctive mode of *theatricality in performance*, one that is materially immanent, technological, and artificial in form. The Trauerspiel-book shows that the baroque theater "has its god in machination," in both senses of the word, as intrigue and as stage machinery (*OGT* 69), showing that the Trauerspiel (or "mourning play"; pluralized as *Trauerspiele*) demands a material and spatial field for staging. In this, Benjamin suggests that the baroque theater corresponds to that moment in the history of Western performance when the stage becomes an independent physical medium in its own right, and not just a conduit for the transmission of literary dramas.

This liberation of the *stage* from the tyranny of *drama* marks a break with Greek tragedy and the beginning of a postmythic and increasingly postdramatic modernity. In this respect, Benjamin's Trauerspiel-book deserves to be read as a theory of modern theater that could answer to and supplant Aristotle's authority on ancient tragic drama in the *Poetics*. Like Nietzsche and Mallarmé, Benjamin conceives of baroque style in opposition to Aristotelian dogma, whose influence over the early modern stage he finds "insignificant" (*OGT* 43). Whereas Aristotle prioritized mimetic drama (the tragic plot or *mythos*) over the theater's material and sensual attributes (spectacle and song, *opsis* and *melos* respectively), in the Trauerspiel-book Benjamin shows that the baroque theater overturns this hierarchy, and does so in a way that remains decisive today, centuries later. In this chapter, I show that Benjamin discloses the specific theatricality of baroque theater as anti-"dramatic" in Aristotle's sense, and thus opposed to drama's anthropocentrism, absorption, and mimesis. In Trauerspiel, baroque style unfolds less in scenes of action than through spatial configurations of allegorical devices: stage images (e.g., lopsided crowns) among other sensory stimuli, illustrative scenery, frozen gestures, stolen glances, and modes of address that interrupt the illusion of a fictional or dialogic world. These moments, I argue, suspend the theater's capacity for representation and involve forms of direct-address presentation instead. I demonstrate that Trauerspiel for Benjamin dissolves its protagonists into constellations of figures in tension with one another, creating a spatial dramaturgy of historical setting or landscape rather than a temporal one of efficacious human action. In these observations, Benjamin reveals features of baroque theatricality in performance that anticipate the conventions of the twentieth- and twenty-first-century stage.

Baroque Trauerspiel form, I argue—like Brecht's epic theater and the postdramatic regime of theater that emerged in Brecht's wake—is by degrees freed from Aristotle's demand to subordinate theater's physical elements to its dramatic texts and plots. As Hans-Thies Lehmann has shown, this demand came into existence in modern Europe only with the rise of French classicism in the later seventeenth and eighteenth centuries, reaching culmination and obsolescence in the first half of the twentieth century. Brecht's work, which both prolongs and contests Aristotle's notion of drama as mimesis, thereby creates an opening for a new post-Aristotelian theater to emerge, while also maintaining links to the theater of the seventeenth century, a theater that had not yet discovered neo-Aristotelian principles.[5] For, as Benjamin asserts at the Trauerspiel-book's outset, "in the middle of the seventeenth century, Aristotelian poetics was not yet the simple and imposing set of dogmas with which Lessing came to terms" (*OGT* 44), the same set of dogmas, incidentally, that had become problematic in Brecht's life-

Landscapes of Melancholy

time. In this view, the baroque stage stands for the prehistory of a certain Enlightenment ideology of modern drama, while the theater of Brecht and his inheritors testifies to this ideology's increasingly awkward status in the history of aesthetic forms. While reflecting on the work of Brecht and his contemporaries, Benjamin recognized that Trauerspiel forms a gateway through which the allegorical mechanisms of the baroque may persist into the historical space-time of the twentieth century. In addition, I argue, Benjamin's writing shows that theatrical forms of allegory residual from the early modern baroque become reactivated in the nineteenth and twentieth centuries, after a long "dormancy." In this vein, Benjamin claims Brecht as an inheritor to the tradition of Trauerspiel, one who repurposes baroque methods within a modernist context.

This chapter explores Benjamin's theory of the baroque through a reading of the *Origin of the German Trauerspiel*'s two chapters, "Trauerspiel and Tragedy" and "Allegory and Trauerspiel." Just as Aristotle had done previously with tragedy in the *Poetics*, in the Trauerspiel-book Benjamin treats the form of the Trauerspiel as a philosophical concept. Where Aristotle attempted to describe an ideal form of tragedy, closest in most cases to the *Oedipus* of Sophocles, so too does Benjamin's study treat the Trauerspiel as a generic abstraction that can yoke together widely disparate texts and authors into a single form. And, as Aristotle's *Poetics* was with tragedy, so too is the Trauerspiel-book often tendentious in its claims about baroque theater and its preferred representatives of the Trauerspiel tradition—often favoring plays far removed from the German context: Shakespeare's *Hamlet* and Calderón's *La Vida es sueño*, for example. (It sometimes seems as though Benjamin were attempting to rewrite the *Poetics* for a modern theater, correcting Aristotle's textual bias by emphasizing as much the physical and performative grounds of the modern stage. So, not a *Poetics* but a *Choreographics*, perhaps.) The value of the Trauerspiel-book resides less in its empirical accuracy about early modern theater than in the concepts of performance the book generates. I do not claim to offer anything like a final exegesis of Benjamin's difficult, some might say esoteric, text. I instead propose to give it a reading attuned—perhaps perversely, given Benjamin's prestige as a *literary* critic—to the material practice of theater, aiming to translate him into a performance theorist of baroque theatricality in his own right.[6] The sections that follow center, first, on Benjamin's comments concerning the role of *landscape* and *gesture* on the baroque stage, with particular respect to the figure of the onstage sovereign. I argue that the Trauerspiel form deconstructs the ideology of the sovereign subject, creating the possibility for a theater organized not around characters but around the material playing space of the stage. In this chapter's second section, I turn to the forms of theatrical *allegory* that baroque performance presupposes and to the ways those forms play out in the space of the theater and its audience. I show that Benjamin's notion of allegory depends on a fundamentally theatrical relation, one that requires the presence of an external interpreter, and that allegory thus stands as an antithesis to the idea of drama as mimesis, requiring instead a theater of sumptuous material and media effects.

In the last section and conclusion of this chapter, I shift focus from questions of theater to those of theory and to the political ambiguities of baroque style, its ability both to enshrine and to destabilize established systems of power. While the ideologists of the Counter-Reformation church, the Westphalian state, and the absolutist monarchies of Europe deployed allegory during the seventeenth century to advance their material interests according to a reactionary metaphysics of presence, Benjamin shows that allegory also holds out a liberatory promise, urgent during his own lifetime when forms of tyranny were again on the rise. This faint promise—that theatricality might be more than an instrument of domination but might make possible the undoing of ideologies, dismantling not only absorptive *drama* of its aura but also *sovereignty, authoritarian power*, and even *capital* of theirs—such a promise would only be developed fully in Benjamin's late writings on Baudelaire, Brecht, and Nietzsche. In those texts, with which I conclude, Benjamin offers his readers a glimpse of theater's messianic potentialities. There, he suggests the baroque theater's legacy as a means to seeing the world differently and reconfiguring it anew.

"History Passes into the Setting"—Baroque Spatialization

Benjamin's first forays into the baroque resonances of modernism appear at the end of the Trauerspiel-book's "Epistemo-Critical Foreword," which elaborates its aims, stakes, and philosophical orientation. (The Foreword includes Plato, Leibniz, Hegel, and the neo-Kantian Hermann Cohen as among the book's major influences.) At its outset, the Trauerspiel-book promises to reevaluate the stage dramas of the German seventeenth century in order to make them essential for a radical aesthetics and philosophy of history, but before arriving at any questions concerning the theater itself, the Foreword opens with a claim couched in suggestive, theatrical terms. "It is peculiar to philosophical writing to be confronted anew at every turn with the question

Landscapes of Melancholy

of presentation [*Darstellung*]" (*OGT* 1). The author of philosophical writing must stand at each turn to face the question: How is this material to be presented? Or rather, according to another meaning of *Darstellung*: How should it be staged or given its mise-en-scène, so to speak, in the space of writing?[7] From its outset, the Trauerspiel-book suggests Benjamin will advance his argument through directions other than the typical syllogisms, logical demonstrations, and geometric proofs of academic philosophy. The Trauerspiel-book will instead pursue a directorial or theatrical mode of presentation, its writing style functioning as the synthesis of its theater-historical content, mediating the baroque theater of images into the form of a philosophical treatise. In this respect, Benjamin is only following in the footsteps of Goethe, who provides the prologue's epigraph in a short selection of "Materials" to *History of the Theory of Color* that counsels, "Since no whole can be brought together in either knowledge or reflection, seeing that the former lacks internality and the latter externality, we must necessarily think of science as art if we are to expect from it any sort of wholeness" (*OGT* 1).

Over the book's first pages, the reader gets an initial foretaste of this "artistic," "directorial," or "theatrical" mode of philosophic writing, which appears immediately to proceed by the direct presentation of emblematic imagery. Only in the book's first and second chapters does the relationship between baroque theater and images in Benjamin's thinking become clear, as I demonstrate in the following sections. The Foreword declares his intention to elevate Trauerspiel into a philosophical idea, constructed in the form of what he calls, in one of the first striking thought-images to appear in the book, a *constellation*.[8] Configuring together both acknowledged masterpieces alongside lesser-known works of baroque theater, Benjamin aims for a picture of the Trauerspiel to emerge in the tensions between the genre's extreme outliers, just as a constellation connects far-flung stars into an imaginary picture. Eschewing the "coercive" reasoning of a mathematical proof, Benjamin has structured his treatise into the image of a *mosaic* of discrete and fragmentary bits that come together in a kind of montage effect (*OGT* 2–3). "Just as the majesty of mosaics remains intact when they are disassembled into capricious bits, so philosophical observation fears no dissipation of momentum" (3). The book's procedure will be to ruminate on the nearly lost plays of the German baroque through fragmentary quotations, in aphoristic sentences, and discontinuous sections. A paratactic principle governs the book's arrangement. The effect will be of the author taking apart the material and reconfiguring it into an image whose unity radiates from its inner discontinuity. In still another image, Benjamin compares the "momentum" he desires for his "philosophical observation" to a constant *pausing for breath* on the author's part. Although the text's discontinuities will mark it with a self-interrupting rhythm, it will be as though the author were an embodied performer on foot, standing or perhaps walking while speaking, and needing to stop briefly "at every turn" because "this continual breathing in and out is the form of existence most proper to contemplation."[9] Benjamin is no disembodied analyst of his material, but moves and breathes as a thinker on stage. Meanwhile, his writing takes shape in the form of a staging, an *Inszenierung*, whose methods involve the presentation of image fragments for the reader to ponder.

For the book's rationale, Benjamin turns to the contemporary theater context, naming German Expressionism's recent emergence as a reason for interest in the forgotten Trauerspiel form. "Striking analogies to the current state of German literature have repeatedly given rise to a positively directed, if mostly sentimental, immersion in the Baroque" (*OGT* 36). While the 1915 publication of Franz Werfel's *Trojan Women* spurred debate regarding Expressionism as a baroque revival, drawing comparisons with Martin Opitz's 1625 translation of Seneca's play on the same theme (36-37), elsewhere in Benjamin's various writings, other contemporary figures appear within the sphere of baroque influence as well, including Stefan George, August Strindberg, Franz Kafka, and Hugo von Hofmannsthal.[10] Between these writers and their seventeenth-century forebears, the *Origin of the German Trauerspiel* notes a set of shared rhetorical features, including hyperbole, neologisms, archaisms, and an almost operatic predisposition toward lamentation. Linguistic stylization of this sort is bound to seem "inwardly empty or else deeply agitated, while outwardly occupied with formal technical problems that, at first sight, seem to have little bearing on the existential issues (*Existenzfragen*) of the age" (36). On a closer look, the formalism of baroque Trauerspiel, like that of German Expressionism, bespeaks what Benjamin describes as, borrowing the art historian Alois Riegl's Nietzschean vocabulary, "an unremitting will to art" (*Kunstwollens*).[11] This will, in turn, reflects a "striving for a vigorous style of language that would make it seem equal to the impact of world events" (37). Baroque style only seems disconnected from its historical contexts and their existential concerns: in reality, Trauerspiel, both in its dramaturgical and theatrical forms, functions to mediate history itself.

Landscapes of Melancholy

A shattered experience of historical life, provoked by the devastating wars fought primarily on Germanic territory in the early seventeenth and twentieth centuries, forms the backdrop to and the primary "content" for both baroque Trauerspiel and Expressionist theater.[12] What sense of "history," then, do Trauerspiel and Expressionist theater presuppose? Benjamin's friend and colleague the Berlin theater critic Herbert Ihering offers one way in which this question might be answered. As Ihering put it in 1922, the young generation of which he, Benjamin, and Brecht were a part "had to fight for something that had been denied to no generation except the one that came after the Thirty Years' War: experience itself. The horrors of the last few years were not the collapse of a nation, but the inability to experience the elemental things elementally. People's energy was so exhausted that they accepted apocalyptic events like everyday inconveniences."[13] After the traumas of World War I, whose only close precedent in violence and grief had been the seventeenth-century wars of religion, the Trauerspiel form appeared vital and contemporary again. In return, the earlier historical period threw new light on the postwar artistic context. Expressionism provided German scholars with a new reason to revisit the Trauerspiel. Benjamin's specific interest was to illuminate how baroque form embeds the cataclysms and violence of the age.

The second chapter of Benjamin's Trauerspiel-book will name allegory as the baroque's quintessential trope, that figure of rhetoric most equal to the breakdown of history and the destruction of experience. For the playwrights of baroque Germany, Benjamin claims, allegory is less a "convention of expression"—not simply a discrete rhetorical technique that can be applied, or not, at will—than an "expression of convention"—that is, a way of giving voice to the conventionality of language in relation to the world of things and events (*OGT* 185). Between human language and the objects it seeks to designate, allegory sees a gross inadequacy, even arbitrariness. That this inadequacy of language to the world demands to be expressed or exhibited, even mourned, is what lends baroque works their irreducibly theatrical character. What is baroque theatricality? The word "theatrical" (*theatralisch, theatralisches, theatralischem*) shows up only occasionally in the Trauerspiel-book's working vocabulary, but when it does appear, it arrives rich with significance. To understand what constitutes theatricality in a baroque context, one must first define it negatively, distinguishing it from modern expectations. Benjamin claims that twentieth-century spectators, in their "prurient delight in the action" onstage, have lost the capacity to appreciate Trauerspiele, because with modern spectators, "cheap thrills arising from dramatic tension . . . [are] all that is left of the theatrical."[14] Suspenseful action of this sort was not typically a feature of baroque martyrdom plays, uninformed as they were by Aristotle's emphasis on plot. If modern spectators deem the Trauerspiele as undramatic, this is only because notions of stage theatricality have diminished since the seventeenth century until an avidity for plot is all that remains.

Seventeenth-century Trauerspiele employ different forms of theatricality than those favored by modern playwrights, over whom the influence of eighteenth-century French neo-Aristotelianism looms. Instead of emphasizing plot and the continuity of action, the Trauerspiel's most representative authors created works marked by an internal discontinuity. The form lacks all unity of time, place, or action. Benjamin explains, using a set of scenographic metaphors: "Baroque drama loves to place its antagonists in the glaring light of separate scenes, in which motivation tends to play a minimal role. The Baroque plot unfolds, one might say, like a change of scene before a raised curtain, so little is any illusion intended in it, so insistently is the economy of this counteraction emphasized" (*OGT* 61). In lieu of uninterrupted action, integrated motives, and causality, the baroque stage privileges something like a separation of the elements. Here I wish to underscore that baroque theatricality depends less on consistent plot and character and more on moments of interruption—machinic interludes, scenic transformations, acts truncated from psychological motive, and action brought to a standstill so that music, pathetic language, and gesture may occur.[15] These moments, through which the Trauerspiel gives expression to the destruction of experience and the arbitrariness of signification, demand forms of staging that go beyond absorptive action or mimesis. (In this regard, the hypertheatricality of German Expressionism functioned to recuperate the pro-theatricalism of baroque Trauerspiel as its historical predecessor.[16])

This nonmimetic quality of Trauerspiel owes to its fundamental irreconcilability with ancient tragedy (*Tragödie*), particularly as Aristotle conceived it. Benjamin distinguishes the two genres on linguistic, conceptual, formal, and metaphysical grounds, but notes that the field of modern philology has conflated the two (*OGT* 106–8). The form that seventeenth-century authors described as Trauerspiel has little in common with the Greek *tragoidia*, but names, literally, a play (*Spiel*) of mourning (*Trauer-*), or a mournful stage play. No tragic catharsis of pity and terror are on offer in Trauerspiel; the genre

Landscapes of Melancholy

instead requires inconsolable grief and, paradoxically, playfulness. Tragedy, for Benjamin, remains fixed in the waning days of Greek polytheism and firmly rooted in its Aristotelian conventions.[17] Trauerspiel, meanwhile, emerges in the Counter-Reformation during Christian monotheism's most decisive and unprecedented legitimation crisis. It appears across the entirety of Europe and influences the whole subsequent development of modern drama.[18] Although the Trauerspiel-book attends mostly to the German writers of Trauerspiel—the Silesians Andreas Gryphius (1616-64), Daniel Caspar von Lohenstein (1635-83), and Johann Christian Hallmann (ca. 1640-1716)— Benjamin also includes the English and Spanish traditions of playwriting within its scope. Irreconcilable as forms of drama, the movement between tragedy and Trauerspiel expresses an entire philosophy of history, allowing Benjamin to retrace the loss of the mythic and religious worlds and the rise of secular modernity.[19] Rather than turning to Aristotle's *Poetics*, the seventeenth-century authors of Trauerspiele turned instead to the contemporary stage for their inspiration.[20] If the plays are to be redeemed from historical oblivion, if they amount to something more than awkward precursors of the German literature Goethe would be credited with inaugurating, they must be recognized not as failed attempts at ancient tragedy but as having a different aesthetic value all their own.

For Benjamin, the Trauerspiel's importance resides in a philosophy of history the form encodes; to rescue these plays from centuries of disdain thus requires him to develop their historico-philosophical truth content.[21] In a Counter-Reformation context, what vision of history do these plays enact? In the Trauerspiel-book, the answer pertains as much to the history of world religions as it does to the history of warring states and territories. Benjamin focuses on the secularization of early modern Christendom to assert that shifting conditions of religious belief during the time transformed the nature of theatrical space. In his narrative, the Lutheran renunciation of "good works" introduced a newfound worldliness into modern Christianity, and thus, "[h]uman actions were deprived of all value. Something new came into being: an empty world. . . . Those who dug deeper saw themselves interposed in existence as in a rubble field of half-completed, inauthentic actions" (*OGT* 141). With the divine realm thought to be implacable through human agency, what arose was a void of meaning and a rubbish heap of incomplete and inauthentic action. In this trash pile of broken gestures, all human deeds are divorced from their salvific ends.[22] The Trauerspiele are therefore works of mourning in that they grieve the loss of a more directly accessible Godhead, but they are also works of melancholy in that this mourning can never be brought fully to completion, for, as Benjamin notes, religious questions persisted in both confessions during the period but were met only with secular solutions.[23] What seemed once a royal road of sacred history leading from Creation to Last Judgment, in which every soul had its privileged place, becomes in the baroque an open setting or landscape devoid of clear directional markers: history as a wasteland. In Benjamin's depiction, melancholy takes on a spatial dimension as a form of permanent historical scenery.

In Trauerspiel, the spatial and scenographic dimensions of theater are therefore emphasized, and the period's notion of history takes shape as an immanent, frozen landscape of melancholy. "History passes into the setting," Benjamin claims aphoristically (*OGT* 81). The baroque dramas literalize a situation like that described by Gurnemanz in Wagner's *Parsifal*, in which time has turned into space.[24] This secular sense of historical standstill, of time fossilized into ruinous setting, is how history forms the "content" of the Trauerspiel.[25] Perhaps nowhere is this vision theatricalized better than in the opening stage picture of Andreas Gryphius's Trauerspiel *Catharine of Georgia, or Proven Constancy*, captured in an engraved frontispiece to the 1657 edition of the play. Gryphius's stage directions read: "The stage is strewn with corpses, crowns, scepters, swords, and other insignia of earthly vanity. Heaven is revealed above the stage; hell, below. Eternity descends from heaven and comes to rest on the stage."[26] The stage space appears as a field of tattered emblems, the *membra disjecta* of human arrogance. Eternity addresses the assembled spectators: "Behold, what is this vale of sorrow?/A torture chamber, where noose and pillory/And death are used for pranks. Prince and crown lie before me./I trample on scepter and mace and rely on Father and the Son./Jewels, images, gold, and scholarly documents/are nothing but chaff and worthless dust before me."[27] The passage draws Benjamin's notice specifically for its potential staging: he is especially attracted to the possibility that it might have been performed with puppets.[28] In the baroque dramaturgy of Trauerspiel, it is not enough for the image of history as a melancholy landscape, littered with ruins, to be evoked through printed language via the technology of the book; instead the landscape of history must be made spatial, as a material image. It requires the mediation of a space, as well as the spectator's participation in the performance as a "reader" of sorts. Benjamin emphasizes this point:

Landscapes of Melancholy 113

> Fundamentally, then, the Trauerspiel too, having risen in the realm of the allegorical, is—by virtue of its form—a drama to be read. To recognize this is not to say anything about the value or possibility of its theatrical performances. But such recognition does make it clear that the select viewer of such Trauerspiele immersed himself in them as though brooding on a problem, and in this respect at least was like a reader; that the situations on stage did not change very often, but when they did it was in a flash, like the aspect of a printed page when it is turned; and it makes clear, finally, how it was that earlier scholarship, in a baffled and reluctant intuition of the law of these dramas, persisted in the view that they had never been performed. (198)

With Trauerspiel, as with baroque theater in general, there exists a privileged spectator that the form aims primarily to address. (In this, the Trauerspiel can be compared to the English masque tradition, which typically took James I, sovereign and scholar, as its ideal audience and reader.) This viewer's experience watching the performance comes close to that of an allegorist deciphering the hieroglyphs of an illustrated emblem book. The visual component of the baroque theater is primary, and even beyond the realm of the visual, a depth of space is required for both playing and seeing, so that the Trauerspiel can exhibit its vision of history as a devastated landscape before this hieroglyphic spectator's gaze.

In its necessary spatialization and its dedication to the depiction of history as a setting, the baroque stage thus amounts to an early form of modern landscape theater.[29] Lacking all unity of place, the baroque stage pursues the ideal of the *theatrum mundi*, facilitating shifts from location to location as though to encompass the entire globe in the playing space. If "all the world's a stage," then the baroque concept of history is best described, in spatial terms, as "panoramatic" (*OGT* 82). But physical settings or landscapes are not the only emblem of history common to the Trauerspiel form. The plays also make use of the figure of the onstage monarch to this effect, the personage best suited to visualizing the gestures of sovereignty. For, as Benjamin claims, using the image of a gesture to open a passage that will come to turn decisively on the question of gesture, and so exposing his writing to the danger of an infinite regression, "The sovereign represents history. He holds historical happenings in his hand like a scepter" (48). The baroque vision of history that the stage sovereign allegorizes is, again, a catastrophic one, marked by situations of national crisis and constant threats to the king's physical person. Benjamin significantly invokes the notion of the state

114   Baroque Modernity

of exception, from Carl Schmitt's 1922 study *Political Theology*, to support this view:[30]

> If the modern concept of sovereignty amounts to a supreme executive power on the part of the ruler, the Baroque concept develops on the basis of a discussion of the state of exception and makes it the most important function of the prince to avert this state. Whoever rules is from the beginning destined to be possessor of dictatorial powers if war, revolt, or other catastrophes should bring about a state of exception. This assumption is characteristic of the Counter-Reformation. For, in antithesis to the historical ideal of the Restoration, the Baroque is faced with the idea of catastrophe. And it is on the basis of this antithetic that the theory of the state of exception is conceived. (49–50)

It is the Trauerspiel sovereign's fate to confront an emergency or crisis situation and declare the state of exception that grants him tyrannical authority. "[T]he completion of the figure of the sovereign in the mold of the tyrant [is]," claims Benjamin, "virtually obligatory" (55). This necessary decision in itself exposes the contradictions of early modern kingship and the arbitrary basis of his power, which was never truly absolute but always subject to the prince's creaturely passions.[31] The prince, who is required by the theory of absolute monarchy to be the most independent of actors, proves himself to be dominated by his own fluctuating whims, riven with indecisiveness (56). When he does settle upon a decision, it transforms him into a tyrant and throws the state into civil war, allowing the king's deposition and death. Again and again in the dramaturgy of Trauerspiel, the sovereign is doomed to become a tyrant, then a martyr. "Thus no very deep research is required to see how an element of martyr tragedy lies hidden in every drama of a tyrant" (59).

This pattern reveals that there exists no baroque unity of character. Unlike the humanist theater of the Renaissance, baroque Trauerspiel divests its characters of their seeming human unity and splinters them into allegorical facets: sovereign, tyrant, martyr. Or else, one might say that the Trauerspiel both reveals the baroque sovereign as the prototypical "corporate person," and then proceeds to disincorporate him, occasionally to the point of a literal dismemberment. This process is most vividly dramatized in Gryphius's 1650 Trauerspiel, *Leo Armenius*, which culminates with the titular Emperor's being hacked to bits while he clings to a crucifix at mass: "The hardened Crambonite began only then to really rage; / . . . And thrust his murderous sword up, which came down on the Prince / And in one stroke amputated

Landscapes of Melancholy

both his arm and the cross./As he fell, they stabbed him twice through his breast./. . . And his corpse was mutilated, as the dull dagger/Was forced through his every limb."[32] As in the Prologue to *Catharine of Georgia*, spoken over a field of limbs and stage properties, here again Gryphius emphasizes a scene of bodily fragmentation as a theatrical correlative to allegory's total "dismemberment of language" (*OGT* 224). In this case too, Benjamin is drawn to the likelihood that the king's corpse would have been brought onstage during the final act in the form of a fractured effigy or puppet (122). In the baroque, it is not enough that allegory play out its disintegrating effects within the spectator's imagination: the physical rudiments of theatrical staging are always required. The sovereign's agony—the body natural torn asunder from the body politic so that the former can be sacrificed[33]— must be depicted concretely. Trauerspiel thus demands its onstage figures be decomposed into their surrounding landscapes.

Alongside the figures of tyrant and martyr, Benjamin sets a third "type," the scheming intriguer who seeks the prince's overthrow, and this figure, too, places theatrical and spatial requirements upon the Trauerspiel form. In Benjamin's description, Trauerspiel emplots history as an endless cycle of conspiracy, with conniving courtiers as the main goad for its many palace intrigues. (In the Shakespearean tradition, one thinks of Bolingbroke in *Richard II*, Macbeth, Claudius, Richard III, *Titus Andronicus*'s Aaron, and, more distantly, Iago, and so on.) Such baroque stage intriguers never strive to overthrow monarchical authority; they mostly wish to become monarchs themselves, or else to sow destruction for the sheer pleasure of it. Once the intrigue succeeds and the intriguer himself becomes a sovereign, he then must necessarily become a tyrant, thus giving inspiration to another intriguer. The new tyrant ultimately becomes a martyr, and the cycle begins afresh. (The pattern recalls a number of Elizabethan tragedies, perhaps none more than Shakespeare's *Richard II*, a play Benjamin knew well and saw performed in Berlin, as early as 1909.[34]) The positions of power within the historical landscape remain a fixed constellation while their occupants merely exchange places, so to speak, moving within a field of stasis. There is something patently mechanical about the way these intrigues play out on the stage, both in how they are handled by the playwrights of Trauerspiel and in how they are effectuated by the intriguers themselves. The devilish schemers construct plots of doom in a way that reflects, metatheatrically, the Trauerspiel author's own literary plot constructions. Both draw to a focus the baroque's dependence on engineering, artifice, and the most elemental laws of physics.[35] The best intrigues become so virtuosic in their physical manipulations that they take on the quality of dance. Benjamin alleges: "In contrast to the spasmodic temporal progression that tragedy presents, the Trauerspiel unfolds—choreographically, one might say—in the continuum of space. The organizer of the plot strands, the forerunner of the ballet master, is the intriguer" (*OGT* 85). Whether the intriguer is a choreographer or a designer of infernal machines, his activity requires the space of the stage to play out. Where the "soul" of tragedy is a mimetic plot that unfolds progressively in time, Trauerspiel tracks bodies as they play mournfully on the stage as in a purely physical medium.

Wherever Trauerspiele intensify a dialectic between figures on the stage and their surrounding landscapes, that tension plays out through *gestures*. Hamlet's injunction to the players that they "suit the action to the word, the word to the action," reminds readers that theater during the seventeenth century required both manual and oral delivery at every pronouncement. It was through the sensual medium of gesture that theatrical passions could be excited in the audience.[36] Although Benjamin has little explicit to say in the Trauerspiel-book about the history of gestures on the early modern stage, they functioned during this period in ways akin to the indeterminacies of allegory. The term "gesture" conveys for Benjamin in physical terms what "allegory" conveys for him in linguistic terms. Baroque Europe produced a vast literature on this subject—the gesture manuals of John Bulwer and Franciscus Lang, for example—but its "approach" to acting amounts less to a prescriptive method for communicating the passions than to a general instinct toward gestural signs. By virtue of their very existence and multiplicity, these new handbooks attest to a relationship between gesture and significance understood to be manifestly conventional, rather than natural.[37] A gesture is often supposed to have a legible or referential relationship to whatever passion, action, or characteristic it denotes, but in the baroque this relationship cannot be assumed. The period inspired the proliferation of numerous handbooks to justify and clarify codes of kinesthetic deportment, precisely because the link between a gesture and its meaning needed but eluded precise explication.[38] Like an emblem, a baroque gesture always produces a multiplicity of meanings and interpretations. Even more so, while a gesture may aim to represent some prior idea, action, passion, or condition, it also always threatens to draw the spectator's attention to the performing body's immanent materiality.[39] And there is also the matter of the temporal sequencing of baroque gesture, its punctuality: onstage, it ac-

Landscapes of Melancholy 117

Franciscus Lang. Gesture illustrations I-III, from *Dissertatio de actione scenica* (Munich, 1727). Courtesy Google Books.

quires a stiff, emblematic quality as actors halt periodically to make their rhetorical *points*.[40] Manual action petrifies into a pose while the fluidity of movement is interrupted and brought to a standstill. In these moments of arrest, the gestures of Trauerspiel acquire all the charged stillness of an engraved image.

In Benjamin's account, the stage monarch's catastrophe—the catastrophe of history—unfolds at the stroke of a gesture. "The drama," Benjamin writes, "is completely given over to making the gesture of executive power a characteristic of the ruler and having him appear with the speech and behavior of the tyrant even where the situation does not call for it; similarly, it is only in rare cases that the ruler will enter the scene without full array, crown and scepter" (*OGT* 54). The sovereign is identified only in part by his regal insignias, which require lavish costumes and stage properties for their emblematic purpose. (Benjamin writes that "the physical appearance of the actors themselves, particularly of the king, who shows himself in full regalia, could have a rigid, puppet-like effect," akin perhaps to the flatness of playing card kings [123].) Beyond the defamiliarizing effect of these regal ornaments, the onstage monarch exhibits a characteristic executive gesture, a seemingly efficacious gesture of commandment or fiat whereby the sovereign's will can be manifested.[41] In light of the abysmal view of history that suffuses Trauerspiel form, however, the king's command rarely if ever succeeds, but instead misfires or backfires in its very execution. As Trauerspiel was by definition mournful, infelicitous—taken up with everything that can go ruinously awry—its authors took special interest in how a sovereign's commandments go astray of his aims. The prince's melancholy culminates in a paralyzing indecisiveness (56), or else precipitates his violent madness, causing him to erupt like a volcano and destroy his entire court (55). Or otherwise, if the prince overcomes the agony of indecision and assumes absolute power, he then becomes susceptible to deposition and death. The same decision and gesture that make the sovereign also unmake him, setting off unforeseen effects that bring about his undoing.

This law of unintended consequences is not merely a problem for princes. In Benjamin's analysis, the political meanings of Trauerspiel extend beyond the realm of monarchical power and into the more mundane sphere of sovereign subjecthood. As he claims, "If, in fact, the tyrant founders not only in his own person but, as ruler, in the name of historical humanity, then his downfall is enacted as a tribunal in whose judgment the subject too feels himself implicated" (*OGT* 57). The figure of the Trauerspiel sovereign demonstrates the more universal debilities that attend the human subject in its efforts to execute its will. One's actions, as gestures, are never guaranteed to meet their desired ends but must instead enter amid the ironic historical field as into a turbulent flux.[42] Subject to the power of creaturely guilt or original sin, these actions are fated in the baroque to be self-destructive. (127-30). It is not through any heroic fault or error (the classical *hamartia*) of the subject's own, but through the condition of fallen nature that the subject's speech acts go necessarily and disastrously off course. There is something ruinous at work within the Trauerspiel's conception of nature, something queer about the natural context;[43] or, one might say, something particularly baroque that sets the sovereign speech act against itself and causes it to go so spectacularly amiss. The second chapter of Benjamin's *Origin of the German Trauerspiel* will designate this ambiguous force as *allegory*.

Baroque Allegory as Nonmimetic Theatricality

Although Trauerspiel may seem a purely dolorous affair at best, its name testifies not to purity but to baroque hybridity. It forces its two opposing moods, mournfulness and playfulness, into a single affect immanently po-

Landscapes of Melancholy

119

larized within itself and communicable as spectacle. The greater the mournfulness, the greater the play of ostentation.[44] Because the form's display value is paramount, so is the necessity of its audience. As Benjamin observes, "The very name of the Trauerspiel already indicates that its content wakens mourning in the viewer . . . [but] they are not so much plays that make one mournful as plays through which mourning finds satisfaction: plays for the mournful. What is peculiar to them is a certain ostentation. Their images are made to be seen, and are arranged according to the way they are to be seen" (*OGT* 115). Somehow, through theater—and through this peculiar kind of theater, crammed with a mass of historical and material fragments—it is possible for a traumatized populace to find solace for the calamities of history, the quotidian Armageddons of wartime, and the sudden withdrawal of divinity into an unclear beyond. The Trauerspiel form acts as a mirror through which its audience's mournfulness attains to satisfaction and, ultimately, to what Benjamin characterizes as a certain redemption. He glimpses the brightest sparks of hope not in the German Trauerspiel but in the English tradition and in the figure of Hamlet specifically, near the close of the Trauerspiel-book's first chapter. "Only in a life of this princely sort is melancholy, on being confronted with itself, redeemed" (163), he claims; and furthermore, only in this English Trauerspiel could the form attain "the bright gaze of self-reflection in its interior" (164). Both the protagonist's interiority and the metadramatic form of *Hamlet* achieve a degree of self-reflexiveness that Benjamin names as redemptive, and the meanings of this weak messianic power are elaborated in the book's second chapter, "Allegory and Trauerspiel."

The dominant stylistic tendency of the baroque age, allegory assumed new importance in the early modern period thanks to a widespread humanist effort to translate ancient pictographic texts, which in turn fueled the creative pursuit of modern hieroglyphic writing systems (170, 175-81). Drawing on Greco-Roman myth and disseminated by means of the printing press, modern emblem books filled with engraved or woodcut illustrations sought to satiate a vogue for new hieroglyphic forms. By such devices did the pagan divinities of antiquity find a curious "afterlife" as objectified elements within the visual and material culture of the Counter-Reformation.[45] Picture, caption, and allegorical explication combined in these emblems to produce a novel format, using image and text as intermedial supplements. An emblem's meaning is not self-evident within the enigmatic image itself but depends upon a corresponding caption and an extended poetic explanation. (This visual mode of allegory still presents itself in the enigmatic-esoteric configurations of images and meanings visible in modern Tarot decks.) That is, the baroque's new, quasi-hieroglyphic model of allegory reveals the relationship between signs and their verbally communicable significances to be obscure in the extreme. To use de Saussure's semiotic vocabulary, for Benjamin, baroque allegory points to a situation in which signifier, signified, and referent are understood to be only conventionally correlated. Allegories thus possess an irreducibly enigmatic character: "Any person, any object, any relation," Benjamin notes, "can signify any other whatever. With this possibility, an annihilating but just verdict is pronounced on the profane world; it is characterized as a world in which not much depends upon detail" (184). The ambiguity of allegory is, properly speaking, demonic (or, even more ambiguously, daimonic): it functions as something akin to a *diabolus in lingua*, the devil in language.[46] Originating from within this context of semiotic confusion, Trauerspiel responds not only to the mournful loss of an accessible divinity but also to that of a transcendent basis for signification altogether.

The second chapter of the Trauerspiel-book casts this loss in the form of another historical secularization narrative, another fall from grace.[47] By means of allegorical devices, language is stripped of its ordinary semblance of immediate meaning and revealed instead as a historical phenomenon. Or, to cast the 1928 Trauerspiel-book in the terms that Benjamin would develop over the 1930s, one could say that in the baroque, language loses its aura of natural signification and acquires another, more complex aura in the process.[48] In the Trauerspiel-book, this process of disenchantment originates in the Reformation but extends into the present by way of nineteenth-century aesthetic theory. Noting the Romantics' artistic preference for symbol over allegory, Benjamin finds that the "genuine concept" of symbol belongs "properly to the field of theology" (*OGT* 164) and involves "an indissoluble union of form and content" (166). Theological symbols, like prelapsarian or Edenic names, partake in an unbroken, metaphysical unity with the objects they designate. (The Trauerspiel-book does not give any specific illustrations, but one thinks of the transubstantiated Eucharist in Catholic dogma as the instance par excellence of such a symbol, wherein, by a miracle, the name "corpus" invests the physical wafer with God's transcendent divinity.)

This theological concept of the symbol, translated into the realm of poetry, authorized the Romantics' suspicion of allegory. In the form of the poetic symbol, the nineteenth century found what the early philologist Georg Friedrich Creuzer (1771-1858) called "momentary totality," in which "a con-

Landscapes of Melancholy

cept itself has descended into the bodily world and is itself what we see immediately in the image" (qtd. in *OGT* 172). In the symbol, the thing and its signification are combined into an indissoluble unity. Not so with allegory. The allegorical form displays only awkward combinations of details, posed alongside one another in ways that can only elicit the viewer or reader's discomfort. For Creuzer's generation, the poetic form of allegory lacks momentary totality and does not permit any immediate unity between object and significance, tenor and vehicle. Instead, one finds in allegory a constant deferral in which sign and idea remain at a distance from each other.[49] Where an artistic symbol supposedly merges the two into a timeless unity, allegory instead demands a spatiotemporal sequence of interpretation.

In the Trauerspiel-book's narrative, with the rise of secular modernity, theological symbols are transformed into aesthetic ones, and all such symbols lose their potency while allegories proliferate. This process occurs within the same context of increasing European secularization that the Trauerspiel-book's first chapter traces. In an early modern episteme, overdetermined by the increased worldliness of Renaissance humanism and the Protestant Reformation, the baroque turn to allegory emerged as part of a quest to recover the diminishing immediacy of theological signs. The humanists' interest in ancient hieroglyphs, their misprision of ancient Egyptian as a prelapsarian language, and their desire to create new forms of mystic image writing—all these historical developments suggest a mournful attitude toward language newly emergent in early modern Europe.[50] Unlike the form of the symbol, allegory registers a sense of human language as *lacking* in theological coherence. When it gains prominence in the baroque, it is no longer a mere rhetorical figure among others ("not a perfunctory illustrative technique"), but rather, it appears as a master trope or a trope of tropes (*OGT* 169). Allegory is "expression, as language is expression, as indeed writing is expression," an expression of the feeling that words are bound to their referents only by human or historical ties, not by any divine immediacy.[51] Hence its usefulness for giving voice to history's unspeakable catastrophes. On the other hand, elsewhere in the Trauerspiel study and in his other unpublished writings, Benjamin suggests that this baroque view of language as empty of divine significance reflects only the ignorance of modern secularism.[52] "Disenchantment" can ever amount only to a historiographical *thesis*. The world of languages and things may in fact be infinitely more interconnected and continuous than allegory ever permitted baroque modernity to perceive, as Benjamin's treatise sometimes implies.[53] But in the time of the historical baroque, which both preconditioned and initiated Europe's modernity, Benjamin detects a situation in which the epistemo-metaphysical relations between beings, meanings, and languages were felt, ubiquitously, to have deteriorated. "Baroque" is thus his name for a certain historical brokenness or ruination. As he puts it, with an imagistic aphorism, "Allegories are in the realm of thought what ruins are in the realm of things" (188).

From all this, allegory may seem a mostly rhetorical or philosophical category, but it also maintains special importance for the practice of theater in the baroque period. As Fredric Jameson writes: "[T]he theatre is . . . a peculiarly privileged space for allegorical mechanisms, since there must always be a question about the self-sufficiency of its representations."[54] It is precisely the mournful, allegorical way of seeing that reveals human history as a ruinous landscape, demanding spatialization on the stage. Benjamin observes:

> Whereas in the symbol, with the sublimation of downfall, the transfigured countenance of nature reveals itself fleetingly in the light of salvation, in allegory there lies before the eyes of the observer the *facies hippocratica* [i.e., the death mask] of history as a petrified primordial landscape. History, in everything untimely, sorrowful, and miscarried that belongs to it from the beginning, is inscribed in a face—no, in a death's head. . . . That is the core of the allegorical vision, of the Baroque profane exposition of history as the Passion of the world—meaningful only in the stations of its decline. So much meaning, so much forfeiture to death, for at the deepest level death incises the jagged line of demarcation between physis and meaning. But if nature has at all times been subject to the power of death, it is also at all times allegorical. (174)

The death mask or skeletal face of history must be staged in spatial arrangements, as "a petrified, primordial landscape." (This rhetoric of petrification is Benjamin's answer to György Lukács's idea of "reification" in *History and Class Consciousness*, a text Benjamin was reading while working on the Trauerspiel-book on Capri in 1924.) Allegory itself necessitates this form of staging, in which the historical process is seen as something immanently physical, even moribund. In the baroque, the melancholy rise of allegory itself brings about a corresponding rise in scenographic spectacle. In the guise of the Grim Reaper, that allegory of time who surrogates the ancient, melancholy figure of Saturn (Kronos, Chronos), Death extends a doleful power over all creation (*OGT* 135), which in turn must be made visible through the medium of the stage. It is this landscape, the natural-historical context of

Landscapes of Melancholy

allegory, that predetermines the onstage sovereign's death. His misfiring executive gesture amounts, at just one level of interpretation, to an allegory for the nature of allegory itself, in which the power that binds language to the things it aims to designate loses performative and referential force, unto the point of disintegration.

At the same time, if allegory shows that "any person, any object, any relation can signify any other whatever," this indeterminacy cannot only be destructive. Within the depths of baroque despair, when all relations between persons and objects are unraveled, there emerges a redemptive potential. Of the strange details that clutter within baroque emblem-images, Benjamin writes—again gesturally—"All of these stage props of signification (*Requisiten des Bedeutens*), precisely by virtue of their pointing to something other, acquire a potency that makes them appear incommensurable with profane things and elevates them to a higher plane, indeed can sacralize them."[55] Drained of their transcendent value, worldly phenomena are simultaneously imbued with a new aura by virtue of their allegorical potential. Allegory transforms nature into what Baudelaire would call "a forest of symbols," with each object of attention breathing confused words for the allegorist to contemplate.[56] In this way, allegorical melancholy can be converted into wonder. Under its influence, the old *theatrum mundi*, whose spectator was the transcendent Godhead, vanishes. There arises in its place an immanent *theatrum* of infinitely networked points, everything in potential communication with itself, everything "meaning" something other than itself. In brief, allegory has the power to disenchant, to reenchant, and so to retheatricalize the world.

All this is to say nothing yet of the specific forms allegory takes on the stage. Much can be derived in theater-historiographic terms from the relatively few comments Benjamin has already offered on this subject. At its baroque origins, Trauerspiel was a form of courtly entertainment comparable with other allegorical forms of private and aristocratic theater during the period (*OGT* 48). In these elite theater venues, where costly spectacle was both desirable and possible, allegory occupied a decisive role in performance, subordinating the mimetic impulse of theater to that of theatrical presentation or parabasis. The allegorical mode is less successful at representing dramatic action, as we have seen, but functions instead by the direct exhibition of sensuous images, addressed to the audience's hieroglyphic contemplation. It subsumes the transcendence of mimesis to the medial immanence of the physical stage as a space—its architecture, proscenium, the bodies of performers and viewers, the hefty material of scenery and machines, the fullness or overrichness of costumes, hair, makeup, decorations, which together compose an allegorical assemblage before the viewer's eyes. For Benjamin, the weightiness of seventeenth-century baroque style is its signature characteristic, and this weightiness results from the theater's efforts at combining various material media into an allegorical synthesis. (In this respect, the baroque stage prepares the way for Wagner's aesthetics: "If the Baroque critic speaks of the *Gesamtkunstwerk* as the summit of the period's aesthetic hierarchy and as the ideal of the Trauerspiel itself, he thereby reinforces in a new way this spirit of heaviness."[57]) The allegories presented onstage acquire aura by virtue of their being ornamental, but they remain ponderous and earthbound nevertheless.[58] Even the passions themselves acquire a certain heavy, fetishized quality in this theater —they "take on the nature of stage properties" and seem almost to become external, objective phenomena—while stage properties come "with unceasing virtuosity to occupy the foreground" of the theatrical event (133).

With allegory, when sign and thing are sundered from each other, their rupture unleashes and perpetuates a series of material effects, some of which may be described in terms of sociopolitical or historical force (i.e., in terms of performativity) while others must be understood as effects of aesthetic style (i.e., theatricality). Where style is concerned, the baroque stage must overflow with materials in excess. To an outsider viewing it through the lens of a "classical," "realist," or "representational" aesthetics, it can only seem hopelessly disordered. Or else, even where the early modern theater made use of the bare stage known to students of Shakespeare, it still required theatrical elements to function as allegories—daggers, handkerchiefs, crowns, and the like—showering the audience with fatal significance from the playing space. For obvious reasons, the invisible fourth wall associated with André Antoine in the nineteenth century and Denis Diderot in the eighteenth century had no purchase over such a theater. To the extent that the baroque theater did stage scenes of dramatic action or absorptive dialogue, as though behind a fourth wall, these had to compete with moments of direct parabasis to the audience in the form of prologue, chorus, epilogue, aside, and interlude.

In other forms of theatrical allegory, such as the English masque, Italian intermezzi and music dramas, Spanish zarzuelas, and French ballets de cour, this boundary between stage and auditorium, performance and offstage life, was violated in other, even more ingenious ways. Courtiers were typically

Landscapes of Melancholy

required to dance both onstage and in the space of the audience, traversing any clear proscenium threshold. Customarily a sovereign spectator seated in the auditorium or stage's centermost point was given royal privilege as the primary viewer to whom all stage discourse needed to be addressed. No fourth wall could be fully observed without insulting the royal presence or making the spoken language of the theater inaudible. Theatrical allegory emphatically requires this external spectator to play the role of interpreter. Their externality is a necessary condition for allegory to function as such. Thus, the baroque theater, as allegory, depends at its most molecular and architectonic levels upon a principle of internal self-difference, rather than self-identity.

Engravings of the baroque stage document that, even in the most absorptive or dialogic of scenes, actors oriented their bodies mostly outward, opening their physical being to the gaze of viewers in the auditorium by a three-quarter turn, assuming something like the fourth position of the feet that would later become widely adopted in the ballet. Or else, as in the English masque form or in the Trauerspiel's choral interludes, baroque conventions of performance required actors' bodies to face entirely outward through the proscenium boundary in order to display themselves and their allegorical attributes to the viewer's gaze, like runway models, eschewing any semblance of absorption in favor of frontal tableaux vivants. These theatrical tableaux form an antithesis to the scenes in which dramatic dialogue occur. "The visionary description of the living image, the *tableau vivant*, is a triumph of the Baroque penchant for the drastic and the antithetical," Benjamin writes (*OGT* 207). Even if the Trauerspiel's dramatic action and its theatrical interludes seem to come from "'two separate worlds,'" nevertheless, "the radical separation of action from interlude does not exist in the eyes of its chosen spectator. Here and there the connection comes to light in the course of the dramatic action itself" (208). With Trauerspiel, dramatic and theatrical elements of theater sit side by side, excluding but also functionally allegorizing each other. These two modalities of performance would diverge over the course of the eighteenth century. In that era, the dramatic features of Trauerspiel would culminate in the form of bourgeois *drame* during Diderot's lifetime, while its theatrical features, as Benjamin observes, gave rise to new forms such as ballet (85) and opera (229).

By commingling mimetic and nonmimetic elements into spectacle, Trauerspiel brings the immanent mediality of the theater to the forefront of the observer's awareness. To borrow a phrase from the deconstructive critic Samuel Weber, what asserts itself in the baroque is its *theatricality as medium*.[59] It is only apparently paradoxical that the theater's theatricality should be so pronounced in those moments when the stage most resembles the flat, illustrated pages of an emblem book: both theater stages and iconologies function as forms of graphic media. Onstage figures in the baroque Trauerspiel possess none of the depth or psychological well-roundedness of human "characters." They instead come to resemble printed images, like those of Cesare Ripa's illustrated emblem books, for example, which present themselves flat on the page, so to be seen.[60] Primary among the factors that permit the theater as a medium to reflect and affirm itself in these allegorical moments is the exchange of gazes between performer and spectator. To phrase this observation another way: when the theater becomes recognizable as a technical medium in its own right during the baroque, this exchange of gazes *is the means* by which this recognizability takes place.[61] With theatrical allegory of the sort found in the Trauerspiel's interludes, the onstage figures return the gaze of their beholders, just as printed emblems from the period typically seem to do from the page. Such emblems are fragments awaiting their interpretation, denying any possibility of "absorption."[62] Where the Renaissance humanist drama venerated symbolic totality in the form of the completed human figure, Benjamin claims that "[i]t is as patchwork . . . that things *stare out from the allegorical construct*" (*OGT* 199; emphasis mine).[63] Such allegories are piecemeal beings. Incomplete in themselves, they refuse to look away from their beholders and instead demand interpretation. The baroque sense of theatricality generates this demand as a dialectical process whenever bodies onstage lock eyes with their audience, returning the spectator's gaze.

At this point, Benjamin's later writings on the concept of aura and its experiential foundations can be invoked to inform this allegorical dialectic.[64] Perhaps most famously, his late aesthetic writings of 1939 define aura as that quality "that withers in the age of the technological reproducibility of the work of art" and, even more germane for the present study, as "the unique apparition of a distance, however near it may be" (*SW* 4:254–55). His notes "On Some Motifs in Baudelaire" from that same year claim the experience of aura arises when "[t]he person we look at, or who feels he is being looked at, looks at us in turn. To experience the aura of an object we look at means to invest it with the ability to look back at us" (*SW* 4:338). When onstage objects of vision become subjects of the gaze, when they address the audience directly, as in a choral interlude between the acts, they be-

Landscapes of Melancholy

come *theatrical* by acknowledging the beholder's presence, as Michael Fried has defined the term. These gazing bodies defamiliarize the process of spectatorship, shocking and distancing the watcher from the action of the play. The baroque epoch is one that has experienced what Benjamin will call "a crisis of the aura" (*AP* J77a,8), and in those moments when the illusory frame of the drama is ruptured, there appear two forms of aura in dialectical contestation with each other.[65] The drama's mimetic aura of reality is dispersed and exposed as a fiction, while the theatrical relation of parabasis generates a newfound auratic intensity between the viewer and the hieroglyphic characters on the stage. If you gaze long enough into the theater, the theater suddenly gazes back at you.

Literal face-to-face moments of this kind occurred often in early modern performance, but allegory involves other, less direct strategies for returning the spectator's gaze as well.[66] Beyond moments of outward-facing theatricality, aura can also result from metatheatrical (or "theatricalist") effects that turn inward toward the depths of the playing space. When a play-within-a-play occurs, for example, and performers turn *away* from the viewing audience to constitute themselves as a miniature audience before a miniature proscenium on the stage, they thereby create an abyssal or recursive movement, as in the Droste Effect. Such moments may be deemed "allegories of spectatorship." The widespread seventeenth-century use of scenery in single-point perspective—organized around a central vanishing point, typically aligned with the king's seat in the auditorium—only heightened the baroque feeling of the theater's *mise-en-scene* as a *mise-en-abîme*. With these effects, the theater could evoke a seemingly endless distance, an ambiguously good or bad infinity. Looking forward to the Romantic irony of Ludwig Tieck and his contemporaries, Benjamin notes the popularity of such metatheatrical maneuvers in the early modern period as the baroque's means of safeguarding a vanishing theological realm: "The element of play in drama was ostentatiously emphasized, and transcendence was allowed to have the last word only in the worldly disguise of a play within the play" (*OGT* 69). Some spark of the divine is preserved at an infinitesimal point, recessed deep within the machine of the theater itself. With baroque metatheater, the stage thus undergoes a process of infinite, internal self-reflection and miniaturization as the stage effectively allegorizes itself.[67]

Benjamin cautions that baroque techniques of play and reflection are "not always obvious, in the sense of erecting the stage itself on the stage or incorporating the spectator's space within the space of the stage" (*OGT* 69).

A gesture can also return the audience's gaze, so to speak, inasmuch as it interrupts the mimetic frame of the drama by calling attention to itself and its own explicit embodiment. And more obliquely metatheatrical maneuvers are common in the Trauerspiel form, especially in those moments that precipitate the final catastrophe, as the critic Charles Rosen has pointed out. Whether it be the mock trial at the end of *King Lear*, Macbeth's "poor player" soliloquy, Hamlet pondering Yorick's skull, or Richard II regarding himself in a looking glass—all these cases, Rosen shows, deploy metatheatrical strategies for their allegorical resonance. For Rosen, "This explicit reference to the stage that Benjamin remarks in the German *Trauerspiel* . . . occurs at the moment of crisis of every one of Shakespeare's major tragedies. . . . The references to the stage, the looking glass, the death's head, are all emblems of illusion and premonitions of death." Metatheater serves Shakespeare in these cases as a *vanitas* motif, emphasizing the ephemeral quality of earthly life. In addition, I would add that all of these premonitions amount to moments of illumination, flashing up "in a moment of danger," as Benjamin would later put it.[68] In the form of the Trauerspiel, whether allegorical moments transpire theatrically through a literal exchange of gazes between performer and audience, or metatheatrically through a play-within-a-play or some other emblematic maneuver, such moments produce for the viewer a sudden, shocking flash of aura.

Still, if a looming threat of catastrophe inheres in these theatricalist moments, so does the hope of salvation. There is special providence in the fall of a sparrow: melancholy is redeemed by being confronted with itself in Hamlet's princely life, at a moment when the Trauerspiel form achieves "the bright gaze of self-reflection in its interior." As Benjamin characterizes it, when the baroque stage attains its maximal powers of theatrical self-reflexivity, it also emits glimmers of messianic or auratic potential. Just as was the case at the end of the Trauerspiel-book's first chapter, with its discussion of Hamlet's melancholy, the book's second chapter ends by returning to allegory's redemptive promise:

> [I]t is precisely in visions of the intoxication of destruction, visions in which everything earthly turns to rubble, that there is revealed not so much the ideal of allegorical immersion as its limit. The bleak confusion of Golgotha, legible as schema of allegorical figures in a multitude of engravings and descriptions of the period, is not simply a symbol of the wilderness of human existence. In it, transience is not so much signified, allegorically presented, as—itself signifying—

Landscapes of Melancholy

presented as allegory. As the allegory of resurrection. At the last, in the death-marks of the Baroque—only now in backward-turning great arcs and as salvific —allegorical vision veers about.[69]

In the book's concluding pages, allegory redeems itself in a miraculous moment of self-rediscovery as the skeletal landscapes of the baroque theater reveal themselves as Golgothas. These landscapes were always allegories of allegory itself, and, as self-reflections, they suggest to Benjamin the possibility that the world might be saved from its ruinous fate. Redemption springs forth immanently, dialectically, from the world's internal contradictions and self-reflections, rather than from any transcendent source. In honor of Calderón, in whose plays the Trauerspiel form achieves its perfection for Benjamin, the final chapter of the *Origin of the German Trauerspiel* gives this miraculous turnabout the Spanish name of an apotheosis, "the *ponderación misteriosa*, the intervention of God in the work of art."[70]

How this baroque turnabout occurs in the theater is a more elusive question, but Benjamin's naming of Hamlet at the end of the Trauerspiel-book's first chapter suggests an answer. A usurped sovereign, a tyrannizing intriguer, and a secular martyr, Hamlet is also, like James I and Benjamin himself, a student or scholar whose action and contemplation are at times indistinguishable.[71] He comprises all of Benjamin's typologies or aspects of baroque character in one figure. His Trauerspiel is that he is divided within himself: not only is he indecisive, but he is also self-theatricalizing, and his inner subjectivity opens up a hall of mirrors within the play.[72] Where transcendent divinity has become inaccessible, a messianic power beckons weakly from within this space of inwardness. Hamlet is at his most allegorical in those moments when he speaks to the audience in self-conscious, self-divided monologue, revealing the abyss of his interiority. His discourse, delivered directly to the viewer, is less referential than self-referential.[73] It creates a series of performative effects within the context of its delivery. The baroque parabases of *Hamlet* hail the audience into being as a collective of similarly self-divided subjects, impressing on them the unbridgeable distance between physical nature and transcendent meaning. As Franco Moretti has argued, in further widening the gap between divinity and creaturely being, Trauerspiele like *Hamlet* helped effectuate the historical possibility of monarchical overthrow.[74] Characters like Hamlet who refuse to stay within the fictional drama, but interrupt it with outward glances, asides, soliloquys, and *apartés*, remind the audience that the given order of things struc-

130   Baroque Modernity

turing representation is not to be taken seriously. There is political potential in all of these theatrical conditions, but Benjamin could not offer it a fuller elaboration at the time of the Trauerspiel-book's publication. Allegory's capacity for radically reconfiguring the world would remain for the time being purely virtual. Only later, in response to the writings of Baudelaire, Nietzsche, and above all, Brecht, would Benjamin discover a vision of baroque form with more radical political potential.

The Catastrophe in Permanence

While he was completing the Trauerspiel-book on the island of Capri in 1924, Benjamin's thought took on its more explicitly Marxist orientation. Lukács's *History and Class Consciousness* nurtured this shift, as did Benjamin's deepening relationship with the Bolshevik theater director Asja Lacis. While never fully abandoning the theological dimension of his early writing, Benjamin found a more political voice in his next work, *One-Way Street* (written 1923-26; published 1928). There he laid claim to the critic's role as "strategist in the literary struggle" (*SW* 1:460) and embraced a new form of "prompt language" with a series of captioned sections modeled after "leaflets, brochures, articles, and placards" (444). In *One-Way Street*, modern life rushed to the foreground of Benjamin's attention as a writer, and allegoresis became a tool for interpreting the space of the city. As Susan Buck-Morss notes, the emblems of the baroque had taught him a new way to approach the urban labyrinth, with all its enigmatic ornaments, passages, arcades, and objects of visual attention.[75] Illuminated by the work he had done in *Origin of the German Trauerspiel*, suddenly, construction sites, advertisements, lighting fixtures, architectural structures, monuments, and vendibles all became privileged objects of Benjamin's study. During these years, he wrote to Scholem that the street scenery of Palladio's Teatro Olimpico in Vicenza was converging for him with the street scenes of Berlin and Paris.[76] The baroque stage was extending its spatiality outside the boundaries of the proscenium and auditorium, suffusing the city with uncanny theatricality.

In the writing that occupied the last decade of Benjamin's life, the primary inhabitant of this urban *theatrum mundi* was Charles Baudelaire, whose embrace of allegorical devices in poetry had attracted Benjamin's interest during the conception phase of his habilitation thesis.[77] With the Trauerspiel-book completed, Benjamin's research on nineteenth-century Paris, which would culminate in the so-called *Arcades Project*, began in earnest by 1927. Convolute (or section) J of the project would be devoted to Baudelaire, and

Landscapes of Melancholy 131

The Teatro Olimpico in Vicenza, designed by Andrea Palladio (1508–80). Courtesy Mondadori Portfolio/Electa/Marco Covi/Bridgeman Images.

would take up the "afterlife" of baroque allegory in the historical space-time of nineteenth-century modernity. In that convolute, Benjamin claims Baudelaire's poetry as the medium through which the mid-nineteenth century absorbed the persistence of allegory, situating Baudelaire's work as a crucial link between seventeenth- and early-twentieth-century modes of cultural production.[78] Amid its reflections on Baudelaire, *The Arcades Project* elaborates a new critique of the commodity form *as* allegorical that attests to the Trauerspiel-book's continuing influence over Benjamin's later, Marxist methods. "The commodity form emerges in Baudelaire as the social content of the allegorical form of perception" (*AP* J59,10), Benjamin observes, adding some pages later that "the ruling figure of his [Baudelaire's] imagination—

allegory—corresponded perfectly to the commodity fetish" (J79a,4). Structured as allegories, commodities give rise to their own forms of spectacle, casting the metropolis as an all-encompassing space of illusion, an immersive phantasmagoria of modern capital.

The description of commodities *as allegory* receives its fullest articulation in notes J80,2 and J80a,1 of the *Arcades Project*, where Benjamin compares allegoresis to the task of assembling a puzzle whose pieces' connections can never be foreseen:

> Through the disorderly fund which his knowledge places at his disposal, the allegorist rummages here and there for a particular piece, holds it next to some other piece, and tests to see if they fit together—that meaning with this image or this image with that meaning. The result can never be known beforehand, for there is no natural mediation between the two. But this is just how matters stand with commodity and price. The "metaphysical subtleties" in which the commodity delights, according to Marx, are, above all, the subtleties of price formation. How the price of goods in each case is arrived at can never quite be foreseen, neither in the course of their production nor later when they enter the market. It is exactly the same with the object in its allegorical existence. (J80,2; J80a,1)

The arbitrariness with which signs and meanings are paired in baroque allegory finds its analog in the arbitrariness with which commercial goods are given prices and endowed as fetishes under capitalism. "Hence, the allegorist is in his element with commercial wares" (J80,2; J80,1). Allegory describes the way in which living processes are transformed into object-commodities, that is, how they are readied for consumption through a force of reification. At the same time, it has the power to strip those commodities of their seeming naturalness and reveal them as the products of socioeconomic convention.

Allegory thus enjoys both regressive and progressive potentials.[79] The "key" to the overthrow of a capitalist regime of commodities is to be found, if anywhere, within the contradictions of the commodity's allegorical form itself. Modern allegory gave Baudelaire the means to mediate in poetry the crises of the commodity economy, and for Benjamin, there is political radicalism incipient in this approach: "Baudelaire's allegory bears traces of the violence that was necessary to demolish the harmonious façade of the world that surrounded him" (J55a3). Yet for all this potential, Baudelaire remained alienated from the urban crowd around him, where collective power might be found. Although Baudelaire could employ allegorical devices, he was not

Landscapes of Melancholy 133

able to *grasp* allegory in a way that would become politically efficacious or that would allow allegory "to incorporate itself into the most immediate realities" of modern life.[80] The closing of Benjamin's essay "On Some Motifs in Baudelaire" likens the poet's fight against his historical circumstances to the uselessness of one walking against the wind and rain (*SW* 4:343).

For a model of allegory in which Baudelaire's rage could be put to use, Benjamin turned to the work of Bertolt Brecht. The two men first met during the spring of 1929, just months after the publication of the *Origin of the German Trauerspiel* and the opening of *The Threepenny Opera*.[81] The play's Berlin premiere took place in August 1928 at the Theater am Schiffbauerdamm —later to become home to Brecht's Berliner Ensemble—both a building and a theater space constructed in the neobaroque architectural style of the late nineteenth century.[82] Brecht was by this time accustomed to describing his playwriting and directing practice as "epic theater."[83] For his part, Benjamin had already begun to consider how artists working outside the Expressionist orbit, as Brecht was during those years, might also be understood as effectively continuing the legacy of baroque style. In his writings outside the Trauerspiel-book, he had begun detecting baroque traces amid such disparate, left-leaning movements as Russian Naturalism and French Surrealism.[84] In this regard, the full panorama of modernist art and literature came ultimately to be associated in Benjamin's view with a diffuse but somehow unavowable baroque inheritance. That seemingly most conservative of aesthetic forms, the aristocratic theater of the baroque seventeenth century, had become a source of innovative and avant-garde experimentation.

In the theater, Brecht forms the cornerstone of this theoretical edifice, whereby baroque aesthetic conventions appear as the secret logic of modernist innovation. By the time of their meeting in 1929, Benjamin's research had led him to understand epic and allegory as formally isomorphic, and thus he was already predisposed to considering Brecht in light of the twentieth-century persistence of baroque conventions. The Trauerspiel-book notes that the observed congruence between epic and allegory had already become commonplace during the Romantic era of Creuzer and Friedrich von Schelling, and in response, Benjamin suggests that "[t]he epic is in fact the classic form of a history of signifying nature, as allegory is its Baroque form. Related as it was to both currents of thought, Romanticism was bound to bring epic and allegory closer together" (*OGT* 175). In the aftermath of Romantic aesthetics, that which appears from one (classical) perspective as epic seems from another (baroque) perspective as allegory. The differences between

134 Baroque Modernity

the two may amount only to a difference in one's philosophy of history, that is, may depend mostly on the question of whether one can admit the viability of epic as a classical form in the modern world. To Benjamin, for whom the specific mythic-polytheistic context of Olympian antiquity remains irretrievably lost, and for whom the twentieth century exists in the long shadow of the baroque, Brecht's theater was bound to seem even more like a form of allegory than one of epic. On Brecht's "epic" stage, where allegorical elements vie for the spectator's attention alongside mimetic ones, and defamiliarizing gestures call into question the veracity of realism in performance, the afterlife of baroque forms in the time of European modernism could be seen with particular vividness.[85]

Benjamin's writings on Brecht make the connection to baroque theater explicit, particularly the 1939 essay "What is Epic Theatre?" which labels Brecht as an "inheritor" to the baroque theatrical tradition. Observing the seventeenth-century custom of reserving a seat on the open stage for royal spectators to appear as "thinking men" in full view of the audience, Benjamin finds a similar tendency in Brecht: "We may go further and say that Brecht has attempted to make the thinking man, or indeed the wise man, into an actual dramatic hero" (*UB* 17). The exemplary onstage thinker or "untragic hero" in Brecht's dramaturgy is, for Benjamin, the figure of Galy Gay in Brecht's 1926 play *A Man's a Man*, whom Benjamin describes as "himself like an empty stage on which the contradictions of our society are acted out. Following Brecht's line of thought, one might even arrive at the proposition that it is the wise man who, in this sense, is the perfect empty stage" (17). Galy Gay begins Brecht's play as a civilian packer during wartime, who is then unwittingly conscripted into the military, dismantled of his identity, and transformed into a ruthless soldier. In a choral interlude, Brecht's play informs its audience: "Tonight, you are going to see a man reassembled like a car / Leaving all his individual components just as they are."[86] In *A Man's a Man*, the physical dismemberment of Gryphius's *Leo Armenius* finds its ideological correlative in militaristic brainwashing. With Galy Gay, Brecht not only follows the baroque practice of placing an onstage thinker at the center of the drama, but, as in Trauerspiel, dismantles that figure's sovereign subjecthood into its constituent pieces, leaving behind an empty space where historical contradictions and action may transpire. Brecht's didactic purpose in *A Man's a Man* could not be realized through the form of the psychologically realistic play, nor is his lesson fully intelligible when the play is read only as a printed drama.[87] For Galy Gay's dismantling to become sensible to

Landscapes of Melancholy 135

the audience as the outcome of a contingent historical process, rather than a necessary fate, that process must be played onstage, so its actors can take a distance from their character's actions and give the spectators the space of performance to interpret the allegory, on their own and collectively.

It is only the twentieth-century spectator's notional conflation of "theatre" with "the dramatic" that makes this *onstage thinker* seem "out of place" in Brecht as in the Trauerspiel (*OGT* 17). Once again, Aristotle is at fault for this conflation, since an opposition to Aristotle's concept of drama unites Brecht with the authors of baroque Trauerspiel.[88] Against Aristotle, both epic theater and Trauerspiel approach instead a *Socratic* tradition of theater, which puts the figure of "the thinker" onstage. In Benjamin's view, this tradition extends from Plato's dialogues, focused on Socrates, to the medieval passion play, focused on Christ.[89] It continues, he claims, into the twentieth century with Brecht as its genealogical heir:

> This important but badly marked road (which may serve here as the image of a tradition) ran, in the Middle Ages, via Hroswitha and the Mysteries; in the age of the baroque, via Gryphius and Calderon. Later we find it in Lenz and Grabbe, and finally in Strindberg. Shakespearian scenes stand as monuments at its edge, and Goethe crossed it in the second part of *Faust*. It is a European road, but it is a German one too. If, that is, one can speak of a road rather than a stalking-path (*Saumpfad*) along which the legacy of medieval and baroque drama has crept down to us. This stalking-path, rough and overgrown though it may be, is visible again today in the plays of Brecht. (*UB* 17–18, *GS* 2.2:534)

In light of the modern secularization of the world, history may appear little more than an open landscape bereft of clear signposts, but the materialist historian can nevertheless appear as a guide, pointing out trail markers through the wilderness, by which the "legacy" of a tradition has come into the present, as though along a *Saumpfad* (a mule track or bridle path, a seam- or hem-like trail, folding through the wilderness). Brecht stands as a terminus of this rough tradition, the exemplary participant in the historical dialectics of the baroque theater within Benjamin's lifetime, even more so than the Expressionists had been.[90]

The inheritance of baroque conventions in Brecht is especially significant in light of the many stylistic ways his theater seems to diverge from Trauerspiel: for example, where baroque style tends toward strong emotions, as Benjamin and Nietzsche both note, Brecht's preference was for a more detached and analytic spectator, smoking cigarettes if possible. Still, both Brecht and his baroque precursors come together in positioning "the thinker" center stage. Whether this contemplative figure be the sovereign spectator of baroque Trauerspiel, or Hamlet, or Galy Gay, it is also the Brechtian actor who disidentifies from their character in order to demonstrate its atomized actions.[91] By extension, this "thinker" is also the spectator who is never an individual, but rather a divided singularity within the larger field of collective life.

In all this, Benjamin joins the redemptive operations of baroque allegory with the revolutionary potential of Brecht's defamiliarization or *gestus*. Both function through the transformation of melancholy into wonder or astonishment. In the Trauerspiel, the purpose of the baroque apotheosis or *ponderación misteriosa* is to awaken wonder in the spectator.[92] This concluding miracle, in which the impossible complications of intrigue are suddenly resolved as though through divine intervention, is the ultimate dramaturgical gesture of the baroque stage, just as individual performers' gestures could provoke wonder in the viewer in each passing moment. By comparison, "the art of epic theatre," Benjamin asserts, "consists in arousing astonishment rather than empathy. To put it as a formula, instead of identifying itself with the hero, the audience is called upon to learn to be astonished at the circumstance within which he has his being."[93] In epic theater, as in Trauerspiel, astonishment may arise dynamically out of the performers' gestural comportment: "'Making gestures quotable' is one of the essential achievements of epic theatre. The actor must be able to space his gestures as the compositor produces spaced type. . . . [Epic] theatre is, by definition, gestural. For the more often we interrupt someone in process of acting, the more gestures we obtain" (*OGT* 19-20). These defamiliarizing gestures awaken astonishment in the spectator and so allow the onstage events to become legible in political terms, as allegory.[94]

Inasmuch as Brecht makes gestural citationality into his theater's method, he repeats and transforms the performance practices of the baroque stage. Benjamin perceived Brecht's desire to make gestures citable: prior to this epic practice, the acting handbooks of the baroque circulated gestural imagery to be quoted or reproduced in performance. (I explore this "citability of gesture" in the following chapter, on Gertrude Stein.) With acting in epic theater and in Trauerspiel, one must *quote* one's gestures; in neither arena is it a matter of actors identifying with their characters. The two theatrical formations stand at the beginning and end, respectively, of a modern history of dramatic theater—culminating in Romanticism, naturalism, and the

Landscapes of Melancholy   137

principles of "method acting"—that aims at absorbing the actor into the character through emotional identification. In some ways prefiguring Brecht's actors, performers in baroque Europe did not necessarily empathize with their "characters" or need to create an illusion of psychological interiority to transmit passions to their beholders. The point of playing was to display the figure's actions through reference to a published code of gestural convention, just as stage allegory had to make reference to a published code of emblems. As baroque gestures come to function like hieroglyphs to be deciphered, so in Brecht's theater does each gesture become a social hieroglyph, like Marx's commodity, for critical contemplation. This necessary gestural dimension requires a stage on which to take place. (In this, Brecht attests to the posthistory of modern drama, while Trauerspiel attests to its baroque prehistory, the two answering each other across the space-time of Europe's supposedly Enlightened modernity.[95]) It does not suffice for these gestures to be described in printed or textual drama: they demand theatricalization, even as they bring the action of spectatorship close to the experience of reading.

Although Benjamin sees Brecht as perpetuating the historical dialectics of the baroque in the modern, post-Aristotelian theater, "allegory" offers him an alternate vision for such a theater and the work it might perform in the world. It designates a counter-Brechtian theater theory, one that takes exception to, and supplements, Brecht's theory of action.[96] While epic theater has as its instrumental aim the training of spectators for revolutionary work, allegory is by contrast a mournful mode, dedicated to all that has been lost, made noninstrumental, rendered useless or defunct. The allegorist grieves whatever has been rendered ungrievable by the historical process. With allegory, Benjamin supplements Brecht's vanguardist emphasis on revolutionary action by insisting on the importance of memory, which "traverses the whole of life like lightning" (112). It is through remembrance that the dead shall be raised and their oblivion redeemed. Or, as Benjamin's theses "On the Concept of History" would put it, "the tradition of the oppressed" (or of "the oppressed past") contains lessons for those engaged in the "struggle against fascism" (SW 4:392; cf. 396), and "*even the dead* will not be safe from the enemy if he is victorious" (SW 4:391; emphasis original).

Whereas, in the Trauerspiel-book, Benjamin insisted on the forgotten baroque theater's importance for a genuinely critical philosophy of history, in his debate with Brecht, allegory appears necessary for revolutionary struggle, which requires historical memory. Above all, the allegorist presupposes no naïve views of what revolutionary action may accomplish. If history is a Trauerspiel, then each action transpires within a given material context and mobilizes that context in ways that are uncontrollable, especially by the actor, whose stable or independent position with respect to that external context cannot be assured.[97] Those struggling against fascism must take cognizance of the ways their "enterprises of great pith and moment" may have, as Hamlet puts it, "their currents turn awry / and lose the name of action." At the same time, they must also not succumb to the temptations of political defeatism, indecisiveness, or what Benjamin will elsewhere describe in evocative terms as "left melancholy." Allegory serves as a reminder of these melancholy realities of revolutionary action.

Understanding Brecht as an inheritor to the legacy of the baroque stage provides an occasion for readers to rethink the fact that many of his most famous plays have a baroque context, including *Edward II* (adapted from Marlowe), *Mother Courage and Her Children* (set in the Thirty Years' War), and *The Life of Galileo* (set during the Inquisition).[98] This understanding should also invite re-readings of Brecht's *Don Juan* (after Molière) and *The Duchess of Malfi* (with W. H. Auden, after Webster). In *Brecht and Critical Theory: Dialectics and Contemporary Aesthetics* (2005), Sean Carney offers one example of such a rereading. He argues that Brecht and Kurt Weill's 1933 music drama (or "sung-ballet"), *The Seven Deadly Sins of the Petty Bourgeoisie*, amounts to a "Brechtian Trauerspiel[,] . . . a series of neo-baroque allegories that dramatize the commodification of the human being under capitalism," "a performance of reification," and "an allegorical journey depicting the action of capitalist allegorization itself."[99] The play does not easily resemble one of Gryphius's Trauerspiele, but is for Carney "a parodic repetition of the baroque."[100]

The Seven Deadly Sins follows Anna I and Anna II, two sisters who declare in the first scene that they are one and the same person, an artist who has been sent on a mission to raise money for her/their Louisiana family. Anna II is a mostly mute dancer, while Anna I acts as her manager and narrates her/their doings in song. On the baroque stage, as with Brecht's repetition of its conventions, "even the absolutely singular, the individual character, is multiplied in the allegorical."[101] (Coincidentally and unintentionally, Gertrude Stein and Virgil Thomson will pursue precisely this same strategy of theatrical *dédoublement* with the figures of Saints Teresa I and II in *Four Saints in Three Acts*, a subject I explore at length in chapter 4.) Over seven scenes in seven American towns, the two Annas confront seven deadly sins,

Landscapes of Melancholy

which Brecht inverts ironically to generate a critique of capitalist society. Anna II succumbs to Pride, for example, when she feels a moment's hesitation about performing in a strip club to earn the money needed to survive her precarious conditions as an artist. She has to learn how to overcome the temptations of these sins in order to become a success in America's capitalist economy. In Carney's description: "Annie I is the seller, Annie II is the object sold; in prostituting herself, Annie depicts the paradigmatic action of commodification, such as Benjamin saw in the dialectical image of the prostitute, who is simultaneously the laborer and the alienated product of labor."[102] Like the sovereign of the Trauerspiel plays, Anna is both sadistic tyrant (Anna I) and mournful martyr (Anna II). As the two Annas fall victim to the depredations of America's economic system, Brecht's play demonstrates that they give their passive consent repeatedly to their own exploitation, suggesting that there are unexplored alternatives to their impotent grief and rage. In *The Seven Deadly Sins*, one sees a vivid, politically engaged example of the Brechtian baroque.

Beyond what the baroque legacy means for Brecht, the question also arises as to what Brecht might mean for modern scholarship vis-à-vis the theater history of the baroque stage. "Brechtian Trauerspiel" should describe more than an approach to reading or staging Brecht. The phrase should imply a way of understanding seventeenth-century theater through a vanguardist or formalist optic, rather than through the antiquarian or historicist one that has become familiar to Anglophone scholars, or through an optic that sees Shakespeare, for example, as more than an antecedent to modern realism in performance. It might then become clear that the early modern stage functioned in ways that were more "experimental" than have often been acknowledged.[103] By rethinking forms of early modern theater and performance through the stereoscope lenses of the baroque, on one side, and defamiliarization, on the other, the well-regarded repertory of seventeenth-century plays that readers feel they know well from their college lecture halls, community playhouses, and regional theaters may come to seem something darker, more unfamiliar, and more politically volatile.

Benjamin's theories of the baroque also offered him an occasion to critique Nietzsche's philosophical viewpoints on political grounds throughout the 1920s and '30s, and these critiques further elucidate the conceptual history of baroque style. In its very title, Benjamin's *Origin of the German Trauerspiel* responds to *The Birth of Tragedy*; and in the Trauerspiel-book's first chapter, "Trauerspiel and Tragedy," Benjamin makes this debt clear. "With its insight into the connection between tragedy and legend, and into the independence of the tragic from the ethos, Nietzsche's work lays the foundation for theses such as this."[104] Having acknowledged its Nietzschean influences, the Trauerspiel-book then alleges that *The Birth of Tragedy* sacrifices a proper historico-philosophical understanding of tragic myth in favor of "the abyss of aestheticism" into which all of Nietzsche's best concepts are lost, along with the "gods and heroes, defiance and suffering" that are characteristic of tragedy (*OGT* 95). To Benjamin, Nietzsche's youthful, Schopenhauerian nihilism undermines the historical concreteness of tragic theater (96), and *The Birth of Tragedy*'s conflation of Trauerspiel with tragedy causes Nietzsche to misconstrue the forms of opera that the baroque period produced. "Just as every comparison with tragedy—not to mention musical tragedy—remains insufficient for an understanding of opera, so too it is incontestable that, from the perspective of literature and particularly of the Trauerspiel, opera must appear as a product of decay" (230). In the context of Benjamin's habilitation thesis, these critical comments may seem like pro forma academic maneuvers, clearing away other writers' views so that his own may emerge. While that may be true, the Trauerspiel-book also lays the groundwork for broader disagreements with Nietzsche that mark those of Benjamin's later works that continue to inflect and reflect questions of baroque style.

In *The Arcades Project*, for example, Benjamin targets Nietzsche's thinking again in a critique of modern capitalism that makes continual reference to elements of baroque style, focusing on Nietzsche's idea of the eternal return. Although Nietzsche's thinking on eternal recurrence developed in opposition to nineteenth-century bourgeois myths of progressive history, Benjamin finds it to be structured according to the logic of an endless, repetitive crisis—that of the modern capitalist economy. This outlook Nietzsche shares with Baudelaire, whose mournfulness surpasses melancholy into all-consuming spleen, "the feeling that corresponds to catastrophe in permanence" (*AP* J66a,4). Within *The Arcades Project*'s convolute titled "Boredom, Eternal Return," Benjamin suggests that Nietzsche's doctrine of eternal recurrence knowingly colludes with the prevailing capitalist order of things: "There is a handwritten draft in which Caesar instead of Zarathustra is the bearer of Nietzsche's tidings (Löwith, p. 73). That is of no little moment. It underscores the fact that Nietzsche had an inkling of his doctrine's complicity with imperialism" (D9,5). And it is not only imperialism to which Nietzsche's philosophy lent its approval, in Benjamin's view, but to the en-

Landscapes of Melancholy

tire system of political economy that necessitated nineteenth-century imperialism to begin with. What emerges from *The Arcades Project* is a critique of Nietzsche's philosophical collusion not only with the crimes of imperialism but with Belle Époque economics writ large.

The "true order of eternal recurrence," which Benjamin's Trauerspiel-book had renamed *fate* (*OGT* 135), enshrines history only as a permanent cycle of crisis to which Nietzsche, like Baudelaire, ultimately surrenders (*AP* D5a,6). In his final analysis, then, Benjamin sees Nietzsche's philosophy of history as symptomatic of the market economy's endless cycles of boom and bust, just one register of the many financial panics that marked the last half of the nineteenth century in Europe. The commodity has an allegorical form akin to that of a baroque emblem, but so does the stock exchange, whose movements can be grasped and graphed as the image of a complex baroque unfolding. In the market's fluctuations between upturn and downturn, like Nietzsche's oscillations between occurrence and recurrence, a view of "history" takes shape as a baroque image that Benjamin names "petrified unrest," fluctuating but frozen.[105] The phrase could similarly describe the fluttering of fabrics in a marble sculpture by Bernini, just as it adequately names the frozen cycles of intrigue found in the Trauerspiel. To Benjamin, Nietzsche's doctrine of eternal recurrence is baroque in its very form, a fact Nietzsche already acknowledged by describing it as a "da capo." Although Nietzsche's idea of the eternal return arguably served him as an existential thought experiment rather than a theory of the historical process, for Benjamin, this idea expresses only a kind of hopelessness that is fully compliant with the permanent catastrophe, the endlessly repeated financial crisis. It was the theater history of the baroque Trauerspiel that offered Benjamin the insights needed to judge Nietzsche's complicity with imperial capital. Against Nietzsche's baroque philosophy of historical cyclicality, Benjamin would seek in his final writings on the concept of history to articulate a messianic view that could make space for revolutionary interruption.

Benjamin did not oppose Nietzsche at every point, however. Despite their political differences, he shares with Nietzsche an understanding that baroque style cannot be considered a uniformly repressive force. Against those who might interpret baroque cultural production as only a means for absolutist or ecclesiastic propaganda, he joins with Nietzsche in finding within the baroque an immanent polarization that renders it politically ambiguous. As I have argued, Nietzsche's writings reveal a distinction between what may be called *resentful* and *affirmative* baroque styles. Benjamin's analysis, in turn, reveals a second dialectic internal to the baroque, between *mournful* and *messianic* uses of allegory. Baroque style acquires, in Benjamin's writings on Brecht, a set of radical potentials that can be made useful for revolutionary political actions when those actions are guided by the light of historical memory. This potential is best expressed in the polyvalence of allegory, its capacity for being refunctioned against its hegemonic purposes. For every cultural force that uses imagery and media to sanctify existing forms of power, there exists a countervailing force that can deconsecrate these forms and strip them of their aura. The same emblem, like an onstage crown in a production of *Le Cid*, can be read both regressively and progressively—its "meaning" ultimately undecidable, but its form still holding out a faint spark of utopian hope.

"Enter, fleeing"

In their respective comments on Wagner and Brecht, Nietzsche and Benjamin stand out as paradigmatic theorists of baroque style, especially attuned to the necessity of theatrical effects in the baroque as an object of their study. Both theorists, moreover, require of themselves a decidedly theatrical approach to the process of writing, a philosophical style that exposes the performative basis of language through the inscriptive act itself. As I outline in chapter 1, the task of conceiving baroque style was bound, for Nietzsche, to an idea of writing given to irony, affective excess, and allegorical mask wearing. This approach amounted to his rejoinder, as a theorist, to Wagner's own histrionics. Benjamin's writings on baroque style involve a different mode of theatricality, one somewhat differently attuned to writing's capacity for defamiliarization. In the first pages of the Trauerspiel-book, Benjamin comments on his own approach to the writing of philosophy with a phrase that contradicts Nietzsche's youthful tendency for Dionysian excitements: "[Philosophical writing's] goal cannot be to enthrall or excite enthusiasm. Only where it obliges the reader to pause at stations of reflection is it sure of itself" (*OGT* 4). Unlike the rhetoric of, say, *The Birth of Tragedy*, which threatens to carry the reader away amid an overflow of powerful feelings, Benjamin's gestic prose subjects thinking to a state of repeated self-interruptions. In the *Origin of the German Trauerspiel*, Benjamin aims through writing to subvert the theatricality of those powerful feelings Nietzsche's work can capably induce in his readers. He seeks instead to defamiliarize the process of reading even further, using formal devices that can thwart any easy readerly absorption into a text's material weave. In Susan

Landscapes of Melancholy

Sontag's view, this writing style is best described as "freeze-frame baroque": a style that "was torture to execute. It was as if each sentence had to say everything."[106] Moreover, the paratactic form of the Trauerspiel-book's aphoristic sentences and discontinuous subchapters mimes the disintegrated structure of the Trauerspiel itself. The book's two chapters emplot a repeated narrative of secularization that reproduces the recurrent catastrophes of Trauerspiel form; and the concluding turn to the subject of redemption at the end of both chapters reenacts a Calderónian apotheosis. In all these ways, the Trauerspiel-book proceeds like the "staging" of a Trauerspiel, all its own: it is philosophical writing conceived according to a baroque theatrical or directorial logic.[107]

There is also the matter of the Trauerspiel-book's intermediations of text and image, its way of incorporating emblems into its linguistic texture. The mosaic, the constellation, the thinker pausing for breath, the sovereign gripping his scepter, the site of Golgotha, and—in Benjamin's later writings—the connector of puzzle pieces, the stalking path: emblems of this sort continually permeated Benjamin's thinking during his work on the Trauerspiel-book and continued to inflect it until his final years. They form, so to speak, the ornaments and scenography of his staged interventions into his historical material. As allegories, they recall the memory of a theater tradition that placed unprecedented emphasis on visual display while they open a space for Benjamin's development of the dialectical image as his method in *The Arcades Project*. In a private letter to Scholem composed from Capri, Benjamin cautioned: "It is quite characteristic of baroque style that anyone who stops thinking rigorously while studying it immediately slips into a hysterical imitation of it" (*CWB* 247). In writing the Trauerspiel-book, his task was to take on attributes of baroque theatrical style, but to do so in a rigorous manner that could illuminate the subject in novel and surprising ways. The book achieves this purpose, in part, through the calculated array of emblem effects, making baroque allegory into a distinctive mode of theatricality.

Nietzsche's and Benjamin's examples illuminate much about the impact of baroque style, both on the rise of modernist theater and on the development of modern critical theory, and this impact would continue to resonate well into the second half of the twentieth century. Both thinkers make clear that there exists a baroque genealogy to modern thought, an early modern theater prehistory to the traditions of theory that Nietzsche and Benjamin helped initiate. In their enigmatic way, that is, the baroque theaters of the seventeenth-century past throw light upon late-twentieth-century poststructural thought, especially deconstruction and its inheritors. This fact owes not only to the legacy of Paul de Man's writings on allegory, which establish a theoretical conjunction between Benjamin's methods and Derrida's, but also to the intermediation of stage and text in baroque theater and deconstruction alike. Just as the baroque theater medium functioned "like the aspect of a printed page" illustrated with allegorical devices, so does deconstruction as a theoretical mode often take on "theatrical" qualities, in the most robust sense of that word. Samuel Weber calls special attention to this fact in *Theatricality as Medium*, when, in reading Derrida's interpretation of Mallarmé in "The Double Session," he describes Derrida as having moved "from a purely 'theoretical' discourse, describing an object independent of it, to a 'theatrical' mode of (re)writing that stages (dislocates) what it also recites: the theatrical movement of Mallarmé's writing."[108] "In the almost four decades since ["The Double Session"] was published," Weber argues, "Derrida's writing has not ceased to demonstrate and explore, with increasing explicitness and variety, its own theatrical quality as a 'staging' or *mise en scène*, rather than as an essentially constative reading of something held to exist independently of it."[109] Grammatology understands and constructs writing, textuality, into a form of theatrical space.[110] Likewise, deconstruction undertakes in the textual field a kind of spatialization (*"espacement"*) that corresponds to the explicit spatialization necessary in baroque Trauerspiel, Brechtian epic theater, and the post-dramatic regime of theater that Brecht made possible.[111] In this respect, Derrida participates in a tradition (or stalking path) of thought that must take shape *in writing as theater*, a tradition that stretches through Benjamin, Brecht, Mallarmé, and Nietzsche to a forgotten baroque history of the stage.

What this conjunction between Benjamin's critical theory and deconstruction reveals, in part, is that performance in the baroque theater does not proceed according to anything like a "metaphysics of presence." In initiating a game of deferrals and substitutions between sign and meaning, play and beholder, the baroque theater instead creates an originary rhythm, a fleeting pulse: not metaphysics as self-presence but metaphysics as difference and repetition. In the final analysis, the idea of such a baroque movement —fugal in its very form—is notably suggested at various points throughout Benjamin's writings, particularly as they concern the subject of messianic power and the figure of the fugitive.[112] A final example serves to illuminate this point. Despite his various criticisms of Nietzsche's philosophical style and political orientation, Benjamin was not opposed to adopting Nietzsche's

Landscapes of Melancholy

practice of casting himself in his own critical writing. His mosaic of aphorisms, *One-Way Street*, published soon after the *Origin of the German Trauerspiel*, includes the following passage near its end, in which Benjamin again takes up a directorial mode of writing, as though staging a Trauerspiel scene in the space of *One-Way Street* as a text. This passage, or scene, is conspicuous for its theatrical references, imagery, and self-reflexiveness:

> Again and again, in Shakespeare, in Calderón, battles fill the last act, and kings, princes, attendants, and followers "enter, fleeing." The moment in which they become visible to spectators brings them to a standstill. The flight of the *dramatis personae* is arrested by the stage. Their entry into the visual field of nonparticipating and truly impartial persons allows the harassed to draw breath, bathes them in new air. The appearance on stage of those who enter "fleeing" takes from this its hidden meaning. Our reading of this formula is imbued with expectation of a place, a light, a footlight glare, in which our flight through life may likewise be sheltered in the presence of onlooking strangers. (*SW* 1:484)

In these lines, there radiates the premonition of a future catastrophe, the barest glimmer of what would become the author's own last act. Within the ruins of the baroque past, whose culture was devoted to the display of power at the grandest possible scale, Benjamin found warnings of the coming collapse of his own Weimar society of spectacle. In this passage, he casts himself in the role of the baroque sovereign-as-fugitive, in a manner that cannot help but seem for his belated interpreters a presentiment of his coming exile from Germany and, later, his final flight across the Pyrenees from Vichy France. Within this imagined Trauerspiel, conducted with heavy tread on foot, by way of overgrown mountain mule paths, amid frequent pauses for breath, Benjamin himself seems to glance upward self-consciously from the text. As he turns his gaze through the proscenium of history to meet the eyes of the future, it is left to his interpreters to return that gaze as it flashes up in the glare of the footlights.

4   The Citability of Baroque Gesture
Unsettling Stein

> I'm reading the signs. I love to read the signs.
>
> —Gertrude Stein, to Alice B. Toklas

Opening on Broadway to great acclaim after its debut at a regional art museum in Hartford, Connecticut, *Four Saints in Three Acts* was Gertrude Stein's first and only dramatic text to receive a major stage production during her lifetime.[1] As a foundational work of avant-garde opera in the United States, *Four Saints'* importance is perhaps rivaled in the history of American modernist theater only by the one-act plays of Eugene O'Neill's early "Expressionist" period (1914-22). Whereas Stein's theater writing, however, has often been eclipsed by O'Neill's (and the American theater's) gradual turn to realism, her opera enjoyed widespread popular appeal during its brief New York run and has proven enormously influential over subsequent generations of the avant-garde. What is more, the Broadway premiere occurred amid the earliest art-historical reevaluations of seventeenth-century Italian visual art by American curators and collectors. This contemporaneous interest in the historical baroque period, far from being merely fortuitous or coincidental, actively shaped the creation and reception of Stein's work. With its Counter-reformation-era protagonists, Teresa of Avila and Ignatius of Loyola, deployed as allegories for the modern-day artist's life, *Four Saints* undertakes a direct dialogue with the conventions of baroque spirituality, art, and theater. Not only was this connection centrally important to the project's collaborators, but it was also recognizable to its 1934 audience, even if it has gone largely undiscussed in subsequent theater scholarship, which has focused instead on questions of poetics, antitheatricality, gender, race, and Stein's place within a larger avant-garde context.[2] Although these are all crucial topics for understanding Stein's project in *Four Saints*, one

The Citability of Baroque Gesture

147

wonders what can account for this critical omission. Reconsidering Stein as a modern inheritor of the baroque stage stands to reframe her involvement with all these various questions, casting both her own theater work and that of her later interpreters into a new light altogether.

This chapter explores *Four Saints in Three Acts* as the first work of American avant-garde theater whose creators were cognizant of modernism's baroque inheritance and sought to claim it in formal terms on the stage. With *Four Saints*, Stein found in the idea of the baroque a means to contest norms of representation across a wide array of registers: linguistic, aesthetic, sexual, racial, and historiographic. Regarding the last of these, I propose to read Stein's opera as a kind of history play, and to do so in spite of the fact—remarkable in itself—that it depicts no clear actions or events. Radically devoid of plot in any traditional sense, *Four Saints* nevertheless enacts the lives of saints in a way that fundamentally redefined normative concepts of mimesis during its time. As I show, the opera's libretto and premiere performance explicitly cited and iterated a wealth of historical gestures, tropes, and images that were once original to the baroque stage, thereby reenacting an entire repertoire of baroque theater forms. But *Four Saints* is something more than a baroque pasticcio or modernist pastiche; rather, the opera bodied forth that repertoire of gestures into the production's modernist moment and beyond.[3] In this way, *Four Saints* puts forward a baroque vision of temporal movement in order to contest progressivist narratives of history and modernity. While doing so, the opera also popularized baroque style as a clear source of inspiration for an ensuing century of theatrical avant-gardists.

As with the Trauerspiel form in Benjamin's analysis, one can say that Stein's opera amounts to both a work of theater and a work of historiography, a play whose material content is history itself. In *Four Saints*, an entire baroque philosophy of historical repetition is itself reenacted on the stage. When the American director Robert Wilson staged *Four Saints* in 1996, the critic Bonnie Marranca wrote that his production amounted to "a virtual casebook, embodying histories of imagery and histories of performance style." For Marranca, the production's real achievement was "the way it frames performance history to elucidate for its spectators the process through which ideas, art, and style are transmitted through artworks."[4] Even without Wilson's intervention, however, Stein's 1927 libretto already posed these very questions. At a crucial moment when the concept of the baroque was first becoming mainstream for American audiences, *Four Saints* dramatized a reflection on history—including art history, theater history, religious history, and the histories of style and taste—and how it comes to be materialized and transmitted from within the arts themselves. Stein and her collaborators issued a summons to the theater forms of the baroque past in order to re-cite them in a new (twentieth-century American) context. As an "allegory of canonization," in Corinne Blackmer's evocative phrase, the opera used text and performance not only to reimagine its baroque materials but to stage the historical process as a movement of reenactment and recursion, iteration and citation.[5]

In what follows, I unfold numerous important aspects of Stein's text in relation to the concept and cultural memory of the baroque during the 1920s. For this task, a primary point of reference will be Benjamin's *Origin of the German Trauerspiel*, a text whose contemporaneity and similarity to Stein's theater theory is remarkable.[6] Numerous important aspects of Stein's opera and the theoretical writings she generated to articulate it (her 1934 essay "Plays," specifically) bear striking resemblances to the concepts of baroque theatricality that emerge from Benjamin's Trauerspiel-book.[7] Most notable among these is the idea of the theater as a landscape, in which history has merged or passed into the setting, as Benjamin claimed had taken place in the case of the German baroque stage. With *Four Saints*, Stein perceived that modern theater needed to realign itself with a new emphasis on space (as in Trauerspiel), one that takes on a distinctly ecological cast in Stein's description. In addition to this quality of spatialization, Stein also grasps the distinct temporality of baroque style, its ever-punctual, ever-convoluted repetitions, which her poetic voice registers in its syntax and diction. In its incessant turns and returns, Stein's libretto seeks a paradoxical experience of immediacy by plunging deeper and deeper into the mess and recursive complexity of mediation: the only transcendence known to the baroque stylist is that which can be found in the immanence of things. These structural elements of Stein's style are not just her most distinctively modernist features (in their resemblance, say, to Cubo-Futurist techniques or to montage); they also link her work to the baroque past.

For all its formal radicalism, Stein's work is, at heart, a saintly miracle play. She found in Saint Teresa of Avila a kindred spirit: a woman, an intellectual, a writer, a visionary, a contemplative, a mystic, perhaps also a crypto-Jewish converso, with whom Stein could radically identify herself. In this light, Benjamin might say that *Four Saints*, like the baroque Trauerspiel "from Calderón to Strindberg," proves that the medieval form of the *mysterium*

The Citability of Baroque Gesture

continues to have an open future into the twentieth century (*OGT* 108). Like Benjamin, Stein sought the theater as a means to remember and redeem the forgotten materials of the oppressed past. Like Mallarmé, she was nourished by the baroque influence of Racine's Phèdre, Catholic liturgy, and the theater of the Book. Like Nietzsche, she embraced baroque style as a vehicle to affirm, joyously, the world as a continual Dionysian flux. Drawing on and analyzing these similarities, this chapter examines how Stein and her collaborators used *Four Saints* to reimagine the baroque theater anew. In this effort, I assert the baroque's notional capacity to enfold affective forms of gaiety and queer modes of sexuality, desire, and affiliation. In sum, I urge us to rethink Stein's miracle play as a paradigm-shifting and uniquely American example of baroque modernism.

"To Mount It Up"—Baroque Citationality on Stage

Upon entering the Wadsworth Atheneum's newly built theater in Hartford, Connecticut, for the 1934 premiere of *Four Saints*, spectators received a printed program made of pink paper and black Spanish lace that set the tone for the events to follow. For its frontispiece, this program featured a photograph of Bernini's *Saint Teresa in Ecstasy* (ca. 1650) along with a lengthy excerpt from Richard Crashaw's hymn to Saint Teresa (also ca. 1650), "The Flaming Heart."[8] These baroque intertexts were no accident. Stein came to be situated alongside Bernini and Crashaw in this way, in no small part, through the influence of the Atheneum's new chief curator, Arthur Everett "Chick" Austin (1900-1957). In the seven years since his appointment as museum director at age twenty-seven, Austin had sought to focus the museum's collecting on two then-undervalued fields of European painting—the same two art-historical periods that were his lifelong passion, namely, the modernist and the baroque. He had already curated the first major American exhibition of Italian baroque paintings, in 1930.[9] Through his efforts, a new awareness of baroque visual art had come sharply into focus among American museumgoers and collectors. On the occasion of *Four Saints'* premiere, Austin also inaugurated the Atheneum's newly completed Avery Memorial Wing, which he had arranged to be built in the austere International Style, and at whose center he had placed an enormous sculpture of Venus, dated 1600, by Pietro Francavilla (1548-1615). The opening-night audience passed through this space while entering the first American retrospective of Picasso's paintings, before heading to the museum's auditorium for the opera premiere.[10] By 1934, Austin had established his reputation by juxtaposing

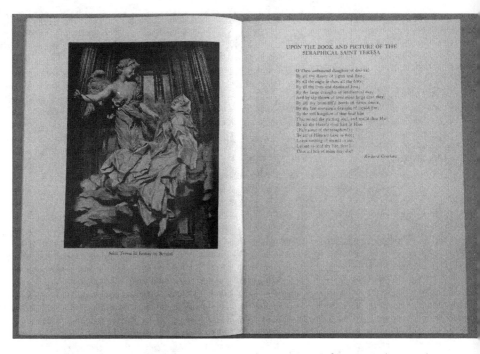

Theatrical program book for *Four Saints in Three Acts* (1927), featuring a photograph of *Saint Theresa in Ecstasy* by Gian Lorenzo Bernini and excerpts from "On the Book and Picture of the Seraphical Saint Theresa" by Richard Crashaw. Photo by Joseph Cermatori. Courtesy Beinecke Rare Book and Manuscript Library, Yale University.

early modern artworks alongside modernist ones. He served as *Four Saints in Three Acts*' host not only in his capacity as museum director but also as its financing producer in his role as founder of the Friends and Enemies of Modern Music (established 1928), a society devoted to programming music by composers both modern (Stravinsky, Satie, Schoenberg) and baroque (Vivaldi, Couperin, Scarlatti). Juxtaposing recent and historical artworks in this way, the museum effectively suggested a historical allegory between the two, highlighting their shared investment in formal experimentation and unexpected shock effects.[11]

Moreover, the choice to contextualize *Four Saints*' premiere within a set of citations to baroque culture was far from an arbitrary one. The subject of the baroque was then still gaining ground among modernists in France with close connections to Stein's circle, a fact that may have influenced her think-

The Citability of Baroque Gesture

ing about the opera while she worked on it in Paris in 1927.[12] As the opera's main collaborators, Stein and Thomson chose to focus the opera on two saints whose ecstatic visions were even then understood to have inspired the programmatic use of theatrical propaganda within the Catholic Counter-Reformation. In the person of Saint Teresa, Stein claims kinship with the baroque as a variety of spiritual experience. An account by Virgil Thomson in 1966 of how the choice of subjects fell to baroque saints is evocative:

> I had asked Miss Stein for an opera libretto, and we had sat together for picking out a subject. The theme we chose was of my suggesting; it was the working artist's life, which is to say, the life we both were living. . . . I thought we should follow overtly, however, the format of classical Italian opera, which carries on the commerce of the play in dry recitative, extending the emotional moments into arias and set-pieces. And since the eighteenth-century opera seria, or basic Italian opera, required a serious mythological subject with a tragic ending, we agreed to follow that convention also, but to consider mythology as including not just Greek or Scandinavian legends, of which there were already a great many in operatic repertory, but also political history and the lives of saints. Gertrude liked American history, but every theme we tried out seemed to have something wrong with it. So that after I vetoed George Washington because of the eighteenth century costumes (in which everybody looks alike), we gave up history and chose saints, sharing a certain reserve toward medieval ones and Italian ones on the grounds that both had been overdone in the last century. Eventually our saints turned out to be baroque and Spanish, a solution that delighted Gertrude, for she loved Spain, and that was far from displeasing to me, since, as I pointed out, mass-market Catholic art, the basic living art of Christianity, was still baroque. And [Thomson's lover, the landscape painter, poet, and scenarist for *Four Saints*] Maurice Grosser was later to remind us that musical instruments of the violin family still present themselves as functional baroque forms.[13]

By this description, then, it is clear that the initial conceptual discussions for the opera centered not only on the baroque setting of its saintly protagonists but also on a number of ways in which the baroque could make a fortuitous dramaturgical concept for the work. Stein and Thomson's collaboration would develop techniques of baroque recitative, elaborate upon the structures of eighteenth-century baroque opera seria, and reprise the mythic scenarios found in early opera and in Wagner.[14] Perhaps most important of all, it would take advantage of the colorful and flamboyant costumes of the period, as opposed to the bland uniformity of Enlightenment- and Revolutionary-era clothing.[15] But it is Grosser's comment (as recollected here by Thomson) on the historical persistence of baroque forms within the physical bodies of modern string instruments that best informs the opera's conceptual gambit. The bodies of these objects, into which the weight of the historical past has sunk or merged, exemplify just one of many ways in which the past can hardly be considered as something absolutely past, but as something materially and continuously present, if in subtly transformed ways.

Stein's love for Spain owed in part to her friendships with Pablo Picasso and Juan Gris and in part to her summer travels of 1912, when she and Alice B. Toklas toured Madrid, Toledo, Barcelona, and Ávila, some ten years' prior to Teresa's canonization. Stein had likewise been interested in Teresa's life and writings since the time of her Radcliffe College days studying psychology under the American philosopher William James, who had written on Teresa as part of his studies in mystical experience.[16] As Lisa Ruddick has demonstrated, the early 1910s were a period during which Stein was reevaluating her relationship to James's thinking and developing her own writing as a form of modern gnostic or mystic experience.[17] The Ávila visit's timing was thus propitious. Making the journey as so many pilgrims and tourists before her had done (and as so many of her own devotees would later do at her apartment in Paris's Rue de Fleurus), Stein found the fantasy landscape of Ávila enchanting. There she and Toklas visited the ornate shrine dedicated to Teresa's honor in the saint's official chapel, a sight that surely left a lasting impression.[18]

Stein would draw even more inspiration from what Thomson describes as the still-baroque status of "mass-market Catholic art," as seen in numerous shop windows during her walks through the streets of Paris. She claimed the opera's roots lay in the Catholic kitsch objects she spotted for sale around town, ones glimpsed while she walked idly through the city streets like Benjamin's flaneur. One display in the Boulevard Raspail, for example—exhibiting a series of First Holy Communion photographs in which a young girl's street clothes are gradually transformed into a nun's habit—provided Stein with the idea for one of the libretto's most memorable moments (*P* li). ("Saint Teresa could be photographed having been dressed like a lady and then they taking out her head changed it to a nun and a nun a saint and a saint so" [*4S3A* 447].) Elsewhere, a porcelain statuette representing a young, unhelmeted soldier showing charity to a beggar offered her an image for the militancy and grace of Saint Ignatius (*P* li). ("Saint Ignatius could be in porcelain actually. Saint Ignatius could be in porcelain actually while he was

The Citability of Baroque Gesture

young and standing" [4S3A 450].) It was from these fragmentary allegories of modernity—the remains of baroque church architecture in Spain, the trace of baroque emblematics hidden ruinously within commodity souvenirs encountered while strolling idly through the streets of Paris—that Stein drew her inspiration for *Four Saints in Three Acts*, her *Gesamtkunstwerk* of the American modernist baroque.[19]

It was to be a baroque *Gesamtkunstwerk* with a difference. Unlike a Wagner or a Bernini, who both consolidated artistic control into one sovereign artist figure, Stein and her collaborators instead pursued another path altogether. Their model of collaboration was something more akin to that of the Ballets Russes under Sergei Diaghilev or the Salzburg Festival under Max Reinhardt. As with both of these forerunners, to varying degrees, distinguished artists from a variety of different mediums would be brought together and each granted relative artistic autonomy from the rest so that no one centrally controlling artistic intelligence could emerge.[20] What was more, Stein and Thomson's methods as musical dramatists would sharply depart from the more straightforwardly representational structure of Wagner's operas. With *Four Saints*, they would contest the relationship between drama and representation altogether, taking theater away from standard forms of dramatic mimesis toward more self-reflexive forms of theatricalism and mime.

Audience members at any of the productions of *Four Saints* in 1934 would have been confronted with the bizarre spectacle of painter Florine Stettheimer's scenery, executed in a "whimsical baroque style."[21] Stettheimer's involvement was secured early on in the collaboration, in 1929, well before any of the other major players had been drawn in. As Thomson would recall many years later in describing Stettheimer's appropriateness for *Four Saints*' subject matter: "Florine's paintings are very high camp, and high camp is the only thing you can do with a religious subject. Anything else gets sentimental and unbelievable, whereas high camp touches religion sincerely and its being at the same time low pop."[22] Stettheimer produced one of American theater's most iconic stage images, unquestionably modern while simultaneously evocative of baroque stage practices. She dressed the stage's overhanging borders, legs, and upstage wall with a draping of blue cellophane that collected in shimmering folds everywhere. (Still a relatively recent invention at that time, the product was patented only in 1912.) Seen from the audience as it formed a background to the symmetrical placement of bodies onstage, it drew attention to the orthogonal vectors

Production photograph from *Four Saints in Three Acts*' premiere, 1934. Florine and Ettie Stettheimer Papers. American Literature Collection, Beinecke Rare Book and Manuscript Library, Yale University. Photo by White Studio © The New York Public Library.

of the theater space itself. In this, it mirrored the use of artificial stage perspective that has been the hallmark of baroque scenic design since the construction of the Teatro Olimpico. The total design's effect is captured pithily in Maurice Grosser's observation that the stage looked like "a Schrafft's candy-box version of Baroque."[23] To reinforce the theatricality of the opera's proceedings, Stettheimer placed an opera box to one side of the stage, allowing the opera's two narrators (called Commère and Compère, inventions of Thomson drawn from the French music hall tradition) a seat from which to watch the onstage events. This effect echoed Bernini's *Teresa in Ecstasy* sculpture group, in which sculptures depicting Bernini's patrons from the Cornaro family flank the enraptured saint from either side as spectators to the miracle, watching from their boxes in a theater loge.

The Citability of Baroque Gesture

The costumes Stettheimer designed for *Four Saints in Three Acts* cited baroque visual culture in similar ways, based largely upon Catholic liturgical dress. In one spectator's description, the nearly forty performers portraying the opera's innumerable saints wore "simple, unshaped robes, with wide sleeves and cowl hoods, varied by lace bordered tunics like ecclesiastical surplices."[24] The opera's two Saints Teresa appeared in its opening act wearing matching cardinal-red cassocks and shoulder capes, their heads crowned with short lace mantillas and rakishly posed, wide-brimmed straw hats that created the appearance of halos. The two resembled a pair of female cardinals who decided to don their finest choir dress for a picnic on the lawn. Other costumes were equally rich and strange. Saint Ignatius of Loyola, for example, made his first appearance in a cassock of bright-green watered silk. Almost all the actors changed costumes—and colors—at each of the production's three entr'actes, creating a veritable pageant with a constantly shifting palette, full of azure, crimson, tan, white, silver, diamond, emerald, and other lavish hues. In David Harris's description, "The sheer number of costumes—approximately two hundred in an opera that ran only one hundred minutes—contributed to the baroque richness of the spectacle."[25]

Beyond the costumes, the actors' gestures and stage movements also cited the visual forms of early modern Catholic culture in deliberate and significant ways. Thomson wrote to Stein in 1933 of the production team's intention for the performers' bodies to conjure "the same magnificence [that bodies] give to classic religious painting and sculpture" (*LST* 208). He charged the British dancer Frederick Ashton with choreographing a continuous repertoire of gestures for the entirety of the spectacle. Ashton brought to the task a deep familiarity with Catholic ritual attained from having spent his childhood in Lima, Peru, where he served as an acolyte to the city's cardinal archbishop, assisted with masses in its grand cathedral, and witnessed countless street processions like the one he staged for the opera's climax.[26] Working with the scenario composed by Maurice Grosser to organize Stein's libretto into "a train of images," Ashton arranged the performers' bodies into a series of tableaux vivants, alternating between continuity of movement and the sort of momentary frozenness that allows a gesture *to settle*.[27] Eschewing the fourth wall, he instead opted frequently for the outward-facing or presentational performance orientation characteristic of onstage allegory.[28] At other moments, Ashton found occasions for dancers to contort their bodies into what Harris describes as a "baroque spiral of a curve" or as "baroque swirls and convolutions of mass."[29]

156   Baroque Modernity

His aims were in no way lost upon the 1934 audience. From the auditorium, Carl Van Vechten perceived that Ashton's choreographed gestures were meant to coordinate with Stettheimer's fanciful scenery, and that they responded to the tradition of Spanish baroque painting—particularly El Greco, Zurbarán, and Velázquez—and he said so in an essay later printed in the *New York Times* and the Broadway production's souvenir program.[30] Another viewer, the Jesuit priest, prominent anti-racist, anti-fascism activist, and sometime art critic John La Farge, joined Van Vechten in perceiving baroque culture as a central touchstone for *Four Saints* and described this aspect of the opera in detail in his 17 February 1934 review of it in the Jesuit weekly *America*. Thomson's short letter to Stein of 2 March 1934 enjoins her to find a copy of La Farge's review in the American Library, noting campily and with evident satisfaction, "Fancy high Jesuit Father La Farge did us proud. He incidentally, was the author of the phrase 'baroque fantasia. Usefully'" (*LST* 227). La Farge's review of the production claims that the text's prevailing idea

> seems to be a baroque fantasia. She [Stein] wishes to convey to the spectator and hearer the vague general impression of how baroque appears to her; of what she particularly loves in baroque; its contained grandeur; its dignity of high noon and blue skies. But this is not done too seriously. It is ironical; seriously ironical or ironically serious.
>
> She conveys too, in a strange way, the impression that a spiritually illiterate person receives from the accidentals of the Catholic liturgy. To such a person, the chanted lessons of the Church, the intonations and movements, appear solemn yet inconsequential grave announcements of the inexplicable. Not that she resents this; she enjoys it, as the most precious element in the baroque. Her attitude toward it is of interest; of pleasure; possibly of something deeper, a sense that there *is* something profound and meaningful beneath these forms. So with an immense number of moderns; a nostalgia for something they have lost. Yet she remains slightly ironical.
>
> St. Teresa and St. Ignatius are but symbols of this something in the baroque which lifts it above a gorgeous garden party. They are the foci of baroque dignity, restraint, expansiveness. They are vaguely reminiscent of a vaguely apprehended period: agreeable figures. St. Teresa is two figures, one who sings, one who postures. They have many conversations: pleasant conversations. (qtd. in *LST* 227-28)

In La Farge's estimation, if *Four Saints* imitates the visual rhetoric of the baroque past, this is not so that it can mock or parody that rhetoric, nor

The Citability of Baroque Gesture

reflect on it with mere humor or with nostalgia alone. In its "serious irony," a phrase that hearkens back to Nietzsche's rhetorical methods and forward to the dawning discourse of camp, something else is at stake. As far as La Farge was able to detect, it was *pleasure*, and profound and meaningful pleasure at that. In performance, Stein's play focuses "baroque dignity, restraint, expansiveness" into a seductive game, a tease of signification. In its material splendor, the performance evoked what Susan Sontag would later call, in "Against Interpretation," an erotics of art.

Like Thomson, the producers of *Four Saints'* later Broadway run saw the usefulness in La Farge's interpretation of the work as a "baroque fantasia" and included the phrase in the final sentence of their press release.[31] Fastening onto this description, Stark Young described the performers' movements quite explicitly in his review of the production as "a baroque composition that is sometimes heavy as in sculpture or sculpturesque painting, sometimes as light as the air of salon walls." In Young's view, Ashton's recognizable citations to the visual culture of the seventeenth century were decisive in determining the choreography's reception in general. "The question is, then," Young continues, "how much does one's enjoyment of this dance design arise from recognition, from the appearance suddenly here, in sum, of tradition? . . . What is the particular response or emotion that the traditional in itself arouses? Does it give a certain dignity to art by achieving a sense of continuity? Is this a sense more of a continuity in art or of a continuity in the type of the mind?"[32] These are questions that must be asked not only of Ashton's choreography but also of Stein's text, alongside other aspects of the production's concept and context.

These various responses to the play in performance from Grosser, Van Vechten, La Farge, and Young record both the nearness and distance between Stein and the baroque theater. A further measure of the distance must also be sought in Ashton's choreography, which incorporated aspects of Harlem's vibrant performance and nightlife scene into its textural weave. Beyond his childhood encounters with Catholic ceremonials in Latin America, Ashton drew inspiration from contemporary social dances like the Charleston, Snake Hips, and the Lindy Hop.[33] In this regard, as in the fact that it was the first Broadway production to feature an all-Black cast, the production offered a further destabilization of norms and aesthetic conventions. Thomson claimed he hit on this casting idea while listening to Jimmie Daniels sing "I've Got the World on a String" during a late-night visit to the Hot-Cha Bar and Grill on 134th Street in 1933.[34] By drawing the Lindy Hop

158   Baroque Modernity

and other Black dance forms into the mix, Ashton developed *Four Saints'* choreographic vocabulary at the conjunction of Blackness and baroque.[35]

Thomson's decision to cast an entirely Black group of singers sprang from a complicated mixture of politically progressive and racially paternalistic attitudes on his part. As the historian Steven Watson notes, the premiere production "offered two breakthroughs for African-American singers": a musical one and a financial one.[36] Surely the opera brought its singers to new degrees of visibility, particularly its principal performers: Edward Matthews as Saint Ignatius, Abner Dorsey and Altonell Hines as the Compère and Commère, and Bruce Howard and Beatrice Robinson Wayne as the twinned Saints Teresa. But Thomson also by turns objectified and idealized the singers he hired from Eva Jessye's Harlem-based choir, and often found himself in conflict with Jessye herself.[37] His erotic interest in the production's male performers occasionally led to conflicts within the creative team, and particularly so surrounding the question of how the singers were to appear onstage in performance. Thomson's letter to Stein of 30 May 1933 mentions the spectacle's planned use of gestures drawn from "religious painting and sculpture" as a way to persuade her that the performers' bodies and movements will be full of magnificence, "sedate and prim" rather than "titillating" (*LST* 208). Although ideas about whitening the performers' skin and clothing them in transparent vestments were ultimately dropped, the citational use of movements remained, intermixed with movements Ashton quoted from the bars and nightclubs of Harlem.

This same period saw the rise of a thriving queer nightlife in New York City, as the historian George Chauncey has carefully recorded.[38] It is likely, given Thomson's frequent visits to Harlem during the time of its literary and artistic renaissance, that the production also reflected the emergent phenomenon of drag or "pansy" balls in northern Manhattan. Thomson, who had attended such balls in Paris for Mardi Gras, journeyed to at least one of these balls with Carl Van Vechten in February 1929 at the Rockland Casino (155th Street and Frederick Douglass Boulevard) while visiting the United States to drum up initial financial support for a production. There he would have witnessed a fantastic, multiracial procession of drag kings and queens parading in extraordinary costumes of black lace, canary satin, spangles, calla lilies, and other extravagances. This potential convergence suggests two interpretations: first, that *Four Saints* functioned as an elaborate pageant in what might be called "historical drag"; and second, that modern drag balls may bear within themselves the performative traces of the ba-

The Citability of Baroque Gesture

roque form of the pageant. Both Stein's opera and drag performance involve the project of "making gestures quotable"—as Benjamin claimed it was the project of Brecht's Epic Theater to do. With drag, this means making quotable the gestures that compose the illusion of a stably gendered identity, whereas Stein's opera made citable the gestures of the baroque repertoire. Drag theatrically exposes gender as a mythical or performative construction. The similarly citable use of gesture in *Four Saints* theatrically exposed as equally mythic and performative those notions of historical progress by which the past can come to be considered as irrecoverably separate from the present. Stein's play thus "synchronizes" the 1920s and the baroque, as Bonnie Marranca once passingly suggested it does.[39] Its premiere performance worked to effect this synchronicity with every pose, in which the history of baroque gesture, through reiterated acts of citation, was bodied forth into the modernist present. Both as a text and in its premiere performance, *Four Saints* produced a queer idea of time as performative, organized according to the rhythms of citation and iteration.[40] With *Four Saints*, Stein enacted a baroque metaphysics of repetition—a metaphysics, in Benjamin's words, of the *origin*.

Allegorical Temporality

The year after *Four Saints'* premiere and subsequent Broadway transfer, Stein composed her only theater-theoretical treatise, the 1935 lecture entitled "Plays," which takes up the phenomenology of spectatorship. This essay both reflects her dramaturgical principles in *Four Saints in Three Acts* and makes a philosophical inquiry into the nature of time. It commences with the following fundamental observation about plays:

> The thing that is fundamental about plays is that the scene as depicted on the stage is more often than not one might say it is almost always in syncopated time in relation to the emotion of anybody in the audience. . . . Your sensation as one in the audience in relation to the play played before you your sensation I say your emotion concerning that play is always either behind or ahead of the play at which you are looking and to which you are listening. So your emotion as a member of the audience is never going on at the same time as the action of the play. . . . That the thing seen and the thing felt about the thing seen not going on at the same tempo is what makes the being at the theatre something that makes anybody nervous. (*P* xxix-xxx)

In this passage, Stein refers to the traditions of dramatic realism and melodrama that she knew as a young playgoer, in which exciting events, suspense, and unexpected plot reversals shape the viewer's affective response. Where "syncopation" is concerned, she credits her sources in the world of Black popular musical performance, claiming that "[t]he jazz bands made of this thing, the thing that makes you nervous at the theatre, they made of this thing an end in itself" (*P* xxx). While Stein feels nervous in the theater, out-of-sync or "in syncopated time" with the play in performance, she also claims that everyday existence gives rise to a similar set of affects. The theater produces a feeling of nervousness and a desire for "relief," while events in everyday life generate a sense of "excitement" that can culminate in a sense of "completion" (*P* xxxii-xxxiii).

Crucially, however, being present to an event in one's daily life is just as impossible outside the theater as it is inside the theater. With exciting events taking place *outside* the theater, Stein claims, "[t]here one progresses forward and back emotionally," just as one might do in a theatrical audience, shuttling to and fro through syncopated time, but "at the supreme crisis of the scene the scene in which one takes part, in which one's hopes and loves and fears take part at the extreme crisis of this thing *one is almost one with one's emotions*" (*P* xxxiii; emphasis mine). This *almost one* is an important nuance in Stein's theory. Things *feel* more immediate and present in everyday life, even if they aren't actually so. This feeling comes, in part because we are participants in our own lives in ways that we are not at the traditional theater, where we are spectators first and foremost. If the theatrical medium is problematic for Stein, its anxiogenic character owes to the mediated and temporal quality of all experience, theatrical or otherwise.

For Stein, these anxieties of theatrical spectatorship are exacerbated by the modern drama's mode of presenting characters. In everyday life and in novels, new individuals are introduced gradually over time. In most drama, by contrast, characters suddenly manifest themselves on the stage or the page in the inexplicable, if apparent, fullness of their presence. To counteract this confusion, one must keep a finger tucked into the script's (or playbill's) list of dramatis personae to help refamiliarize oneself at periodic intervals (*P* xxxviii). Unlike the well-known mythic or divine figures of the ancient or medieval theater, the modern secular theater disorients spectators by confronting them with strangers. Each new presence onstage is ghosted by a certain absence; each new identity is, for a confusing time, a mystery or nonentity. The actor is there, present, but a full understanding of the character's identity is not there yet and takes a frustrating amount of lag time to arrive on the scene. Strangers, of course, can enter suddenly into the flow

The Citability of Baroque Gesture

of one's everyday life just as they can enter abruptly into the narrative flow of a novel, but only in exceptional cases. By contrast, sudden appearances and other "shock effects" are the stock-in-trade of theater. Thus, the theater's anxiogenic quality stems from its capacity to expose and magnify the temporal character of what is supposedly nontheatrical life.

In Stein's theater theory, there is a rhythm to temporal existence, one in which presence is promised but nonpresence is always haunting. The theater is defined by this phenomenological syncopation in opposition to everyday life, but it is also the rebus by which that syncopation's pervasiveness in everyday life is exposed. In these observations, Stein can be seen as a modernist precursor to the contemporary field of performance studies that has sought to develop a range of conceptual rubrics derived from theater and performance for the analysis of everyday life.[41] In the evocative terms of performance theorist Rebecca Schneider, herself drawing on Stein's vocabulary of syncopation, the theater is the mechanism by which the *theatricality of time itself* is touched. If time's partitioning in the theater is structured around no presence, then doubling, rehearsing, reenacting, and repetition (e.g., going again and again to the dramatis personae) must be acknowledged in everyday life as well.

Although Stein finds the syncopation of time in jazz performance, there is a baroque philosophy of time—and of history—implicit in her view of temporal recursion, one close to Nietzsche's concept of eternal return as a baroque da capo (*BGE* 56 [50-51]). As Benjamin articulated it in the Trauerspiel-book, the word "origin" designates a kind of movement in the historical process marked by "restoration" and "restitution," in which "singularity and repetition prove to be reciprocally determined" (*OGT* 24-25). For Stein, as for the authors of the baroque Trauerspiel in Benjamin's assessment, events playing out in time become susceptible to repetitive play and thus possess a peculiar theatrical quality. Just as Stein shares a baroque preoccupation with the cyclicality (and theatricality) of temporo-historical life, so too does her writing incorporate the possibility for difference or revision within repetition.[42] Her concept of repetition as insistence, articulated in the 1934 lecture "Portraits and Repetition," echoes Benjamin's concept of origin, in which singularity and repetition condition each other mutually. There she takes up the question of whether repetition itself can be said ever to actually take place, a question at least as old as Heraclitus. As Stein puts it, what we typically consider repetition must instead be understood as *insistence*, in which each new re/iteration differs slightly from the ones before and after.[43]

It is as a form of emphatic insistence that Stein's writing (re)turns upon itself so regularly, as in the much-parodied line from her 1913 poem *Sacred Emily*: "Rose is a rose is a rose is a rose." This sentence is hardly a dumb tautology. It is instead a statement of identity that calls into question what identity can be when it is constituted through repetition and self-difference.[44] Stein's kinship with the allegorists of Benjamin's Trauerspiel study can be gauged in the fact of self-difference as her basic point of departure. In Stein, as in the baroque Trauerspiel, the self-sufficient wholeness of things has always already been violated, and language and theater are the mechanisms for its attempted repair. When each new "rose" asserts itself insistently, it was Stein's belief, "in that line the rose is red for the first time in English poetry for a hundred years."[45] In revivifying the rose's lost redness, her insistent repetition functions as an almost Shklovskyan defamiliarization, the kind that rescues for stone its forgotten stoniness.[46] Deploying repetition as a bulwark against oblivion in this way, Stein's writing expresses an acute awareness of the ephemerality of entities and phenomena when they are subject to the ruinous effects of time. In response, her poetics sought the establishment of what she described as a "continuous present."[47] To be clear, this concept of presence should not be confused with a more traditionally theological concept of the "eternal present," a space outside time and extension in which transcendent divinity might reside. Rather, for Stein, it comes closer to the grammatical form of the present continuous tense or the present participle, which appears throughout *Four Saints*, as in the bizarre, non sequitur sentence fragment, "Saint Teresa advancing" (4S3A 448). In such cases, an action becomes an image, a gesture. A figure is frozen in the medial nowhere *between* two positions and two moments, unfolding as part of a continuous process.

This immanent *between* is where the continuous present is to be sought, not in the transcendent realm of sempiternity. For Stein, this domain appears full of meditative and intellectual power, of a sort that comes close to a form of esoteric wisdom.[48] Everything in *Four Saints* relates differentially to some other thing or set of things, even to its own "self." This can be noted in the play's declaration that "There is a difference between Barcelona and Avila./There is a difference between Barcelona" (4S3A 471). Everything in the opera's "world" mediates everything else and itself as well. Each particularity, no matter how infinitely small, is both separated from and linked to every other, hanging together as through a kind of pre-established harmony,

The Citability of Baroque Gesture

like threads in a textile. In this vibrant plenum, the continuous present takes place as a betweenness or liminality, a *suspension* of presence. In the fold of this suspension, the spectator can seek refuge from being *either* ahead of *or* behind the event, by being *both* ahead of *and* behind it at once.[49] What is made most vividly apparent through this operation is the flux of time itself.[50] As it turns out, continual presence—"staying on quite continuously," as one saint phrases it, using another present participle (*4S3A* 446)—entails a dynamic process of continual becoming, rebecoming, and intensification.

Theatricality is a privileged medium for effecting this paradoxical form of presence, and specifically the theatricality of the baroque stage, reconceived anew. The theater both registers, like a seismograph, the uncanny and theatrical syncopations of time, and offers Stein a means to ameliorate her anxiety. She gives reasons for why this is so in her essay "Plays." In terms that recall Benjamin's descriptions of the Trauerspiel form, she describes how her dramaturgy deliberately merges time into a natural landscape:

> I felt that if a play was exactly like a landscape then there would be no difficulty about the emotion of the person looking on at the play being behind or ahead of the play because the landscape does not have to make acquaintance. . . . The landscape has it [*sic*] formation and as after all a play has to have formation and be in relation one thing to the other thing and as the story is not the thing as any one is always telling something then the landscape not moving but being always in relation, the trees to the hills to the fields the trees to each other any piece of it to any sky and then any detail to any other detail. . . . And of that relation I wanted to make a play and I did, a great number of plays. . . . The only one that has been played is Four Saints. In Four Saints I made the Saints the landscape. All the saints that I made and I made a number of them because after all a great many pieces of things are in a landscape all these saints together made my landscape. These attendant saints were the landscape and it the play really is a landscape. A landscape does not move nothing really moves in a landscape but things are there, and I put into the landscape the things that were there.[51]

In Stein, as in baroque Trauerspiel (as in Wagner's *Parsifal*), time becomes space, passing into the setting. Unlike a portrait, a landscape is a multifocal immanence without any single central point. Likewise, as a landscape play, *Four Saints* is not organized around the central Aristotelian criterion of plot as an imitation of action. Instead, it uses the theater to present a plot in the spatio-geographic sense of the term: a plot of land. Taking place, as the opera does, in some saintly realm apart from normative conceptions of time, events do not progress in any causal manner within this plot. Nothing can be said to "happen" in *Four Saints* in the conventional sense of the word. As drama, it *takes place* in an entirely different way. In Stein's theater each element of the landscape forms a component of a larger allegorical vision. Each object of attention is "relatable" to every other object: "the trees to the hills to the fields the trees to each other any piece of it to any sky and then any detail to any other detail."[52] The overall landscape does not move, but the constellation of saints and other beings within it does continuously shift positions, just as a breeze through any seemingly static natural prospect might send tree limbs and leaves fluttering. Stein writes that she "wanted it to have the movement of nuns very busy and in continuous movement but placid as a landscape has to be" (*P* lii). Like the emblems of baroque allegory, Stein's landscape incorporates into itself an internal dialectic of stasis and movement. She underlines this point in her essay by remarking that the landscape of *Four Saints* "moves but it also stays" (*P* lii).

The possibility that Ashton's choreography might have given Stein the idea for this sense of stasis-in-movement makes clear that gestures must take their place as allegorical components of Stein's landscape.[53] Like a landscape, a gesture moves but also stays. It is, as Benjamin reminds us, the image of movement interrupted. In a gesture, the movement must compose itself and settle into an image, however fleetingly, before continuing. The various accounts by Van Vechten, Young, La Farge, and Harris of the premiere production serve as eyewitness testimony to the way it unfolded as a landscape of gestures in continual variation. Here, it is salient that a viewer like John La Farge detected the trace of the baroque inheritance not only in Stein's text but also in the production's obscure and ritualistic use of gesture. With the libretto moving flirtatiously between sense and nonsense, the spectator is left to concentrate even more on the stage as a field of gesticulating bodies, like La Farge's "spiritually illiterate person" observing the arcane rituals of a Catholic Mass. One's experience watching *Four Saints* is similar to the experience Stein's "Plays" recalls of a time in her youth when she witnessed Sarah Bernhardt play Racine's Phèdre in a touring production in San Francisco. She writes, "I knew a little french of course but really it did not matter, it was all so foreign and her voice being so varied and it all being so french I could rest in it untroubled. And I did. . . . The manners and customs of the French theatre created a thing in itself and it

The Citability of Baroque Gesture

existed in and for itself. . . . . It was for me a very simple direct and moving pleasure" (*P* xlii).

For Stein watching *Phèdre*, as for La Farge watching *Four Saints*, or for a "spiritually illiterate" person watching any religious ritual, the general incomprehensibility of language in performance functions as a powerful defamiliarization effect. Language and gestures together form a larger field of sensory stimulus. With *Four Saints* in performance, the spectator's attention is turned toward the action's performance components, its *liturgy*. These components appear as immanent densities unto themselves (just as Stein calls Bernhardt's French-language performance "a thing in itself") whose mediating status is irreducible. There is not a way to get interpretively *beyond* the performance as a constellation of foreign visual and auditory media, or to reach a tantalizing truth-content lingering somewhere "behind" it. The only way to feel at-home in an experience of this sort is by accepting the feeling of being not-at-home; the only escape from mediation, a further plunge into hypermediacy.[54] The performance's various signifiers all *suggest* a referent, all flirt with mimesis, but that referent has receded to a point of obscure inaccessibility. Mimesis thus gives way to metatheater and mime.

In short, with *Four Saints* in performance, Stein effectively created a hieroglyphic situation for the audience, a Trauerspiel in a different key. In her work, as in the allegorical theater of the baroque, the viewer is confronted with an interpretive enigma in which language, gesture, and every other material element of performance are rendered opaque, thus requiring the spectator's contemplation. (Not coincidentally, this dependence on a time-bound spectator was a large part of Diderot's disdain for both allegory and "theatricality," as Michael Fried's work reminds us.[55]) But where Benjamin's baroque spectator observes the melancholic, allegorical gestures of Trauerspiel with a mix of mournfulness and "satisfaction," Stein's spectator is supposed to respond to this hermeneutic situation with what both she and La Farge describe as "pleasure." As we shall see, the vision of baroque style Stein glimpsed in *Four Saints* is one that transmutes mournfulness, miraculously, into gaiety.[56]

Functional Baroque Forms in Performance

In *Four Saints in Three Acts*, the time of All Saints' Day merges with the space of the stage.[57] While Stein's title promises four saints, the opera's spectator may be treated instead to forty-four (the number given in Thomson's score), though the total number is left indeterminate. Stein's prologue offers a litany of twenty-one fancifully named saints, apparently divided up by gender:

Saint Teresa	Saint Ignatius
Saint Martyr	Saint Paul
Saint Settlement	Saint William
Saint Thomasine	Saint Gilbert
Saint Electra	Saint Settle
Saint Wilhelmina	Saint Arthur
Saint Evelyn	Saint Selmer
Saint Pilar	Saint Paul Seize
Saint Hillaire	Saint Cardinal
Saint Bernadine	Saint Plan
	Saint Giuseppe (4S3A 444)

Others are added to this list throughout the subsequent scenes and acts, forming a veritable panorama. Throughout, the question of how many saints appear within the piece even becomes a point of self-reflexive fun— "How many saints are there in it. . . . There are very many saints in it. . . . There are as many saints as there are in it. . . . There are as many saints as there are saints in it." (4S3A 458)—while the total sum of saints is constantly deferred in favor of the pleasure of counting endlessly without ever reaching a goal.[58] Their proliferation over the course of the piece forms a poetic analogue to the baroque concept and practice of *horror vacui*.[59] The reader's ability to enumerate them baffles against passages that suggest an unstable or painterly relation between the discrete figures conjured by the text. "Can two saints be one" (4S3A 448) the text asks, and elsewhere, one saint seems to become two—as in "How many are there halving" (449) and "Saint Teresa with Saint Teresa. . . . Saint Teresa and Saint Teresa" (457-58)—or even three —"Saint Teresa and Saint Teresa and Saint Teresa" (448). Are there three Saints Teresa here, or one in a process of insistent self-re-presentation and intensification? In Thomson's musical setting, there are two Saints Teresa, in constant dialogue and harmony with each other. The saints merge with one another, or multiply themselves, or divide as if by mitosis in ways that are unstageable in traditional dramatic terms.[60]

The text furthermore gives no clear indications as to who sings or speaks what lines, or how many actors would be needed in total. At times the libretto uses the traditional speech prefixes that are conventional to printed

The Citability of Baroque Gesture

dramatic literature in a way that seems to indicate that a certain line of text is to be uttered by a certain "character," as, for example, when a line appears that reads "Saint Teresa. Nobody visits more than they do visits them" (*4S3A* 446). This could be a line designated for Saint Teresa to speak, or it could be a line to be spoken by someone else to Saint Teresa, or it could be something else altogether: no clear indications are given. The matter is complicated by the text's provocative lack of differentiation between stage directions and lines to be spoken; for instance, when the phrase "Saint Teresa. Leave later gaily the troubadour plays his guitar" (*4S3A* 446) appears on the page without any clue as to whether these words are meant to indicate an utterance to be spoken or an onstage event to be enacted. Frequently, these stage directions take on an expressly metatheatrical character, as in "This is a scene where this is seen" (*4S3A* 453). For his part, Thomson elected to set the majority of the written lines as melodic texts to be sung, and so anything that could be construed as a stage direction is given over to explicit vocalization when the opera is performed, including the indications for each new act and scene.

As with the opera's proliferating saints, a similar principle animates the number of acts. The play's title promises *Four Saints in Three Acts*, a phrase that itself suggests an irregular, asymmetrical, brocaded structure—every bit as off-center as the nonspheroid baroque pearl. This promise turns out to be a ruse as well. As the play proceeds, the number of acts varies continually along with the constantly shifting quantity of saints, sometimes condensing —as in "Could Four Acts be Three. / Saint Teresa. Could Four Acts be three. / Saint Teresa Saint Teresa Saint Teresa Could Four Acts be three Saint Teresa" (*4S3A* 462)—and at other times spiraling outward and expanding, as in "Could Four Acts be when four acts could be ten Saint Teresa. Saint Teresa Saint Teresa Four Acts could be four acts could be when when four acts could be ten" (462). Linear chronology no longer serves to connect one scene straightforwardly to the next: no sooner is a "Scene II" declared than the poem sings back rhymingly, "Would it do if there was a Scene II" (*4S3A* 455).

Furthermore, the point where each new act begins and ends follows no numerically progressive path. The libretto does not unfold in an initial first act followed by a subsequent second, third, and fourth, in that order. Rather, after a few pages of a prologue, the libretto declares "Act I," only to proceed, some ten or so lines after, to the words "Repeat First Act" and, a page or so later, to the words "Enact end of an act." Some pages later, the beginning of

"Act Two" is announced, and after just a few more lines, the text declares once again "Act One," and then, another page or so later, "Act Two" once again. Along the way, scenes are declared in a way that similarly abolishes any notion of linear or chronological progress, in this order: "Scene Two" (4S3A 448), "Scene III" (448), "Scene III" again (449), "Scene IV" (450), "Scene II" again (452), "Scene III" again (450), "Scene IV" again (452), and so forth. At times, two scenes occur, as it were, simultaneously, as when an indication is given (on 455) for "Scene III and Scene IV" to take place. As if in exasperation at all this numerical play, a voice in the text asks somewhat impatiently, "How much of it is finished" (4S3A 461) and "How many acts are there in it" (478). Although Thomson and Grosser divided the textual material into large chunks that could be considered "acts" for the simple purpose of partitioning the music and evening into more manageable bits, the playfulness and repetition of Stein's text belie this decision making.[61]

Time does not *progress* in the world of *Four Saints*, but neither is it perfectly immobile. The saints are idle, leisurely, as if at an afternoon garden party with croquet mallets, but they are not entirely static. Instead they are caught *between* stasis and flux. They are both fixed and in motion. This inbetweenness, this (both-and) doubleness, lends them an iridescent quality. Stein highlights the saints' liminal or processual nature with lines that allude frequently to the characters caught somewhere between two states, as in the opera's central and emblematic opening image of "Saint Teresa half in and half out of doors" (4S3A 445), "Saint Teresa very nearly half inside and half outside outside the house and not surrounded" (445–46). For some readers, these moments are interpretable as indicating a scene in which an onstage actor representing the historical Theresa of Avila is visible entering her convent for the first time as a young woman.[62] What is more important is the literal liminality given here, the image of the saint caught in a doorframe, between two spaces, an image echoed in other freeze-frame images-in-motion throughout the text, as in the enigmatic fragments of text "Saint Teresa about to be" (4S3A 446), "Saint Teresa in moving" (447), "Saint Teresa has begun to be in act one" (453), and "Saint Teresa in a cart drawn by oxen moving around" (454).

At other times, the text catches its figures in the fold between two incommensurable gestures or positions, as in a long passage near the opera's beginning that depicts Teresa somewhere between sitting and standing and surrounded and not surrounded at various sequential instances through a kind of constant process of montage. Shortly after the libretto's first dec-

The Citability of Baroque Gesture

laration of "Act I," a kind of cine-seizure effect occurs as Saint Teresa is described, in lines spanning just over two pages, as "Saint Teresa seated. . . . Saint Teresa seated. . . . Saint Teresa seated and not surrounded.. . . Saint Teresa not seated. . . . Saint Teresa not seated at once. . . . Saint Teresa at once seated. . . . Saint Teresa seated and not surrounded."[63] Here the effect is of an *unsettling*—a continuous folding and unfolding, as when a piece of cloth at rest is ruffled violently, or as in Bernini's ecstatic depiction of the saint. (In fact, "Saint Teresa seated and not surrounded might be very well inclined to be settled" *4S3A* 447.) Like allegorical emblems and the baroque infinitesimal method of Leibniz's calculus, these images incorporate movement into the spatial frame of single instant—an instant whose stasis is punctuated with a series of constant repetitions and revisions. As with the boundaries between saints and acts, the boundaries between one temporal moment and another seem to blur together in this allegorical treatment, like a sequence of slowly metamorphosing photographs in a flipbook or like frames in a reel of film. Each image appears distinct and separate from—while also seeming to merge into—the next.[64] Self-dividing, and riven by an internal tension between frozenness and fluidity, Stein's text formally translates into poetic terms the experience of the tableau vivant that Benjamin describes as a hallmark of allegory in baroque theatrical performance.

Stein's "presence" as the text's author also makes itself felt in the libretto of *Four Saints*, and she too is subject to this same manner of allegorical treatment and this form of self-division. Her vocal being in the text not single, but contrapuntal. Rather than taking the form of an internal monologue, large parts of the text unfold as an internal conversation for numerous debating voices, transpiring in multivocal converse with one another, as the process of writing the text is inscribed into the written text itself.[65] This is particularly true of the opera's prologue, whose discourse suggests the author focusing a hermetic consciousness upon the task at hand, to "prepare for saints," that is, to prepare to write the opera itself. The opera has already begun, and its beginning is a rumination on how to begin. Its beginning is already behind itself. Ulla Dydo has effectively described this prologue as a meditative act, and as reflecting an author's struggle to grasp an image that could effectively ground an opening scene. The libretto is thus the written record of a form of spiritual exercise, based on the experience of an artistic vision. Just as the opera includes a Saint Plan and a Saint Settlement, much of the action of *Four Saints* revolves around the author's process of planning the text and settling upon textual decisions. "Imagine four benches separately," a poetic voice or set of poetic voices intones: "One in the sun./Two in the sun./Three in the sun./One not in the sun./ Not one not in the sun./Not one./Four benches used four benches used separately./Four benches used separately" (4S3A 441). Each possibility is considered in its turn. In imagination and in conversation with herself, the author is attempting "to mount it up"—that is, she is laboring toward a mental staging of sorts. Should benches appear? If so, how many? And how many illuminated? There seems not to be an internal consensus on the poet's part. Then, after a brief digression of two lines, the question of how many benches returns briefly, only to be forcibly set aside in an abrupt self-interruption: "Four benches with leave it" (4S3A 441). The matter has been *settled*, however provisionally: four benches, no more, no fewer. On to the next passage, on to the next imagistic component.

The poetic vision approaches like a wonder, as another passage suggests —"It is very close close and closed"—and Stein's self-divided text proposes a next plan: "Begin suddenly not with sisters" (4S3A 441). "Imagine imagine it imagine it in it," (443) the libretto's voices command themselves and, thereby, the audience. Much of *Four Saints* unfolds in this way, not a single poetic speaker but a multitude in polyphonic responsiveness with itself.[66] The overall effect is of a radical defamiliarization of the conventions of language use through an emphatic break with traditional forms of syntax and punctuation. In this way, *Four Saints'* libretto continually and playfully exposes the work of writing itself, thereby exhibiting and reveling in writing's temporal nature as a processual act. *Four Saints* could, on one hand, be considered a form of what Della Pollack has described as *performative writing* or an early instance of postmodern écriture.[67] But it is more accurately a text that exposes and theatrically stages the performative processes of all writing.[68] Like the two Saints Teresa of Thomson's musical setting, Stein's plural poetic voice is always in conversation with itself. For Stein, as for the two Saints Teresa, identity is always already "dividual" and nonunitary. In the betweenness of the continuous present, the author of *Four Saints* is always in a semifixed, semifluid state of continual becoming (like "St. Teresa about to be," or "Saint Teresa having not commenced" [4S3A 447]), an emblem divided imminently within herself. In *Four Saints*, identity is not a matter of something being indivisibly itself. Rather, it is a function of difference and repetition.

The Citability of Baroque Gesture

But it is the markedly imagistic character of *Four Saints*' text that suggests its most productive affinities with baroque theatrical allegory. In order to make any sense of the work at all, one must approach Stein's libretto the way Benjamin's baroque allegorist approaches his own emblematic puzzle pieces, as a kind of bricoleur. "Through the disorderly fund which his knowledge places at his disposal, the allegorist rummages here and there for a particular piece, holds it next to some other piece, and tests to see if they fit together—that meaning with this image or this image with that meaning. The result can never be known beforehand, for there is no natural mediation between the two" (*AP* J80,2; J80a,1). The same is true of Stein's plays, whose fragmentary images and meanings suggest no necessary connections but compel the creative work of allegoresis on the part of a reader or spectator or director. "What is the difference between a picture and pictured," the libretto asks quizzically, then moments later spills forth into a veritable cascade of paratactic images: "One a window. / Two a shutter. / Three a palace. / Four a widow. / Five an adopted son. / Six a parlor. / Seven a shawl. / Eight an arbor. / Nine a seat. / Ten a retirement" (*4S3A* 452). The meanings of this constellation are left open to enigmatic reflection. The same holds for the nails that appear in the text's central section ("How many nails are there in it. / Hard shoe nails and silver nails and silver does not sound valuable," *4S3A* 455.) These might be the nails of Christ's crucifixion, imagined as in one of Ignatius's meditative exercises, or else the building implements of a heavenly mansion, as Grosser's scenario indicates. The text authorizes neither of these readings singly or fully. Elsewhere, these thingly images themselves wax almost surreal, as when "[t]he envelopes are on all the fruit of the fruit trees" (*4S3A* 479).

The sheer number of these visual devices almost cries out for lush onstage spectacle, blurring boundaries between performance, poetry, and the visual arts, but (as with Mallarmé's concrete poetry) the work's most productive meanings occur in the space *between* images and words.[69] In the description of Teresa being photographed and changed into a nun, for example, the poetic text aspires via ekphrasis to the condition of image. The theater suggests itself as a medium that can overcome the discontinuity between mediums by holding out the allure of a plentiful, simultaneous presence. As Stein's theoretical writings suggest, however, this allure of simultaneity is always a ruse. In the theater, things heard are constantly replacing things seen and things seen replacing things heard, over and over again in sequence, with only rare moments in which both seem to go on together (*P* xxxiv). As in all allegorical theater, the relationship between verbal text and onstage spectacle that accompanies it remains apparently arbitrary to the spectator, more emblematic than illustrative.

It is therefore not the case, as Hans-Thies Lehmann has claimed, that Stein evinces an early form of a *postdramatic theater* unprecedented prior to the twentieth century.[70] Certainly, it is true that the dramatic text of *Four Saints* cannot authoritatively govern its realization in performance. But it is the allegorical dimension of *Four Saints*' libretto, which has origins in the early modern period and which combines images and texts with what David Harris calls an "almost aleatory manner," that governs this open relationship between text and enactment.[71] Long before the emergence of what Lehmann calls postdramatic theater in the twentieth century, the baroque allegorical stage already functioned in this promiscuously open manner.[72] In its baroque setting, Stein's libretto both makes clear and embodies this historical precedence. Rather than being anti-theatrical closet dramas in any traditional sense of the term, Stein's work vigorously redefines theatricality altogether, reorienting it along the horizon of baroque allegory. With a certain queer or sadistic glee, these allegories defy any straightforward translation into stage images.[73]

Regardless of how the text is meant to be materialized through performance into stage imagery, the question of vision remains crucial within *Four Saints*' libretto. It is through the opera's frequent returns to the subject of visionary experience that Stein comes into closest contact with her saintly and baroque protagonists. As Ulla Dydo describes it, the opera *Four Saints* seeks continually a kind of visionary experience in and through its fixation on landscape: "Did Stein believe in visions? The details [of the landscape] are not sacred but entirely commonplace. Visions are possible for those who are willing to look at the ordinary. To those who are able to see, an unexceptional, still, bare landscape offers the possibility of vision that is the essence of Stein's meditation."[74] Thomson and Grosser actualized this aspect of Stein's writing within the text, creating not only a series of so-called "tableaux" but a number of scenic moments quite clearly put forward as sacred visions. For the passage in which the text describes something like the radiance of a spring afternoon with trees in full flower—"Pear trees cherry blossoms pink blossoms and late apples and surrounded by Spain and lain," asserting that "[t]here can be no peace on earth with calm with

The Citability of Baroque Gesture

173

calm" (4S3A 451)—Thomson and Grosser envisioned a scene in which one of the Saints Teresa would appear "in ecstasy, seated, with angel hovering," as though in homage to the Bernini sculpture of Teresa's famous vision seen in that evening's theatrical program.

Near the end of the opera, Thomson created an aria for Saint Ignatius and gave it the title "St. Ignatius predicts the Last Judgment." This musical scene has none of the terror-stricken pathos of El Greco's treatment of Saint John envisioning the opening of the fifth seal of the apocalypse. Rather it jubilates and is performed almost as a musical round or baroque voluntary. A triumphal trumpet fanfare resounds the singer's melody back to him as both rejoice together in language's sonic, playful, echoic nature: "Once in a while and where and where around is a sound and around is a sound and around is a sound and around. Around is a sound around is a sound around is a sound and around" (4S3A 475). This vision of the Last Judgment leads into a remarkable linguistic enactment of Stein's continuous present, endlessly punctuating, reiterating, and deferring itself: "Around differing from anointed now. Now differing from anointed now. Now differing differing. Now differing from anointed now" (4S3A 475). This is an extraordinary manifestation of the continuous present as the end of (progressive) time. Although Saint Ignatius's aria leans heavily on the sonic playfulness of *Spiel*, Stein elsewhere introduces a more mournful, apocalyptic vision. In a striking and eerie exchange, the opera sets two saints in idle chitchat. The first: "If it were possible to kill five thousand chinamen by pressing a button would it be done." The second: "Saint Teresa not interested." Here, as in Herbert Ihering's commentary on Brecht's *Drums in the Night* and the historical traumas of the Thirty Years' War, an apocalyptic event is encountered as an everyday inconvenience, a banal obviousness. With the bombardments of World War I still a recent memory, the instantaneous slaughter of thousands becomes a subject for daily conversation that either elicits one's interest or does not. It is the opera's most strikingly gestic moment. For all the whimsy of this garden landscape, *Four Saints'* world is still haunted by catastrophe.

Even if all causes for mourning are ineradicable from *Four Saints'* sundrenched landscape, Stein still emphasizes gaiety. This emphasis is evident in what is undoubtedly the most famous of the opera's several visionary moments, the famous "Pigeons on the grass alas" passage that Thomson set as an aria for Saint Ignatius. The composer and scenarist conceived of this passage, under Stein's advisement, as a vision of the Holy Ghost.[75] Together with a company of saints, Ignatius intones:

> Pigeons on the grass alas.
>
> Pigeons on the grass alas.
>
> Short longer grass short longer longer shorter yellow grass Pigeons large pigeons on the shorter longer yellow grass alas pigeons on the grass.
>
> If they were not pigeons what were they.
>
> If they were not pigeons on the grass alas what were they. He had heard of a third and he asked about it it was a magpie in the sky. If a magpie in the sky on the sky can not cry if the pigeon on the grass alas can alas and to pass the pigeon on the grass alas and the magpie in the sky on the sky and to try and to try alas on the grass alas the pigeon on the grass the pigeon on the grass and alas. (453A 468)

As Stein explained in an interview, this moment had its genesis during one of her walks in the gardens of the Luxembourg Palace in Paris: "It was the end of summer the grass was yellow. I was sorry that it was the end of summer and I saw the big fat pigeons in the yellow grass and I said to myself, pigeons on the yellow grass, alas, and I kept on writing pigeons on the grass, alas . . . until I had emptied myself of the emotion."[76] The words "Pigeons on the grass alas" serve Stein as a mantra of sorts, a means to meditative nonattachment that can elicit spiritual joy. They give rise to an experience of semantic satiation, that defamiliarizing moment when repeating a word or a phrase effectively drains it of its meaning, laying bare language's conventionality and sensuous materiality. Here, in contrast to Stein's "Rose is a rose is a rose," insistent repetition serves not to intensify an image or the poetic feeling it embodies, but to heighten the affect of play and redeem the word from its melancholic nonidentity with its referent. "Pigeons on the grass alas pigeons on the grass alas pigeons on the grass alas!" All of a sudden, mourning ("alas") miraculously becomes the pleasure of a rhyme—round sound answering round sound.

It is significant that this redemptive moment—in which mourning is canceled and then sublated into elation—should occur at the moment of Stein's vision of the Holy Ghost. For, if the pigeons on the grass suggest themselves as a ludicrous allegory of baroque mournfulness, they are juxtaposed with the "magpie in the sky on the sky," which Stein explained as follows:

> Magpies are in the landscape that is they are in the sky of a landscape, they are black and white. . . . When they are in the sky they do something that I have never

seen any other bird do they hold themselves up and down and look flat against the sky. A very famous French inventor of things that have to do with stabilization in aviation told me that what I told him magpies did could not be done by any bird but anyway whether the magpies at Avila do do it or do not at least they look as if they do do it. They look exactly like the birds in the Annunciation pictures the bird which is the Holy Ghost and rests flat against the side sky very high.[77]

For Stein, all of nature puts itself forward as a baroque text to be read allegorically.[78] The magpie in/on the sky asserts itself as one example of this kind of reading: its flatness is like that of an image on a canvas or on a page. With it, Stein "reads the signs," translating imaginatively between signs and referents, transcendent and material beings. Although the Pentecostal dove suspended flat against the backdrop of the sky is a familiar icon within the Christian tradition for a vision of the Holy Spirit, what is pictured in such a vision is not a sign but the Holy Spirit itself. The flattened bird—whether dove or magpie—is thus less an allegorical emblem than a remembered theological symbol, a prelapsarian *logos* in which word and thing attain a sacred, reparative unity. Stein is unsure whether the magpies in physical reality are actually capable of pausing midflight to rest flat in a moment of midair standstill, but it is enough that they *look as if they do do it*. In this moment, physical reality has become art, just as in Stein's dramaturgy ecological land becomes artistic landscape.

Stein and Thomson claimed artists to be the modern-day correlative to saints, a fact that suggests a shared secular orientation. Still, all these elements of *Four Saints* point to a more complicated perspective, on Stein's part, toward the sacred as such. The garden setting of *Four Saints* is both a reminder of the *hortus conclusus* of baroque poetry and an Edenic "enclosure," where language can be resanctified in a new way.[79] It is also a "garden inside and outside of the wall" a space both closed and open to its outside; that is to say, not self-contained or self-identical, but both enclosed and porous simultaneously. In this paradisiacal space, one finds no Father divinity present.[80] The space amounts instead to a kind of queer heterotopia. It flows and teems with myriad creatures—male, female, of seeming nonbinary gender, and dazzling in their variety (Saint Answers, Saint Two, and Saint Ten). Presiding over this numinous scene is a mysterious winged animal-spirit that manifests the spiritual within nature itself. The physical world is depicted in *Four Saints* not as something fallen and baneful but as extraordinary and charged with significance. At just the moment when Stein's discourse in *Four Saints* nearly succumbs to mournfulness over the transitory nature of the world, the magpie spirit-animal appears in Ignatius's song and in Stein's imagination. One might say it *flashes up* momentarily, and like a deus ex machina, to illuminate another possibility. Perhaps the apparently broken, allegorical relationship between language and world was an illusion all along, obscuring the reality of a more fully integrated and harmonious immanence of things.

Music has a role to play, too, in this peculiar spirituality. Whereas Nietzsche's writings on Wagner express extreme worry over the theological and political regressiveness of subordinating music to dramatic text and theatrical gesture, in *Four Saints* these elements are all granted an almost unprecedented degree of autonomy from one another.[81] For Stein's dissonant syntax, Thomson produced consonant, tuneful harmonies, as Daniel Albright has observed, drawing abundantly on popular musical forms: glees, marches, fairground waltzes, and hymns.[82] Added to these were those elements of recitative that Thomson borrowed from baroque opera, with an important difference. Whereas baroque monody, the *stile rapprasentativo*, developed to ensure that sung words would be intelligible over their musical underscore (often as a way to appeal to the audience's emotions, as Nietzsche observed), Thomson strove for melodic clarity so that Stein's challenging text could be heard as a separate, autonomous element of the larger work. With *Four Saints*, the music does not serve to heighten the emotional intensity of any given plot or action, but rather seeks only to make the text clear so its peculiar formal dynamics can be perceived and contemplated. As Thomson observed, "'Gertrude was wonderful to set to music because there was no temptation to illustrate the words. . . . For the most part you didn't know what it meant anyway . . . you had to set it for the way the grammar went and for the clarity of the words."[83]

As independent as the score and libretto are in *Four Saints*, the opera is hardly an abstract étude that forecloses any emotional responsiveness. Moments of extraordinary sensuousness and emotion abound, even if they offer no straightforward path to a single, authoritative interpretation. The greatest of these comes in the third act of Thomson's score, during Ashton's saintly procession tableau. In this climactic moment, the saints seem to cross the stage while remaining immobile, carrying a draped baldacchino over their heads in the manner of a baroque *trionfo*. Meanwhile, the text intones a Dies Irae-like dirge whose words are based on continual combina-

Production photograph from *Four Saints in Three Acts*' premiere, 1934. Florine and Ettie Stettheimer Papers. American Literature Collection, Beinecke Rare Book and Manuscript Library, Yale University. Photo by White Studio © The New York Public Library.

tions and recombinations of the words "led," "let," "wet," and most significant, "wed" and "dead."[84] Equal parts wedding and funeral procession, the essential comedic and tragic finales conflated into a single moment, the text and music alternate between passages of solemnity and frivolity. Suddenly a shift occurs, and singers and orchestra join together at the high point of the score, a lush maestoso passage that, onstage, communicated something of "the ecstasy of ritual," in Ashton's words.[85] It is a moment full of strain and sincerity, bliss and longing, soaring to a powerful crescendo like a great spiritual, and its performance by Black singers likely reinforced this association for its first audiences. Although they may seem nonsensical, the words of the libretto that Thomson chose for this musical passage are marked by the traces of a certain messianic longing: "With be there all their all their time there be there vine there be vine time there be there time there all their time there" (4S3A 476). The climax interweaves Stein's imagery of vines—evoking the Christian symbol of the redemptive wine and blood—with the language of a utopian futurity—somewhere "there" but also "all their time."[86] For a moment, as Stein might say, "it all feels abreast," everything working together as simultaneously as possible. It is a moment of splendid theatrical excitement, and a culmination into completeness.

But, although the audience might feel *something* splendid at this moment, the text holds open what that splendid something might be. No single interpretation is possible; instead the opera proposes only multiple, contradictory meanings. (The libretto is in contradiction with itself, for one example, and Stein's "intentions" were at times in contradiction with Thomson's, for another.[87]) Stein's work does not proselytize or propagandize on any matters whatsoever, but instead creates a space for enjoyment and for critical contemplation.[88] In its conclusion, her opera effects a defamiliarization of language and gesture that unfolds as a kind of baroque wonder. It is in this sublime moment and in this sense of the wonder-full that *Four Saints* most propitiously occasions what Bonnie Marranca has described as "the vernacular marvelous."[89]

Last Act./Which is a fact?

Just as *Four Saints* begins repeatedly once it has begun, the opera ends just as ambiguously—with a fourth act in spite of its title's promised three. In Thomson's score, this fourth act functions almost as an encore, a short coda to end the piece and upset the audience's assumption that it had already finished. In the opera's final moments, the saints line up laterally and exclaim: "Last act./Which is a fact" (4S3A 480). Against the Aristotelian dogma that dictates dramas must have clear beginnings, middles, and ends, this blunt announcement of the last act's factual status is enough on its own to call into question just how final the moment actually is. How and when can an opera end when it is so thoroughly preoccupied with repetition?

Sure enough, *Four Saints* has gone on to have a storied afterlife. Stein continued her engagements with baroque opera dramaturgy in her 1938 libretto, *Doctor Faustus Lights the Lights*, based loosely on Marlowe's English Trauerspiel (ca. 1592).[90] *Four Saints* would also go on to draw the admiration of John Cage and many of his followers in the post–World War II American avant-garde, inspiring restagings by Robert Wilson and Mark Morris, each in his own signature way. Stein's work continues to be cited regularly by

The Citability of Baroque Gesture 179

artists and critics alike as being germinal to the development of a uniquely American vanguardism in late-twentieth-century ("postmodern") theater.[91] That is, *Four Saints* allows us to think of Stein as an artist not only participating in the ongoing tradition of the baroque in her own right but also transmitting that tradition to her postwar inheritors.

Without needing to search quite so far afield from the opera's premiere, we can note that it was likely in his dialogues with Stein that Thornton Wilder developed his own admiration for baroque style. In November 1934, just months after *Four Saints'* premiere, Stein had the opportunity to meet the young, Pulitzer Prize-winning novelist and to begin a lifelong friendship. Although Wilder likely missed seeing *Four Saints* in performance, Stein sent him an inscribed copy as a Christmas gift in 1934. The letters that ensued from this initial gift make clear their shared love of baroque art and culture at that time. He was then preparing to stage a production of Handel's 1738 opera *Xerxes* at the University of Chicago in February 1935 to honor the composer's two hundredth birthday. In the ensuing years, he would mention to Stein the baroque art and architecture he encountered during his travels, often in a worshipful key. In his letter from Salzburg dated 28 April 1937, for instance, he writes: "Pleasure comes in all shapes and sizes and it's now what I live for. For instance: there are two polychrome baroque archangels on the altar of the Peterskirche in poses of flight and ecstasy that no human body could ever assume, and as far as I'm concerned they're my definition of ART."[92]

In the concluding sentences of Wilder's handwritten essay "The Barock," the author takes up the question, "What is the subject-matter of masterpieces?" This phrasing echoes the title of Stein's 1935 essay, "What Are Master-pieces and Why Are There So Few of Them?" suggesting yet another crosscurrent between the two writers. As Wilder asserts: "[T]he subject-matter of masterpieces is the Action of the Poet's Mind. . . . The hero of every work of art is the mind of its poet: it is that mind we watch."[93] Although Stein is not named in the "Barock" essay, these sentences describe her approach to composition precisely. Even more to the point, Wilder's concept of the baroque as "the art of seeing the supernatural appearing continuously in the daily life" links him ever more directly to Stein's dramaturgy. For Wilder and Stein alike, the baroque involves a way of seeing "the ordinary" as itself already extraordinary. *Four Saints* is nearest to Wilder's idea of baroque in that it allows the extraordinary attributes of a landscape or any other, seemingly unexceptional vision to come forward. Like any good

180   Baroque Modernity

miracle play or baroque apotheosis, *Four Saints* suspends the representational norms of realism, suggesting that neither saints' lives nor queer lives can be accommodated into realism's dramaturgical conventions.[94]

Doing so, the opera exposes the ways the "exceptional" or the "miraculous" resides *within* the space of the seemingly "normal" and normative. Just as Brecht presented his audience with the ordinary conditions of life in such a way that allowed them to be seen with astonishment and critical questioning, Stein's work for the theater pursues a similar goal: both approaches conjoin baroque wonder with modernist defamiliarization. Like Brecht, Stein's capacity for defamiliarization involves a political potential, one that performance theorist Elin Diamond has productively described (by way of both Brecht and Derrida's deconstruction) as a prototype for a "gestic feminist criticism."[95] For Diamond, Stein's writing puts itself forward as the kind of critical praxis that can pleasurably mark sites of indeterminacy within texts in order to contest heterosexual patriarchal hegemony.[96] This political potential can be extended to Stein's ecological consciousness as well. When Stein glimpses the world of physical nature, she recognizes it as being always already supernatural, and this recognition is consequential not only for eco-poetics but for political environmentalism as well.

I wish to close by returning briefly to Stein's meanings for queer and racial politics. It is not only that Stein herself identified as Jewish and lesbian, though these identifications are not inconsequential for her own relationship to the violence of heteropatriarchy and white nationalism in her own time.[97] *Four Saints* was also possible in part due to the large cohort of queer men who attached themselves to her work, including Thomson, Grosser, Austin, and Ashton, who collaborated to produce *Four Saints'* Hartford premiere.[98] This fact suggests that a common taste or queer sensibility played some role in this group's shared affection for baroque style in the arts. By the 1960s, a new critical vocabulary was coming into being. Whereas Thomson had once felt drawn to Stettheimer's paintings because they seemed suitable to an opera on baroque themes, by the second half of the twentieth century he was able to speak of them as "high camp." As the New York intellectual Susan Sontag would have it, it is the *camp* way of seeing things that glimpses the extraordinary within the ordinary, a way of seeing cultivated largely by an elite, urban, queer vanguard.[99] The gay novelist Christopher Isherwood would write in *The World in the Evening* (1954), "Low Camp' is to be distinguished from "High Camp" in that the former pertains to "a swishy little boy with peroxided hair, dressed in a picture hat and a feather

The Citability of Baroque Gesture

181

boa, pretending to be Marlene Dietrich," while the latter "is the whole emotional basis for the ballet, for example, and of course of baroque art."[100] By the 1970s, an even clearer relationship between same-sex desire and baroque style was already evident in the writings of the gay Cuban novelist Severo Sarduy and in Sontag's ability to speak blithely about a category of "homosexual baroque."[101] As *Four Saints* was the brainchild of a host of gay modernists, it was well ahead of its time in anticipating this relationship.[102]

Something similar is surely true for artistic work that takes place at the conjunction of "Black and baroque," as the premiere of *Four Saints in Three Acts* undoubtedly did, with its entirely African American cast in drag as a cabal of European mystics. Although *Four Saints'* score and libretto were by Thomson and Stein, the work's enactment on Broadway by an all-Black group of performers involved a radicalism all its own. Even more than *Porgy and Bess's* premiere would do some months later, the Broadway production of *Four Saints* would reveal to its audience a situation in which the rituals of performance could expose race as a fictional construction.[103] Still to this day, the lived experience of deviating from the racial, sexual, or religious norms of the time makes possible an outsider status that carries with it a critical potential. As with baroque ways of seeing, this potential begins with the capacity for regarding the ordinary and everyday from a distance and perceiving the trace of the extraordinary within it. (*Queerness* as such reminds us that, as with allegory, this defamiliarization takes place at the level of a nonidentity between materiality and meaning, in which bodies and the set of meanings culturally assigned to them have no necessary relationship.) From this vantage, the kind of baroque theatricality one sees on display in *Four Saints* functions less as the propagandistic style of Church, State, or Capital than as a form of deconstruction that exposes the highly extraordinary processes by which the ordinary itself comes to be established as such. Stein's baroque serves not to sediment ideology but to theatrically expose and call it into question. This deconstructive baroque is already at work in Nietzsche, Mallarmé, and Benjamin's writings, and with Stein's *Four Saints in Three Acts*, it moves into a new and ever gayer direction.

Epilogue

Glancing Back, Reaching Forward

> The present of art is always in the past and in the future. Its presence is always in two places at once.
>
> —Jacques Rancière, "Painting in the Text"

In the preceding pages, I present a fourfold allegory of modernism as it unfolded in the sixty years surrounding the last century's turn. More chronological time now separates our present moment from Gertrude Stein than separated her from Friedrich Nietzsche, but the maelstrom of modernity continues to roar. The petrified unrest of market fluctuation has reached ever new and unprecedented levels. In environmental terms, the storm blowing from paradise has been upgraded to proportions previously unimaginable, with discussions of our current "climate emergency" and impending "climate collapse" coming to the fore as a lived reality of our time. The looming potential for disaster gives new credence to Benjamin's sense of eschatological terror in the time of the Reformation, in which one "holds fast to the world because he feels himself being driven along with it toward a cataract" (*OGT* 50). Today, as in the heyday of the Jesuit theaters and of Bernini, propaganda and spectacle are still deployed as means to advance the interests of the powerful, and today the expectation of apocalypse only draws closer. It is not surprising, then, that over the past sixty years, the persistence of baroque conventions has not ceased to animate artists working at the forefront of their fields. With each new generation, this inheritance must be taken up and posed again as a question in the search for ever-original solutions. I do not expect this quest to end in the near future. "The return of the baroque" was never really a return at all, not the reappearance of something lost that has since resurfaced, but an insistent reemphasis occurring within a continuum of human existence that was never fully in-

Epilogue

terrupted to begin with. We find ourselves within the deep time scales of geological time, as Stephen Jay Gould once explained it: "Consider the Earth's history as the old measure of the English yard, the distance from the King's nose to the tip of his outstretched hand. One stroke of a nail file on his middle finger erases human history."[1] What we call "modernity" measures only a few nanometers' length on this filed fingernail: it unfolds within the actuality of the baroque as a (manicurial) fact of life.

With this sense of an ending in mind, I offer a final set of emblems for the reader's contemplation. In the space of this epilogue, I can compose only a brief sketch, but will configure it around several crucial developments of the 1960s and '70s, a period in which the various movements of early-twentieth-century modernism culminated and decisively changed in form. During that decade, the subject of baroque became compelling once again to a new generation of artists and intellectuals, at a time when the future not only of modernism but of modernity writ large was being hotly debated. Popular studies of early modern visual art and music appeared in print, and the emerging field of theater studies saw its own groundbreaking scholarly inquiry into the subject with Margarete Baur-Heinhold's *Theater des Barock* (1966; published in English in 1967 as *Baroque Theater: A Cultural History of the 17th and 18th Centuries*).[2] Within a few years, this epistemic shift was already shaping American graduate students' research for some of the first major American doctoral theses on the subject.[3] Over and against this academic context, the topic of theater and theatricality in art and public life again occasioned vigorous controversy. Whether this debate focused on the values of "spectacle" and "illusion" or "minimalism" and "camp," it played out in some of the most significant artistic and theoretical tracts of the time.[4]

Over the course of the 1960s, Samuel Beckett's plays grew increasingly spare (*Happy Days*, *Play*, *Come and Go*, and *Breath*), ruthlessly denying and subtracting many of the usual means of scenographic spectacle from the physical stage. The Fluxus artist George Maciunas demanded in 1963 that artists "PURGE the world of dead art, imitation, artificial art, abstract art, illusionistic art." As if in rejoinder, Susan Sontag hailed camp in 1964 as a sign of the times, a new mode of conjoining art and life through "theatricality," and a twentieth-century name for a long-standing modern sensibility whose "soundest starting point" can be traced to the seventeenth century. In turn, the choreographer Yvonne Rainer, herself rejecting the methods of Martha Graham, declared in 1965 an adamant sequence of negations: "No to spectacle./No to virtuosity./No to transformations and magic and make-believe. . . . / No to involvement of performer or spectator. / No to style. / No to camp." In the modern visual arts, Donald Judd began describing his sculptural works as "Specific Objects" around the year 1965, and in 1967, Michael Fried derided those same works for approaching the condition of *mere theater*, warning that theatricality as such was the enemy modernism needed to overcome.

In France, Guy Debord announced in the opening pages of *The Society of the Spectacle* (1967), that "[t]he whole life of those societies in which modern conditions of production prevail presents itself as an immense accumulation of *spectacles*," and that "[a]ll that once was directly lived has become mere representation."[5] Many of Debord's generation adopted something of this critical gesture, sharing in the sense that all of life had receded into a new and confounding form of the *theatrum mundi*.[6] Debord himself opined that "Baroque was the art of a world that had lost its center with the demise of the last mythic order recognized by the Middle Ages," and the emphasis on the baroque in aesthetic discussions of the 1960s reflected mostly "a growing awareness of the impossibility of classicism in art."[7] Debord elaborates this point, in polemical terms that only continue to reverberate today: "[F]or three centuries all efforts to create a normative classicism or neoclassicism have never been more than brief, artificial projects giving voice to the official discourse of the state—whether the State of the absolute monarchy or that of the revolutionary bourgeoisie draped in Roman togas."[8] Writing very nearly at the same time, but from another critical vantage, Theodor Adorno disparaged the 1960s turn to "baroque" or "historically accurate" Early Music as a product of the culture industry and a regression in musical consciousness.[9] By the end of Adorno's life, "baroque" had become for him a symptom of administered culture, little more than a marketing ploy.

The new theater that sprang from this context perpetuated the baroque's historical dialectics in a variety of ways. As the period saw a widening rift between what Hans-Thies Lehmann has called "dramatic" and "post-dramatic" practices onstage, the forms of allegory and theatricality that had fallen into disregard during the nineteenth-century ascension of realist mimesis continued, with mounting force, to reassert themselves onstage. The modernist approaches of most recent European theater—still sometimes called, however vaguely, *Regietheater*, or "director's theater"—only attest to this enduring life of allegory in a contemporary or postdramatic frame. One can trace a continued intensification since the late 1960s of these strategies in performance, carried over from those early-twentieth-century thinkers pro-

Epilogue

filed in the preceding chapters. In New York, for example, the playwright, performer, and director Charles Ludlam (1943-87) described his own aesthetic program with the following suggestive summary: "Modern art up through Beckett is the reduction of form—the elimination of things. There's no way to go beyond Beckett, because you can't get any more minimal. You reduce and reduce until there's nothing. It's like being in a labyrinth with no exits: the only way out is to fly. I'm moving in the other direction, to a maximal, more baroque vision."[10] The dialectical pendulum had reversed its course. Beckett's stark and subtractive aesthetics had yielded a new zeal for addition and excess in unabashedly queer works like Ludlam's *Conquest of the Universe, When Queens Collide* (1969). The deconstructive wit with which Ludlam tore through mainstays of the European dramatic canon involved an allegorical operation all its own, doubling the dramatic forms of *Hamlet*, the *Ring* cycle, Molière, Ibsen, Flaubert, and Strauss with elements of popular culture and original material of his own, juxtaposed in excessive and irreverent ways. Inspired though Ludlam's ambition was, nothing could be further from the case than to suggest that his camp "maximalism" belonged to a "more baroque" logic than Beckett's dramaturgy. The "minimalism" of Beckett's melancholy landscapes (and, in the visual arts, Judd's sculptures) cannot escape the demand that modern art unfold in the pursuit of its utmost extremes.[11] By Icarus's flight, we escape only from one labyrinth into another.

In a related vein of the American theater during this time, the early works of Robert Wilson (b. 1941) witness a contemporaneous, late modernist turn to baroque strategies in performance. Beginning with his "silent opera" *Deafman Glance* (1970), the hybrid director-designer-playwright began creating works on a grand scale that could rival those of a Bernini or Wagner. His productions have frequently been cited as extending the tradition of the *Gesamtkunstwerk*, or Total Artwork, and they are just as demonstrably indebted to the theater practices of the Symbolists, the Expressionists, Brecht, and Stein, those baroque-modernist theater makers I survey in the present study.[12] The eight-hour-long *Deafman Glance* explored the foundations and experience of human consciousness through the perception of Raymond Andrews, the Black deaf child Wilson adopted as his son, opening onto an expansive vista of dream images saturated in color and light. When it premiered in Nancy, France, Wilson was hailed by the aging Surrealist Louis Aragon, in a famous open letter to the then long-dead André Breton, as embodying the next generation of the theatrical avant-garde.[13] In Aragon's suggestive phrase, Wilson's theater embodied a "strange proximity . . . of science and art" that he named "a baroque of the future."[14] A century earlier, Nietzsche's *Birth of Tragedy* had already hailed the merger of science and art as the future of philosophical thought. What Aragon discovered in Wilson was then an already established cultural project. He has not been the only observer to note Wilson's proximity to the baroque stage. More recently, several others have done so as well, including Lehmann, for whom Robert Wilson stands as a paradigmatic artist of the "postdramatic theater."[15] What seems most absolutely original in Wilson's theater, most worthy of founding an entire paradigm shift in modern performance, is also, in Lehmann's own estimation, evidence of Wilson's place in a centuries-old theater tradition.

In commenting on his directorial vision, Wilson has echoed these critics. In one of his favorite and most-often-repeated ways of describing his process, he has spoken implicitly in the terms of allegory, the yoking of heterogeneous visual components together as if by violence. "If you place a baroque candelabra on a baroque table, both get lost. You can't see either. If you place the candelabra on a rock in the ocean, you begin to see what it is. Usually in the theater the visual repeats the verbal. The visual takes second place to language. I don't think that way."[16] This thought-image amounts to more than an example of modernist defamiliarization. Torn from its customary context and resituated elsewhere, as in a process of citation or montage, the candelabra also becomes an emblem in Benjamin's ruinous sense. It testifies not only to the primacy of the visual in Wilson's theater and the arbitrariness with which images and texts can be conjoined with meanings, but also to the theater as a sensuous medium for addressing the affect Benjamin calls melancholy. On Wilson's stage, a candelabra atop a lonely rock in the middle of the sea evokes a "'landscape waiting for the gradual disappearance of man.'"[17] Although Wilson is hardly a political theater artist in any simple sense of that term, his lavish productions attain an urgency through their ongoing formal preoccupation with just this sort of evacuated, posthuman landscape. Not only is his ecology post-anthropocentric, but, as allegory, it forecasts the world after the end of the Anthropocene. The formalist theater he envisions offers few comforting or didactic solutions to the viewer but is better characterized as conservationist. It is as if, by displaying the ecological and cultural phenomena of this world upon the stage, Wilson seeks a momentary preservation of those phenomena in all their richness and diversity, against the looming threat of oblivion. For him, as in Trauerspiel, allegory holds out a hope of rescue and survival, preservation and adaptation.[18] And the threat of oblivion is becoming ever more relentlessly present today.

Epilogue 187

Throughout the preceding chapters of this book, the languages of the baroque stage appear repeatedly in reaction to a pervasive crisis across a range of modern spheres: in belief, everyday experience, language, representation, politics, and political economy. These crises are already incipient in the era of the justaucorps, the full-bottomed wig, and the lace cravat; and, although those outward accoutrements have changed their shape or vanished, the crises remain ongoing. As Benjamin declared: "Every age must strive anew to wrest tradition away from the conformism that is working to overpower it" (*SW* 4:391). Within this ever-present and self-renewing struggle resides what he might term the messianic dimension of baroque style, its perennial openness to a world that is to come. This openness was never more embodied during the period of the 1960s than in the art and life of the queer film- and performance maker Jack Smith (1932-89), who exerted a marked influence on both Wilson and Ludlam.[19] But while Wilson and Ludlam advanced the cause of the contemporary avant-garde in theater, Smith pushed it further into the field of performance art. He, moreover, brought the twentieth-century rhetoric of the baroque into an ever more activist dimension, one that may hold open a lesson for our own twenty-first-century moment.

In Mary Jordan's 2006 documentary, *Jack Smith and the Destruction of Atlantis*, the artist is heard in archival voiceovers repeatedly describing himself and his work, unironically, as participating in a baroque tradition. "Andrew Sarris in one of his columns said something about the deliberately boring orgy scene in *Flaming Creatures* [1963]. In other words, he believes that that was cutie-pie art and he could not detect that it was baroque art," Smith intones in his unmistakable, moose voice. Inveighing against the patron class that by turns fetishized and ignored him, he continues: "That's the trouble if you're making baroque art. People—their criminality is brought out by the jewel-like work that you're making. It's the only American response to real art. They become criminal."[20] Elsewhere he claims: "It only reveals the power of baroque art. That's all I was doing. I was the only one really continuing baroque art. . . . [I]t seems so incredible, but that's all it was." On a photocopied poster produced by Smith's studio—of uncertain dating but exhibited in 2018 as part of a retrospective of his work at the downtown Manhattan gallery Artists Space—a photograph of an aging Smith in a camp orientalist setting sits above the words "Interns Become Baroque Apprentices at Jack Smith's Academy of Baroque Studies." The flyer advertises internships for "two summer sessions" and lists a telephone number for applicants to call. The only other text to appear on this homemade advertisement

Jack Smith. "Interns Become Baroque Apprentices." Advertisement flyer. Fales Library and Special Collections, New York University. Courtesy Gladstone Gallery, New York.

is an unattributed quote, presumably Smith's words: "You may never master baroque art but you can at least be told about it." When I phone the Manhattan-based number on the flier, I reach an automated message: "The number you have dialed is not in service."[21]

Before his untimely death in 1989, the result of HIV/AIDS-related com-

Epilogue

plications, Smith was to make the unmasterability of baroque artistic forms his general wheelhouse. His scandalous works of performance mingled camp and literal trash, avant-garde and kitsch, modernity and myth. In *Flaming Creatures* and in *Normal Love* (1963), he limned the contours of another world full of polymorphous perversity and gender mutability, one every bit as colorful and lined with arabesques as 1960s Manhattan was gray and gridlike. As William Morris had done before him, Smith called for a new decorativeness in modern art, aligned with socialist principles. The outrageousness of his style courted controversy and misrecognition from the beginning. Replete with erotic imagery and depicting a desublimated queer sexuality, his films were deemed obscene by the authorities. Even as he helped found American underground cinema, his personal eccentricity and critiques of modern capital made him increasingly a pariah in the downtown art world; but this outsider status only amplified his prophetic voice. As the queer and performance theorist José Esteban Muñoz once wrote, in Smith's work, "dime-store glitter became diamond dust, and cheap polyester was transformed into silken veils. In Jack Smith's world, dumpster diving became treasure hunting. . . . Smith is the exemplary figure of the queer utopian artist and thinker who seeks solitariness yet calls for a queer collectivity."[22] Smith's art called for more than just sexual liberation: it launched a broader and more intersectional critique of American political economy. In the mercenary form of scavenger capitalism (which he decried as *landlordism* and *lobsterism*), he identified and railed against "the one giant social problem." More a Diogenes than a Baudelaire, he filmed and photographed himself taking to the streets in flamboyant attire, raging against the complacency of bourgeois culture, demanding a social awakening on the part of the populace. As he saw it, the ownership of property was little more than exploitation. "But if the population has no conception of how irrational this is, that's how far they are from doing anything about any of the other things that oppress them." In his life and work, the sensuality of baroque style became a vehicle for demanding that all existing social and material conditions be emancipated.

In one of his performances, titled *Jack Smith's Fear Ritual of Shark Museum* (1974), Smith appears in several public spaces attired in a white cape, tropical shirt, and feathered headpiece of enormous construction. Lamenting the commodification of artworks to the heavens from the public lawns of the Cologne Zoo, he bellows in a stilted and dramatic voice: "Art scavengers and other kinds of dealers can also see what is considered far out and can decide what to buy in the next year based on what is similar to what they have seen at the art festival. The artists of course see in which direction to copy. So the artists compete for more and more useless ideas and the art becomes thinner and thinner." In the recording, several passersby regard Smith's theatrical remonstrations as they would a lunatic raving at the moon. In another clip of the same performance, Smith stands on an urban rooftop, shouting and casting accusatory gestures in the direction of a nearby building, addressing the camera directly. His voice is filled with a kind of "hopeless hopefulness."[23] He thunders: "As it is, the museums give nothing. They pretend to give you art and then take it away after two or three weeks. This is a disgusting performance when you think that art should be free. Everything should be free, and it could begin with art. Make that goddamn place open 'til midnight or put something interesting in it and keep it open *'til five in the morning!"*

As the 1960s wore on, Smith gradually stopped making movies, which he found could be transformed into the property of private film archives and so commodified at his own expense. In touring his 1963 project, *Normal Love*, he chose instead to edit the film and sound together in the real time of its projection, creating an open and unfinished work that would be different at every showing. By 1970, he had moved even more fully into the creation of live multimedia work, beginning a two-year-long series of free performances in his East Village loft. The hybrid home and studio space, which Sylvère Lotringer describes in Jordan's film as "a film shoot, a theater, a palace, a dreamland," became his utopian Atlantis, a stage for acting out new visions of modern art and life. In such a playing space, the aesthetic sphere promised a realm of freedom, of human activity engaged in for its own intrinsic value and pleasure. The autonomy of artists and of artworks would open the radical possibility of an even greater human liberation: "Everything should be free, and it could begin with art." For Smith, then, as for Friedrich Schiller, the modern domain of the aesthetic has a crucial, educational function to perform. For this to be the case, however, a revolution in consciousness must first occur. Artists would need to stop making "schlock" and "cutie-pie art" (which Smith aligned with Andy Warhol's commercialism) and turn to making something else instead, something more unfamiliar and unsettling to the order that governs our everyday lives. That dissident "something" would be genuine, autonomous art itself.[24] More specifically, for Smith, it would be art that takes an unapologetically baroque form, in opposition to the petrified unrest of the market economy. If, in allegory,

Epilogue

Wilson's theater offers his audience the interpretive tools with which to face a post-human world, Smith's performances urge us to rage ever more furiously against the dying of the light. For both, questions of style amount to a means for life. Ultimately, the baroque is a gay science.

In a recent *Artforum* section devoted to revisiting the question "What is Enlightenment?" the magazine assembled a panel of luminary thinkers, including the decolonial theorist Boaventura de Sousa Santos, whose response to the prompt was titled, laconically, "Stay Baroque."[25] Must we reject Enlightenment altogether? That is not entirely what the modernist baroque demands, nor is it exactly what Sousa Santos recommends, and it would, of course, be a false step, as others have argued before me.[26] As it turns out, staying baroque or reaffirming the baroque remains difficult advice to follow, requiring a stubborn persistence in the effort. All these many years after Smith and his predecessors in baroque modernism, we still need better ways of seeing, feeling, and acting. The modernist desire to awaken new forms of consciousness and critique remains still unfulfilled. At a time when the market for art grows more massive but the ideas behind it stagnate under the weight of their own commodification, when collective practices (like theater) and entire species (including human beings) are endangered with extinction, when spectacle and simulacra are mobilized to authoritarian ends, a hunger for alternate visions of the world is still present and ever new. The question of how to think and act in order to reapportion the means to future planetary life only grows more urgent, demanding a collective effort. On this stratified field of enduring contradiction, the baroque's future will play out, if there is to be a future at all. Artists like those documented here glimpse its ecstasies as a transit to a less repressive world. Their work is not only an avant-garde in the sense of pure futurity; rather, they advance the cause of art and justice by the remembrance of a forgotten past. In laying claim to baroque style, their aim is not, or not primarily, to re-create it "accurately." They do not seek to recognize the past "the way it really was." Instead, as Benjamin's theses "On the Concept of History" urge, these artists aim toward "appropriating a memory as it flashes up in a moment of danger," grasping it as "a revolutionary chance in the fight for the oppressed past" (*GS* 4:391, 396). Such a chance offers us a fitting model for glimpsing the baroque as that form of art which sees the miraculous potential within the everyday life. In the springing motion that has characterized writers and artists reaching out to seize that chance, we reconnect pasts and futures, beginnings and endings, in the full now-time of history.

Note on Translations and
Abbreviations for Primary Sources

Throughout this book, I regularly reproduce quotations from authoritative English-language translators of my German and French source materials. In some cases it was necessary to make modifications to these translators' work, and wherever I have done so, the changes are indicated and explained in the notes. In those cases where I cite material for which no published English translation exists, I offer, if appropriate, the original texts in the notes to clarify my own translations.

Chapter 1

Citations to Nietzsche's writings follow guidelines set by the *Journal of Nietzsche Studies*. I have mostly consulted the "Cambridge Texts in the History of Philosophy" translations and have used other editions as necessary for those few texts that do not appear in a Cambridge edition. For those published writings and letters that do not appear in an English translation, I cite the Colli and Montinari *Kritische Gesamtausgabe* (*KGW*) and *Briefwechsel: Kritische Gesamtausgabe* (*KGB*). Numerals that immediately follow the abbreviations below refer to Nietzsche's own volume, chapter, and section numbering systems, whereas numbers that appear in parentheses in text or in the notes refer to pages in the English translations. For example, with the abbreviation *AOM* 131 (245), *AOM* 131 designates section 131 of the *Assorted Opinions and Maxims*, and (245) refers to page 245 in the Hollingdale translation listed below.

AOM   *Assorted Opinions and Maxims*. Volume 2 of *Human, All Too Human: A Book for Free Spirits*. Translated by R. J. Hollingdale. Cambridge: Cambridge University Press, 1996.

BGE	*Beyond Good and Evil*. Edited by Rolf-Peter Horstmann. Translated by Judith Norman. Cambridge: Cambridge University Press, 2002.
BT	*The Birth of Tragedy*. In *The Birth of Tragedy and Other Writings*. Edited by Raymond Geuss and Ronald Speirs. Translated by Ronald Speirs. Cambridge: Cambridge University Press, 2002.
CW	*The Case of Wagner*. In *The Anti-Christ, Ecce Homo, Twilight of the Idols, and Other Writings*. Edited by Aaron Ridley and Judith Norman. Translated by Judith Norman. Cambridge: Cambridge University Press, 2010.
DD	*Dithyrambs of Dionysus*. Translated by R. J. Hollingdale. London: Anvil Press Poetry, 1984.
EH	*Ecce Homo*. In *The Anti-Christ, Ecce Homo, Twilight of the Idols, and Other Writings*. Edited by Aaron Ridley and Judith Norman. Translated by Judith Norman. Cambridge: Cambridge University Press, 2010.
GM	*On the Genealogy of Morality*. Edited by Keith Ansell-Pearson. Translated by Carol Diethe. Cambridge: Cambridge University Press, 2010.
GMD	*The Greek Music-Drama*. Translated by Paul Bishop. New York: Contra Mundum Press, 2013.
GS	*The Gay Science*. Edited by Bernard Williams. Translated by Josefine Nauckhoff. Cambridge: Cambridge University Press, 2001.
HH	*Human, All Too Human: A Book for Free Spirits*. Translated by R. J. Hollingdale. Cambridge; Cambridge University Press, 1996.
KGB	*Briefwechsel: Kritische Gesamtausgabe*. Edited by Giorgio Colli and Mazzino Montinari. Berlin: De Gruyter, 1967-2005. (Letters sent by Nietzsche are designated *BVN: Briefe von Nietzsche*.)
KGW	*Kritische Gesamtausgabe*. Edited by Giorgio Colli and Mazzino Montinari. Berlin: De Gruyter, 1967-2005. (Nietzsche's posthumous fragmentary texts are designated *NF: Nachgelassene Fragmente*.)
LR	*Lectures on Rhetoric* [otherwise known as the "Description of Ancient Rhetoric" (1872-73)]. In *Friedrich Nietzsche on Rhetoric and Language*. Edited and Translated by Sander L. Gilman, Carole Blair, and David J. Parent. Oxford: Oxford University Press, 1989.
NCW	*Nietzsche contra Wagner*. In *The Anti-Christ, Ecce Homo, Twilight of the Idols, and Other Writings*. Edited by Aaron Ridley and Judith Norman. Translated by Judith Norman. Cambridge: Cambridge University Press, 2010.

Note on Translations

PTAG *Philosophy in the Tragic Age of the Greeks.* Translated by Marianne Cowan. Washington, DC: Regnery, 1998.

TI *Twilight of the Idols.* In *The Anti-Christ, Ecce Homo, Twilight of the Idols, and Other Writings.* Edited by Aaron Ridley and Judith Norman. Translated by Judith Norman. Cambridge: Cambridge University Press, 2010.

TL "On Truth and Lying in a Non-moral Sense." In *The Birth of Tragedy and Other Writings.* Edited by Raymond Geuss and Ronald Speirs. Translated by Ronald Speirs. Cambridge: Cambridge University Press, 2002.

UM *Untimely Meditations.* Edited by Daniel Breazeale. Translated by R. J. Hollingdale. Cambridge: Cambridge University Press, 2006.

WP *The Will to Power.* Edited by Walter Kaufmann. Translated by Walter Kaufmann and R. J. Hollingdale. New York: Vintage, 1968.

Z *Thus Spoke Zarathustra.* Edited by Adrian Del Caro and Robert Pippin. Translated by Adrian Del Caro. Cambridge: Cambridge University Press, 2006.

Chapter 2

The difficulties that Mallarmé's writing poses to translation is a subject of considerable notoriety for his English-language critics. I have consulted the translations below.

C *Correspondance.* Edited by H. Mondor, J. Richard, and L. Austin. Paris: Gallimard, 1985.

CP *Collected Poems: A Bilingual Edition.* Translated by Henry Weinfield. Berkeley: University of California Press, 1994.

D *Divagations.* Translated by Barbara Johnson. Cambridge, MA: Harvard University Press, 2009.

OC *Oeuvres Complètes.* Edited by H. Mondor and G. Jean-Aubry. Paris: Gallimard, 1945.

SL *Selected Letters of Stéphane Mallarmé.* Edited and translated by Rosemary Lloyd. Chicago: University of Chicago Press, 1988.

Chapter 3

Citations to Benjamin's work use the abbreviations that follow. For those writings that do not appear in an English translation, I have used the seven-volume *Gesammelte Schriften* (*GS*), edited primarily by Rolf Tiedemann. In

citing the authoritative Harvard translation of Benjamin's *Arcades Project*, I
have used Benjamin's own idiosyncratic section designations.

AP   *Arcades Project*. Translated by H. Eiland and K. McLaughlin.
      Cambridge, MA: Harvard University Press, 1999.
B   *Briefe*. Edited by G. Scholem and T. Adorno. Frankfurt am Main:
      Suhrkamp Verlag, 1978.
CWB   *Correspondence of Walter Benjamin*. Edited by G. Scholem and
      T. Adorno. Translated by M. Jacobson and E. Jacobson. Chicago:
      University of Chicago Press, 1994.
GS   *Gesammelte Schriften*. Edited by R. Tiedemann. Frankfurt am
      Main: Suhrkamp Verlag, 1991.
OGT   *Origin of the German Trauerspiel*. Translated by H. Eiland. Cam-
      bridge, MA: Harvard University Press, 2019.
SW   *Walter Benjamin: Selected Writings*. Edited by M. Jennings,
      M. Bullock, H. Eiland, and G. Smith. Cambridge, MA: Harvard
      University Press, 1996-2003.
UB   *Understanding Brecht*. Translated by Anna Bostock. London: NLB,
      1966.
UDT   *Ursprung des deutschen Trauerspiels*. Edited by R. Tiedemann.
      Frankfurt am Main: Suhrkamp Verlag, 1978.

Chapter 4

Unless otherwise indicated, all citations to Stein's writings refer to *Last
Operas and Plays*, originally published in 1949, which contains both the 1935
edition of Stein's lecture "Plays" (originally included in *Lectures in America*)
and the 1927 edition of *Four Saints*.

4S3A *Four Saints in Three Acts*, in *Last Operas and Plays*. Edited by Carl
      Van Vechten. Baltimore: Johns Hopkins University Press, 1994.
LST   *The Letters of Gertrude Stein and Virgil Thomson: Composition as
      Conversation*. Edited by Susan Holbrook and Thomas Dilworth.
      Oxford: Oxford University Press, 2010.
LSW   *The Letters of Gertrude Stein and Thornton Wilder*. Edited by
      Edward M. Burns and Ulla Dydo with William Rice. New Haven,
      CT: Yale University Press, 1996.
P   "Plays," in *Three Acts*. In *Last Operas and Plays*. Edited by Carl Van
      Vechten. Baltimore: Johns Hopkins University Press, 1994.

Notes

Preface

1. My initial notes encompass a wide range of contemporary fields: playwrights, theater directors and collectives, dancers and choreographers, performance artists, filmmakers, multimedia and installation artists, photographers, and fashion designers. See, for example, on Jean Genet: Fredette, *Figures baroques de Jean Genet*; on Tony Kushner and "baroquosity": Kushner, *Death and Taxes*, 34; on Richard Foreman: Rabkin, *Richard Foreman*, 60; on the Wooster Group: Jakovljevic, "Wooster Baroque"; on Reza Adboh: Lehmann, *Postdramatic Theater,* 166; on Yvonne Rainer: "Eine barocke Party" (A baroque party); on Marina Abramović: "Marina Abramović"; on Derek Jarman and Peter Greenaway: Calloway, *Baroque Baroque*, 229; on Nam June Paik: Paik, *Nam June Paik*; on Gordon Matta-Clark: "Gordon Matta-Clark"; on Cindy Sherman: Schor, *Wet*, 76; and on Christian Lacroix: Kotzamani, "Red," 105, 107.

2. Numerous examples can be named in this regard. Contemporary artists in the expanded performance field described in note 1 whose work is often described (or self-described) as baroque include Lars Jan, David Levine, Jacolby Satterwhite, and Ryan Trecartin, to name just a few. On Jan, see "ABACUS"; on Levine, see Byrnes et al., "Babylon Is Everywhere"; on Satterwhite, see Fateman, "Satterwhite"; on Trecartin, see Cooper, "Ryan Trecartin." See also the Wingspace Salon hosted in Brooklyn in April 2015 on the theme "Designs for a Contemporary Baroque Stage," which included talks by contemporary theater and performance artists Andrew Ondrejcak, Julian Crouch, Troy Herion, Yanira Castro (of A Canary Torsi), and Alexandro Segade (of My Barbarian). See "Salon #16."

3. See, for example, the foreword to Lyotard, *Postmodern Condition*, where Jameson praises Jean-François Lyotard for being "unwilling to post a postmodernist stage radically different from the period of high modernism and involving a fundamental historical break with this last" (xvi). One classic, contrary example of a starkly drawn demarcation between modern and postmodern cultural production

198   Notes to Pages xiv–3

would be Ihab Hassan's oft-reproduced table of differences between the two isms, but even Hassan noted that "the dichotomies this table represents remain insecure" (*Dismemberment of Orpheus* 269).

4. For the form of these questions, I have taken influence from the excellent introduction to Weber, *Theatricality as Medium*, 1–3.

5. On the "afterlives" (*Nachleben*) of artistic forms in a dialectical-materialist view of history, see Walter Benjamin's essay "Eduard Fuchs, Collector and Historian" (especially *SW* 3: 261–62). I am grateful to Isabel von Holt for reminding me of this well-known concept in Benjamin's work.

6. On "ever new modernisms," see Jameson's foreword to Lyotard, *Postmodern Condition*, xvi.

Introduction

1 As one measure, the word "baroque" appears in three of Wilder's novels, spanning the full length of his career, from *The Cabala* and *The Bridge of San Luis Rey* in 1926–27 (Wilder, *The Bridge of San Luis Rey and Other Novels*, 10, 119) to *Theophilus North* in 1973 (Wilder, *The Eighth Day, Theophilus North, Autobiographical Writings*, 695). The *Bridge* is also set in baroque Peru.

2. Niven, *Thornton Wilder*, 399. On the rediscovery and dating of Wilder's manuscript, see Cermatori, "Thornton Wilder's Baroque Visions." Note that Wilder uses the German *Barock* for his essay's title, but the English-French spelling, "baroque," for its body.

3. Stein, *Letters of Gertrude Stein and Thornton Wilder*, 16–17, 356–58.

4. Unless otherwise indicated, all Wilder citations in this introduction are to his manuscript essay "The Barock." Wilder most likely learned of the Jesuit theater from René Fülöp-Miller's comments on it in *The Power and Secret of the Jesuits* (409–21), published in German in 1926 and then in English translation in 1930. His own travels in Austria are documented in Zacharasiewicz, *Transatlantic Networks*, 104–7, 209–18, 284–90.

5. See Barthes, *Critical Essays*, 26.

6. For other claims of baroque style as an evolving stylistic paradigm during this period, see d'Ors, "Debate on the Baroque," in Zamora and Kaup, *Baroque New Worlds*, 75–92; Focillon, *Life of Forms in Art*, 58–61.

7. From the "Preface to *Three Plays*" (1957): "Toward the end of the 'twenties I began to lose pleasure in going to the theater. I ceased to believe in the stories I saw presented there. . . . I became dissatisfied with the theater because I was unable to lend credence to such childish attempts to be 'real.' I began writing one-act plays that tried to capture not verisimilitude but reality" (Wilder, *Thornton Wilder*, 682, 685). From "Some Thoughts on Playwriting": "The stage is fundamental pretense and it thrives on the acceptance of that fact and in the multiplication of pretenses" (ibid., 701).

Notes to Pages 3–5   199

8. Cf. Gaonkar, *Alternative Modernities*, 1–23. Drawing on Sarduy's example, Echeverría also speaks of the baroque as an "alternative modernity" to the one advanced by capitalism in *La modernidad de lo barroco*, 15, and in *Modernity and "Whiteness,"* 79.

9. On "magic realism" as a literary concept and its historical connections to "baroque," see Zamora and Kaup, *Baroque New Worlds*, 13–14. See also Alejo Carpentier's 1975 essay "The Baroque and the Marvelous Real," in Zamora and Faris, *Magical Realism*, 89–108.

10. Krauss, *Originality of the Avant-Garde*, 157.

11. In this line of questioning, I take my cues from Douglas Mao and Rebecca Walkowitz's call for a "New Modernist Studies" with expanded temporal frameworks, pushed beyond "the core period of about 1890 to 1945" to include "the late twentieth century" and "even . . . the early seventeenth" (*Bad Modernisms*, 738).

12. Mao and Walkowitz identify one form of "bad modernism" in "work deemed inferior or inadequate *as* modernism" (*Bad Modernisms*, 15). On the historical relationship between kitsch and baroque, see Frank Wedekind, qtd. in Calinescu, *Five Faces of Modernity*, 225.

13. For Wilder's other writings on seventeenth-century drama, see the essays "New Aids toward Dating the Early Plays of Lope de Vega" (1952) and "Lope, Pinedo, Some Child Actors, and a Lion" (1953), in Wilder, *American Characteristics*, 257–77.

14. On the "new baroque," see Willoughby, "Architect Recalls Genesis." On the sort of inheritance I have in mind throughout this book, see Richter, *Inheriting Walter Benjamin*, 1–14. Summarizing Benjamin's views of tradition as transmission, Richter writes: "There can be no inheriting of a tradition without a perpetual transformation, in which the one who receives ('der Lernende') also becomes the one who passes on ('der Lehrende')" (See ibid., 5–6). On this subject, see also Buck-Morss, *Dialectics of Seeing*, 223–26.

15. I borrow the chronological bookmarks of 1600 and 1750 from the field of historical musicology, which conventionally situates baroque between the birth of opera (in Jacopo Peri's Florence) and the death of Bach. A robust debate has grown up around the question of whether the term "baroque" as a period concept should usefully encompass *mannerism* (as an early, initiatory period of baroque) or *rococo* (as its late style, as Wilder's manuscript suggests). On the subject of the former, see, for example, Erwin Panofsky's lecture "What Is Baroque?" in *Three Essays on Style*, 19–88. On the latter, see Wellek, "Concept of Baroque," 77–86.

16. Eliot: "[I]f the only form of tradition, of handing down, consisted in following the ways of the immediate generation before us in a blind or timid adherence to its successes, 'tradition' should positively be discouraged." (*Sacred Wood*, 43). On Eliot's dialectical vision of tradition, see Brooker, *T. S. Eliot's Dialectical Imagination*, 75–89. On allegory in Eliot's "tradition" essay, see Halpern,

Shakespeare among the Moderns, 2-3. For an analysis of "the contemporary" that echoes Eliot's "historical sense," see Agamben, *What Is an Apparatus?* 39-41. Though distancing himself from Eliot's aesthetics, the dance theorist and historian Mark Franko nevertheless argues that "the return of the baroque in the twentieth century could be considered a modernist project" and claims this return as a species of what he calls "the post-modern archaic" ("The Baroque Body," in Kant, *Cambridge Companion to Ballet*, 47).

17. This point bears additional clarification. In the ritual performance of transubstantiation, presence is configured not as self-presence or self-identity but as dissemination. Counter-Reformation theology understands divinity as presenting itself in a "myriad" of disarticulated sites, separated in time and space, day after day. In this observation, Wilder is close to the claim the deconstructive critic Samuel Weber makes in *Theatricality as Medium* when he describes the present participle as the grammatical hallmark of theatricality: "Why the present participle? For two interrelated reasons, at least. First, because its 'presence' is suspended, as it were, in and as the interval linking and separating that which is presented from the presentation 'itself.' The 'presence' of the present participle is thus bounded, or defined, by the convergence of its articulation with that which it articulates. But in thus being defined by its own redoubling—and this is the second reason—it is also constituted by and as a series of repetitions, each of which is separated from the others and yet is also bound to them in sequence" (15). On the importance of the doctrine of Real Presence to medieval spectacle, and consequently, to baroque theater, see Egginton, *How the World Became a Stage*, 33-46.

18. Wilder, *Three Plays*, 110.

19. Shepherd, "Why I Write," in *Orpheus in the Bronx*, 195. Shepherd here recalls Walter Benjamin's *Origin of the German Trauerspiel*: "Origin, though a thoroughly historical category, nevertheless has nothing in common with genesis. By 'origin' I meant not the coming-to-be of what has originated but rather what originates in the becoming and passing away. The origin stands as an eddy in the stream of becoming and vigorously draws the emerging material into its rhythm. In the naked, manifest existence of the factual, the original never allows itself to be recognized; its rhythm stands open only to a dual insight. On one hand, it demands to be recognized as restoration, restitution, and on the other hand—and precisely on account of this—as something incomplete and unclosed" (*OGT* 24). I am indebted to Joseph Roach's writings on the Orphic qualities of performance in "Performance" and in Cermatori et al., "Teaching African American Dance/History."

20. See Berman, *All That Is Solid Melts into Air*, 15-16. A full historiography of early-twentieth-century modernism far exceeds the scope of this inquiry. Nevertheless, Cody and Sprinchorn usefully distinguish between *modern* drama on one hand, centering on realism as a movement (with Ibsen's 1879 *A Dollhouse* as a landmark example), and *modernist* theater on the other, which eschewed realistic

Notes to Pages 7-8

conventions (*Columbia Encyclopedia*, 915-17). Admittedly, this schema reprises the distinction between realist and "formalist" modernisms introduced by Lukács (see Adorno et al., *Aesthetics and Politics*). For other useful work in defining "modernism" (and "avant-garde"), see Albright, *Untwisting the Serpent*, 29-36; Berman, *All That Is Solid Melts into Air*, 6; Bradbury and McFarlane, *Modernism*; Calinescu, *Five Faces of Modernity*; Knowles, Tompkins, and Worthen, *Modern Drama*; Koss, *Modernism after Wagner*, xii-xxviii; Latham and Rogers, *Modernism*, 62-65; Levenson, *Cambridge Companion to Modernism*; Lewis, *Cambridge Introduction to Modernism*, 95-97; Mao and Walkowitz, "New Modernist Studies"; Melville, *Philosophy beside Itself*, 3-33; Puchner, *Stage Fright*, 7-12; Rancière, *Politics of Aesthetics*, 26-31; Roberts, *Total Work of Art*, 77-79; Schulte-Sasse's foreword to Bürger, *Theory of the Avant-Garde*, vii-xlviii; Walker and Odom, "Comparative Modernist Performance Studies"; Williams, *Politics of Modernism*, 31-35.

21. "The modernisms of the past can give us back a sense of our own modern roots. . . . They can help us connect our lives with the lives of millions of people who are living through the trauma of modernization thousands of miles away, in societies radically different from our own—and with millions of people who lived through it a century or more ago" (Berman, *All That Is Solid Melts into Air*, 35).

22. Melville, *Philosophy beside Itself*, 18

23. Baudelaire, *Painter of Modern Life*, 13-14.

24. See the opening of the "Preface for *Our Town*": "For a while in Rome I lived among archaeologists, and ever since I find myself occasionally looking at the things about me as an archaeologist will look at them a thousand years hence. Rockefeller Center will be reconstructed in imagination from the ruins of its foundations. How high was it? A thesis will be written on the bronze plates found in New York's detritus heaps—'Tradesmen's Entrance,' 'Night Bell.' . . . It was something of this method that I brought to a New Hampshire village" (Wilder, *Thornton Wilder*, 657).

25. On baroque style as an "archaeology of modernity," see Buci-Glucksmann, *Baroque Reason*, 41. On "historical allegory," see Halpern, *Shakespeare among the Moderns*, 4-14. On archaeology and genealogy as contemporary historiographic terms, see Foucault, *Archaeology of Knowledge*, 3-19; and Foucault, *Language, Counter-memory, Practice*.

26. Wellek, "Concept of Baroque in Literary Scholarship," 77.

27. See Underwood, *Why Literary Periods Mattered*, 84-85, 112-13. This attention to periodization is itself attributable to a new, modern understanding of historical time; see Berger, *Bach's Cycle, Mozart's Arrow*, 1-19; Habermas, *Philosophical Discourse*, 1-23; and Koselleck, *Futures Past*, 222-54.

28. As part of this particular dyad, "baroque" functions to advance the sort of cultural work that Sedgwick once described as "minoritizing" (see *Epistemology of the Closet*, 1). For her deconstructive analysis of binaries oppositions, see ibid., 9-11.

202   Notes to Pages 8-10

29. On the British distaste for the term "baroque," see Wellek, "Concept of Baroque in Literary Scholarship," 85; Davidson, *Universal Baroque*, 11. In American theater studies, which would establish itself as a formal discipline nationwide only in the early 1950s (as Marvin Carlson notes in his introduction to Fischer-Lichte, *Transformative Power of Performance*, 2-3), "baroque" gained popularity after the publication of Margarete Baur-Heinhold's 1967 survey, *Baroque Theatre*, but lost ground with the rise of new historicist methodologies in the 1990s.

30. Deleuze, *The Fold*, 33.

31. For Deleuze and Guattari on philosophy as the work of "forming, inventing, and fabricating concepts," see *What Is Philosophy?* 2. (For a summary outline of Deleuze's concept of baroque, see Deleuze, *The Fold*, 3-13.) On concept-formation as "performance," see Spivak, "Foreword," 112; Ophir, "Concept."

32. I am indebted to Judith Butler's reading of catachresis in *Bodies That Matter* (37-39, 217-18). Butler contends that, in Luce Irigaray's writing, "the feminine" is a catachresis in that it functions as a name whose referent "cannot be said to *be* anything, to participate in ontology at all" (ibid., 39).

33. Deleuze, *The Fold*, 33.

34. Wellek, "Concept of Baroque in Literary Scholarship," 87.

35. These transformations date to the rise of the French court ballet (in Paris in 1581, for example, with the *Ballet Comique de la Reine*), the earliest experiments in opera (circa 1600 in Florence with Jacopo Peri's *Dafne* and *Euridice*), and the publication of technical tracts for the widespread use of forced scenic perspective, special effects, and gestural acting (by Niccolò Sabbatini in Ravenna, 1638, and John Bulwer in London, 1644, for example).

36. Abel, *Tragedy and Metatheatre*.

37. Most recently, the view that theatricality forms an important stylistic component of the baroque has been advanced by William Egginton, who argues in *The Theater of Truth* that "the Baroque is theater, and theater is baroque" (39). On "theatricality" as an aesthetic value, see Davis and Postlewait, *Theatricality*; Egginton, *How the World Became a Stage*; Fischer-Lichte, "Theatricality"; Fischer-Lichte, *The Show and the Gaze of Theatre*, 61-72; McGillivray, "Discursive Formation of Theatricality as a Critical Concept"; Turner, *Early Modern Theatricality*; and Weber, *Theatricality as Medium*. See also the essays and bibliography collected in the special "Theatricality" issue of *SubStance*, edited by Josette Féral in 2002. For a summary of the persistent poststructuralist preoccupation with questions of theatricality, see Fuchs, *Death of Character*, 144-57; see also the essays collected in Murray, *Mimesis, Masochism, and Mime*.

38. Bernini scholar Irving Lavin describes a view of Bernini that has by now become something of an art-historical commonplace: "Although he had had many predecessors as artist-scenographer (not so many as artist-playwright and artist-actor), it is with Bernini that the relationship between art and theater

Notes to Pages 10-13   203

becomes a critical question. The epithet 'Baroque theatricality' has often been leveled at his work in general and the Teresa chapel in particular, implying a kind of meretricious stagecraftiness that transfers formal and expressive devices from the domain of ephemeral and artificial to that of permanent and 'serious' arts, where they have no proper business. It might almost be said that our view of the whole period, as well as of the artist himself, has been colored by Bernini's activity in the theater" (Lavin, *Visible Spirit*, 16).

39. Quoted in Petersson, *Bernini and the Excesses of Art*, 34.

40. Bredekamp, *Lure of Antiquity*.

41. Although modern aesthetic theory emerges only around 1750 with figures such as Baumgarten, and though early modern theories of emotion are a complex subject in their own right, the experience of *wonder* occupies a defining place in many of the theoretical dialogues on art from the early modern period, particularly among interpreters of Aristotle. For one synoptic overview of the English context, see Platt, *Reason Diminished*, 1-18.

42. Smith, *Business of Alchemy*, 267. Maurice Slawinski offers further description of several other Bernini spectacles: "In another, the curtain opened to reveal a second crowded auditorium identical to the real one, after which it closed again, and a *zanni* appeared in front of it to perform a comic routine, but periodically, sounds of laughter could be heard, as if something much more amusing was being performed in the 'other' theatre. [In yet another of Bernini's stage plays,] the audience about to leave the auditorium was treated to the spectacle of its own departure, as the curtain went up for a final time to reveal a replica of the square facing the theatre, full of the bustle of carriages which gradually disappeared, leaving the space empty and dark. No better metaphors could be found for the fear that what took place on stage, for all its contrivance, might overwhelm real life, the anxiety as to where a truly effective drama might be found, and the suspicion that the audience itself could be the real spectacle, unwitting performers in a play not of their making, and destined to fade into nothing." (Slawinski, "The Seventeenth-Century Stage,' in Farrell and Puppa, *History of Italian Theatre*, 141).

43. Lavin, *Visible Spirit*, 22.

44. Drawing on Paul Fréart de Chantelou's diary, Mary Ann Frese Witt observes that, while Bernini was often employed in lavish settings for sumptuous audiences, he "produced most of his own plays with low budgets, at his own expense, in his own home or in the Vatican foundry where he did his sculpture. . . . [These productions were] often 'homegrown and home-staged,' often featuring members of his family and his workshop" (Witt, *Metatheater*, 80).

45. I rely upon Beecher and Ciavolella's translation: Bernini, *The Impresario*, 43. The play was first published as the appendix to Cesare d'Onofrio's *Gian Lorenzo Bernini, Fontana di Trevi*.

46. Cf. Deleuze: "The Baroque entails neither falling into nor emerging from

illusion but rather *realizing* something in illusion itself, or of tying it to a spiritual presence that endows its spaces and fragments with a collective unity. The prince of Homburg, and all of Kleist's characters, are not so much Romantic as they are Baroque heroes. Prey to the giddiness of minute perceptions, they endlessly reach presence in illusion, in vanishment, in swooning, or by converting illusion into presence: Pethesilea-Theresa? The Baroque artists know well that hallucination does not feign presence, but that presence is hallucinatory" (Deleuze, *The Fold*, 125).

47. Fried, *Art and Objecthood*, 153.

48. Fried, *Moment of Caravaggio*, 122.

49. Fried, *Absorption and Theatricality*, 100. Fried's narrative of modernity shares certain similarities with one influentially advanced by Péter Szondi. Over the eighteenth century, Szondi asserts, the theater came increasingly to emphasize an onstage "world of the interpersonal," a dramatization of what Habermas would later call "the bourgeois public sphere," in which direct addresses to the spectator on the other side of the proscenium boundary were forbidden (Szondi, *Theory of the Modern Drama*). See also Cermatori, "Allegories of Spectatorship," 92–95.

50. Fried put forward this argument over the course of his influential trilogy of books on modern painting: *Absorption and Theatricality: Painting and Beholder in the Age of Diderot* (1980); *Courbet's Realism* (1990); *Manet's Modernism; or, The Face of Painting in the 1860s* (1996). Notably, Fried cites Nietzsche's contemporary Édouard Manet as a decisive turning point when the quest for an autonomous realism in anti-theatrical painting had to be abandoned.

51. Fried, *Art and Objecthood*, 163. Fried elaborates his theses in three axioms: "1. *The success, even the survival, of the arts has come increasingly to depend on their ability to defeat theatre.* . . . 2. *Art degenerates as it approaches the condition of theatre.* . . . 3. *The concepts of quality and value—and to the extent that these are central to art, the concept of art itself—are meaningful, or wholly meaningful, only within the individual arts. What lies* between *the arts is theatre*" (ibid., 163–64; emphasis in original).

52. Puchner, *Stage Fright*, 7.

53. Puchner admits pro-theatricalism as a possible orientation among modernists in *Stage Fright* but attends more exclusively to anti-theatricality (2), preferring to link pro-theatricalism to the more limited domain of the avant-gardes as a subset of modernism (7–8). For an argument opposing Puchner's anti-theatricalism, see von Held, "Brecht's Anti-theatricality?" 38–40.

54. Von Held, *Brecht's Anti-theatricality?* 40.

55. On the seventeenth century as a period of crisis, see Aston, *Crisis in Europe*; Parker and Smith, *General Crisis of the Seventeenth Century*. Berman characterizes the period from 1500 to the 1790s as one that saw the initiatory crises of modernity, resulting from a changed understanding of the cosmos and the place of

Notes to Pages 15–17

humankind in it (*All That Is Solid*, 16-17), with those transformations accelerating in the later eras of Rousseau (17), Marx, and Nietzsche (19-23). In my reading, the experience of modernity can be said to align with the deconstruction of Aristotelian metaphysical systems held over in the scholastic monotheism of medieval Europe. The philosophical movement known as deconstruction emerges from this modern matrix and carries forth its hidden baroque trace. On deconstruction's ties to modernism, see Melville, *Philosophy beside Itself*, 18-19.

56. For a recent study of the reemergence of Pyrrhonianism in the time of Michel de Montaigne, Thomas Hobbes, and their eighteenth-century successors in skepticism—one of particular interest to the tradition of left anti-foundationalism in the twentieth century—see Thorne, *Dialectic of Counter-Enlightenment*. For other comments on early modern skepticism and its effect upon the arts, see Bell, *Shakespeare's Tragic Skepticism*; Cavell, *Disowning Knowledge in Seven Plays of Shakespeare*; Fried, *Moment of Caravaggio*, 106-7.

57. Wellek, "Concept of Baroque in Literary Scholarship," 77.

58. This view is elaborated in José Antonio Maravall's *Culture of the Baroque*: "The baroque monarchy made use of a large repertory of means [*medios*] to succeed in dominating the tension of adverse forces; this, along with the novelty of some of these means, revealed what was constitutive of baroque culture. It included aspects all the way from physical constraint, based on military force, which is the ultima ratio of political supremacy, to psychological expedients [*resortes*] that acted on consciousness and created within it a repressed psyche" (36).

59. For Debord's comments on baroque, see *Society of the Spectacle*, 133-35.

60. Echeverría, *Modernity and "Whiteness,"* 131. See also Cheng, *Ornamentalism*.

61. Echeverría, *Modernity and "Whiteness,"* 131. Echeverría's comments on "the decorative" deserve to be considered alongside the theoretical hostility toward decoration in the classical, tendentious modernism of Adolf Loos, Clement Greenberg, and Michael Fried. This hostility came under new scrutiny with the rise of so-called postmodernism in the 1970s. See, for example, Jeff Perone's essay "Approaching the Decorative" (1976); and Melville's discussion of Fried's theatricality and "wallpaper" in "Notes on the Reemergence of Allegory," 64-65.

Curiously, the theater director Richard Foreman, who has at times compared his own stage dramaturgy to an idea of the baroque theater, has discussed his approach to decoration and mise-en-scène in terms that recall Deleuze's interest in baroque folds: "There is a prejudice against decoration in art and architecture, because there is an awareness that the decorative allows the ornamental (or visual) aspect to take on a life of its own, which then threatens to interfere with the basic thrust of, say, a Le Corbusier building that declares, 'I am purely hospital,' or 'I am a home that is like a hospital because here we lead focused, uncluttered lives.' The unspoken assumption is that if we allow a little squirly-gig up in the decorative

molding to reproduce itself throughout the entire room, it would introduce
something into the environment that threatens to run out of control. But the fact is
that our brains are secretly powered by those little squirly-gigs. . . . So more power
to the decorative. Which is really to say that man is not the only possible center of
the universe; there are other energies, other forces, at work" (*Unbalancing Acts*,
65-66). Here, Foreman's argument echoes Mallarmé's fascinations with the baroque
scrollwork of Versailles, a subject I introduce in chapter 2.

62. For recent book-length, scholarly efforts at unpacking baroque style (or
the so-called neobaroque), see Bal, *Quoting Caravaggio*; Calabrese, *Neo-baroque*;
Calloway, *Baroque Baroque*; Daddario, *Baroque, Venice, Theatre, Philosophy*;
Egginton, *Theater of Truth*; Golub, *The Baroque Night*; Lahiji, *Adventures with the
Theory of the Baroque and French Philosophy*; Lambert, *On the (New) Baroque*; Lyons,
Oxford Handbook of the Baroque; Murray, *Digital Baroque*; Ndalianis, *Neo-Baroque
Aesthetics and Contemporary Entertainment*; Scholz-Hänsel, *El Greco and Modernism*;
Snyder, *L'estetica del Barocco*; Stevenson, *Baroque between the Wars*; and Zamora
and Kaup, *Baroque New Worlds*. See also the chapters devoted to "Baroque and
Neo-Baroque Enigmas" in Perniola, *Enigmas*, 91-126.

63. Egginton, *Theater of Truth*, 1-2.

64. Egginton, *Theater of Truth*, 2. In a series of disconnected observations, the
theater historian Herbert Blau drew attention to this irreducibility, both as the
molecular problem of theater as such and, in a linguistic sense, as the source of
Genet's "baroque" style of discourse. "Genet has suffered the solitary confinement
of a displacement so severe it causes him to *see* words, as Sartre had pointed out,
as irreparably separated from what they name. . . . [T]he great mission of theatre
[is] to grant meaning to appearances, the appearances in which we commonly live,
the feeling that we have about whatever constitutes reality, that we're always in the
immanence of theater, that we may be perceiving at any moment . . . merely the
appearances of what should be transparencies" (qtd. in Cermatori, "Essential
Ruptures," 3).

65. In Egginton's definition, the modern theater that emerged in baroque
Europe can be understood as *"that medium of interaction whose conventions structure
and reveal to us our sense of space or spatiality*. The spatiality so revealed is theatricality." *How the World Became a Stage*, 3 (emphasis in original).

66. Egginton, *Theater of Truth*, 2.

67. Fried, *Art and Objecthood*, 47; cf. Fried, *Moment of Caravaggio*, 121, 179, 262.

68. Buci-Glucksmann, *Baroque Reason*, 41. Here I must bracket a broader
question, namely, whether "aesthetics" as a concept whose history developed in
northern European philosophy through the systematic writings of Kant, Hegel,
and others—capital *A* aesthetics, one might say—can designate a theoretical field
sufficiently capacious for understanding baroque style at all. If "baroque" amounts
to an "aesthetics," as Buci-Glucksmann suggests, it cannot be one fully subsumable

Notes to Pages 17-18

to this (Enlightenment) sense of the word, or to what Hegel called in *Introductory Lectures on Aesthetics* "the science of art" (13). Here some of Brenda Machosky's skepticism as to whether allegory constitutes an aesthetic category can be redirected to the notion of baroque as well. "Allegory is not an aesthetic category," Machosky writes. "As the phenomenon that 'says one thing and means another,' as the phenomenon in which two things (impossibly illogically) occupy the same space at the same time, allegory is the work of art with which Aesthetics simply cannot contend" (*Structures of Appearing*, 26). Susan Buck-Morss expresses similar reservations in *Dialectics of Seeing* (225).

69. In the present study, I avoid "neobaroque" for three reasons. First, the term creates confusion with the revivalist architectural style of the nineteenth century, epitomized in the Palais Garnier opera house (completed 1875). Second, "neobaroque" has been affiliated with notions of "postmodernism" that unduly distort discussions of modernity. Third, the term has sometimes been used as a way to stereotype the literatures of the Global South, and Latin America in particular. (At the same time, much important baroque scholarship has been produced by postcolonial and decolonial scholars of Hispanophone and Latinx cultures. See, for example, the seminal essays included in Zamora and Kaup, *Baroque New Worlds*.)

70. Here I wish to offer a parenthetical clarification. In my description of "baroque" as a condition, some readers may detect an echo of Lyotard's vocabulary in *The Postmodern Condition*. Although Lyotard has his own importance for my subject matter (for example, his comment in 1971, in *Discourse, Figure*, that "the space of this book is no more than Baroque"), the following chapters should make clear, in a variety of ways, that I do not share Lyotard's concept of postmodernism as a theory of late-twentieth-century cultural production.

71. As Lehmann has argued, the bases for drama's hegemony during this time were already being prepared as early as 1667-77, when Racine's neoclassical tragedies were first written and performed (Lehmann, *Tragedy and Dramatic Theatre*, 253-86). For him, Racine amounts to "pure dramatic tragedy" (253), though this view obscures those elements in Racine's dramaturgy that resist the closure of drama in favor of greater theatrical efficaciousness. On French neoclassicism as itself baroque, see Wellek, "Concept of Baroque in Literary Scholarship," 80.

72. See also Cermatori, "Allegories of Spectatorship"; and Brown, *Persistence of Allegory*, 6-7, 183-221. On the cultural renunciation of allegory and ornamentation, beginning with the bourgeois revolutions of the eighteenth century and continuing "across the nineteenth century all the way to the triumph of a literal-minded 'realism' (and to Adolph Loos's manifesto *Ornament and Crime*)," see Jameson, *Allegory and Ideology*, 22. On Hegel's mediation of baroque philosophy during the late eighteenth century, see Tom Conley's introduction to Deleuze, *The Fold*, xiii; and Plotnitsky, "Curvatures: Hegel and the Baroque," in Rajan and Plotnitsky, *Idealism without Absolutes*, 113-34.

208 Notes to Pages 18-19

73. Weigel, *Body- and Image-Space*, 88.

74. For arguments depicting the modernization process as self-undermining, the classical texts are, of course, Freud's *Civilization and Its Discontents* and Weber's *Protestant Ethic and the Spirit of Capitalism*. See also Adorno and Horkheimer's *Dialectic of Enlightenment*, where the dialectic of myth and Enlightenment is narrated in ways that usefully illuminate the dialectics of myth and disenchantment within baroque modernity writ large. Alina Payne argues that everyday objects have come to take over the same rhetorical function once espoused by architectural ornamentation. Her claims in *From Ornament to Object* echo Fried's *Art and Objecthood* and Jameson's writings on allegory (e.g., in *Allegory and Ideology*, 22-26).

75. See, in particular, de Man's analysis of Nietzsche in *Allegories of Reading*, 103-18. For a discussion of the fin de siècle linguistic turn as that moment when language "invaded the universal problematic," see Derrida, *Writing and Difference*, 280; and Foucault, *The Order of Things*, 303-7. Derrida's few comments on baroque style include his rejoinder to structuralist literary criticism in "Force and Signification," citing Jean Rousset: "Has not a 'structural poetics' 'founded on a rhetoric' been mentioned in relation to the baroque? But has not a 'burst structure' also been spoken of, a 'rent poem whose structure appears as it bursts apart'?" (Derrida, *Writing and Difference*, 6). For other participants in the late-twentieth-century reevaluation of allegory, see Fletcher, *Allegory*; Honig, *Dark Conceit*; Kantrowitz, *Dramatic Allegory*; Nuttall, *Two Concepts of Allegory*; Quilligan, *Language of Allegory*; Tuve, *Allegorical Imagery*; Van Dyke, *Fiction of Truth*.

76. Greenblatt, *Allegory and Representation*, vii-viii. On the opposition of allegory to mimesis, see de Man, *Resistance to Theory*, 61-70. On modernism's inheritance of a modern "crisis of representation" extending back to the time of Kant, see Lewis, *Cambridge Introduction to Modernism*, 3-10.

77. For relevant discussions of Freudian *Nachträglichkeit* (afterwardness), see Laplanche, *Essays on Otherness*, 264-69; and Donald Marshall's introduction to Melville, *Philosophy beside Itself*, xvi. For Walter Benjamin's signal discussion of historical afterwardness, see *SW* 3: 261-62.

78. For an account that traces the prehistory of the "death of God" motif, locating it in Hegel's writings and in German baroque hymnody, see Von Der Luft, "Sources of Nietzsche's 'God Is Dead!'"

79. Barthes, *Critical Essays*, 26; cf. Julia Gros de Gasquet, "Baroque Theatricality" in Lyons, *Oxford Handbook of the Baroque*, 65-87. Elsewhere, Henry Turner and Simon Palfrey have written of "theatricality" as describing "not a technology of mimesis nor even a kind of enacted philosophy but rather a kind of physics: a world in which bodies, ideas, affects, and figures combine and recombine to generate the plays we watch, read, react to, and think about today" (Turner, *Early Modern Theatricality*, 18).

80. On the subject of decoration as an expression of *eros*, see Rae Beth Gordon's

essay "Ornament as Veiled Language of Desire" in her *Ornament, Fantasy, and Desire*, 78-79.

81. Bersani, *A Future for Astyanax*. (Whether Bersani's theory of modernity is fully compatible with an aesthetic theory that takes its cues from Walter Benjamin's rhetoric of redemption is the subject for another essay.)

82. On the suggestive historical queerness of the letter *Q*, see Masten, *Queer Philologies*, 1-38.

83. On formalism and abstraction in modern and contemporary queer art, see Doyle and Getsy, "Queer Formalisms"; Getsy, "Ten Queer Theses on Abstraction"; Lancaster, "Queer Abstraction"; Ruiz, "Radical Formalism"; and Simmons, "Notes on Queer Formalism."

84. Getsy suggests that queer or camp style and "minimalism" in the contemporary arts (of the sort criticized by Michael Fried) amount only to an *apparent* antithesis (Doyle and Getsy, "Queer Formalisms"). For further commentary on the conjunctions of queerness and minimalism, see Jonathan Flatley's chapter "Allegories of Boredom" in his *Like Andy Warhol*, 137-78.

85. Jameson, *Allegory and Ideology*, 313-17.

86. The context for Deleuze's claim echoes much of Michael Fried's argument precisely, and sheds rich light on the place of Fried's anti-theatricality within a larger historical dialectics of the baroque: "This extensive unity of the arts forms a universal theater that includes air and earth, even fire and water. In it sculptures play the role of real characters and the city a décor in which spectators are themselves painted images or figurines. The sum of the arts becomes the Socius, the public social space inhabited by Baroque dancers. Perhaps we rediscover in modern abstract art a similar taste for a setting 'between' two arts, between painting and sculpture, between sculpture and architecture, that seeks to attain a unity of arts as 'performance,' and to draw the spectator into this very performance (*minimal* art is appropriately named following a law of extremum)" (Deleuze, *The Fold*, 123).

87. Rebecca Schneider offers a summary of the recent queering of historiographic methods in *Performing Remains*: "[R]ecent scholars in queer historiography, such as Carolyn Dinshaw, Chris Nealon, Louise Fradenberg, Carla Freccero, Elizabeth Freeman, Heather Love, and Judith Halberstam build on materialist, post-colonial, psychoanalytic, and post-structural theories to argue for an inquiry and analysis that challenges received modern conventions of temporal linearity (conventions Dipesh Chakrabarty calls 'modern historical consciousness' and Ann Pellegrini and Janet Jakobson call 'secular time'). Such scholars argue for the value of crossing disparate and multiple historical moments to explore the ways that past, present, and future occur and recur *out of sequence* in a complex crosshatch not only of reference but of affective assemblage and investment" (35).

88. Roach, *It*, 13. Cf. Michel Serres and Bruno Latour: "Time doesn't flow; it percolates" (qtd. in ibid., 13).

89. For a sample of recent book-length scholarly works at the conjunction of theater and philosophy, or in the new "interdiscipline" of performance philosophy, see Cull and Lagaay, *Encounters in Performance Philosophy*; Cull, *Theatres of Immanence*; Gobert, *The Mind-Body Stage*; Kornhaber, *The Birth of Theater from the Spirit of Philosophy*; Kottman, *A Politics of the Scene*; Puchner, *Drama of Ideas*; Rokem, *Philosophers and Thespians*; and Weber, *Theatricality as Medium*. In an even more expanded field of philosophically inclined theater and performance theory, one might also cite Camp, *First Frame*; Harries, *Forgetting Lot's Wife*; Hoxby, *What Was Tragedy?*; Jarcho, *Writing and the Modern Stage*; Ridout, *Stage Fright, Animals, and Other Theatrical Problems*; Sack, *After Live*; and Smith, *Total Work of Art*.

90. For select recent writings on and in the vein of this return, see Boyle, Cornish, and Woolf, *Postdramatic Theater and Form*; Levine, *Forms*, 11–16; Kramnick and Nersessian, "Form and Explanation"; Levinson, "What Is New Formalism?"; Macpherson, "A Little Formalism"; North, *Literary Criticism*, 140–48; and Wolfson and Brown, *Reading for Form*. On the relation of *style* to *form*, see Kramnick and Nersessian, 667–68; see also, Focillon, *Life of Forms in Art*, 44–48.

91. See, for example, the anachronic approach undertaken in Schneider, *Performing Remains*. Schneider's intervention in the performative dimension of Civil War battles takes place with a strategic belatedness: "I went to Civil War. I did not go to an archive, though that would have been the most legitimate path to set for myself as a scholar interested in history. Instead I went to witness battles mounted in the *again* of a time out of joint, as a scholar interested in history's theatrical returns" (1). Adapting this method, I have studied the performance history of the baroque "in the again of a time out of joint," by focusing on documents from the early twentieth century.

92. On Pirandello, Genet, Stoppard, and Kushner's relationship to baroque, see Witt, *Metatheater and Modernity*. On Craig, Duncan, Lewis, and Barnes, see Armond, *Modernism and the Theater of the Baroque*. See also Pérez-Simón, *Baroque Lorca*.

93. Sontag, "Artaud," xliii–xliv.

94. Nagel, *Der Skandal des Literalen*.

95. I likewise acknowledge that this book's argument could be expanded into other fields. In classical music, for example, one might conscript the works of Richard Strauss, Ferrucio Busoni, Paul Hindemith, Benjamin Britten, or Pierre Boulez to a study of baroque style in modernist form. In poetry, one might trace similar lineages from Gerard Manley Hopkins, Elizabeth Bishop, and W. H. Auden to Richard Wilbur, James Merrill, and John Ashbery, among others. For this study's purposes, I have restricted my focus to the modernist theater and some of its primary theorists.

96. MacDonald, "Masscult and Midcult," in *Against the American Grain*, 3–75.

97. Watson, *Prepare for Saints*, 112.

98. Already in 1946, René Wellek's "Concept of Baroque in Literary Scholarship"

Notes to Pages 25–28

was able to depict the long-standing refusal among French and English critics to acknowledge any baroque qualities in the early modern literatures of their countries (83–95). This tendency is still widely felt, for example, in American academic departments of English or Anglophone literatures, where baroque continues to be an uncommon period descriptor.

99. Echeverría, *La modernidad de lo barroco*, especially 11–18, 32–56. See also Echeverría, *Modernity and "Whiteness,"* 38–73, 128–49. Notably, Echeverría describes the Jewish diaspora of Nazi Germany as pursuing "a strategy of resistance . . . characterized by an anti-capitalist baroque expression within capitalism" (*Modernity and "Whiteness,"* 46). An even more radical alignment of this baroque ethos with an opposition to racial and ideological whiteness is also registered in the present book's conclusion on Gertrude Stein's *Four Saints in Three Acts*.

100. See Édouard Glissant's "Toward a Baroque Abroad in the World" (1990), in Zamora and Kaup, *Baroque New Worlds*, 626. For a further baroque elaboration of Glissant's theory of "relation," see Diawara, "Conversation with Édouard Glissant"; Moten, *Black and Blur*, xv; and Moten, *Universal Machine*, 135.

101. While Echeverría grants baroque style a certain radical promise, his characterization of it as a liberatory force minimizes the ways in which hegemonic power today also assumes markedly baroque characteristics. The philosopher and trans activist Paul Preciado has, for example, described global technopatriarchy as a baroque assemblage of sorts.

102. See Severo Sarduy's 1972 "Baroque and Neobaroque," in Zamora and Kaup, *Baroque New Worlds*, 290. See also Egginton's description of the *minor* baroque, which maintains a subversive or critical potential, in *Theater of Truth*, 7–8.

103. "Paradoxically, but also with great promise, the subject who is 'queered' into public discourse through homophobic interpellations of various kinds *takes up* or *cites* that very term as the discursive basis for an opposition. This kind of citation will emerge as *theatrical* to the extent that it *mimes* and *renders hyperbolic* the discursive convention that it also *reverses*. . . . To oppose the theatrical to the political within contemporary queer politics is, I would argue, an impossibility" (Butler, "Critically Queer," 23).

Chapter 1. Overcoming Ascetic Style

1. These details are recounted in Barth, Mack, and Voss, *Wagner*, 116; Koss, *Modernism after Wagner*, 30–65; Millington, *Sorcerer of Bayreuth*, 221–32; Spencer, *Wagner Remembered*, 217–18; Spotts, *Bayreuth*, 38–42; Payne, "Beyond *Kunstwollen*: Alois Riegl and the Baroque," in Riegl, *Origins of Baroque Art*, 5–6; and, of course, in Nietzsche's own telling of the occasion in *Richard Wagner in Bayreuth* (*UM* IV 1 [199]). Koss, especially, details Wagner's aversion to baroque architecture (Koss, *Modernism after Wagner*, 40) and to Gottfried Semper's neobaroque revivalist style.

212 Notes to Pages 29-31

Wagner initially collaborated with Semper on a theater in Munich, but parted ways with him in disapproval of his monumental designs, which he passed on to Brückwald as blueprints for the more austere Bayreuth Festspielhaus.

2. Nietzsche's physical copy of the 1869 edition of Burckhardt's *Der Cicerone*—currently residing in the Duchess Anna Amalia Archives in Weimar, Germany—shows atypical margin markings in the sections devoted to *Barockstyl*. I am grateful to the archivists at Weimar's Goethe-Schiller Archiv, particularly Anne Fuchs and Karin Ellermann, for bringing this volume to my attention. Nietzsche requested a new copy of the book from his sister in summer 1883 after an extended stay in Rome, where he encountered much baroque art and architecture firsthand. He was also likely influenced by the music historian August Wilhelm Ambros (1816-76), who in his posthumously published *Geschichte der Musik* (vol. 4, 1878) became the first to use the word "baroque" as a period term for music (Wellek, "Concept of Baroque in Literary Scholarship," 78). Ambros, upon hearing a preview of *Die Walküre*'s first act at a Wagnerite gathering in February 1874, hailed Wagner as a "modern Monteverdi" (Gregor-Dellin, *Richard Wagner*, 726). Nietzsche was acquainted with Ambros's writings, referring to them as early as 1870 in his lecture *The Greek Music Drama*, and again in his letters of 1872 and 1878, but it is unclear if he was in attendance at this 1874 gathering.

3. For notable exceptions, see Waite, *Nietzsche's Corps/e*, 189-90; and Zamora and Kaup, *Baroque New Worlds*, 41-43.

4. The connection between the terms *baroque* and *theatricality* has since become a critical commonplace, even if Nietzsche's foundational role in forging it is barely remembered. See, for example, Michael Fried's claim: "By the 1630s theatricality of an obvious sort did become a conspicuous strain in what we have come to call baroque art—not only in painting, but more importantly, in sculpture and architecture (the great exemplar is of course Gian Lorenzo Bernini)—but it remained for a future age, the mid-eighteenth century and after, to criticize that art specifically on those grounds" (Fried, *Moment of Caravaggio*, 122.)

5. For a discussion of Nietzsche, Burckhardt, and Wölfflin as a "Basel Baroque" triumvirate, and of the connections between baroque style and the Dionysian drive, see Zamora and Kaup, *Baroque New Worlds*, 32, 42.

6. Whether Nietzsche's concept of eternal recurrence is finally compatible with Fried's narrative of modernity as the rise and fall of mimetic absorption is a question that exceeds the scope of this chapter. For fuller analysis of Fried's historiography, see Cermatori, "Allegories of Spectatorship."

7. Nietzsche's theatrical style, experience as a public speaker, and conception as a performer are considered in Sloterdijk, *Thinker on Stage*. On university lecturing as performance, see McKenzie, *Perform or Else*, 20-22, 196.

8. The conjunction of Nietzsche's physical body and body of works is explored in Waite, *Nietzsche's Corps/e*, 51-58.

Notes to Pages 31–35

9. Schneider, *Performing Remains*, 17. Nietzsche's valuing of error as a way of knowing is ubiquitous throughout his early and late writings alike. For a mid-career instance, see *GS* 107 (104).

10. . Danto, *Nietzsche as Philosopher*, 63. For a complementary depiction, see Safranski, *Nietzsche*, 106–7.

11. Danto, *Nietzsche as Philosopher*, 45.

12. Shaw, *Perfect Wagnerite*, 25–31; Millington, *Sorcerer of Bayreuth*, 98.

13. Wagner wrote to his physician, the prominent Wagnerite Otto Eiser, in October 1877 expressing concern that Nietzsche engaged in excessive masturbation. Nietzsche, who had consulted Eiser at Wagner's urging, was outraged to learn of this correspondence, interpreting the charge to mean that Wagner suspected him of practicing pederasty. Rumors of Nietzsche's perversion were circulating around Bayreuth by the 1882 Festival. See Young, *Friedrich Nietzsche*, 239–40; Köhler, *A Lesson in Subjugation*, passim; Sedgwick, *Epistemology of the Closet*, 161–62.

14. See Aristotle's censure: "Whenever delivery comes to be developed as an art, it will have the same power as acting (*hypokritikí*). . . . To be an actor (*hypokritikón*) requires natural talent and is less a matter of training, but delivery in rhetoric is more a matter of training in the technique of art." Aristotle, *Rhetoric*, 3.1.7 (1404a); Plato's similar views are found in *Gorgias*, notably 502d.

15. I have altered Hollingdale's translation of Nietzsche's title, "Das Aufregende in der Geschichte der Kunst," which he renders as "the seditious in the history of art."

16. For Nietzsche's history of Asianism, see *LR* Appendix, 233–36. On the Roman distinction between the Attic and Asianist styles, see Cicero, *Brutus* §325, and Quintilian, *Institutio Oratoria* §XII.10. On Asianism and Sophistry, see Pernot and Eggins, *Rhetoric in Antiquity*, 82–83. See also Large, "Nietzsche's Orientalism."

17. In defining baroque style in terms of a Sophistic, anti-Platonist conception of language, Nietzsche prefigures an argument later put forward by Christine Buci-Glucksmann. See "The Work of the Gaze," in Zamora and Kaup, *Baroque New Worlds*, 151. In *Spurs: Nietzsche's Styles*, Derrida pursues "style" as a primary deconstructive category in Nietzsche's writing. On philosophy and style, see also Frank, "Style in Philosophy"; and Sontag, *Against Interpretation*, 15–36.

18. From "On the Nonexistent; or, On Nature," in Bizzell and Herzberg, *Rhetorical Tradition*, 24.

19. The view that language functions only by shared social and rhetorical convention dates to antiquity; see Hermogenes's position in Plato's *Cratylus* dialogue, 383a–385e. Nietzsche incorporates Kant's vocabulary into this argument in *TL* 1 (144). Elsewhere he characterizes Sophistic culture as "realist culture" (*TI* "Ancients" 2 [225]). For analyses of his general linguistics and debts to Sophism, see Deleuze, *Nietzsche and Philosophy*, 58–59, 76–77; and Brobjer, "Nietzsche's Relation to the Greek Sophists."

214   Notes to Page 36

20. See *LR* III (25). Nietzsche frames this position as a direct rebuttal to Aristotle: "We call an author, a book, or a style 'rhetorical' when we observe a conscious application of artistic means of speaking; it always implies a gentle reproof. We consider it to be not *natural*, and as producing the impression of being done deliberately. . . . But it is not difficult to prove that what is called 'rhetorical,' as a means of conscious art, has been active as a means of unconscious art in language and its development [*Werden*], indeed, that the *rhetorical is a further development*, guided by the clear light of the understanding, of *the artistic means which are already found in language.* There is no obviously unrhetorical 'naturalness' of language to which one could appeal; language itself is the result of purely rhetorical arts. The power to discover and to make operative that which works and impresses, with respect to each thing, a power which Aristotle calls rhetoric, is, at the same time, the essence of language" (*LR* III [21], emphasis original).

21. For similar arguments deriving the modern preoccupation with the baroque from the linguistic turn, or from the arbitrariness of the signifier, see Bryan S. Turner's introduction to Buci-Glucksmann, *Baroque Reason*, 4–7. See also Zamora and Kaup, *Baroque New Worlds*, 266; and Severo Sarduy, "Baroque and Neo-baroque," in ibid., 288.

22. Translating Nietzsche's views into J. L. Austin's vocabulary of the performa-tive, one might say that words—like *snake* or *Schlange*, to use one of Nietzsche's recurring examples—do not report upon the world as constatives but instead *posit* that world through rhetorical figures, thus acquiring the illocutionary character of performatives. Nietzsche explains that the Greek word (*drakōn*) designates only the thing's shiny quality, whereas the Latin words (*serpens* and *anguis*) designate its crawling and constrictive abilities respectively, while the Hebrew word means "that which hisses or winds or creeps," and so forth. See *LR* III (23) and *TL* 1 (144). One says, "This is a snake," and believes oneself to be representing the world through a constative utterance, but the *is* of one's speech, closer to the rhetorical *is* of metaphor than to the grammatical *is* of predication, simply posits and propagates a trope. (See de Man, *Allegories of Reading*, 120–24, and *passim*.) In describing baroque style as "bedecked and masked," however, Nietzsche offers a crucial supplement to Austin's terms, building on the fact that language's inherent rhetoricity operates without the speaker's conscious noticing. Whenever a word is thus recognized as harboring covert performative force, this recognition exposes a *certain* theatrical status, "unmasking" that word of the disguises of truthfulness and revealing it to be a trope. Everywhere in language one looks, however, one finds only more such masks. Where the referent once stood, available to be represented, there now appears a chaotic surplus of energies, language systems, and signifying practices. When sign and thing are sundered, certain effects that are by turns *performative* and also *theatrical* in nature are unleashed upon the world. Such effects can be said to constitute what are normatively understood as the phenom-

Notes to Pages 36-37

ena of baroque style. For further reflections on the distinction between performativity and theatricality, see Davis and Postlewait, *Theatricality*, 27-28; Féral, "Performance and Theatricality"; and Reinelt, "The Politics of Discourse."

23. See Butler, *Performative Theory of Assembly*, 62-63.

24. *BGE* 289 (173). See the similar rhetoric of *PTAG* 12 (83), where Nietzsche claims: "Through words and concepts we shall never reach beyond the wall of relations to some sort of fabulous primal ground of things." Biographer Gary Elsner suggests that Nietzsche acquired this materialist view of language from the neo-Kantian Friedrich Lange (*Nietzsche*, 29). Nietzsche's notion of a world aestheticized through rhetoric resonates with his claim in *BT* 24 (113): "Only as an aesthetic phenomenon do existence and the world appear justified."

25. Nietzsche's decentered *theatrum mundi* is not fully reducible to, say, Calderón's Christian-theistic one in *La Vida es Sueño*, as the closing section of this chapter makes clear. Still, in Nietzsche's essay "On Truth and Lying," written contemporaneously with his early lecture notes on rhetoric, the baroque sense that life is a dream (*la vida es sueño*) is made even more explicit: "Actually the human being is only clear about the fact that he is awake thanks to the rigid and regular web of concepts, and for that reason he sometimes comes to believe that he is dreaming if once that web of concepts is torn apart" (*TL* 2 [151]).

26. Martin Puchner points out that in Greek, the concepts of *gesture* and *figure* were both connoted in the same word, *schema* (σχημα) ("Gestures of Modernism," 1). For a discussion of this displacement of signification from language to body through gesture, see Agamben, "Gesture, or the Structure of Art."

27. Nietzsche's philosophical rejection of *ascesis* is at its most pronounced in the famous concluding sentence of the *Genealogy*, where the ascetic ideal is said to involve "this hatred of the human, and even more of the animalistic, even more of the material, this horror of the senses, of reason itself, this fear of happiness and beauty, this longing to get away from appearance, transience, growth, death, wishing, longing itself." (*GM* III.28 [128]).

28. For an analysis of the functions of primary narcissism, self-excitation, and self-glorification in Nietzsche's theory of speech, see Sloterdijk, *Nietzsche Apostle*, 8-10, 13. Sloterdijk describes Nietzsche's notion of rhetoric in terms that resonate amply with the phenomenon Leo Bersani has described as "self-swelling" or "psychic tumescence" ("Is the Rectum a Grave?" 25). On the ubiquity of *dilation* as a performance principle in performance, see Barba and Savarese, *Dictionary of Theatre Anthropology*, 52-61. On the necessary relation of feeling and enjoyment as a means to increasing power in Nietzsche's philosophy, and on Nietzsche's debts to Spinoza's baroque metaphysics in this regard, see Deleuze, *Nietzsche and Philosophy*, 61-64. (Cf. Deleuze, *Spinoza*, 48-51). On the discursive conjunction of power and pleasure, see also Foucault, *History of Sexuality*, 36-50.

29. Critchley and Webster, *Stay Illusion!* 17. In similar terms, Mario Untersteiner

216   Notes to Page 39

describes Sophistic rhetoric as "a tragedy for the intellect" in which "only through a
sort of deception—through allowing oneself to be persuaded—can a person feel
that he or she knows anything" (Untersteiner, *Sophists*, 35). In *Nietzsche and
Philosophy*, Deleuze likewise claims that the Sophists (e.g., Hippias) possessed
knowledge of "the tragic question" par excellence (76–77).

30. From *UM* IV 5 (214): "First of all [Wagner] recognized a state of distress
extending as far as civilization now unites nations: everywhere *language* is sick,
and the oppression of this tremendous sickness weighs on the whole of human
development. . . . Man can no longer express his needs and distress by means of
language, thus he can no longer really communicate at all" (emphasis original).
For Erika Fischer-Lichte, this passage diagnoses a situation in which "single words
appear as turbulences that do not lead to the perception or interpretation of
reality, but instead, to a complete void." She asserts that the "re-theatricalization
of theatre" clamored for by Georg Fuchs and heralded by Wagner amounts to an
attempt "to open up possible solutions to this crisis" (Fischer-Lichte, *The Show and
the Gaze*, 62–63).

31. "Shepherd" and "brigand" are, of course, significant terms in Nietzsche's
lexicon. See, for example: *Z* "Prologue" 9 (14): "To lure many away from the
Herd—for that I came. The people and the herd shall be angry with me: Zarathustra wants to be called a robber by shepherds."

32. *CW* 9 (249). These claims echo Nietzsche's views of 1870: "Ancient tragedy
was, in comparison [with French classical tragedy], poor in action and tension: one
could even say that, in its earlier developmental stages, it was not interested at all
in action, in drama, but in suffering, in pathos. The plot was only added when the
dialogue arose: and every genuine and serious deed took place off-stage in the
prime of the drama. . . . What was the tragedy originally other than an objective
lyric, a song that was sung from the condition of certain mythological beings, and
moreover in their costume? First of all, a dithyrambic chorus, composed of men
disguised as satyrs and sileni, had to make what had put it into such a state of
excitement: it pointed, in a way that was immediately comprehensible to the
spectators, to an episode from the story of the struggles and sufferings of
Dionysos" (*GMD* [28, 30]).

33. On Nietzsche's anti-mimetic bias, which favors the theater's "presentational" over its "representational" capacities, see Barish, *Antitheatrical Prejudice*,
403; and Puchner, *Drama of Ideas*, 139. See also de Man, *Allegories of Reading*,
which describes Nietzsche's *Birth of Tragedy* as one of the "pre-expressionist
critical documents in which a non-representational art is being prepared" (95).

34. For the irreducibility of theater to drama, see Roland Barthes's essay
"Baudelaire's Theater," which characterizes theatricality as "theater-minus-text"
(*Critical Essays*, 26). Borrowing Hans-Thies Lehmann's distinction between theater
and drama, we may rephrase this definition as "theater-minus-dramatic-text."

Notes to Pages 40-43

35. Fried, *Absorption and Theatricality*, 149; cf. *The Moment of Caravaggio*, 122. On Nietzsche's relationship to Fried, modernist theatricalism, and the collapse of referential or communicative language, see Cermatori, "Allegories of Spectatorship," 94-95.

36. *AOM* 144 (246). For Eugenio d'Ors's similarly transhistorical view, see Zamora and Kaup, *Baroque New Worlds*, 78-92.

37. The letters to Fuchs and Seydlitz, and the first letter to Maier, appear in Nietzsche, *Selected Letters*, 162, 166, 168; the second note to Maier (which appears here in my translation) appears in German in *KGB/BVN*-1878, 741.

38. The first letter to Fuchs appears in Nietzsche, *Selected Letters*, 307. The second letter to Fuchs and the letter to Spittler appear in *KGB/BVN*-1888, 1104, 1189.

39. For Wagner's theoretical development of the *Gesamtkunstwerk* concept, see Wagner, *The Art-Work of the Future* and *Opera and Drama*. For an analysis of the competing priorities of music and drama in these theories, and over the course of Wagner's lifetime, see Dieter Borchmeyer's essay "Wagner and Nietzsche," in Müller and Wapnewski, *Wagner Handbook*, 333-336.

40. In brief, Hofmannsthal, Wilder, Benjamin, and Aercke argue in various ways that the *Gesamtkunstwerk* concept has roots in the baroque theater. (See Hofmannsthal, qtd. in Smith, *Total Work of Art*, 189-90n5; Wilder, "On the Barock"; *OGT* 192; Aercke, *Gods of Play*, 67.) A similar view is put forward by the contemporary arts curators Muriel Pérez, Filine Wagner, and Gabrielle Schahad, who claim that the baroque stage anticipated the aesthetics of the *Gesamtkunstwerk* by harnessing painting, sculpture, and architecture in the stage set (glossary in Curiger and Zürich, *Deftig Barock*, 162). Smith holds out a dissenting but supplementary view in *The Total Work of Art*, 11.

41. For Nietzsche's analysis of the liquid, immersive dynamics of Wagner's metrics, the effects of which he compares to the experience of gradually walking into the ocean until one is submerged, see *AOM* 134 (244). See also *UM* IV 9 (239), which describes the "passionate empathy" (*Miterleben*) Wagner effects through combining word, gesture, and music.

42. On theatricality as the mingling space between the arts, see Fried, *Art and Objecthood*, 164; on the Wagnerian stage as technological medium, see Friedrich Kittler, "World Breath," in Levin, *Opera through Other Eyes*; on theatricality itself as a medium, see Weber, *Theatricality as Medium*; on the dynamic by which the proliferation of technical mediums seeks to redress (or "remediate") the problem of mediation in itself, see Bolter and Grusin, *Remediation*, 2-20.

43. Nietzsche's contemporaries identified the feeling of empathy, or *Einfühlung* (feeling-into), as a characteristic component of Wagner's stagecraft (See Koss, *Modernism after Wagner*, 68). But the concept of *Einfühlung* had developed previously among such architectural theorists as Semper and Wölfflin from the

218   Notes to Pages 43-44

study of seventeenth-century baroque architecture, as Alina Payne has shown (see "On Sculptural Relief" in Riegl, *Origins of Baroque Art*, 42-43).

44. The connection between Wagner and Asianism, hinted at in *AOM* 131, was already apparent to Nietzsche as early as the 1870 lecture notes on rhetoric, in which he compares Wagner's periodics with those of the ancient Asianists (*LR* "History of Greek Eloquence" 233). He recalled this connection again in his 29 July 1877 letter to Carl Fuchs. His consciousness of the Asianists' preference for short utterances illuminates both his preference for a more aphoristic style and his view of Wagner as a "miniaturist" in music (*CW* 7 [246]). Furthermore, from the standpoint of theatricality, it might also be said that Nietzsche's aphoristic style in itself functions to direct his reader toward thinking in ways more elliptical and participatory. In this regard, aphoristic and allegoric writing function in markedly similar ways.

45. For a history of the fourth wall from Diderot to Antoine, and for the rise of the idea of the proscenium arch as a window rather than a mirror, see Camp, *First Frame*, 63-70, 180.

46. See Koss, *Modernism after Wagner*, 58-66.

47. For Nietzsche's description of baroque recitative as "only half-sung declamation," see *BT* 19 (89). For his claim that Wagner's "endless melody" amounts only to a new form of recitative in the older, baroque style, see *CW* 8 (248). Nietzsche also characterizes the Asianist oratory as being "sing-song" in its vocal quality, see *LR* XVI (165).

48. Adorno, *In Search of Wagner* 18, 24, 26. A clear example of this effect, which Wagner drew from the coordination of music and gesture in the melodramatic theater, is the famed Longing and Desire motiv sequence in *Tristan*. The melody phrase rises initially alongside the physical raising of the fateful love potion, descends while Tristan and Isolde down the drink, lands on the opera's signature Tristan Chord at the moment of ingestion-enchantment, only to continue rising in a further upward motion miming the development of their enflamed passion.

49. See Della Pollack, "Performative Writing," in Phelan and Lane, *Ends of Performance*, 73-103. On textual performativity, see McGann, *Textual Condition*, 88-100. On theatricality in theoretical writing, see Weber, *Theatricality as Medium*, 14.

50. See Barish, *Antitheatrical Prejudice*, 400-417. For treatments of Nietzsche as a preeminently theatrical thinker and writer, see Agamben, *Means without End*, 52; Deleuze, *Nietzsche and Philosophy*, 78; Kornhaber, *The Birth of Theater from the Spirit of Philosophy*, passim; Puchner, *Drama of Ideas*, 138-48; Rokem, *Philosophers and Thespians*, 88-102, 113; Sloterdijk, *Thinker on Stage*, passim; and Witt, *Nietzsche and the Rebirth of the Tragic*, passim.

51. One thinks of Empedocles, Dionysus, Apollo, Silenus, the music-making Socrates, Zarathustra, Ariadne, and the Anti-Christ in this company of philosophi-

Notes to Pages 44-48

cal personae. Even the Francophile aphorist behind *Human, All Too Human* amounts to another such mask device.

52. De Man, *Allegories of Reading*, 96. Elinor Fuchs makes a similar observation in *Death of Character*, 28.

53. De Man, *Allegories of Reading*, 93-94.

54. For a later, explicit parabasis, see *EH* "Preface" 2 (71): "Just between us, this seems to be a point of pride for me." For a more implicit instance, see *EH* "Books" 5 (105): "The fact that a *psychologist* without equal is speaking in my works, this is perhaps the first thing a good reader will realize—the sort of reader I deserve, who reads me as good old philologists read their Horace."

55. Although Nietzsche likely inferred residual clues about early modern theater practice from the theater of his lifetime, it is clear he also conceived the practice of baroque gesture on the basis of examples drawn from visual art, since Bernini (both a sculptor and a theater maker) is the most consistent baroque reference across his writings. For analyses of Nietzsche's relationship to the theater of his time, see Kornhaber, *The Birth of Theater from the Spirit of Philosophy*, 5, 24, 28-33.

56. "He would declaim [what he had written] in order to experience its cadence, its accent, its tonality and metrical movement, also in order to test out the clarity and precision of the idea expressed." (Curt Paul Janz, qtd. in Parkes, "Introduction," to Nietzsche, *Thus Spoke Zarathustra*, xxix.) On the relation between text and performance, and the necessary performativity of texts, see Worthen, "Disciplines of the Text / Sites of Performance," 16-17.

57. Derrida, *Spurs*, 69.

58. On Nietzsche's relation to the disappearance of gestures from modern life, see Agamben, *Means without End*, 53.

59. Qtd. in Andreas-Salomé, *Nietzsche*, 77-78 (emphases original). Nietzsche offers similar insights into his own rhetoric in *EH* "Books" 4 (104).

60. For a (relatively unbiased) view of the early Florentine opera, see Nietzsche's 1870 lecture notes on "Sophocles and Tragedy," in *KGW/NF*-1871, 9 [5]. See also Nietzsche's notes on "die antike Tragödie und die Oper" in the Musarion Ausgabe, *Friedrich Nietzsche*, 2:262-65.

61. *BT* 19 (89). Nietzsche's condemnation of Italian luxury in *Birth of Tragedy* ("die zerstreuungssüchtige Üppigkeit jener Florentiner Kreise") directly echoes Wagner's views in *Opera and Drama*, which claims that opera arose "in the luxurious courts of Italy" ("an den üppigen Höfen Italiens"); see Wagner, *Oper und Drama*, 20. On Wagner's minimal familiarity with baroque drama, see Ellis, "Introduction," to Wagner *Opera and Drama*, 18.

62. *BT* 19 (91). Nietzsche complains that baroque opera sacrificed music's autonomy to the authority of dramatic poetry and the rhetorical manipulation of passions by developing recitative, text-painting, and the so-called doctrine of

"affects" (*BT* 19 [89-91]). On his attitudes toward absolute music, see Borchmeyer, "Nietzsche and Wagner," 333-35. See also Clemens Risi, "The Operatic Stage," in Schramm, Schwarte, and, Lazardzig, *Collection, Laboratory, Theater*, 146-61.

63. Cermatori, "Allegories of Spectatorship," 98.

64. Roach, *Player's Passion*, 46.

65. It must be acknowledged that Nietzsche was not interested to possess what modern scholars would consider a thoroughly historicist understanding of the early modern passions. His interest in this subject owes debts to Spinoza and, to a lesser degree, Descartes, but his *Nachlass* pays less attention to other early modern theories of emotion—for example, those of Hume, Hobbes, and Shaftesbury. For analyses of the relative historicity of early modern discourses on passion, see Paster, Rowe, and Floyd-Wilson, *Reading the Early Modern Passions*.

66. Roach, *Player's Passion*, 47: "The passions are easily summoned from the lower regions, but, like devils, once summoned they cannot so easily be put back. In this view the actor, like the Sorcerer's Apprentice, toys with enormous forces that he can evoke quickly but not easily subdue."

67. Fried, *Absorption and Theatricality*, 92.

68. The rediscovered *L'Orfeo* first attracted scholarly attention between 1825 and 1850, but was not published until 1881, when it appeared in a modern study version in Berlin. See Nigel Fortune, "Rediscovery of *Orfeo*," in Whenham, *Claudio Monteverdi*, 80-81.

69. "Or mentre i canti alterno, or lieti or mesti, / Non si mova augellin fra queste piante, / Nè s'oda in queste rive onda sonante, / Ed ogni auretta in suo cammin s'arresti." Monteverdi, *L'Orfeo* (translation mine).

70. "Griechische Dithyrambus ist der Barockstil der Dichtkunst" (*KGB/NF*-1878, 30 [26]).

71. The finer doctrinal points of this claim are debatable and have been discussed by numerous commentators. Nietzsche himself insinuates Wagner's ultramontanist or crypto-Catholic sympathies in *NCW* "Music without a Future" (271). Thornton Wilder agrees with the general view of Wagner's dramaturgy as quasi-Catholic, describing *Parsifal* as "the last Jesuit play" ("On the Barock"). Matthew Wilson Smith connects *Parsifal* to the liturgies of medieval Catholicism (Smith, *Total Work of Art*, 42). George S. Williamson observes that the mature Nietzsche himself shows signs of a strong attraction to Catholicism as over and against Protestantism; if this is so, his attribution of a "Counter-Reformation spirit" to Wagner can hardly be understood as a simple criticism (*Longing for Myth*, 272-73). George Bernard Shaw, on the other hand, argues that Wagner's many heroes instead should be understood better as typifying the Protestant individual (*Perfect Wagnerite*, 58). Richard Bell and Theodor Adorno both claim that what irritated Nietzsche in *Parsifal* was a certain insincere, cynical stance on Wagner's part toward the subject of religion altogether. (See Bell, *Wagner's Parsifal*, 237; and

Notes to Pages 51-56

Adorno, *In Search of Wagner* 12). Bell also argues that Wagner's *Parsifal* is better understood as advancing a pantheistic, rather than a monotheistic, metaphysics (*Wagner's Parsifal*, 252).

72. From the start, he had confessed misgivings about Wagner in a letter to his friend Carl von Gersdorff (dated 11 October 1866) after having a mixed reaction to the vocal score of *Die Walküre*—finding the opera's merits outweighed by its equally great "ugliness and defects." *KGB/BVN*-1866, 523 (translation mine).

73. Nietzsche, *Selected Letters*, 260.

74. On the role of gesture in Wagner's music and theory, see Smart, *Mimomania*, 163-204.

75. See Barish, *Antitheatrical Prejudice*, 400-418; Puchner, *Stage Fright*, 2-3, 31-40.

76. *CW* "Preface" (234). I have here amended Judith Norman's translation, which reads: "It's no use, you need to start out as a Wagnerian." Nietzsche writes: "Es hilft nichts, man muss erst Wagnerianer sein."

77. Sedgwick, *Epistemology of the Closet*, 169 (emphasis original).

78. *CW* 8 (247); emphasis original. I have altered Judith Norman's translation, which reads "histrion" and "scenicist."

79. Nietzsche's attacks on Wagner's desire for the intelligibility of lyrics over music reprises the precise argument he made in *BT* 19 (89) against baroque opera, which invented recitative "in order to satisfy the listener's wish to hear the words clearly amidst the singing," but it also reflects upon him as a philosopher of rhetoric and communication in a time when truth can no longer be understood as correspondence or as communicable.

80. Samuel Weber has demonstrated that Wagner's *Ring* cycle borrows its dramaturgical structure, whether wittingly or not, from the allegorical form of the baroque Trauerspiel, or mourning play. See Weber, *Benjamin's -abilities*, 281-96.

81. On the importance of Dionysus to the late Nietzsche's thought and the irreconcilable differences between Christian and Dionysian outlooks in his analysis, see Girard, "Dionysus versus the Crucified"; and Sokel, "On the Dionysian in Nietzsche."

82. "Guided culture" is Geoff Waite's description for the way Nietzsche may have understood his contemporary readers; I here adapt the term (perhaps polemically, with respect to Waite's larger argument) to apply instead to Wagner's aesthetics (*Nietzsche's Corps/e*, 188-90).

83. *CW* 6 (243). Here Nietzsche seems to have in mind the "ugly feeling" Sianne Ngai designates as *stuplimity*, "a synthesis of excitation and fatigue." See Ngai, *Ugly Feelings*, 36, 248-98. The impetus to astound can be traced through the history of baroque art and literature to Marino, whose impetus for the poet to stupefy ("*far stupire*") his audience can be taken as an aesthetic slogan for much baroque art. On the "Sublime" as a significant category for Nietzsche's aesthetics, see Waite, *Nietzsche's Corps/e*; and Roberts, *Total Work of Art*, 201-6.

84. On the relationship of ressentiment to actual, Dionysian violence, see Girard, "Dionysus versus the Crucified," 824-26.

85. On Wagner's oceanic sound, see *AOM* 134 (244); on Wagner's soupiness, see *CW* 8 (248).

86. On Nietzsche's "aristocratism," see Brandes, *On the Aristocratic Radicalism of Friedrich Nietzsche*; for a more critical view, see Losurdo, *Nietzsche, il ribello aristocratico*. For Nietzsche's interest in baroque morals, see Merrow, "Nietzsche and the Baroque."

87. See, for example, *WP* 61, where Nietzsche asserts that those called rich in our modern world are actually the poorest and most bankrupt of all.

88. Brown, "Nietzsche for Politics," in Schrift, *Why Nietzsche Still?* 208.

89. In the da capo aria, whose use is unique to baroque opera, an "A" section of musical material is followed by a contrastive "B" section, which then returns to repeat the initial "A" section with virtuosic embellishment. Other examples of Nietzschean baroque should include *Thus Spoke Zarathustra*, which Peter Sloterdijk has likened to a kind of autobiographical hagiography or Vita ("Entitled Opinions") of the sort that Saint Theresa of Ávila wrote during the Counter-Reformation; Nietzsche's late dithyrambic poetry, including his pseudo-Catholic hymn "Saint Januarius" (1882), which opens Book Four of *The Gay Science* and can be read alongside baroque devotional poetry (for example, that of Richard Crashaw); and his "Night Song" (1883), inspired by the sound of Bernini's Triton Fountain in Rome's Piazza Barberini (Parkes, "Explanatory Notes," in Nietzsche, *Thus Spoke Zarathustra*, 299n91).

90. See Carter, *Monteverdi's Musical Theatre*, 5; Lorenz, *Musik und Nihilismus*, 1.4-1.4.3.

91. Karsten Harries, "Nietzsche's Labyrinths," in Kostka and Wohlfarth, *Nietzsche and "an Architecture of Our Minds*, 39. See also Harries, "World-Picture and World-Theater," in Schramm, Schwarte, and, Lazardzig, *Collection, Theater, Laboratory*, 507-35.

92. Harries elaborates: "The close link between these metaphors becomes visible in the relationship between the stage designs by the Bibienas and Piranesi's labyrinthine *Carceri*" ("Nietzsche's Labyrinths," 39).

93. Harries, "Nietzsche's Labyrinths," 36, 42, 45.

94. For this distinction between various modes of address, I am indebted to Leo Bersani's thoughts on the enigmatic signifier in Dean et al., *A Conversation with Leo Bersani*, 11.

95. Nietzsche's 1876 essay on Wagner expresses anxiety about the presence of fate in Wagner's naturalistic dramaturgy: "[O]ne feels only the *necessity* of it all"; and "his music subjugates itself to the course of the drama, which is as inexorable as fate" (*UM* IV 9 [244]; emphasis original).

96. Agamben adduces the opening of the second meditation in support of this reading: "This meditation is untimely . . . because it seeks to understand as an

Notes to Pages 63-66

illness, a disability, and a defect something which this epoch is quite rightly proud of, that is to say, its historical culture, because I believe that we are all consumed by the fever of history and we should at least realize it" (Nietzsche qtd. in Agamben, *What Is an Apparatus?* 1).

97. For Wagner's central place of influence over the history of modern culture, see Puchner, *Stage Fright*, 1-13, 31-55; Koss, *Modernism after Wagner, passim*; and Smith, *Total Work of Art, passim*.

98. See Kornhaber, *The Birth of Theater from the Spirit of Philosophy*; Witt, *Nietzsche and the Rebirth of the Tragic*.

Chapter 2. The Matter of Spectacle

1. For a handful of critics who have remarked on Mallarmé's difficulty, see Bowie, *Mallarmé and the Art of Being Difficult*; Mauron, *Mallarmé l'obscur*; Ross, "Stéphane Mallarmé"; Steiner, "On Difficulty."

2. Bernstein, *A Poetics*, 31.

3. Translation mine. "Il y a à Versailles des boiseries à rinceaux, jolies à faire pleurer; des coquilles, des enroulements, des courbes, des reprises de motifs—telle m'apparaît la phrase que je jette d'abord sur le papier en un dessin sommaire, que je revois ensuite, que j'épure, que je réduis, que je synthétise." Quoted in Scherer, *L'Expression litteraire dans l'oeuvre de Mallarmé*, 79.

4. On the place of decoration in Mallarmé's aesthetics, see Reynolds, "Mallarmé and the Décor of Modern Life."

5. See Thibaudet, *La poésie de Stéphane Mallarmé*, 74; Wellek, "Concept of Baroque in Literary Scholarship," 96; Eco, *Open Work*, 13-14; and Paz, *Sor Juana*, 381. For Borges, see Zamora and Kaup, *Baroque New Worlds*, 173.n.v.

6. See Richard, *L'Univers Imaginaire*, 177-80. For an uncomplicated discussion of Mallarmé's love of folds (*plis*), particularly relevant to theater, see McGuinness, "Mallarmé Reading Theatre," in Freeman et al., *Process of Art*, 83. Notably, Harold Bloom calls Derrida's *Dissemination* "a baroque elaboration" all its own in Bloom, *Stéphane Mallarmé*, vii). For a rich summary of recent critical debates surrounding the faulty role of modern linguistics (including de Saussure, Derrida, and others) in illuminating Mallarmé's poetry, see Weintraub, "Mallarmé in Light of Art History," 8-11, 16-18.

7. Deleuze, *The Fold*, 30-31.

8. Weber, *Theatricality as Medium*, 16.

9. For pro-theatrical scholarly arguments depicting Mallarmé as a visionary of the form, see Block, *Mallarmé and the Symbolist Drama*, 13, 20, 104-5, 131; Deak, *Symbolist Theater*, 58-94; 100-103; Lehmann, *Postdramatic Theater*, 57-58; Charles Lyons, "Mallarmé and Representation in the Theater," in Cohn, ed. *Mallarmé in the Twentieth Century*, 92-101; and McGuinness, *Maurice Maeterlinck*, 162-68.

224   Notes to Pages 66-68

10. See, for example, Gould, *Virtual Theater*, 141-78; Puchner, *Stage Fright*, 59-80; and Szondi, *Lyrische Drama*, 73-141.

11. Puchner, *Stage Fright*, 59. Lacoue-Labarthe offers a view different from Puchner's. He claims that Mallarmé's criticisms of theater "must not be misunderstood" and are largely "sociological." But he also specifies that Mallarmé's criticisms of theater target bourgeois theater's inability "to elevate itself to the height of allegory, of emblem, or of myth. And consequently of Idea" (*Musica Ficta*, 60-61).

12. Some performance theorists might argue that Mallarmé evinces a growing gap between *drama/theater* and nonmimetic *performance*. But, as this chapter shows, Mallarmé is demonstrably suspicious of the notion of *presence* that has traditionally grounded performance art and performance studies, and for this reason, along with others I have outlined in "Allegories of Spectatorship," I focus instead on the schism between *drama* and *theater* during modernism. On performance and performativity in Mallarmé, there have been many important scholarly opinions. See Johnson, *Critical Difference*, 52-66; Norman, *Mallarmé's Sunset*, 57-62; Shaw, *Performance in the Texts of Mallarmé*; and Puchner, *Stage Fright*, 64. On performative language as a hallmark of modernist literature across the board, see Barthes, *Image, Music, Text*, 114.

13. That is, Mallarmé's supposedly initiatory position with respect to modernism raises questions about modernism's *systemic* debts to the baroque past, its immanence or saturation within a baroque impulse of style. Authors who claim him as having inaugurated modernist aesthetics include Cohn ("Mallarmé's Wake"); Johnson ("Mallarmé Gets a Life"); Lehmann (*Postdramatic Theater*, 57-58); Steiner (*After Babel*, 186-87); and Ross ("Terrifying Beauty of Mallarmé").

14. Although explicit references to Hegel are few in Mallarmé's writing, his Hegelian debts are important, even though a full discussion of them exceeds this chapter's scope. See Jameson, *Modernist Papers*, 323; Philippe Sollers, "Literature and Totality," in Bloom, *Stéphane Mallarmé*, 54; Langan, *Hegel and Mallarmé*, especially 42-53; Norman, *Mallarmé's Sunset*, 1-11; Reynolds, "Mallarmé and Hegel," 71-89; and Weintraub, "Art History in Light of Mallarmé," 10-11. See also Weinfield's commentary, in *CP* xiv-xv.

15. For a concise biographical account of Mallarmé's spiritual crisis, see Pearson, *Stéphane Mallarmé*, 64-88.

16. *SL* 60. I have modified Rosemary Lloyd's translation slightly to adhere more closely to Mallarmé's original grammar and syntax. Lloyd's translation reads: "I want to gaze upon matter, fully conscious that it exists, and yet launching itself madly into Dream, despite its knowledge that Dream has no existence." "Oui, *je le sais*, nous ne sommes que de vaines formes de la matière,—mais bien sublimes pour avoir inventé Dieu et notre âme. Si sublimes, mon ami! que je veux me donner ce spectacle de la matière, ayant conscience d'elle, et, cependant, s'élançant forcenément dans le Rêve qu'elle sait n'être pas, chantant l'Ame et toutes les divines

Notes to Pages 68-72

impressions pareilles qui se sont amassées en nous depuis les premiers âges, et proclamant devant le Rien qui est la vérité, ces glorieux mensonges!" (*C* 297-98).

17. Weinfield commentary, *CP* xiii.

18. "La littérature ici subit une exquise crise, fondamentale" (*OC* 360).

19. Although *A Throw of the Dice* effectively allegorizes the shipwreck of traditional Western metaphysics and Mallarmé's desired use of performance as a life raft of sorts in that wreckage's wake, a discussion of it far exceeds the scope of this chapter. Still, its title suggests an affinity between structures of secularized feeling in Mallarmé's lifetime and Pascal's in baroque France. For discussion of Mallarmé's closeness to Pascal, see Weinfield's comments in *CP* 266; and Deleuze, *Nietzsche and Philosophy*, 25-34.

20. *D* 205. "Les langues imparfaites en cela que plusieurs, manque la suprême: penser étant écrire sans accessoires, ni chuchotement mais tacite encore l'immortelle parole, la diversité, sur terre, des idiomes empêche personne de proférer les mots qui, sinon se trouveraient, par une frappe unique, elle-même matériellement la vérité" (*OC* 363-64). These claims echo uncannily those found in Nietzsche's fragment "On Truth and Lying"; and Walter Benjamin later cites precisely this passage from Mallarmé as the cornerstone of his essay "The Task of the Translator." (*SW* 1:253-63).>

21. Derrida also makes this connection explicitly: "Mallarmé is then perhaps a very great rhetorician; a sophist, doubtless, but a sophist who is not deceived by the image of himself which philosophy has wanted to hand down to us" (*Acts of Literature*, 126).

22. Bersani, *The Death of Stéphane Mallarmé*, 1-2.

23. *Musica Ficta*, 49.

24. On the central importance of allegory to Mallarmé, see de Man, *Blindness and Insight*, 173-75; Johnson, *Critical Difference*, 13-20; and Jameson, *Modernist Papers*, 313-19, 333.

25. Wölfflin, *Principles of Art History*, 20 (emphasis original).

26. See, primarily, Lyons, "Mallarmé and Representation in the Theater," 92-103. See also Anna Balakian, "Hérodiade and Virtual Reality," in Cohn, *Mallarmé in the Twentieth Century*; Block, *Mallarmé and the Symbolist Drama*, 6-10, 16; and Lacoue-Labarthe, *Musica Ficta*, 60-61.

27. In *Postdramatic Theater*, Lehmann calls Mallarmé "a step on the way to postdramatic theatre" (57). See also Lehmann's discussion of postdramatic "performance texts" (85-86) and the Symbolist use of scenic elements to create not just "lyric drama" (Szondi's term) but "stage poetry" (57-60). Derrida also productively observes that the libretto was "reflecting the mimodrama rather than programming it" (*Dissemination*, 199).

28. An analysis of "Pierrot, Assassin of His Wife" lies beyond the scope of this chapter, but a brief summary clarifies its plot. The play is a pantomime for a single

226 Notes to Pages 72-73

actor, Margueritte himself as Pierrot, the white clown of French *commedia*, whose figure suggests a photonegative image of Hamlet in his "customary suits of solemn black." The 1882 printed text of the play consists of a single lengthy monologue for Pierrot to speak, but it also opens paradoxically with the stage direction: "*Pierrot is mute, and this drama from start to finish,* mimed" ("Pierrot, Assassin of His Wife," in Gerould, *Doubles,* 45). Thus, in a dumbshow like the one Hamlet orchestrates, Pierrot reenacts his murder of his adulterous wife, Columbine, whom he has tickled to death prior to the play's beginning. Alongside a gravedigger, Pierrot appears at the play's outset having just buried his wife. She haunts the onstage business while Pierrot repeatedly steps in and out of her position to demonstrate, gesturally, the effect of his tickling upon her. Eventually the murderer is himself tickled to death by unseen forces. His dying laughter mixes with evil cackling from Columbine's onstage portrait, while their marriage bed bursts into infernal flames. Pierrot at once both perpetrates and suffers the main action of the play, but never fully represents it. Although Columbine's death is not directly staged, its gestures are, as Walter Benjamin might say, *quoted*. For further discussion of the connections between Hamlet and Margueritte's Pierrot, see Derrida, *Dissemination,* 195-97.

29. *D* 140. "Le silence, seul luxe après les rimes, un orchestre ne faisant avec son or, ses frôlements de pensée et de soir, qu'en détailler la signification à l'égal d'une ode tue et que c'est au poëte, suscité par un défi, de traduire! le silence aux après-midi de musique; je le trouve, avec contentement, aussi, devant la réapparition toujours inédite de Pierrot ou du poignant et élégant mime Paul Margueritte. Ainsi ce Pierrot Assassin de sa Femme composé et rédigé par lui-même, soliloque muet que, tout du long à son âme tient et du visage et des gestes le fantôme blanc comme une page pas encore écrite. . . . La scène n'illustre que l'idée, pas une action effective, dans un hymen (d'où procède le Rêve), vicieux mais sacré, entre le désir et l'accomplissement, la perpétration et son souvenir: ici devançant, là remémorant, au futur, au passé, *sous une apparence fausse de présent*. Tel opère le Mime, dont le jeu se borne à une allusion perpétuelle sans briser la glace: il installe, ainsi, un milieu, pur, de fiction" (*OC* 310).

30. For overviews of Symbolist mise-en-scène, see Deak, *Symbolist Theater,* 58-93; and Gerould, *Doubles, Demons, and Dreamers,* 7-13. On the Symbolist preoccupation with pantomime, see Symons, *Studies in Seven Arts,* 381-83.

31. Hans-Thies Lehmann argues that Mallarmé initiates a "neo-lyrical theatre that understands the scene as a site of an 'écriture' in which all components of the theatre become letters in a poetic 'text'" (*Postdramatic Theater,* 58). In Lehmann's depiction, Mallarmé seems to recall Benjamin's claim that a Brechtian actor "must be able to space his gestures as the compositor produces spaced type" (*UB* 19-20).

32. On "écriture corporelle," see Mallarmé's essay "Ballets," in *Divagations* (*OC* 304); and Derrida, *Dissemination,* 194-98. Likewise, Lacoue-Labarthe claims that for

Mallarmé, "the ballet is the purest form of theater, that is to say the closest to the presentation of the Idea" (*Musica Ficta*, 61). For a critical reading of Derrida on Mallarmé from the field of dance and performance studies, see Franko's essay "Mimique," in Noland et al., *Migrations of Gesture*, 241-58).

33. For a list of emblematic images that dance creates (knives, goblets, flowers—and, elsewhere, waves, clouds, jewels), see the essay "Ballets," in *Divagations* (*OC* 304). In a similar vein, Walter Benjamin observes that ballet eventually supplanted the emblematic-allegorical theater of the baroque (*OGT* 85). Likewise, Lacoue-Labarthe sees Mallarmé's preference for ballet over theater as stemming from "the incapacity of the drama to elevate itself to the height of allegory, of emblem, or of myth. And consequently of Idea. . . . Allegory: this is what a fundamental Platonism here . . . imposes as the very modality of the sensual presentation of the image" (*Musica Ficta*, 61).

34. Derrida, *Dissemination*, 219. The American critics Barbara Johnson and Samuel Weber have further advanced Derrida's view. In a reading of "La Déclaration Foraine," Johnson argues that Mallarmé's writing exposes both the performativity of poetic language and the abyssal self-referentiality of performative utterances (*Critical Difference*, 57). For Johnson, the performative speech act seeks but fails to exclude "theatricality" (65). Weber, however, suggests that Mallarmé puts the notion of the performative itself into question altogether, asserting instead that "Mimique" and Mallarmé's mime expose "the *theatrical* movement of Mallarmé's writing" (14).

35. Jameson, *Modernist Papers*, 317.

36. On Mallarmé and Fuchs, see Lyons, "Mallarmé and Representation in the Theater," Cohn, *Mallarmé in the Twentieth Century*, 97.

37. On the Symbolist scenography, and particularly their use of the scrims, see Deak, *Symbolist Theater*, 117. For Derrida's reading of Mallarmé's Wagnerian debts, particularly as they relate to "Mimique," see *Dissemination*, 214.

38. *Dissemination*, 213 (emphasis mine).

39. Only the second of *Hérodiade*'s three movements appeared during Mallarmé's lifetime, and only the second was maintained in his final plan for *Les Noces d'Hérodiade, mystère*. A fuller history of the poem's manuscript variants and publication history is given in Block, *Mallarmé and the Symbolist Drama*, 9-10; Norman, *Mallarmé's Sunset*, 18; and Weinfield commentary in *CP* 168-71.

40. See, for example, Block, *Mallarmé and the Symbolist Drama*, 7-10, 18; Puchner, *Stage Fright*, 59; and Shaw, *Performance in the Texts of Mallarmé*, 105.

41. Deleuze, *The Fold*, 31.

42. Puchner, *Stage Fright*, 59-80. In a similar vein, Evelyn Gould and Anna Balakian have variously argued that *Hérodiade* creates a form of "virtual theater" in the reader's mind. Gould, *Virtual Theater*; Balakian, "Hérodiade and Virtual Reality," 131-41.

228 Notes to Pages 76-78

43. The French text reads "non *possible au théâtre*, mais *exigeant le théâtre*." As Weinfield notes, this could "mean either 'not just capable of being staged but demanding the stage,' as Rosemary Lloyd translates it, . . . or 'not . . . playable on the stage, but needing the stage,' as Bradford Cook renders it" (*CP* 179). For more on the Symbolists' desire "to put on stage what common sense declared to be nondramatic and undramatizable," see Gerould, *Doubles, Demons, and Dreamers*, 7-8.

44. On spatiality in *Hérodiade*, see Marshall Olds, "From Stage to Page," in Benston and Olds, *Essays in European Literature*, 92-94; Balakian, "Hérodiade and Virtual Reality," 133. See also the discussion of externality in Bersani, *Death of Stéphane Mallarmé*, 17.

45. For Hans-Thies Lehmann's comments on Mallarmé, especially with respect to Mallarmé's scenic and gestural qualities, and on Symbolism's prefiguration of the postdramatic, see *Postdramatic Theater*, 93-94, 164.

46. Deleuze, *The Fold*, 30.

47. "le sujet de mon oeuvre est la Beauté, et le sujet apparent n'est qu'un prétexte pour aller vers Elle." (*C* 279).

48. Weinfield commentary in *CP* 169. On poetic self-abandonment in the historical baroque, see Fish, *Self-Consuming Artifacts*, 1-5.

49. On spacing, *mise-en-page*, and choreographic poetry in *Hérodiade* and *A Throw of the Dice*, see Puchner, *Stage Fright*, 63-64. For an extended discussion of Salome's dance and its importance for modernism—particularly considering the connections between Mallarmé, the broader Parisian Salome craze of the 1870s-80s, and Oscar Wilde's influential depiction of the myth in *Salomé* (1891)—see Dierkes-Thrun, *Salome's Modernity*, 16-25. In intermediating text and emblem or image, Mallarmé owes debts to the baroque pattern poetry (or *carmen figuratum*) tradition of George Herbert, as Puchner observes (*Stage Fright*, 191n30), a tradition that also inspired Dick Higgins and Intermedia. See Higgins, *George Herbert's Pattern Poems*.

50. Samuel Johnson famously defined *discordia concors* as "a combination of dissimilar things, or discovery of occult resemblances in things apparently unlike. . . . The most heterogeneous ideas are yoked by violence together" (*Lives of the English Poets*, 12). On the necessity of violence for the work of allegorical figuration, see Teskey, *Allegory and Violence*.

51. On Salome as a crucial figure at the intersection of modernist and baroque literature and theater, see Christine Buci-Glucksmann, "Salome, or the Baroque Scenography of Desire," in *Baroque Reason*, 144-62.

52. On the poem's alternative title, *Les Noces d'Hérodiade, mystère*, see Block, *Mallarmé and the Symbolist Drama*, 18; Shaw, *Performance in the Texts of Mallarmé*, 104-5. Benjamin describes the baroque tradition (from Calderón to Strindberg) as attempting a modern "form of the mystery play" (*OGT* 108).

Notes to Pages 78-82   229

53. Unsettlingly, the "Don du Poëme" also alludes to the birth of Mallarmé's daughter Geneviève some months before, in November 1864. Weinfield notes that the poet referred to Geneviève and Hérodiade as his "daughters" (*CP* 176).

54. Derrida, *Writing and Difference*, 294.

55. See "Tennyson Viewed from Here" (*D* 86–90); Smith, "The Mirror of Art"; and Cohn, *Toward the Poems*, 62.

56. Bersani explains: "The poem's difficulty is largely due to the sliding identities of persons and things, to casual and unexplained shifts in the register of being. This is particularly true of the 'Ouverture ancienne.' I am thinking, for example, of the metamorphoses of *plis*" (*Death of Stéphane Mallarmé*, 11). "A certain narrative logic . . . is disrupted by the rhetorical wandering of the word *plis*: from its merely denoting the tapestry's visible folds to a metaphorical status in 'les plis jaunes de la pensée,' and finally back to a denotative function within the elaborate metaphor of the shroud" (ibid., 12). In a similar reading of rhetorical mobility of *Hérodiade*, Barbara Johnson claims the poem for a species of allegory, describing it as "dramatizing sexuality as a rhythm of multiplications, divisions, and fusions, a series of trespassings over the bounds of unity and property" (*Critical Difference*, 18) the ultimate division being a theatrical one, between "golden conscious stage and a dark populous house" (ibid., 19). This is, as Benjamin might say, a space bedecked "in the myriad folds of an allegorical garment" (*OGT* 205).

57. Marshall Olds remarks that in Mallarmé's poetics of crisis, the sense of an individual self "is no longer channeled through the inner life. Instead the approach is from the outside through gesture, scenic context, and a relationship to things" ("From Stage to Page," 85). For similar readings, see Bersani, *Death of Stéphane Mallarmé*, 17; and Jameson, *Modernist Papers*, 326–27.

58. This is Arthur O'Shaughnessy's 1876 translation, approved and emended by Mallarmé himself. (The original text is lost.) See Moffett, *The New Painting*, 30. See also Lyons's discussion of this passage (which, like my analysis here, owes debts to Michael Fried's *Manet's Modernism*) in "Mallarmé and Representation in the Theater," 99–102.

59. *Death of Stéphane Mallarmé*, 11.

60. *Death of Stéphane Mallarmé*, 5. On this subject, Barbara Johnson makes an important qualification: "What is revolutionary in Mallarmé's poetics is less the elimination of the 'object' than [a] type of construction of a systematic set of self-emptying, nonintuitive meanings. Mallarmé's famous obscurity lies not in his devious befogging of the obvious but in his radical transformation of intelligibility itself through the ceaseless production of seemingly mutually exclusive readings of the same piece of language. *This* is what constitutes Mallarmé's break with referentiality, and not the simple abolition of the object, which would still be an entirely referential gesture. Reference is here not denied but suspended" (Johnson, *Critical Difference*, 65).

230   Notes to Pages 83-90

61. *CP* 27. "Reviendra-t-il un jour des pays cisalpins!/Assez tôt? Car tout est présage et mauvais rêve!" (*OC* 43).

62. "Comme les mit le vieux cygne en sa plume, allée/De la plume détresse, en l'éternelle allée/De ses espoirs, pour voir les diamants élus/D'une étoile mourante, et qui ne brille plus" (*OC* 43).

63. On the relation of (macro) *kosmos* to (micro) *kosmoi*, see Fletcher, "The Cosmic Image," in *Allegory*, 69-147.

64. See Weinfield's comments in *CP* 176; and Puchner, *Stage Fright*, 189n6.

65. Phèdre's entrance occurs in Act One, Scene Three, of Racine's play: "Que ces vains ornements, que ces voiles me pèsent!/Quelle importune main, en formant tous ces nœuds,/A pris soin sur mon front d'assembler mes cheveux? / Tout m'afflige et me nuit, et conspire à me nuire" (lines 6-9). Jean Racine, *Phèdre*, 38. Her entrance effectively allegorizes a desire to do "away with the ornaments" (to recall Wagner's phrase, anticipating Adolf Loos).

66. See Puchner, *Stage Fright*, 62-63; and McGuinness, *Maurice Maeterlinck*, 92; By comparison, Barnaby Norman interprets the three gestures of refusal to mean that the "Scène" allegorizes the poem's own attempt at "leaving behind a theological writing, separating itself from its past . . . and the heavy burden of a tradition associated with that past (La Nourrice), and announcing the coming of a new poetics" (*Mallarme's Sunset*, 50).

67. See Praz, *Romantic Agony*, 289; and Gerould, *Doubles, Demons, and Dreamers*, 18-19.

68. For this reason, Deleuze writes that Hérodiade, unlike Nietzsche's Dionysus, is a "frigid creature of ressentiment and bad conscience, the spirit which denies life, lost in her bitter reproaches to the Nourrice" (*Nietzsche and Philosophy*, 33). Deleuze thus suggests Hérodiade still figures the baroque of the past, not yet that of the future.

69. This phrase—"*vivante allégorie*" (*OC* 282)—comes from the prose poem "La Déclaration Foraine."

70. For analyses sensitive to the role of jouissance in *Hérodiade*, see Robillard, *Désir de la vierge*, 179; and Bersani, *Death of Stéphane Mallarmé*, 16.

71. Thibaudet, qtd. in Weinfield commentary in *CP* 176.

72. "Mallarmé and Representation in the Theater," 97.

73. This phrase in French is "virginité de site pas songé" *OC* 309. ("Virginity of undreamt-of places" is Rhonda Garelick's translation in *Rising Star* 114). Barbara Johnson renders this passage, "a spatial virginity undreamed of" (D 136).

74. Qtd. in Derrida, *Acts of Literature*, 112; For further analysis of the queer appeal of Fuller's performances, see Farfan, *Performing Queer Modernism*, 36-38.

75. Lyons, "Mallarmé and Representation in the Theater," 97.

76. *Death of Stéphane Mallarmé*, ix.

Notes to Pages 90–95

77. Lyons, "Mallarmé and Representation in the Theater," 97.

78. *D* 255. "Qu'une Banque s'abatte, du vague, du médiocre, du gris. / Le numéraire, engin de terrible précision, net aux consciences, perd jusqu'à un sens. / . . . [O]n cherche, avec cet indice que, si un nombre se majore et recule, vers l'improbable, il inscrit plus de zéros: signifiant que son total équivaut spirituelle- ment à rien, presque" (*OC* 398).

79. This maxim, from Shakespeare's *Merchant of Venice*, reflects a revised but commonplace example of the far-fetched BAROCO syllogism of classical logic (1. All P are M; 2. And some S are not M; 3. therefore some S are not P). Thus: "1. All gold has value. 2. Some things that glitter have no value. 3. Therefore, some things that glitter are not gold."

80. On Mallarmé's interest in the Panama scandal, see Johnson, *World of Difference*, 57–67. In dialogue with Michael Fried, Walter Benn Michaels has also spoken about Mallarmé's preoccupation with French monetary policy and the gold standard. See Centre Pompidou, "Walter Benn Michaels"; see also Benn Michaels, *Gold Standard and the Logic of Naturalism*; and Pearson, "Les Chiffres et les Lettres." For a Marxist account of the Symbolists' relationship to the "deferentialization" of currency from monetary value, see also Berardi, *The Uprising*, 18–30.

81. Jameson, *Modernist Papers*, 326.

82. On the connection between *Hérodiade* and the "Sonnet allégorique de lui-même," see Norman, *Mallarmé's Sunset*, 49.

83. On Mallarmé's meanings for écriture, it is notable that one of Jacques Derrida's 1968–69 seminars (as yet untranslated) is titled *L'écriture et le théâtre: Mallarmé/Artaud*. Although the philosophical connections between Mallarmé and Artaud, in particular concerning their shared preoccupations with cruelty, are significant, the subject lies outside the scope of this chapter.

84. Shaw writes that Jacques Scherer's 1978 *"Livre" de Mallarmé* (first published in 1957) "should not be equated with the text of Mallarmé's Book, not because Mallarmé did not intend [the Book] to be published but because [his manuscript] does not present itself either as a literary text in the ordinary sense or as the text of the literary/theatrical work that it describes. For those who still regard some measure of intentionality as relevant in determining the status of a work, it should be noted that there is no apparent order to the collection of sheets and notes that constitute *Le Livre*. . . . Moreover, there is no reason to think that this manuscript includes *all* of the notes pertaining to the Book, since many of Mallarmé's notes were burned as he had requested" (Shaw, *Performance in the Texts of Mallarmé*, 186n3). Taking an opposing view, the translator Sylvia Gorelick writes, in the introduction to her English translation of Mallarmé's *Livre* manuscript: "The manuscripts that compose *The Book* constitute, in a significant respect, the precise material realization of the idea that preoccupied Mallarmé for over thirty years.

232   Notes to Pages 96-98

They show a material ideality that has not yet had its time—they communicate an injunction to the reader-participant to theatrically fabricate a present in which it could take place" (xiv).

85. Often—for example, as with RoseLee Goldberg's history *Performance Art*—the prehistory of performance in Europe is said to begin with Marinetti and the Futurist evenings of the 1910s, but Mallarmé's imagined *Livre* performances predate Marinetti by two decades.

86. On Mallarmé's interest in the Catholic mass as a true form of drama, see Meillassoux, *Number and the Siren*, 107-13; Lacoue-Labarthe, *Musica Ficta*, 51-59; and Deleuze, *Nietzsche and Philosophy*, 33. Mallarmé's views on Catholic ritual are primarily, and ambiguously, set out in his prose poem "Catholicism" (*D* 243-48; *OC* 390-95). His notes describe the ritual of the *Livre* as a *mystère*, a term he uses elsewhere for his *Hérodiade*, recalling the medieval and baroque theater of Catholicism.

87. Puchner, *Stage Fright*, 68-69.

88. For discussions of the performance components of the *Livre*, see Deak, *Symbolist Theater*, 89-93; and Puchner, *Stage Fright*, 69-75.

89. Puchner, *Stage Fright*, 75-76.

90. Deak offers this reading in *Symbolist Theater*, 92.

91. Orgel, *Illusion of Power*, 24.

92. Deak sees a connection between Mallarmé's Book and the *Book of Fate* dreamed of by Leibniz (*Symbolist Theater*, 85).

93. Edward Said observes, in "The Problem of Textuality," that the notion of textuality found in Derrida's writing has consistent reference to ideas of theater and theatricality (691). Fuchs makes a similar observation about deconstruction in the chapter "Postmodernism and the 'Scene' of Theater" in her *Death of Character*, 147-49.

94. See, for example, Borges, *Total Library*, 214-16; and Borges, "The Library of Babel," in *Collected Fictions*, 112-18. On Borges's complex relationship to baroque style, see Johnson, "On Borges's B/baroque."

95. Meillassoux, *Number and the Siren*, 106-7. Mary Lewis Shaw observes that Mallarmé initially and explicitly "tied his reflections on the ideal Book with the date 1889 and the opening of the centennial celebrations for the French Revolution," but later shifted the focus of its intentions toward the dawning of the twentieth century (*Performance in the Texts*, 1n1).

96. For French theorists (other than Meillassoux, Derrida, and Deleuze) concerned with Mallarmé's politics, see, for example, Badiou, *Being and Event*, 191-98; Lacoue-Labarthe, *Musica Ficta*, 41-84; Rancière, *Mute Speech*, 128-44; and Rancière, *The Politics of the Siren*, passim. On Mallarmé's relationship to Wagner, see Block, *Mallarmé and the Symbolist Drama*, 54-75, 79-81; Jameson, *Modernist Papers*, 315, 320; Lacoue-Labarthe, *Musica Ficta*, 41-84; Meillassoux, *Number and the Siren*,

Notes to Pages 98-101   233

108; Puchner, *Stage Fright*, 71-72; Roberts, *Total Work of Art*, 131-36; Shaw, *Performance in the Texts of Mallarmé*, 1, 87-96; and Weinfield commentary, in *CP* 227-29.

97. This phrase appears amid a discussion of poetry's need to compete with the theater of Bayreuth. Mallarmé writes that the Book will need to become a kind of theater: "The pleasure vainly sought by the late Dreamer-King of Bavaria in solitary attendance at the unfolding of scenery, is found, in retreat from the baroque crowd rather than in its absence from the bleachers, achieved by restoring the text, in its nakedness, to the spectacle" (*D* 160-61).

98. See Jameson, *Modernist Papers*, 326. Meillassoux (*Number and the Siren*, 118) and Dudley Marchi ("Participatory Aesthetics") have offered similar opinions.

99. See Jameson, *Modernist Papers*, 326-27. Jameson's concepts of constellation and allegory derive from a reading of both Walter Benjamin and Mallarmé's "Sonnet allégorique de lui meme," in which the constellation figure appears significantly in the poem's closing moments (as it does in *A Throw of the Dice*).

100. *D* 215; *OC* 369. "[Agir signifia] produire sur beaucoup un mouvement qui te donne en retour l'émoi que tu en fus le principe, donc existes: dont aucun ne se croit, au préalable, sûr."

101. "The pure work implies the disappearance of the poet speaking, who yields the initiative to words, through the clash of their ordered inequalities" (*D* 208). "L'oeuvre pure implique la disparition élocutoire du poëte, qui cède l'initiative aux mots, par le heurt de leur inégalité mobilisés" (*OC* 366). For Mallarmé's foundational role in modern discussions of "The Death of the Author," see Barthes, *Image, Music, Text*, 143.

102. For the classic articulation of the performativity of political action without a transcendent subject, which Mallarmé here seems to anticipate, see Butler, *Gender Trouble*, 194-203.

103. Puchner notes Mallarmé's vision of acting approaches what Michael Kirby calls "non-matrixed performance" (Puchner, *Stage Fright*, 190n22). It is also clear that Mallarmé's theater is one that witnesses what Fuchs calls "the death of character" in its stable, anthropocentric sense.

104. Here Mallarmé's usefulness goes beyond his theory of avant-garde theatricality on the stage or in the poetic text. He also seems to entertain an inchoate thought of gender performativity, since most of Mallarmé's personae in *La Dernière Mode* were female. It should not go without saying that several were also not white: "A Creole Woman," "Zizi, good mulatto woman of Surat," "Olympia, the negress" (Mallarmé, *Mallarmé on Fashion*). I mention this fact, bearing in mind Judith Butler's precaution that "race and gender ought not to be treated as simple analogies. . . . [N]o single account of construction will do, and that these categories always work as background for one another, and they often find their most powerful articulation through one another" (*Gender Trouble*, xvi-xvii). Butler cites

234   Notes to Pages 102-107

the work of Kobena Mercer, Kendall Thomas, Hortense Spillers, and Greg Thomas
as influential in shaping her thinking on this subject. I wish only to note here that
Mallarmé's racial consciousness and the sense of easiness with which he adopts
aspects of racial masquerade may be the subject of another study, but the potential
he saw in writing to destabilize and resignify otherwise fixed categories of identity
must nevertheless be marked as an important dimension of his political aesthetics.

Chapter 3. Landscapes of Melancholy

1. *UB* 115. In this chapter I leave the word Trauerspiel untranslated, unitalicized,
and capitalized. For its plural, I prefer the German *Trauerspiele* over the Anglicized
"trauerspiels," the latter of which appears in Eiland's new translation of Benjamin's
baroque study. When quoting passages that include this word, I have silently
regularized spelling, capitalization, and formatting so the word appears consistently across the chapter.

2. For an echo of this lopsided crown, see Benjamin's comments on Chaplin
circa 1934: "[H]is bowler hat which no longer sits so securely on his head, betrays
the fact that the rule of the bourgeoisie is tottering" (*SW* 2.2:793).

3. See Steiner's introduction to Benjamin, *The Origin of German Tragic Drama*,
13-14.

4. For performance scholars who draw influence from Benjamin, see Auslander,
Liveness, 50-55; Reinelt and Roach, *Critical Theory and Performance*, 192-93; and
Taussig, *Mimesis and Alterity*. The Trauerspiel-book's continuing neglect within
American performance historiography owes largely to early modern German
drama's continuing marginality in Anglophone academic circles. For an example of
laudable recent work in early modern theater studies that shows few traces of the
Trauerspiel-book's direct influence, see Turner, *Early Modern Theatricality*.

5. Lehmann identifies Racine with originating a modern regime of dramatic
theater (*Postdramatic Theatre*, 34; *Tragedy and Dramatic Theatre*, 253-87).

6. For Benjamin's status as a "literary" writer, see Wellek, "The Early Literary
Criticism of Walter Benjamin"; and Grossman, "The Reception of Walter Benjamin
in the Anglo-American Literary Institution." For analysis of Benjamin's importance
for theater, by contrast, see Asman, "Return of the Sign to the Body: Benjamin and
Gesture in the Age of Retheatricalization"; and Asman, "Theater and *Agon/Agon*
and Theater." See also Fehér, "Lukács, Benjamin, Theatre"; Friedlander, "On the
Musical Gathering of Echoes of the Voice"; and Rokem, "'Suddenly a stranger
comes into the room.'"

7. "Es ist dem philosophischen Schrifttum eigen, mit jeder Wendung von
neuem vor der Frage der Darstellung zu stehen" (*UDT* 9). As Eiland explains in a
footnote: "'Presentation' translates *Darstellung*, which also means 'representation'"

Notes to Pages 107–110

(*OGT* 1n1). Osborne's translation also translates *Darstellung* as "representation." See Benjamin, *Origin of German Tragic Drama*, 27.

8. "Ideas are to things as constellations to stars. . . . Ideas are eternal constellations, and inasmuch as the elements are grasped as points in such constellations, the phenomena are simultaneously divided out and saved" (*OGT* 10–11). Péter Szondi defines the Benjaminian idea as "the figure of the unity of the diverse semantic nuances of a word" (qtd. in Bernstein, *Frankfurt School*, 36n21). In this way, Benjamin's idea constellations respond to Nietzsche's philology, in which different languages use different words for the same referent. See also the discussion of *Brot* and *pain* in Benjamin, "The Task of the Translator," *GS* 4.1:13–14.

9. *OGT* 3. On embodiment in Benjamin's work, see Richter, *Walter Benjamin and the Corpus of Autobiography*.

10. On George and Strindberg, see *OGT* 36 and 108, respectively. On Hofmannsthal's connections to the baroque, see the letter of 11 June 1925 in *CWB* 270–71. On baroque resonances in Kafka, see Weber, *Theatricality as Medium*, 76–82. For Benjamin's views on Expressionism in the visual arts, see his letter to Scholem, 22 October 1917, in *CWB* 97–102. See also Newman, *Benjamin's Library*, 7–8.

11. *OGT* 37; *UDT* 37. On Benjamin's admiration for Riegl, see his final curriculum vitae of 1939–40 (*SW* 4:381). See also Riegl, *Origin of Baroque Art in Rome*. On his dismissive views of Wölfflin, by contrast, see Smith, *Benjamin*, xxxviiin96; and Levin, "Walter Benjamin and the Theory of Art History," 79–81.

12. Expressionism arose in Germany during the First World War, reaching what Mel Gordon describes as a culmination between 1919 and 1921 in Berlin. (Benjamin was residing in Berlin during these years, having completed his doctorate.) See Gordon, *Expressionist Texts*, 11, 20–22. For Benjamin's description of "history as content of the Trauerspiel," see *OGT* 45–48.

13. This evocative passage comes from Ihering's review of the premiere of Brecht's play *Drums in the Night*. Kaes, Jay, and Dimendberg, *Weimar Republic Sourcebook*, 534. See also Wellek, "Concept of Baroque in Literary Scholarship," 79–80.

14. *OGT* 40. "Denn der ärmliche Affektrest der Spannung, der diesem Typus als einzige Evidenz von Theatralischem geblieben ist, kommt in der Vorführung der Märtyrergeschichte nicht auf seine Kosten" (*UDT* 56).

15. The Trauerspiel-book explicitly questions if musical performance in Trauerspiel "plays a role other than merely theatrical (*anders als rein theatralisch*)" (*OGT* 230; *UDT* 189). On the relationships between Trauerspiel, sound, and music, see Vélez, "Allegory, Noise, and History"; and Friedlander, "On the Musical Gathering of Echoes of the Voice."

16. On the pro-theatricalism of Expressionism in Benjamin's lifetime, see Fuchs, *Revolution in the Theater*; and Kracauer, *Theory of Film*, 36–39. On the tension between Expressionism and realism, see Davis and Postlewait, *Theatricality*, 12–13.

236 Notes to Pages 111-112

17. Benjamin draws on Franz Rosenzweig's *Star of Redemption* to note that "in tragedy pagan man becomes aware that he is better than his gods, but the realization robs him of speech, remains unspoken" (*OGT* 104). By contrast, the figures of Trauerspiel are compelled into lamentation and prolixity.

18. Throughout the Trauerspiel-book, Benjamin observes elements of Trauerspiel in a wide range of later theater forms: Viennese farces, the Christian tragedy of fate, popular puppet theaters, the Sturm und Drang and Weimar classicism movements, and the *Haupt- und Staatsaktion* (a southern German subgenre about affairs of state).

19. With this narrative of secularization, Benjamin draws on both Nietzsche's *Birth of Tragedy* and Lukács's *Theory of the Novel*. For similar narratives of European secularization, see Goldmann, *The Hidden God*; and Weber, *Protestant Ethic and the Spirit of Capitalism*. Against Nietzsche, George Steiner, and others, Hans-Thies Lehmann has argued that tragedy ought to be considered a modality not of drama but of theater, and that doing so reveals it as a persistent phenomenon throughout European history, from antiquity through Racine to the present (*Tragedy and Dramatic Theatre*, 1-16).

20. "No one looked to the Greek author for serious instruction concerning technique and subject matter, such as, since the time of Gryphius, Dutch classicism and the Jesuit theater, above all, had time and again provided" (*OGT* 43). In addition to Jesuit and Dutch theater scenes, English influences on Trauerspiel can be traced to itinerant acting companies from London touring the continent starting in the 1580s, whose numbers swelled with the closing of the English playhouses in 1642.

21. "It is precisely the dramatic form that, more decisively than any other, makes an appeal to historical resonance. The Baroque dramatic form has been denied such resonance" (*OGT* 28).

22. Agamben, in *Means without Ends*, defines gesture, after Varro, as the presentation of a means that evades the possibility of an end (57) and as "*the exhibition of a mediality: it is the process of making a means visible as such*" (58; italics in original).

23. *OGT* 65-67. Cf. Freud's essay "Mourning and Melancholia," in *General Psychological Theory*, 161-78.

24. Wagner, *Parsifal*, 7.

25. On the role of space in Benjamin's argument, see Weber, *Theatricality as Medium*, 172-73.

26. Gryphius, "Catharine of Georgia, or Proven Constancy," I.1. I thank Janifer Stackhouse for her scholarly work on Gryphius's plays and for generously sharing her translation with me. "Der Schauplatz liegt voll Leichen-Bilder/Cronen, Zepter, Schwerdter etc. Vber dem Schau-Platz öffnet sich der Himmel/vnter dem Schau-Platz die Helle. Die Ewigkeit kommet von dem Himmel/vnd bleibet auff dem Schau-Platz stehen" (Gryphius, *Catharina von Georgien*, 13).

27. Gryphius, "Catharine of Georgia, or Proven Constancy," I.1.62-69. "[S]chaut

Notes to Pages 112-115

was ist diß Threnenthal/Ein FolterHauß da man mit Strang vnd Pfahl/Vnd Tode schertzt. Vor mir ligt Printz vnd Crone/Ich tret auff Zepter vnd auff Stab vnd steh auff Vater vnd dem Sohne./Schmuck, Bild, Metall vnd ein gelehrt Papir/Ist nichts als Sprew vnd leichter Staub vor mir" (Gryphius, *Catharina von Georgien*, 16).

28. *OGT* 122. Benjamin's interest in puppetry reflects a modern preoccupation with puppets as a means to dehumanize the modern stage. See also Kleist, "On the Marionette Theater"; and the discussion of the *Übermarionette* in Craig, *On the Art of the Theatre*.

29. In this regard, Trauerspiel anticipates the twentieth-century theater, particularly in the latter's development of "landscape" dramaturgies. See Fuchs, *Death of Character*, 12; Lehmann, *Postdramatic Theater*, 62-63).

30. See Schmitt, *Political Theology*, 5-7. Schmitt responds to Benjamin in *Hamlet or Hecuba*, 59-65. On Benjamin and Schmitt's relationship, see Agamben, *State of Exception*, 52-64; Weber, *Benjamin's -abilities*, 176-94.

31. "The plane of the creaturely state, the terrain on which the Trauerspiel unfolds, quite unmistakably determines the sovereign as well. As highly enthroned as he is over his subjects and his state, his status is circumscribed by the world of creation; he is the lord of creatures, but he remains a creature" (*OGT* 72).

32. Gryphius, *Leo Armenius*, in Gillespie, *German Theater before 1750*, 128. "Der harte Crambonit begont' erst recht zu wütten:/. . . Vnd schwung sein Mordschwerd auff das auf den Fürsten kam/Vnd jhm mit einem streich so Arm' alß Creutz abnahm./Man stieß in dem er fiel jhn zweymal durch die brüste:/. . . Wie man die Leich vmbriß wie man durch jedes glied/Die stumpfen Dolchen zwang." (Gryphius, *Leo Armenius: Trauerspiel*, 95).

33. Benjamin's discussion of the allegorical divisions within the sovereign body show a clear resonance with the later claims of his colleague Ernst Kantorowicz in *The King's Two Bodies*. On the intersections of their thought, see Kahn, *Future of Illusion*, 55-82; and Halpern, "King's Two Buckets," 72-75. In an English context, the early modern notion of the king's double body as an allegorical entity already appears in the prefatory letter to Raleigh of Edmund Spenser's *Faerie Queene*, where Elizabeth I is described as one who "beareth two persons, the one of a most royall queene or empresse, the other of a most vertuous and beautiful lady" (Spenser, *Faerie Queene*, 16).

34. Zenón Luis-Martínez advances the argument, in "Shakespeare's Historical Drama as *Trauerspiel*," that *Richard II*, even more than *Hamlet*, deserves to be understood as that Shakespearean play which conforms most recognizably to Benjamin's description of Trauerspiel ("Shakespeare's Historical Drama as *Trauerspiel*"). (Benjamin mentions in the *Berlin Chronicle* that he saw the Austrian actor Josef Kainz in the role of Richard II at the Theaters am Nollendorfplatz in 1909. I am grateful to Nadine Werner, formerly of the Akademie der Künste in Berlin, for bringing to my attention this footnote of performance history.)

238 Notes to Pages 116-120

35. The intriguer's dramaturgical-philosophical interest resides in the situation of immanence his plots expose and depend on. His skullduggery prevails because of his superior understanding of his victims' subjection to the state of physical, creaturely being (*OGT* 85). Benjamin offers Machiavelli as an exemplary philosopher of immanence in this respect, citing Dilthey's views on Machiavelli to make his point (ibid., 85-86).

36. See Turner, *Early Modern Theatricality*, 568-78.

37. In *The Player's Passion*, performance theorist Joseph Roach documents extensively how the rise of Cartesian mechanism initiated a centuries-long process by which the supposedly "natural" relationship between gesture and passion could be fixed with increasing scientific specificity (23-58).

38. On the problems of interpreting gesture manuals, see Peters, *Theatre of the Book*, 281-82.

39. That is, allegorical gesture (like postdramatic gesture) can be said to expose, above all, what Hans-Thies Lehmann calls "a *self-dramatization of physis*" (*Postdramatic Theater*, 163; emphasis original).

40. For a discussion of the frozen or statuesque quality of baroque gesture, see Roach, *Player's Passion*, 67-70.

41. For a discussion of gestures of commandment, see Agamben, "Gesture, or the Structure of Art."

42. Although human and natural history *seem* like a frozen landscape to the authors of Trauerspiel, Benjamin's notion of origin as "an eddy in the stream of becoming" suggests historical movement along more Heraclitan lines, as a turbulent flow in which human action may have its currents turned awry (*OGT* 24).

43. On the conceptual relationship between queering and ruination, see Herring, *Queering the Underworld*, 21.

44. "To become aware of the lack of freedom, the imperfection and brokenness of the sensuous, of the beautiful physis, was something forbidden to classicism by its very nature. But this is precisely what Baroque allegory, beneath its mad pomp, proclaims with unprecedented insistence" (*OGT* 186).

45. Benjamin describes the comingling of Egyptian, Greek, and early Christian visual elements in baroque allegory throughout the Trauerspiel-book, drawing influence from Aby Warburg and Erwin Panofsky's iconological scholarship (*OGT* 153-59, 181, 247).

46. See *OGT* 103-4, 241-48; and Fletcher, *Allegory*, 39-47.

47. To be clear, the Trauerspiel-book does not argue that language was once full of divine significance that it lost during the baroque. Rather, it claims that this *felt* loss of linguistic fullness, whether justified or not, was a defining characteristic of early modern European life, unprecedented in its pervasiveness.

48. Benjamin's 1940 essay on Baudelaire defines aura, via footnote, as follows: "Whenever a human being, an animal, or an inanimate object thus endowed by the

Notes to Pages 121-123

poet lifts up its eyes, it draws him into the distance. The gaze of nature, when thus awakened, dreams and pulls the poet after its dream. Words, too, can have an aura of their own. This is how Karl Kraus described it: 'The closer one looks at a word, the greater the distance from which it looks back'" (*SW* 4:354n77).

49. Benjamin's rethinking of allegory's relationship to symbol in light of Romanticism should be understood in the context of a broader academic reassessment of this subject by German philologists such as Ernst Robert Curtius, Erich Auerbach, and others, as Paul de Man has argued. *Blindness and Insight*, 171, 191.

50. To name one example, Benjamin cites Marsilio Ficino's idea of Egyptian hieroglyphs as image characters of divine thought in which words express things in perfect fullness (*OGT* 178).

51. For Nietzsche's similar (Benjamin would say allegorical) concept of truth as a mobile army of metaphors and a sum of human power relations, see *TL* 145.

52. *OGT* 5-8. See also Benjamin's essay "On Language as Such and on the Language of Man," which echoes the Kabbalistic tradition in claiming that "all language communicates itself *in* itself" (*SW* 1:64). For Benjamin, human language may appear arbitrary and broken from its divine source, but it is nevertheless part of an immanent linguistic medium in which words and things are always interconnected and in constant communication with each other. Such correspondences are the "antidote" to allegory's destructive and nihilistic arbitrariness (*AP* J86,2).

53. See, for example, Benjamin's discussion of Johann Wilhelm Ritter's Romantic philosophy of language, developed in response to Ernst Chladni's experiments with music, acoustics, and sound. Of Chladni's "sound plates," Benjamin cites Ritter's assertion "The whole of creation is really language, and thus literally created through the word, and [is] the created and creating word itself" (qtd. in *OGT* 231-32). This passage may be fruitfully read alongside Benjamin's argument in "On Language as Such and on the Language of Man" (*SW* 1: 62-75).

54. Jameson, *Brecht and Method*, 153. Similarly, Weber sees Benjamin as claiming that theater "assume[d] a radically new role" in the Reformation, namely "that of restaging history and politics . . . as allegories" (*Theatricality as Medium*, 172); and that "[i]f allegory marks the more or less forced convergence of phenomenon and meaning, it does not achieve their fusion or unification. Such convergence remains, therefore, *disjunctive*. This disjunction defines the specifically *theatrical* medium of the German baroque *Trauerspiel* as irreducibly allegorical" (ibid., 174).

55. *OGT* 184. Samuel Weber offers a provocative reading of this passage with respect to Benjamin's comments on *detail*: "That strict attention to detail is no longer favored in the world of the German baroque, however, does not mean that details themselves have lost all meaning; indeed, precisely the opposite is the case. . . . [Details are] anything but insignificant or superfluous: they are required of baroque allegory, but as *Requisiten des Bedeutens*, indispensable theatrical props of signification" (*Benjamin's -abilities*, 241-42).

240   Notes to Pages 123–127

56. "La Nature est un temple où de vivants piliers / Laissent parfois sortir de confuses paroles; / L'homme y passe à travers des forêts de symboles / Qui l'observent avec des regards familiers" (Baudelaire, *Flowers of Evil*, 18). The place of allegory and melancholy in Baudelaire's poetry preoccupied Benjamin during the early 1920s. Baudelaire's poem corresponds to Scholem's claim that "the world of Kabbalism is full [of theological symbols]," and moreover, "the whole world is to the Kabbalist . . . a *corpus symbolicum*" (qtd. in Buck-Morss, *Dialectics of Seeing*, 236).

57. *OGT* 192. For Benjamin's comments on baroque allegory as an early effort at the *Gesamtkunstwerk*, see his discussion of Harsdörffer and Winckelmann (ibid.). Benjamin also detects the *heaviness* of allegory within the domain of baroque poetry: "Its language is full of material display. Never has poetry been less winged" (ibid., 217).

58. On the relationship of ornament to aura, see Hansen, "Benjamin's Aura," 359.

59. Weber, *Theatricality as Medium*, 1–31, 175–80.

60. The first (1593) edition of Ripa's *Iconologia* was published without woodcuts and described the allegorical figurations in printed text alone. This fact in itself indicates a robust, early modern awareness of language's emblematic nature.

61. Miriam Bratu Hansen argues that, for Benjamin, the concept of aura "is not an inherent property of persons or objects but pertains to the *medium* of perception. . . . [A]ura is itself a medium that defines the gaze of the human beings portrayed" ("Benjamin's Aura," 342).

62. "In order to counter the absorption, the allegorical has to unfold itself in constantly new and surprising ways" (*OGT* 195). In other words, as the Trauerspiel-book explains in a passage later reproduced in the *Arcades Project*, "[a]llegories become dated because it is part of their nature to shock" (*AP* J54,3).

63. "Als Stückwerk aber starren aus dem allegorischen Gebild die Dinge" (*UDT* 164).

64. As Hansen notes, the concept of aura first appears in Benjamin's writing in 1930 ("Benjamin's Aura," 336).

65. Hansen distinguishes between "genuine" and "simulated" forms of aura in Benjamin's writing. The former holds out a utopian political promise but is "irrevocably in decay," while the latter deploys "art, technology, and the masses" to oppose any such utopian politics. With this distinction, it may be said that theatrical parabasis permits genuine aura to flash up, while dramatic mimesis threatens to perpetuate simulated aura ("Benjamin's Aura," 356).

66. Hansen argues this point with respect to Benjamin's writings on photography. Notwithstanding the differences between theater and photography as mediums or between the 1650s and the 1850s as historical contexts, her comments illuminate the exchange of gazes that can occur with theatricality in performance. "The auratic return of the gaze does not depend upon the photographic subject's

Notes to Pages 127-130　　　　　　　　　　　　241

direct look at the camera (or, for that matter, the later injunction against that direct look which voyeuristically solicits the viewer as buyer)" ("Benjamin's Aura," 343).

67. For Benjamin's notion of reflection and miniaturization, see his comments on the baroque volute in architecture, which "repeats itself to infinity and reduces to the unfathomable the sphere which it delimits" (*OGT* 71).

68. See Benjamin's thesis "On the Concept of History," where he writes, in opposition to the nineteenth-century academic historicism of Leopold von Ranke: "Articulating the past historically does not mean recognizing it 'the way it really was.' It means appropriating a memory as it flashes up in a moment of danger" (*SW* 4:391). On "the notion of aura as a premonition of future catastrophe," see Hansen, "Benjamin's Aura," 342.

69. *OGT* 254. For a version of this passage that offers greater syntactical clarity, see Osborne's translation: "For it is precisely visions of the frenzy of destruction, in which all earthly things collapse into a heap of ruins, which reveal the limit set upon allegorical contemplation, rather than its ideal quality. The bleak confusion of Golgotha, which can be recognized as the schema underlying the allegorical figures in hundreds of the engravings and descriptions of the period, is not just a symbol of the desolation of human existence. In it transitoriness is not signified or allegorically represented, so much as, in its own significance, displayed as allegory. As the allegory of resurrection. Ultimately in the death-signs of the baroque the direction of allegorical reflection is reversed; on the second part of its wide arc it returns, to redeem" (Benjamin, *Origin of German Tragic Drama*, 232).

70. *OGT* 258. Benjamin adapts this notion of *ponderación misteriosa* from German literary historian Karl Borinski's *Geschichte der deutschen Literatur*. He notes elsewhere that "the Baroque apotheosis is dialectical. It is achieved in the turnabout of extremes" (*OGT* 166).

71. On students' importance for history and revolutionary struggle, see "The Life of Students," in *SW* 1:37-47.

72. Benjamin's claim echoes Hegel's conclusion in the lectures titled "Tragedy as a Dramatic Art," which locate the actual tragic-dialectical collision of the play not between Hamlet and Claudius but in Hamlet's subjective inwardness, his "inner life." See Hegel, *Hegel on Tragedy*, 83.

73. As Franco Moretti writes: "A single voice speaks in [Shakespeare's] soliloquys—or better, a single function: not referential, as in the speeches of Gorboduc's counsellors . . . but *self-referential*, forcibly released from all that surrounds it and henceforward painfully absorbed in itself" (*Signs Taken for Wonders*, 71).

74. Moretti, *Signs Taken for Wonders*, 45-50, 70-71.

75. Buck-Morss, *Dialectics of Seeing*, 18.

76. See Benjamin's letter of 18 September 1926, in *CWB* 305. Elsewhere, Benjamin writes that, to the flaneur, the city represents "a theatrical display"

242 Notes to Pages 130-133

(*AP* J66a,6). As Susan Sontag summarized this shift, "The successor to the baroque stage set is the Surrealist city" (*Under the Sign of Saturn*, 116.)

77. Benjamin's translation of Baudelaire's "Tableaux parisiens" first appeared in print in 1923, alongside Benjamin's introduction, "The Task of the Translator." The latter notably cites Mallarmé's essay "The Crisis of Verse": "Les langues imparfaites en cela que plusieurs, manque la supreme." (*SW* 1:263n1).

78. On 13 January 1924, Benjamin wrote to Hugo von Hofmannsthal, "In the final analysis, it is [Baudelaire's] style that fascinated me more than anything else and that I would be inclined to call baroque banality in the same sense that Claudel called it a mixture of the style of Racine and that of a reporter of the 1840s" (*CWB* 230).

79. "Baudelaire's destructive impulse is nowhere concerned with the abolition of what falls to it. This is reflected in his allegory and is the condition of its regressive tendency. On the other hand, allegory has to do, precisely in its destructive furor, with dispelling the illusion that proceeds from all 'given order,' whether of art or of life: the illusion of totality or of organic wholeness which transfigures that order and makes it seem endurable. And this is the progressive tendency of allegory" (*AP* J57,3).

80. *AP* J81,6. These comments recall those Benjamin makes elsewhere concerning Kafka's incapacity to comprehend *gestus*: "Kafka could understand things only in the form of a *gestus*, and this *gestus* which he did not understand constitutes the cloudy part of the parables. Kafka's writings emanate from it" (*SW* 2.2:808).

81. In his letter to Scholem of 24 June 1929, Benjamin claims that he was familiar at the time only with Brecht's *Threepenny Opera* and ballads. This letter does not appear in the published Benjamin correspondence edited by Scholem and Adorno, but is reproduced in Wizisla, *Benjamin and Brecht*, 1. The circumstances of Brecht and Benjamin's initial meeting are described ibid., 1-8.

82. The Theater am Schiffbauerdamm was completed by architect Heinrich Seeling in 1892. Dorita Hannah describes it as "[a] classic bourgeois concoction, its opulent multilevel horseshoe auditorium, painted red and gold, faces a proscenium stage flanked with caryatids. The only spatial gesture to a Brechtian 'theatre of alienation' is the slash of a defiantly painted red cross on the royal box's coat of arms: a performative statement within a sea of plush velvet and gilded figures" (*Event-Space*, 163).

83. By his own account, Brecht began conceiving of his work as "*episches Theater*"—originally Erwin Piscator's term, coined in 1924, during his first year as artistic director of the Berlin Volksbühne—in the rehearsals for his production of *Edward II*, also in 1924. His narrative of "the moment at which the idea of epic theatre first came into his head" is given in "Conversations with Brecht," in *UB* 115.

84. For Benjamin's remarks on the baroque elements of Russian Naturalism, see

Notes to Pages 134–136   243

"The Political Groupings of Russian Writers" (1927), in *SW* 2.1:7. On the closeness of baroque emblems to both Surrealism and montage as artistic methods, see Buck-Morss, *Dialectics of Seeing*, 225–31; and Bürger, *Theory of the Avant-Garde*, 68–82. On the distinction between allegorical images and dialectical images, see Buck-Morss, *Dialectics of Seeing*, 241.

85. To be clear, it is not the case that allegory *triumphs* over mimesis in the time of European modernism. Instead, the form of allegory, residual since the early modern period, reasserts itself in Brecht's work and so contests the primacy of dramatic mimesis as a theatrical mode. Nor does the crisis of mimesis in European modernism signal a situation in which the external, objective world has disappeared as a point of stable reference. Susan Buck-Morss addresses these problems of Benjamin interpretation in *Dialectics of Seeing*, 222–27.

86. Brecht, *Collected Plays*, 2, 38.

87. Regarding realism, Benjamin's interest in the baroque may usefully be described as formalist inasmuch as baroque theater, like epic theater, typically resists the primacy of any straightforwardly absorptive representation. For primary texts in the 1930s debate over realism and formalism, sometimes referred to as the Brecht-Lukács or Frankfurt School-Lukács debate, see the contributions in Adorno et al., *Aesthetics and Politics*.

88. Erdmut Wizisla writes: "Benjamin pointed out that Baroque tragedy and epic theatre were linked by a related anti-Aristotelian aesthetic; in both dramatic forms it was rather a question 'of the social sphere of interaction' than 'of individual characters'" (*Benjamin and Brecht*, 109). For Brecht's own self-described opposition to Aristotle, see, for example, "Indirect Impact of Epic Theatre," in Brecht, *Brecht on Theatre*, 57–62).

89. On this Socratic tradition of theater, see Puchner, *Drama of Ideas*.

90. Although Benjamin lists Trauerspiel here alongside a number of other historical influences over Brecht, such as Hroswitha of Gandersheim and Jakob Lenz, he gives indications elsewhere that the baroque aspects of Brecht's work are especially noteworthy. See, for example, the letter to Werner Kraft of 30 January 1936: "Tradition is surely present in Brecht's work. It is just that we must look for it where we have not often looked before: I am thinking primarily of Bavarian folk poetry, not to mention manifest characteristics that can be traced back to the didactic and parabolic sermon of the south German baroque" (*CWB* 520–21).

91. In describing "the death of character" that takes place in the time of modernism, the dramaturgical critic and theorist Elinor Fuchs has suggested three major directions the dissolution of autonomous character has taken as "allegorical, critical, and theatricalist," positing "Strindberg, Brecht, and Pirandello" as providing "the seminal examples." But if Benjamin's theory of Trauerspiel can be credited, all of these developments (including Galy Gay as a "critical" character and Hamlet as a "theatricalist" one) are actually forms of allegory. See Fuchs, *Death of Character*, 32.

92. Benjamin cites the historians Wilhelm Hausenstein and Karl Borinski, respectively, on this point: "[T]here is no turn of events which the baroque style would not conclude with a miracle"; and: "It is the Aristotelian idea of the *thaumaston*, the artistic expression of wonder (the biblical *sēmeia* [sign]), that, since the Counter-Reformation and especially since the Council of Trent, has dominated [architecture and sculpture as well]" (qtd. in *OGT* 257).

93. *UB* 18. Benjamin offers similar comments in his essay "The Author as Producer" (*UB* 100). On wonder as a critical method, see also his letter to Adorno of 9 December 1938, which claims that the "wide-eyed presentation of bare facts" is "the genuinely philological stance" (*CWB* 587).

94. Benjamin's "The Author as Producer" makes clear that the production of astonishment in epic theater coincides with the execution of gestures. There he explains that "the interrupting of the action" through gesture should "work against creating an illusion among the audience," and instead should distance "the conditions of our life," so that those conditions can be recognized "not, as in the theatre of naturalism, with complacency, but with astonishment" (*UB* 99-100). Benjamin's term throughout is *Gestus*, not strictly reducible to *Gebärde* as manual gesticulation. Brecht distinguishes between these two terms in his essay "On Gestic Music" (*Brecht on Theatre*, 104).

95. On Brecht's hinge status as the "renewal and completion" of the dramatic theater, see Lehmann, *Postdramatic Theatre*, 33. On spatiality in the post-Brechtian theater, see ibid., 150-52.

96. The debate between Brecht and Benjamin over *action* arises in their conversations over Kafka's politics. Brecht asserts that the correct question to raise about Kafka's stories is what behaviors his characters model for the reader and what "practicable suggestions" can be "extracted" from them (*UB* 110), while Benjamin counters that, in Kafka, "the true measure of life" is not practicable action but "memory" (ibid., 112). I am grateful to Judith Butler for drawing my attention to this distinction.

97. To adapt Judith Butler's argument, allegory can be understood as Benjamin's way of countering Brecht's theater practice, in that "the decomposition of the speech act into gesture is not only the sign of critical capacity, but of grief for what decomposes us as we compose, and for what is no longer possible, for the loss of those traditional supports, and tradition itself, that cannot be restored." See her essay "When Gesture Becomes Event," in Street, Alliot, and Pauker, *Inter Views in Performance Philosophy*, 190-91. (By contrast, others have argued that Benjamin embraced Brecht precisely to have done with melancholy in favor of action. See Eagleton, *Walter Benjamin*, 23; and Stanley Mitchell's introduction in *UB* xiii.

98. For a reading of *Galileo* as Brechtian allegory, see Jameson, *Brecht and Method*, 154-60.

99. Carney, *Brecht and Critical Theory*, 71

Notes to Pages 138-144

100. Carney, *Brecht and Critical Theory*, 72. For Jameson's reading of *Threepenny Opera* as allegorical pastiche (rather than parody), see *Allegory and Ideology*, 320-23.

101. Carney, *Brecht and Critical Theory*, 72.

102. Carney, *Brecht and Critical Theory*, 71-72.

103. As the editors of *Collection, Laboratory, Theater* suggest, the theater during the seventeenth century maintained connections to the analogous space of the early modern laboratory, where the principles of mechanistic science were first discerned empirically. See, for example, "*Kunstkammer*—Laboratory—Theater in the 'Theatrum Europaeum,'" in Schramm, Schwarte, and Lazardzig, *Collection, Laboratory, Theater*, 9-34.

104. *OGT* 94. Benjamin wrote most of the Trauerspiel-book under the mentorship of Florens Christian Rang (1864-1924), a specialist in Nietzsche's work. On the connections between Nietzsche and Benjamin, see Asman, "Theater and Agon/Agon and Theater," 606-10; Fenves, *Arresting Language*, 230-33; Fehér, "Lukács, Benjamin, Theatre," 415-25; Friedlander, "On the Musical Gathering of Echoes of the Voice," 637-38; McFarland, *Constellation*; and Ponzi, *Nietzsche's Nihilism in Walter Benjamin*.

105. See, for example, *AP* J54,5, in which Benjamin quotes his earlier writings in the Trauerspiel-book: "The image of petrified unrest, in the Baroque, is 'the bleak confusion of Golgotha, which can be recognized as the schema underlying the allegorical figures in hundreds of the engravings and descriptions of the period.'" Comparing Nietzsche to Blanqui (in *AP* D5a,6), Benjamin suggests Nietzsche's theory of history is one in which "petrified unrest becomes the status of the cosmos itself. The course of the world appears, accordingly, as one great allegory" (*AP* J55a,4; cf. *AP* J78a,2). As Howard Caygill has written, Benjamin's notion of petrified unrest can be called upon "to stand for the stabilized instability of the capitalist economy in which values are perpetually being assigned and reassigned" (Caygill, "Walter Benjamin's Concept of Allegory," in Copeland and Struck, *Cambridge Companion to Allegory*, 251.)

106. Sontag, "Under the Sign of Saturn," in *Under the Sign of Saturn*, 129.

107. Here again, I am in agreement with Samuel Weber, who characterizes Benjamin's treatment of the baroque as a "staging" (*Theatricality as Medium*, 171).

108. Weber, *Theatricality as Medium*, 14.

109. Weber, *Theatricality as Medium*, 14.

110. For Edward Said's analysis of deconstruction as "establish[ing] a sort of perpetual interchange in Derrida's work between the page and the theater stage," see Said, "Problem of Textuality," 691-92. Said writes: "The grammatological attitude . . . [is] a visual, theatrical one, and its consequences for intellectual production (Derrida's in particular) are quite specific and quite special" (ibid., 685). And further "Many of Derrida's essays employ not only . . . spatial metaphors . . . but, more specifically, theatrical ones. Writing, écriture, is seen in Freud's work, for

246   Notes to Pages 144-148

example, to have a kind of textuality that attempts to emulate a stage setting"
(ibid., 691).

111. With regard to Derridean textual *"espacement"* and physical spatiality in
postdramatic theater, see Lehmann, *Postdramatic Theater*, 148, 153-58.

112. The figure of the fugitive as a personification for messianic power appears
most notably in Benjamin's essay on Kafka, where he relates the parable of a fleeing
king, passing through a Hasidic village by night. See *SW* 2.2:812.

Chapter 4. The Citability of Baroque Gesture

1. As Ulla Dydo observes, *"Four Saints* was the only one of Stein's eighty plays
performed anywhere in her lifetime. It was not one success among many but *the
one* success, which puts a different light on it even as it enlarges its reputation"
(*Gertrude Stein*, 172).

2. On Stein's relationship to antitheatricality (and to the genre of closet drama),
see Puchner, *Stage Fright*, 101-18; and Salvato, *Uncloseting Drama*, 99-137. On her
gender identity and sexuality, see Blackmer, "Ecstasies of Saint Teresa," in Blackmer
and Smith, *En Travesti*, 306-47; Coffman, *Gertrude Stein's Transmasculinity*; and
Salvato, *Uncloseting Drama*. On her poetic practice, see Dydo, *Gertrude Stein*. On
the racial politics of *Four Saints'* premiere, see Barg, "Black Voices / White Sounds."
On Stein's influence on later-twentieth-century avant-gardes, see Bay-Cheng,
Mama Dada, 114-41; and Fuchs, *Death of Character*, 92-96.

3. On pastiche as the hallmark of "postmodern" or late capitalist cultural
production, see Jameson, *Postmodernism*, 17-25. The discipline of performance
studies has usefully elaborated the means whereby performance can operate as a
medium of historical transmission for embodied knowledge and kinesthetic
imagination. For various influential theories on this subject, see Roach, *Cities of the
Dead*, 1-6; Schneider, *Performing Remains*, 87-110; and Taylor, *The Archive and the
Repertoire*, 1-52.

4. Marranca, *Performance Histories*, 78.

5. See Blackmer's essay "Saint as Queer Diva," in Blackmer and Smith, *En
Travesti*, 327. For critical attention to Stein's philosophy of history, see Jayne
Walker's essay "History as Repetition," in Bloom, *Gertrude Stein*, 177-200.

6. Because the Trauerspiel-book first appeared in print in January 1928, several
months after Stein composed the libretto for *Four Saints* in June 1927, there is little
possibility of Benjamin having influenced Stein's opera. Stein may have encountered Benjamin's book in the years between 1927 and 1934, when she was preparing
her explanatory lecture on her dramaturgy, "Plays," but this possibility is also
unlikely, given that she seems to have read little in her parents' native German.

7. These resemblances are all the more pronounced for the fact that Stein and
Benjamin never met or corresponded. The intellectual and biographical similarities

Notes to Pages 149–151

between the two thinkers are notable. Both Stein and Benjamin were expatriate Jews born to wealthy families and living in Paris during the 1930s; both were collectors; both cultivated an interest in esoteric spirituality; and in their various ways, both advanced the banner of abstraction in modern writing. Critics concerned with their connections include Bassoff, "Gertrude Stein's 'Composition as Explanation,'" 76–80; Bernstein, "Disfiguring Abstraction," 486–97; and Perloff, *Poetics in a New Key*, 20. At another, more metadiscursive level, the work of the contemporary art collective the Museum of American Art in Berlin has put Benjamin and Stein's thinking into direct conversation in a variety of performative ways in recent years. See Wetzler, "Walter Benjamin."

8. For contemporary claims of Richard Crashaw's baroque status, see Eliot, *For Lancelot Andrewes*, 117–25; and Wellek, "Concept of Baroque," 82–86, 94–97. See also Warren, *Richard Crashaw* (1939). For the connections between Bernini and Crashaw's treatments of Teresa, see Petersson, *Art of Ecstasy*.

9. For relevant biographical contexts for Austin, and particularly his long-standing interest in juxtaposing seventeenth- and twentieth-century artworks, see Gaddis, *Magician of the Modern*, 4, 119, 111–13, 132–37.

10. See Watson, *Prepare for Saints*, 6.

11. Austin's efforts at juxtaposing modern and baroque forms anticipated later the historiographic writings of, for example, Siegfried Giedion, who, in *Space, Time, and Architecture* (1941), would juxtapose photographs of the cupola of Borromini's Sant'Ivo alla Sapienza with a Picasso sculpture bust: "The continuous inner surface of the dome is broken up. It is made to transmit the movement which runs throughout the whole elevation. . . . Borromini's intersection of the continuous inner surface of the dome must have had the same stunning effect upon his contemporaries that Picasso's disintegration of the human face produced" (117).

12. See, for example, Stein's letter to Thomson of 28 May 1927: "The Sitwells [Edith and Sachaverell] are here and we are giving a party an early tea Monday and you can get here any time after half past three preferably about that time. They are much xcited about the Opera ad like the sound of your name. . . . Life is too strenuous I have not even been able to write in a diary let alone a saint" (*LST* 34). On the Sitwell siblings as vehement promoters of baroque taste during the mid-1920s, see Calloway, *Baroque Baroque*, 34–35, 56.

13. Qtd. in Dydo, *Gertrude Stein*, 176–77. According to Watson, the idea to focus on saints was apparently Stein's (*Prepare for Saints*, 42).

14. "Beneath its apparently simple surface are finely calculated repetitions of musical phrases associated with syntactical units, bits of neo-Baroque recitative, and melodic lines that shift as meter shifts" (Watson, *Prepare for Saints*, 50). Watson also records that Thomson composed *Four Saints* almost after the manner of a baroque composer, following the technique of "setting down the vocal parts and figured bass lines, leaving harmonies for a later point" (ibid., 51).

248 Notes to Pages 152-157

15. This disagreement recurred with Stein and Thomson's later collaboration, *The Mother of Us All*. In their initial planning discussions, "Stein again proposed George Washington as a subject, and again Thomson refused on the grounds that everyone in the eighteenth century looked alike" (Watson, *Prepare for Saints*, 319). On the eighteenth-century renunciation of ornament as an opposition to baroque decoration, see Jameson, *Allegory and Ideology*, 22.

16. For James's writings on Teresa of Avila and Ignatius of Loyola, see *Varieties of Religious Experience*, 319-25.

17. Ruddick, *Reading Gertrude Stein*, 3, 39-40, 234-35. Ruddick claims, for example, that "[t]he author of *Tender Buttons* [1914] is a gnostic reader, who unlocks within the master text of Western culture a buried, alternative truth. At the same time, she is a gnostic writer, who half hides her own subversive thinking, yet in a way that readers who devote themselves to her text can learn to follow her." On Gnosticism's relationship to allegory, see Fletcher, *Allegory*, 95-96.

18. Stein's Ávila visit is documented in Watson, *Prepare for Saints*, 44.

19. On *Four Saints* as a modern response to the Wagnerian *Gesamtkunstwerk*, see Watson, *Prepare for Saints*, 76; Blackmer, "Saint as Queer Diva," 329.

20. On Diaghilev's influence on the *Four Saints* collaboration, see Gaddis, *Magician of the Modern*, 133; Watson, *Prepare for Saints*, 156-57; Harris, "Original 'Four Saints in Three Acts,'" 103. On Reinhardt's efforts at reimagining baroque theater conventions for the modern stage, see Fleischmann, *Die Wiederentdeckung des Barocktheaters*.

21. Gaddis, *Magician of the Modern*, 186. This interpretation is echoed throughout Harris, "Original 'Four Saints in Three Acts'"; and Van Vechten, "How I Listen to *Four Saints in Three Acts*."

22. Qtd. in Watson, *Prepare for Saints*, 74.

23. Qtd. in Watson, *Prepare for Saints*, 225.

24. Qtd. in Harris, "Original 'Four Saints in Three Acts,'" 109.

25. Harris, "Original 'Four Saints in Three Acts,'" 109.

26. Watson, *Prepare for Saints*, 238.

27. Watson, *Prepare for Saints*, 134.

28. Harris relates this flat, two-dimensional method of staging to the bas relief approach taken in Nijinsky's ballet (after Mallarmé) *L'Après-midi d'un Faune*, which Ashton had seen in Europe previously ("Original 'Four Saints in Three Acts,'" 121, 127). The bas relief style furthered the Symbolist effort to reorganize stage space according to a criterion of flatness, thus remaking spectatorship into a kind of reading or allegoresis.

29. Harris, "Original 'Four Saints in Three Acts,'" 125, 128.

30. See Van Vechten, "'How I Listen to Four Saints in Three Acts.'"

31. The press release reads: "It remained for a priest, Father La Farge, to give it

Notes to Pages 157–158

249

[*Four Saints*] its most interesting and complete appellation. He called it a 'baroque fantasy.'" See Moses, "'Background Notes and Data.'"

32. See Young, "Reading Lesson." Young's other essay on *Four Saints*, "One Moment Alit" (*New Republic* 78 [3 July 1934]), suggests that the phrase "baroque fantasy" was "passed out by the producer as a hint to the wise" and "is a good one for this piece of theater art"; he also comments that the scenery by Stettheimer blended baroque with "whimsical Victorian coquetry."

33. The use of social dance forms imported from Harlem is described in detail in Harris, "Original 'Four Saints in Three Acts,'" 124–25. He writes: "Just as Stein in her libretto had alluded to passages from nursery rhyme and 'My Country Tis of Thee,' and Thomson had quoted them again in the music, Ashton quoted passages from popular dance and from known types. . . . [These allusions] were the only acknowledgment in *Four Saints*—with the possible exception of the Gospel music quality (itself a sort of quotation of style)—of the traditions of the Black performers" (ibid., 124).

34. Watson, *Prepare for Saints*, 199, 206.

35. On the intersections of Blackness and baroque, see Harris, "Original 'Four Saints in Three Acts,'" 130; Joan Copjec, "Black Baroque," in *Imagine There's No Woman*, 98–103; and Moten, "'Black Optimism/Black Operation.'"

36. Watson notes that the opera's music director, Eva Jessye, ensured her singers were compensated for rehearsal, a practice not in keeping with the norms of the time, though Watson also notes that some chorus members later recalled never receiving their full pay (*Prepare for Saints*, 245–6). Where the opera's musical breakthrough is concerned, Watson cites Jessye's recollection: "With this opera we had to step on fresh ground, something foreign to our nature completely. Not like *Porgy and Bess* that came the next year—that was our inheritance, our own lives. But what did we know about the minds of Gertrude Stein and Virgil Thomson? We really went abroad on that" (ibid., 245).

37. Of his desire for an all-Black cast, Thomson wrote: "They [i.e., singers of color] alone possess the dignity and the poise, the lack of self-consciousness that proper interpretation of the opera demands" (qtd. in Watson, *Prepare for Saints*, 200). For a discussion of Thomson's ingrained racist and sometimes fetishistic attitudes toward Black people, and the conflicts these attitudes generated among the production's collaborators, see *Prepare for Saints*, 202–8. For a detailed backstory of the premiere's African American participants, see Watson, *Prepare for Saints*, 241–63. For a critique of the premiere production's logic of racial objectification, particularly concerned with Thomson's musical contributions to it, see Barg, "Black Voices/White Sounds," 151–53.

38. *Gay New York*, 309–10. On Thomson's attendance at Harlem's drag nightlife scene, see Watson, *Prepare for Saints*, 68.

250   Notes to Pages 159-162

39. Marranca, *Performance Histories*, 75.

40. On performativity and temporality, see Tracy Davis's essay "Performative Time," in Canning and Postlewait, *Representing the Past*, 142-67; and Schneider, *Performing Remains*, 10, 93. On Stein's philosophy of history, see Jayne Walker's essay "History as Repetition," in Bloom, *Gertrude Stein*, 177-200.

41. For example, in summarizing this disciplinary development, Judith Butler writes: "In recent years, we have seen the growth of Performance Studies throughout the world, and this has compelled many of us to rethink what we mean by performance and where we find it. It has become important to distinguish Performance Studies from theater studies precisely to foreground performance as a kind of action or practice that does not require the proscenium stage. Performance can and does happen in the street, or in the mall, in ordinary life, and even, we might say, in every possible instance of motion and stillness. Although it has been important to distinguish Performance Studies from theater so as to expand our conception of what the platform for bodily action can be, we make a mistake by failing to see the necessary overlaps between theater and performance, since the 'stage is hardly an unmovable plane, and there are ways of acting in the theater that move both actors and audience on and off the stage. In other words, there are kinds of theater that allegorize the very distinction between theater and performance, and sometimes, a found object on the street—a random plank—can suddenly become a stage or a platform, and that happens within demonstrations on the street as well when a toppled tank becomes a platform for speech. In the latter case, certain surfaces become provisional and improvised supports for movement and speech, assuming the status of the stage. Indeed, why not understand the proscenium as itself a roving or moveable element? Perhaps when the proscenium does move, or withdraw, or turn up in spaces or on surfaces where it is not expected, we are already in the orbit of performance art and performance studies without having left the theater altogether. Theatrical street politics bears this out." Butler, "When Gesture Becomes Event," in Street, Alliot, and Pauker, *Inter Views in Performance Philosophy*, 171-72.

42. Stein's concept of repetition as *insistence*—as a differential form of repetition that entails the possibility of revision—notably anticipates the dramaturgical principle that Suzan-Lori Parks has more recently described as "Rep & Rev" (Parks, *America Play*, 9-10).

43. "[T]here is also the important question of repetition and is there any such thing. Is there repetition or is there insistence. I am inclined to believe there is no such thing as repetition. And really how can there be. . . . [T]here can be no repetition because the essence of that expression is insistence." Stein, *Lectures in America*, 166-67.

44. With Stein's concept of repetition, we are brought into close proximity with what Peggy Phelan describes as "the ontology of performance: representation

Notes to Pages 162-163

without reproduction" (Phelan, *Unmarked*, 146-66). In its attentiveness to that which cannot be directly reproduced or repeated, but only re-presented in time, Stein's work testifies to the very ephemerality of performance. Where the concept of *identity* is concerned, even the word's very etymology—from the Latin *idem(et) idem*, meaning literally "same (and) same"—depends on the fact of repetition. See Mendelsohn, *Elusive Embrace*, 41. See also Stein's "Idem the Same. A Valentine to Sherwood Anderson," first published in *The Little Review* (1923), in Stein, *Writings, 1903-1932*, 475-79.

45. Stein, *Four in America*, v. With this comment, Stein seems to allude, however loosely, to T. S. Eliot's idea of a modern "dissociation of sensibility" beginning in the seventeenth century, a process by which modern poets no longer "feel their thought as immediately as the odour of a rose." (Eliot, *Sacred Wood*, 125-29). Repetition, then, would play a salvific role in Stein's poetics, rescuing the rose from oblivion and restoring its lost, auratic sensuousness.

46. See Victor Shklovsky's "Art as Technique" (1917), in Lemon and Reis, *Russian Formalist Criticism*, 12.

47. Stein's concept of the continuous present is given in *Writings, 1903-1932*, 524. See also the passage in "Plays" in which she writes that the business of Art is "to live in the actual present, that is the complete actual present, and to completely express that complete actual present" (*P* xxxvi).

48. On Stein's writing as a practice of gnosticism, see Ruddick, *Reading Gertrude Stein*, 229-32. More recently, the American theorist of mindfulness Jon Kabat Zinn has written eloquently on the metaphysics of the present participle in the context of guided meditation practices. As Zinn explains, drawing on Buddhist scholarship, the "virtue" of the present participle "is that it transcends duality." See McCown, Reibel, and Micozzi, *Teaching Mindfulness*, xvi.

49. Here I depend and elaborate upon Samuel Weber's conception of the present participle as theatricality's grammatical hallmark. "If theatrical performance does not simply reproduce or accomplish something that exists in and of itself or that is at least intrinsically self-contained, the reiterative openness of the present participle is always both ahead of and behind itself" (*Theatricality as Medium*, 5).

50. As Marc Robinson writes, "Stein succeeds at getting an elusive abstraction—time—into her plays, making it as vivid a presence as Saint Ignatius or a hilltop in Mexico. . . . [In Stein's own words, t]he work should have 'an existence suspended in time' rather than merely 'a sense of time'" (*Other American Drama*, 22).

51. *P* xlvii-l. Much critical ink has been spilled over this curious passage. Jane Palatini Bowers explores Stein's poetics of landscape (as *lang*-scape, textual spatialization), in "The Composition That All the World Can See," in Fuchs and Chaudhuri, *Land/Scape/Theater*, 121-85. The baroque proscenium stage drew visual inspiration from the early modern tradition of landscape painting as well. For other readings of Stein's landscape dramaturgy, see Bowers, *"They Watch Me*

252 Notes to Pages 164-168

as They Watch This," 25-71; Fuchs, *Death of Character*, 92-107; and Marranca, *Ecologies of Theater*, 3-24, 49-58.

52. Stein's principle of landscape conveys in compositional terms what Benjamin's description of the antinomies of allegorical interpretation conveys in hermeneutic terms: "Any person, any object, any relation can signify any other whatever. With this possibility, an annihilating but just verdict is pronounced on the profane world." (*OGT* 184).

53. Harris has argued that Stein drew inspiration for this description from seeing Frederick Ashton's choreography in performance, particularly the Act Three climax, in which the entire company appears in an extended procession, seeming to walk forward while simultaneously remaining in place through a marvelous trick of choreography ("Original 'Four Saints in Three Acts,'" 130). The effect here recalls one later devised by Brecht (with a rotating stage) for his production of *Mother Courage and Her Children*. For an excellent philosophical analysis of this scenic device in *Mother Courage*, see Rokem, *Philosophers and Thespians*, 128.

54. For a useful recent analysis of the dynamics of mediation in Stein's opera, see Clements, "How to Remediate." Summarizing Bolter and Grusin's recent argument in *Remediation* and applying it to Stein's work, Clements writes: "[R]emediation comprises the logic of *hypermediacy* (which reveals the multiplicity of media and, in the process, foregrounds their materiality) and the logic of *immediacy* (in which the medium itself seems to disappear through the 'ignoring or denying [of] the presence of the medium and the act of mediation)" (47). Egginton's notion of the *minor strategy of the baroque* echoes this logic of hypermediacy; see *Theater of Truth*, 6-8.

55. See Fried, *Absorption and Theatricality*, 89-90; and Cermatori, "Allegories of Spectatorship," 96.

56. For a comprehensive history of gaiety in lesbian drama and performance, see Warner, *Acts of Gaiety*.

57. Blackmer, "Saint as Queer Diva," 332.

58. On this point, Dydo claims: "What is meaningless to Stein is not counting but adding up totals, whether nails, windows or doors in houses, followers, acts in a play, all patriarchal activities with numbers substituted for what can only be understood qualitatively" (*Gertrude Stein*, 192).

59. On horror vacui as a device in baroque visual art, see David Castillo, "Horror (Vacui): The Baroque Condition," in Spadaccini and Estudillo, *Hispanic Baroques*, 87-104.

60. In so doing, they actualize a fundamental truth of the theater as a medium in which performers and audiences "consent not to be a single being," to borrow Édouard Glissant's eloquent phrase, with which he described what could be deemed a baroque poetics of relation. See Diawara, "Conversation with Édouard Glissant aboard the Queen Mary II."

61. For example, in the section of text that Thomson and Grosser designated as

Notes to Pages 168–170   253

the opera's second act, a "Scene V" is declared no fewer than nine consecutive times in the space of a single page. (Thomson set all nine to be sung.)

62. Dydo, *Gertrude Stein*, 190.

63. See *4S3A* 446. This effect is repeated some lines later: "Saint Teresa seated and not standing half and half of it and not half and half of it seated and not standing surrounded and not seated and not seated and not standing and not surrounded and not surrounded and not not not seated not seated not seated not surrounded not seated not surrounded not seated and Saint Ignatius standing standing not seated Saint Teresa not standing not standing and Saint Ignatius not standing standing surrounded as if in once yesterday" (ibid., 446–47).

64. On this subject, Marc Robinson has written: "Stein learned her technique from the cinema, then in its fledgling days and for her the most intoxicating development in art. A film's collection of frames—so many nearly identical, yet crucially different—is the clearest expression of the present tense in performance. Each frame announces the situation, the composition, the characters anew; the 'story' starts over each time; only when the parts are taken together and followed sequentially does the film move and seem to breathe" (*Other American Drama*, 19).

65. Ulla Dydo observes that Stein herself likened her use of grammar to a kind of musical counterpoint, possibly inspired by Marcel Brion's 1930 essay, which Stein and Toklas translated, "Le Contrepoint poétique de Gertrude Stein" (Dydo, *Gertrude Stein*, 209n72, 405, 405n80).

66. Some further examples: The poetic discourse emends itself ("Have saints./ Said saints./As said saints./And not annoy./Annoint" [*4S3A* 442]). It muses over and justifies the decisions it has settled upon ("Why should every one be at home./ In idle acts . . . There is no parti parti-color in a house there is no parti parti parti color in a house" [443]). It gets distracted ("Supposing she said that he had chosen all the miseries that he had observed in fifty of his years what had that to do with hats. They had made hats for her. Not really" [443]). It tosses off ideas casually as they arise ("Saint Teresa something like that." [444]). It makes notes to itself and makes note of writerly uncertainties. ("Saint Ignatius not there. Saint Ignatius staying where. Never heard them speak speak of it" [445]). It registers the extra-ordinary emotional vulnerabilities that attend the act of writing ("Come panic come./Come close" [443]). It poses powerful political questions ("Can women have wishes" [448]). Elsewhere, it engages in extended *wordplay*, as in the follow-ing passage, in which *to-two* and *for-four* are thrown gleefully into homophonic uncertainty: "Two saints./Four saints./Two saints prepare for saints it two saints prepare for saints in prepare for saints" (440.)

67. On "performative writing," see Della Pollack, "Performing Writing," in Phelan and Lane, *The Ends of Performance*, 73–103; see also McGann, *The Textual Condition*, 88–100. On Stein's links to *écriture*, see Ruddick, *Reading Gertrude Stein*, 3, 86–90.

254   Notes to Pages 170-176

68. Blackmer writes: "[M]uch of the opera is a reenactment of the work of writing an opera" ("Saint as Queer Diva," 332). Puchner writes that "a large portion of Stein's text depicts, not St. Teresa, but the process of writing an opera about her" (*Stage Fright*, 113). Of the landscape-langscape dramaturgy concept, Bowers argues "the plays are not about Bilignin nor about any other place. Rather they are about language and its relationship to the performance event; they are about writing for the theater, thus, my alteration of the prefix—from 'land' to 'lang'—to give some sense of the true subject of these plays" (*"They Watch Me As They Watch This,"* 25).

69. Of the intermedial tensions and exchanges between word and image implicit within baroque allegory, see Benjamin's discussion of Harsdörffer and Winckelmann (*OGT* 192).

70. Lehmann, *Postdramatic Theater*, 49, 62-63.

71. "Original 'Four Saints in Three Acts,'" 111.

72. Here I borrow and extend an argument originally put forward in Jerzy Limon's essay "Performativity of the Court: Stuart Masque as Postdramatic Theater," in Cefalu and Reynolds, *Return of Theory*, 258-77.

73. On Stein's sadism, see Salvato, *Uncloseting Drama*, 104-5. On the sadism of allegorists, see *OGT* 197.

74. Dydo, *Gertrude Stein*, 196. For Stein's interest in Saint Theresa, Bernini, baroque art, consciousness, visionary experience, hallucination, meditation, and other related topics, see ibid., 180-81.

75. Watson, *Prepare for Saints*, 48.

76. Qtd. in Fuchs and Chaudhuri, *Land/Scape/Theater*, 138.

77. Qtd. in Fuchs and Chaudhuri, *Land/Scape/Theater*, 140.

78. Marranca writes: "In the Steinian ecology, language exists everywhere in the landscape, as if all space were semantic, the world a book" (*Performance Histories*, 76). This "ecology" reflects Mallarmé's enduring influence.

79. Of the Edenic resonance here, Marranca notes: "What Stein does in *Four Saints* is transform the idea of theological space into a spatial conception of drama. Read as an allegory, the 'four saints' of the title act as the four pathways of the garden, echoing the biblical four rivers of Eden. (In her autobiography St. Teresa describes the four kinds of prayer as four ways to water a garden.) The garden is Stein's perfect universe, a paradise, a frame. The Persian word *pairidaeza* (paradise) means enclosure, and from this form the cloister garden plan of Catholic monasteries took shape as a place of learning and meditation and cosmological principle. In *Four Saints* the garden space is now a performance space, the plot of a garden the plot of a play" (*Ecologies of Theater*, 55).

80. On Stein's effective "negation of organized religion and belief in God," see Bay-Cheng, *Mama Dada*, 8.

81. As Watson records, Stein and Thomson worked on the piece's libretto and score in near-total isolation from each other (*Prepare for Saints*, 54).

Notes to Pages 176-178

82. On Stein's "consonant harmony, dissonant syntax," see Albright, *Untwisting the Serpent*, 343. For a discussion of Thomson's musical influences, see Watson, *Prepare for Saints*, 25, 49-50.

83. Qtd. in Watson, *Prepare for Saints*, 38-39.

84. For example: "Letting pin in letting let in let in in in in let in wet in wed in dead in dead wed led in led wed dead in dead in led in wed in said in said led wed dead wed dead said led led said wed dead wed dead led in led in wed in wed in said in wed in said in dead in dead wed said led led said wed dead in" (*P* 476).

85. Quoted in Harris, "Original 'Four Saints in Three Acts,'" 129.

86. This moment deserves to be considered as an instance of what Jill Dolan has called the "utopian performative." See Dolan, *Utopia in Performance*. Despite Thomson's appropriating interest in the musical form of the African American spiritual, it might be said that this culminating moment of musical performance effects the sound of utopia in another sense as well. Here I have in mind the subjunctive utopianism Tavia Nyong'o finds in Trajal Harrell's choreographic work, namely, a "commingling" of "black and white aesthetic forms . . . across class divides, aesthetic hierarchies, and the color line," opening onto a vision of futurity (in the sense described by Muñoz in *Cruising Utopia*). See Tavia Nyong'o, "Dancing in the Subjunctive: Trajal Harrell's Twenty Looks," in *Vogue Not*, 257; see also Nyong'o, *Afro-Fabulations*, 42; and Muñoz's longing for a more fully integrated historiography of the New York avant-gardes in dance, in *Cruising Utopia*, 83-85.

87. Here Stein's divergence from Thomson on matters of race is worth remarking on. Lisa Barg, for instance, has analyzed the way Thomson's score traffics in "expressive vocabularies" linked to avant-garde "primitivism" and blackface minstrelsy ("Black Voices / White Sounds") and thus helps reassert the fixedness of racial identity positions and hierarchies. Stein's attitudes on the subject of race appear to have been more radically deconstructive. While *Four Saints* was not written with Black performers in mind, numerous scholars have linked the depictions of racially marked characters in her fictional writings (e.g., *Melanctha*) to an effective disruption and reconfiguration of racial categories and power structures. See, for example, Doyle, "The Flat, the Round, and Gertrude Stein," 263-71; Leslie, "Melanctha Was Too Many for Him," 262-307; Wu, "Stein's *Melanctha*," 178-80.

88. The distance between Stein and Wagner can be gauged in the way certain moments of *Four Saints'* premiere performance seemed to parody Wagnerian opera. For example, the final tableau in Grosser's score—in which the Saints appear together in their heavenly mansion and share a quasi-Eucharistic cup while singing "it is very nearly ended with bread" and "When this you see remember me" (*P* 479-80)—recall, in parodic terms, the ends of both *Das Rheingold* and *Parsifal*.

89. Marranca, *Performance Histories*, 79.

90. See Kastleman, "An Acquaintance with Religion," 349.

91. Bay-Cheng documents the following artists as a catalog of those who have drawn influence from Stein: the Living Theatre, the Judson Church Poets' Theater, Richard Foreman, Robert Wilson, Peter Sellars, the Wooster Group, Anne Bogart, Suzan-Lori Parks, Mac Wellman, Laurie Anderson, Karen Finley, Cindy Sherman, Andy Warhol, Jack Smith, Michael Snow, Stan Brakhage, Adrienne Kennedy, Maria Irene Fornes, Mark Morris, The Wooster Group, and many others (*Mama Dada*, 114-40).

92. See also 7 October 1935, from Vienna: "Vienna buildings are fine, I kneel to the Baroque" (*LSW* 61); and 8 May 1941, from Lima: "A month in Ecuador. Everywhere the noiseless scurry of the long-enduring Indian. Glittering baroque churches" (*LSW* 287).

93. With this claim in his "Barock" text, Wilder echoes a point made elsewhere, during roughly this same period, by Morris Croll, who argued in 1929 that baroque prose style sought "to portray, not a thought, but the mind thinking." Wilder may have met or studied with Croll while a graduate student at Princeton, where Croll taught in the English Department. This view of baroque style would also famously influence Elizabeth Bishop. See Croll, *Style, Rhetoric, and Rhythm*, 207. See also Pickard, *Elizabeth Bishop's Poetics of Description*, 172-76.

94. Concerning this point, see Blackmer's claim: "Since the lives of saints are, by their very nature, miraculous and extraordinary, an artistic 'exact resemblance' of Teresa and her community of Spanish mystics, such as Stein endeavors to body forth in *Four Saints*, must invariably 'disrupt' the conventions of realism and narrative paradigms of conflict and resolution" ("Saint as Queer Diva," 326). Blackmer further suggests that "aesthetic representations of lesbian lives are not reducible, without politicized distortion and cloying diminution, to the common-place private romances of bourgeois heterosexuality but discover, rather, their 'true reflection' in the resplendent artifice of art forms such as opera" (ibid., 325).

95. Diamond, "Brechtian Theory/Feminist Theory."

96. Elin Diamond's essay "Brechtian Theory/Feminist Theory" takes as a point of departure an instance in which Stein read landscape allegorically as text: "In the 1930s, Gertrude Stein and Alice Toklas, on their American lecture tour, were driving in the country in Western Massachusetts. Toklas pointed out a batch of clouds. Stein replied, 'Fresh eggs.' Toklas insisted that Stein look at the clouds. Stein replied again, 'Fresh eggs.' Then Toklas asked, 'Are you making symbolical language?' 'No,' Stein answered, 'I'm reading the signs. I love to read the signs.'" (Catharine Stimpson, qtd. in "Brechtian Theory/Feminist Theory," 82). For Diamond, the sort of *gestus* Stein's writing enacts "marks a site, in the text, of indeterminacy, of multiple meanings—a pleasurable moment for reading the clouds" (ibid., 92). For other foundational writings on *gestus* as a critical practice, see Rokem, *Philosophers and Thespians*, 127-31, 143-45.

97. Stein's Jewishness deserves consideration in light of the rise of antisemitism

Notes to Pages 180-183

in Europe during the 1920s and '30s. For the classic account of antisemitism as a form of racism in Europe, see Arendt, *Origins of Totalitarianism*, 158-84. On the perception of Jews as a nonwhite "race" during the early twentieth century, see Painter, *History of White People*, 383. On the radical queerness of Stein's gender presentation, see Coffman, *Gertrude Stein's Transmasculinity*.

98. On the subject of this gay modernist "mafia," see Watson, *Prepare for Saints*, 7, 113.

99. See Sontag, "Notes on Camp," §50, in *Against Interpretation*.

100. "You see, true High Camp always has an underlying seriousness. You can't camp about something you don't take seriously. You're not making fun of it; you're making fun out of it. You're expressing what's basically serious to you in terms of fun and artifice and elegance. Baroque art is largely camp about religion." Isherwood, *World in the Evening*, 110. It is worth noting that Sontag found Isherwood's definition of camp "lazy" ("Notes on Camp," 277).

101. See Severo Sarduy, "The Baroque and the Neobaroque" and "Baroque Cosmology: Kepler," both in Zamora and Kaup, *Baroque New Worlds*, 265-315; for Sontag, see "Syberberg's Hitler" (originally published in the *New York Review of Books*, 21 February 1980).

102. For a queer-theoretical reading of the opera, with particular attention to Teresa's status as a "queer diva" as early as the time of Crashaw, see, again, Blackmer, "Saint as Queer Diva," 325-36.

103. The subject of race, performance, and performativity has generated considerable discussion in recent years. See, for instance, Bernstein, *Racial Innocence*, 69-91; Butler, *Bodies That Matter*, 189n15, 206n18; Ehlers, *Racial Imperatives*; Nadine George Graves, "Diasporic Spidering: Constructing Contemporary Black Identities" in DeFrantz and Gonzalez, *Black Performance Theory*; Hartman, *Scenes of Subjection*, 56-59; Nyong'o, *Afro-Fabulations*, 201-12; Roach, *Cities of the Dead*, 179-239; Shirley Anne Tate, "Performativity and 'Raced' Bodies," in Murji and Solomos, *Theories of Race and Ethnicity*, 180-97.

Epilogue

1. Gould, *Time's Arrow, Time's Cycle*, 3. (Gould attributes this quotation to John McPhee's *Basin and Range*.)

2. See also Bazin, *Baroque and Rococo* (1964); Kitson, *The Age of Baroque* (1966); and Palisca, *Baroque Music* (1961).

3. For example, Joseph Roach's Cornell University dissertation, "Vanbrugh's English Baroque: Opera and the Opera House in the Haymarket," was completed between 1970 and 1973, but never published.

4. The sources cited in the following paragraph are Beckett, *Collected Shorter Plays*; Maciunas, "*Fluxus Manifesto*, 1963"; Sontag, "Notes on Camp" in *Against*

Interpretation (cf. §§12, 28, and 43); Rainer, *"Trio A"*; Judd, "Specific Objects—Donald Judd"; Fried, *Art and Objecthood*, 148-72.

5. Debord, *Society of the Spectacle*, 12.

6. For a comprehensive analysis of this poststructuralist concern with theater, see Fuchs, *Death of Character*, 144-57.

7. Debord, *Society of the Spectacle*, 133.

8. Debord, *Society of the Spectacle*, 134. Debord's critique of neoclassicism is once again timely today. In February 2020, the White House drafted an executive order to "make classical architecture the only style permitted for future government buildings." The EO was titled "Making Federal Buildings Beautiful Again" (see "Proposed Executive Order"), but it has since been reversed by the forty-sixth US president.

9. See Adorno's essay "Der Mißbrauchte Barock" (1968), in *Ohne Leitbild*, 133-55. See also Walls, *Baroque Music*, 502n2.

10. Ludlam, *Ridiculous Theater*, 31.

11. See, again, Deleuze's comments on minimalism as an "extremum" in *The Fold* (123) and Jameson's comments on minimalism and maximalism in *Allegory and Ideology* (313-17). See also Benjamin's comments on "extremes" as the foundation of the constellational method in his study of baroque (*OGT* 11).

12. For authors describing Wilson's various influences, see Barnett, *Brecht in Practice*, 214-15; Bay-Cheng, *Mama Dada*, 135; Holmberg, *Theatre of Robert Wilson*, 1, 52-53, 104-5, 162; and Innes and Shevtsova, *Cambridge Introduction to Theater Directing*, 161, 178. Bonnie Marranca, has also remarked copiously on Wilson's influences; see her "Introduction" to Stein, *Last Operas and Plays*, xxv; Marranca, "Robert Wilson and the Idea of the Archive Dramaturgy as an Ecology," 70-71; and Marranca, *Theatrewritings*, 120.

13. To Aragon, Wilson's work was "what we [Surrealists] dreamed it [Surrealism] might become after us, beyond us" ("Open Letter to Andre Breton," 4).

14. Aragon, "Open Letter to Andre Breton," 7. Aragon elaborates on *Deafman Glance*: "It is neither ballet, nor mime drama, nor opera (although it is perhaps a deaf man's opera, a deaf opera, as if we were at this moment in a world like sixteenth century Italy which had seen Cardan and watched the birth from Caccini to Monteverdi, l'opera serio [*sic*], baroque of the ear, passing from the vocal counterpart of religious chants to this new form of art, profane in its essence)" (ibid., 6).

15. Lehmann, in *Postdramatic Theater*, claims, "Wilson is part of a long tradition, from the baroque theatre of effects, the 'machines' of the seventeenth century, Jacobean masques" (81). Similarly, Bonnie Marranca calls Wilson (in *Theatrewritings*, 120-21) the "Inigo Jones of the avant-garde" and describes *Einstein on the Beach* as "mannerist," a "refunctioned" form of the masque, and "a modern allegory." Wilson is also described as an allegorist in Melville, "Notes on the Reemergence," 56, 74.

Notes to Pages 186-190

His debts to baroque landscape pictorialism are noted in Robinson, *The Other American Drama*, 159-88. Umberto Eco notes the similarity between Wilson's idea of spectatorship—in which spectators may leave and return, pay attention or not, as they choose—and the idea that prevailed in the baroque auditoriums of the seventeenth and eighteenth centuries, "with people making love in their loge with the *rideau* closed" (Wilson, "Robert Wilson and Umberto Eco: A Conversation," 96). Wilson has more recently become a sought-after director for new productions of baroque operas, including Monteverdi's trio *L'Orfeo, Il Ritorno d'Ulisse in Patria*, and *L'Incoronazione di Poppea*—in gala, season-opening productions cosponsored by the Teatro la Scala in Milan and the Paris Opera in 2009, 2011, and 2014, respectively.

16. Qtd. in Holmberg, *Theatre of Robert Wilson*, 53.

17. Heiner Müller, quoted in Lehmann, *Postdramatic Theater*, 81.

18. On this preservationist or conservationist impulse in Wilson's work, see Marranca, "Robert Wilson and the Idea of the Archive Dramaturgy as an Ecology," especially 66-67, 70-71, 77; and Schechner, "Conservative Avant-Garde," 895, 898, 909. On a related note, concerning the syncretic use of allegory to preserve vanishing cultural materials, see Fletcher, "Allegory in Literary History."

19. In *Jack Smith and the Destruction of Atlantis*, Wilson explains, "Our whole sensibility, our whole way of thinking, Jack brought to our consciousness." Smith also performed in Wilson's *The Life and Times of Sigmund Freud* (1969) and *Deafman Glance*. Where Ludlam's debts to Smith are concerned, see Rabkin, "Theatre of the Ridiculous," 41.

20. In this epilogue, Smith's quotations are, unless otherwise indicated, from Jordan's film *Jack Smith and the Destruction of Atlantis*.

21. The curiosity that motivated my phone call was inspired by the conclusion of Hai-Dang Phan's poem, "My Father's 'Norton Introduction to Literature,' Third Edition (1981)": "When I dial, the automated female voice on the other end/tells me I have reached a non-working number."

22. Muñoz, *Cruising Utopia*, 169.

23. Muñoz, *Cruising Utopia*, 183. For Benjamin's comments on *hopeless hope*, see SW 1:356; SW 2.2:798.

24. On this subject, see the similar position adopted by Rancière in his critical readings of Lyotard. To Rancière, Lyotard highlights the "tradition of Marxist argumentation linking the radical purity of art and its one-way movement with the promise of political and social emancipation, a tradition championed by Adorno and Greenberg. . . . [This argument presupposes that] art is political to the extent that it is only art, to the extent that its products are different from objects or consumption and are endowed with a character of unavailability" (Rancière, "The Sublime from Lyotard to Schiller," 11). In a broader frame, Rancière's criticisms of Lyotard—which focus on the latter's claim of "postmodernism" as an era preoccu-

pied with the sublime loss of the Kantian thing—respond to this loss (the heteron-omy of language which Benjamin calls allegory) by insisting on the radical autonomy of the aesthetic sphere. See Lyotard, *The Inhuman*, 135-43; and Rancière, "The Sublime from Lyotard to Schiller," 8-15.

25. Sousa Santos, "Stay Baroque."

26. In his lecture "What Is Enlightenment," Foucault describes the demand to be either "'for' or 'against' the Enlightenment" as a kind of "blackmail" (*Foucault Reader*, 43). As he argues, "[O]ne must refuse everything that might present itself in the form of a simplistic and authoritarian alternative: you either accept the Enlightenment and remain within the tradition of its rationalism (this is considered a positive term by some and used by others, on the contrary, as a reproach), or else you criticize the Enlightenment and then try to escape from its principles of rationality (which may be seen once again as good or bad)" (43).

Bibliography

"ABACUS." Early Morning Opera. Accessed February 3, 2020. http://earlymorning opera.com/wp/projects/abacus/.

Abel, Lionel. *Tragedy and Metatheatre: Essays on Dramatic Form*. Teaneck, NJ: Holmes & Meier, 2003.

Ackerman, A., and M. Puchner. *Against Theatre: Creative Destructions on the Modernist Stage*. New York: Palgrave Macmillan, 2016.

Adorno, Theodor W. *In Search of Wagner*. Translated by Rodney Livingstone. New York: Verso, 2005.

———. *Ohne Leitbild: Parva Aesthetica*. Berlin: Suhrkamp Verlag, 1968.

Adorno, Theodor W., Walter Benjamin, Ernst Bloch, and Bertolt Brecht. *Aesthetics and Politics*. New York: Verso, 2010.

Aercke, Kristiaan. *Gods of Play: Baroque Festive Performances as Rhetorical Discourse*. Albany: State University of New York Press, 1994.

Agamben, Giorgio. "Gesture, or the Structure of Art." YouTube. Accessed March 5, 2016. https://www.youtube.com/watch?v=v4bKAEz3TF0.

———. *Means without End: Notes on Politics*. Translated by Vincenzo Binetti and Cesare Casarino. Minneapolis: University of Minnesota Press, 2000.

———. *State of Exception*. Translated by Kevin Attell. Chicago: University of Chicago Press, 2008.

———. *What Is an Apparatus? and Other Essays*. Translated by David Kishik and Stefan Pedatella. Stanford, CA: Stanford University Press, 2009.

Albright, Daniel. *Untwisting the Serpent: Modernism in Music, Literature, and Other Arts*. Chicago: University of Chicago Press, 2000.

Andreas-Salomé, Lou. *Nietzsche*. Translated by Siegfried Mandel. Urbana: University of Illinois Press, 2001.

Aragon, Louis. "An Open Letter to Andre Breton on Robert Wilson's 'Deafman Glance.'" Translated by Linda Moses, Jean-Paul Lavergne, and George Ashley. *Performing Arts Journal* 1, no. 1 (1976): 3-7. https://doi.org/10.2307/3245181.

Arendt, Hannah. *The Origins of Totalitarianism*. New York: Harcourt, 1979.

Aristotle. *On Poetry and Style*. Translated by G. M. A. Grübe. Indianapolis: Hackett, 1989.

Armond, Kate. *Modernism and the Theatre of the Baroque*. Edinburgh: Edinburgh University Press, 2018.

Asman, Carrie L. "Return of the Sign to the Body: Benjamin and Gesture in the Age of Retheatricalization." *Discourse* 16, no. 3 (Spring 1994): 46-64.

———. "Theater and Agon/Agon and Theater: Walter Benjamin and Florens Christian Rang." *MLN* 107, no. 3 (1992): 606-24. https://doi.org/10.2307/2904948.

Aston, Trevor Henry. *Crisis in Europe, 1560-1660*. New York: Routledge, 1965.

Auslander, Philip. *Liveness: Performance in a Mediatized Culture*. New York: Routledge, 1999.

Badiou, Alain. *Being and Event*. Translated by Oliver Feltham. London: Continuum, 2007.

Bal, Mieke. *Quoting Caravaggio: Contemporary Art, Preposterous History*. Chicago: University of Chicago Press, 1999.

Barba, Eugenio, and Nicola Savarese. *A Dictionary of Theatre Anthropology: The Secret Art of the Performer*. Translated by Richard Fowler. New York: Routledge, 2011.

Barg, Lisa. "Black Voices/White Sounds: Race and Representation in Virgil Thomson's Four Saints in Three Acts." *American Music* 18, no. 2 (2000): 121-61. https://doi.org/10.2307/3052481.

Barish, Jonas A. *The Antitheatrical Prejudice*. Berkeley: University of California Press, 1981.

Barnett, David. *Brecht in Practice: Theatre, Theory, and Performance*. New York: Bloomsbury, 2014.

Barth, Herbert, Dietrich Mack, and Egon Voss. *Wagner: A Documentary Study*. Oxford: Oxford University Press, 1975.

Barthes, Roland. *Critical Essays*. Translated by Richard Howard. Evanston, IL: Northwestern University Press, 1981.

———. *Image, Music, Text*. Translated by Steven Heath. New York: Noonday, 1988.

Bassoff, Bruce. "Gertrude Stein's 'Composition as Explanation.'" *Twentieth Century Literature* 24, no. 1 (1978): 76-80. https://doi.org/10.2307/441065.

Baudelaire, Charles. *The Flowers of Evil*. Edited by Jonathan Culler. Translated by James N. McGowan. Oxford: Oxford University Press, 2008.

———. *The Painter of Modern Life and Other Essays*. 2nd revised edition. London: Phaidon, 1995.

Baur-Heinhold, Margarete. *Baroque Theatre: A Cultural History of the 17th and 18th Centuries*. Translated by Mary Whittall. London: Thames & Hudson, 1967.

Bay-Cheng, Sarah. *Mama Dada: Gertrude Stein's Avant-Garde Theater*. New York: Routledge, 2004.

Bazin, Germain. *Baroque and Rococo*. Translated by Jonathan Griffin. New York: Praeger, 1964.

Bibliography

Beckett, Samuel. *Collected Shorter Plays*. New York: Grove Press, 1984.

Bell, Millicent. *Shakespeare's Tragic Skepticism*. New Haven, CT: Yale University Press, 2002.

Bell, Richard H. *Wagner's Parsifal: An Appreciation in the Light of His Theological Journey*. Eugene, OR: Cascade Books, 2013.

Benjamin, Walter. *The Arcades Project*. Translated by Howard Eiland and Kevin McLaughlin. Cambridge, MA: Harvard University Press, 199AD.

——. *Briefe*. Edited by Gershom Scholem and Theodor W. Adorno. Frankfurt am Main: Suhrkamp Verlag, 1978.

——. *The Correspondence of Walter Benjamin*. Edited by Gershom Scholem and Theodor W. Adorno. Translated by M. Jacobson and E. Jacobson. Chicago: University of Chicago Press, 1994.

——. *Gesammelte Schriften*. Edited by R. Tiedemann. 7 vols. Berlin: Suhrkamp Verlag, 1991.

——. *The Origin of German Tragic Drama*. Translated by John Osborne. New York: Verso, 2003.

——. *Origin of the German Trauerspiel*. Translated by Howard Eiland. Cambridge, MA: Harvard University Press, 2019.

——. *Understanding Brecht*. Translated by Anna Bostock. London: NLB, 1966.

——. *Ursprung des deutschen Trauerspiels*. Edited by Rolf Tiedemann. Berlin: Suhrkamp Verlag, 1978.

Benston, Alice N., and Marshall Olds, eds. *Essays in European Literature for Walter A. Strauss*. Studies in Twentieth Century Literature, 1. Manhattan: Kansas State University, 1990.

Benn Michaels, Walter. *The Gold Standard and the Logic of Naturalism*. Berkeley: University of California Press, 1988.

Berardi, Franco "Bifo." *The Uprising: Poetry and Finance*. Los Angeles: Semiotext(e), 2012.

Berger, Karol. *Bach's Cycle, Mozart's Arrow: An Essay on the Origins of Musical Modernity*. Berkeley: University of California Press, 2007.

Berman, Marshall. *All That Is Solid Melts into Air: The Experience of Modernity*. New York: Verso, 1983.

Bernini, Gian Lorenzo. *The Impresario (Untitled)*. Translated by Donald Beecher and Massimo Ciavolella. Carleton Renaissance Plays in Translation 6. Ottawa: Dovehouse Editions Canada, 1985.

Bernstein, Charles. "Disfiguring Abstraction." *Critical Inquiry* 39, no. 3 (2013): 486-97. https://doi.org/10.1086/670042.

——. *A Poetics*. Cambridge, MA: Harvard University Press, 1992.

Bernstein, Jay, ed. *The Frankfurt School*. New York: Routledge, 1994.

Bernstein, Robin. *Racial Innocence: Performing American Childhood from Slavery to Civil Rights*. New York: New York University Press, 2011.

264   Bibliography

Bersani, Leo. *A Future for Astyanax: Character and Desire in Literature*. New York: Columbia University Press, 1984.

——. "Is the Rectum a Grave?" *October* 43 (1987): 197-222. https://doi.org/10.2307/3397574.

——. *The Death of Stephane Mallarmé*. Cambridge: Cambridge University Press, 1982.

Bizzell, Patricia, and Bruce Herzberg. *The Rhetorical Tradition: Readings from Classical Times to the Present*. New York: Bedford / St. Martin's, 2000.

Blackmer, Corinne E., and Patricia Juliana Smith, eds. *En Travesti: Women, Gender Subversion, Opera*. New York: Columbia University Press, 1995.

Block, Haskell. *Mallarmé and the Symbolist Drama*. Detroit: Wayne State University Press, 1963.

Bloom, Harold, ed. *Gertrude Stein*. New York: Chelsea House, 1986.

——, ed. *Stéphane Mallarmé*. New York: Chelsea House, 1987.

Bolter, J. David, and Richard Grusin. *Remediation: Understanding New Media*. Cambridge: MIT Press, 1999.

Borges, Jorge Luis. *Collected Fictions*. Translated by Andrew Hurley. New York: Penguin, 1999.

——. *The Total Library: Non-Fiction, 1922-1986*. Edited by Eliot Weinberger. Translated by Esther Allen, Suzanne Jill Levine, and Eliot Weinberger. London: Penguin, 2007.

Bowers, Jane Palatini. *"They Watch Me As They Watch This": Gertrude Stein's Metadrama*. Philadelphia: University of Pennsylvania Press, 1991.

Bowie, Malcolm. *Mallarmé and the Art of Being Difficult*. Cambridge: Cambridge University Press, 2008.

Boyle, Michael Shane, Matt Cornish, and Brandon Woolf, eds. *Postdramatic Theatre and Form*. New York: Bloomsbury, 2019.

Bradbury, Malcolm, and James McFarlane, eds. *Modernism: A Guide to European Literature, 1890-1930*. 1976. Reprint, London: Penguin, 1991.

Brandes, Georg Morris Cohen. *An Essay on the Aristocratic Radicalism of Friedrich Nietzsche (1889)*. Translated by A. G. Chater. New York: Haskell House, 1972. https://archive.org/details/essayonaristocra00bran/mode/2up.

Brecht, Bertolt. *Brecht Collected Plays, 2: Man Equals Man; Elephant Calf; Threepenny Opera; Mahagonny; Seven Deadly Sins*. Edited by John Willett and Ralph Manheim. New York: Bloomsbury, 2015.

——. *Brecht on Theatre: The Development of an Aesthetic*. Edited by John Willett. New York: Macmillan, 1964.

Bredekamp, Horst. *The Lure of Antiquity and the Cult of the Machine*. Translated by Allison Brown. Princeton, NJ: Markus Wiener, 1995.

Brobjer, Thomas. "Nietzsche's Relation to the Greek Sophists." *Nietzsche-Studien* 34, no. 1 (2005): 255-76.

Bibliography

Brooker, Jewel Spears. *T. S. Eliot's Dialectical Imagination*. Baltimore: Johns Hopkins University Press, 2018.

Brooks, Peter, and Hilary Jewett, eds. *The Humanities and Public Life*. New York: Fordham University Press, 2014.

Brown, Jane K. *The Persistence of Allegory: Drama and Neoclassicism from Shakespeare to Wagner*. Philadelphia: University of Pennsylvania Press, 2006.

Buci-Glucksmann, Christine. *Baroque Reason: The Aesthetics of Modernity*. Translated by Patrick Camiller. Introduction by Bryan S. Turner. Thousand Oaks, CA: Sage, 1994.

Buck-Morss, Susan. *The Dialectics of Seeing: Walter Benjamin and the Arcades Project*. Cambridge, MA: MIT Press, 1991.

Bürger, Peter. *Theory of the Avant-Garde*. Translated by Michael Shaw. Minneapolis: University of Minnesota Press, 1984.

Butler, Judith. *Bodies That Matter: On the Discursive Limits of Sex*. New York: Routledge, 1993.

———. "Critically Queer." *GLQ: A Journal of Lesbian and Gay Studies* 1, no. 1 (November 1, 1993): 17–32. https://doi.org/10.1215/10642684-1-1-17.

———. *Gender Trouble*. 1990. Reprint, New York: Routledge, 2008.

———. *Notes toward a Performative Theory of Assembly*. Cambridge, MA: Harvard University Press, 2015.

Byrnes, Michael, Gordon Dahlquist, David Levine, and Joe Diebes. "Babylon Is Everywhere, or Petrolia Restor'd." *Theater* 34, no. 2 (Summer 2004): 14–27.

Calabrese, Omar. *Neo-Baroque: A Sign of the Times*. Translated by Charles Lambert. Princeton, NJ: Princeton University Press, 1992.

Calinescu, Matei. *Five Faces of Modernity: Modernism, Avant-Garde, Decadence, Kitsch, Postmodernism*. Durham, NC: Duke University Press, 1987.

Calloway, Stephen. *Baroque Baroque: The Culture of Excess*. London: Phaidon Press, 2000.

Camp, Pannill. *The First Frame: Theatre Space in Enlightenment France*. Cambridge: Cambridge University Press, 2014.

Canning, Charlotte M., and Thomas Postlewait, eds. *Representing the Past: Essays in Performance Historiography*. Iowa City: University of Iowa Press, 2010.

Carney, Sean. *Brecht and Critical Theory: Dialectics and Contemporary Aesthetics*. London: Routledge, 2005.

Carter, Tim. *Monteverdi's Musical Theatre*. New Haven, CT: Yale University Press, 2002.

Cavell, Stanley. *Disowning Knowledge: In Seven Plays of Shakespeare*. Cambridge: Cambridge University Press, 2003.

Cefalu, Paul, and Bryan Reynolds, eds. *The Return of Theory in Early Modern English Studies: Tarrying with the Subjunctive*. New York: Palgrave Macmillan, 2011.

Centre Pompidou. "Walter Benn Michaels: Diversity, Equality, Theatricality." In "According to Michael Fried: Artists and Other Thinkers." Accessed December 10, 2020. https://www.centrepompidou.fr/en/program/calendar/event/cKxojG9.

Cermatori, Joseph. "Allegories of Spectatorship: On Michael Fried's Theory of Drama." *Journal of Dramatic Theory and Criticism* 32, no. 2 (July 17, 2018): 89-103. https://doi.org/10.1353/dtc.2018.0007.

———. "Essential Ruptures: Herbert Blau's Power of Mind." *PAJ: A Journal of Performance and Art* 42, no. 1 (January 2020): 1-9. https://doi.org/10.1162/pajj_a_00497.

———. "Thornton Wilder's Baroque Vision." *PMLA* 136, no. 2 (March 2021): 246-48.

Cermatori, Joseph, Emily Coates, Kathryn Krier, Bronwen MacArthur, Angelica Randle, and Joseph Roach. "Teaching African American Dance/History to a 'Post-racial' Class: Yale's 'Project O.'" *Theatre Topics* 19, no. 1 (March 2009): 1-14.

Cheng, Anne Anlin. *Ornamentalism*. Oxford: Oxford University Press, 2019.

Cicero, Marcus Tullius. *Brutus*. Translated by G. L. Hendrickson. Loeb Classical Library. Cambridge, MA: Harvard University Press, 1971.

Clements, Elicia. "How to Remediate; or, Gertrude Stein and Virgil Thomson's *Four Saints in Three Acts*." *Modern Drama* 62, no. 1 (Spring 2019): 45-72.

Cody, Gabrielle H., and Evert Sprinchorn, eds. *The Columbia Encyclopedia of Modern Drama*. New York: Columbia University Press, 2007.

Coffman, Chris. *Gertrude Stein's Transmasculinity*. Edinburgh: Edinburgh University Press, 2019.

Cohn, Robert Greer, ed. *Mallarmé in the Twentieth Century*. Teaneck, NJ: Fairleigh Dickinson University Press, 1998.

———. "Mallarmé's Wake." *New Literary History* 26, no. 4 (1995): 885-901.

———. *Toward the Poems of Mallarmé*. Berkeley: University of California Press, 1981.

Cooper, Dennis. "Ryan Trecartin." *Artforum*. Accessed February 3, 2020. https://www.artforum.com/print/200601/ryan-trecartin-10046.

Copeland, Rita, and Peter T. Struck, eds. *The Cambridge Companion to Allegory*. Cambridge: Cambridge University Press, 2010.

Copjec, Joan. *Imagine There's No Woman: Ethics and Sublimation*. Cambridge: MIT Press, 2002.

Craig, Edward Gordon. *On the Art of the Theatre (1911)*. Edited by Franc Chamberlain. New York: Routledge, 2009.

Critchley, Simon, and Jamieson Webster. *Stay, Illusion! The Hamlet Doctrine*. New York: Knopf Doubleday, 2014.

Croll, Morris W. *Style, Rhetoric, and Rhythm: Essays by Morris W. Croll*. Edited by J. Max Patrick and Robert O. Evans. Princeton, NJ: Princeton University Press, 2015.

Cull, Laura. *Theatres of Immanence: Deleuze and the Ethics of Performance*. New York: Palgrave Macmillan, 2012.

Cull, Laura, and Alice Lagaay, eds. *Encounters in Performance Philosophy*. New York: Palgrave Macmillan, 2014.

Bibliography

Curiger, Bice, and Kunsthaus Zürich, eds. *Deftig Barock: From Cattelan to Zurbarán—Tributes to Precarious Vitality.* Cologne: Snoeck, 2012.

Daddario, Will. *Baroque, Venice, Theatre, Philosophy.* London: Palgrave Macmillan, 2017.

Danto, Arthur C. *Nietzsche as Philosopher.* New York: Columbia University Press, 2005.

Davidson, Peter. *The Universal Baroque.* Manchester: Manchester University Press, 2007.

Davis, Tracy C., and Thomas Postlewait, eds. *Theatricality.* Cambridge: Cambridge University Press, 2003.

Deak, Frantisek. *Symbolist Theater: The Formation of an Avant-Garde.* Baltimore: Johns Hopkins University Press, 1993.

Dean, Tim, Hal Foster, Kaja Silverman, and Leo Bersani. "A Conversation with Leo Bersani." *October* 82 (1997): 3-16. https://doi.org/10.2307/778995.

Debord, Guy. *The Society of the Spectacle.* Translated by Donald Nicholson-Smith. New York: Zone Books, 1994.

DeFrantz, Thomas F., and Anita Gonzalez, eds. *Black Performance Theory.* Durham, NC: Duke University Press, 2014.

Deleuze, Gilles. *Nietzsche and Philosophy.* New York: Columbia University Press, 1983.

———. *Spinoza: Practical Philosophy.* San Francisco: City Lights Books, 1988.

———. *The Fold: Leibniz and the Baroque.* Translated by Tom Conley. Minneapolis: University of Minnesota Press, 1993.

Deleuze, Gilles, and Félix Guattari. *What Is Philosophy?* Translated by Hugh Tomlinson and Graham Burchell. New York: Columbia University Press, 2014.

De Man, Paul. *Allegories of Reading: Figural Language in Rousseau, Nietzsche, Rilke, and Proust.* New Haven, CT: Yale University Press, 1979.

———. *Blindness and Insight: Essays in the Rhetoric of Contemporary Criticism.* 2nd ed. Minneapolis: University of Minnesota Press, 1983.

———. *The Resistance to Theory.* Minneapolis: University of Minnesota Press, 1986.

Derrida, Jacques. *Acts of Literature.* Edited by Derek Attridge. New York: Routledge, 1992.

———. *Dissemination.* Translated by Barbara Johnson. Chicago: University of Chicago Press, 1981.

———. *Spurs: Nietzsche's Styles.* Translated by Barbara Harlow. Chicago: University of Chicago Press, 1981.

———. *Writing and Difference.* Translated by Alan Bass. Chicago: University of Chicago Press, 1978.

Diamond, Elin. "Brechtian Theory/Feminist Theory: Toward a Gestic Feminist Criticism" *TDR: The Drama Review* 32, no. 1 (Spring 1988): 82-94.

Diawara, Manthia. "Conversation with Édouard Glissant aboard the Queen Mary II." *Black Atlantic* (University of Liverpool). Accessed 15 March 2021. https://www.liverpool.ac.uk/media/livacuk/csis-2/blackatlantic/research/Diawara_text_defined.pdf.

Dierkes-Thrun, Petra. *Salome's Modernity: Oscar Wilde and the Aesthetics of Transgression*. Ann Arbor: University of Michigan Press, 2011.

Dolan, Jill. *Utopia in Performance: Finding Hope at the Theater*. Ann Arbor: University of Michigan Press, 2005.

D'Onofrio, Cesare. *Gian Lorenzo Bernini, Fontana di Trevi: commedia inedita*. Rome: Staderini, 1963.

Doyle, Jennifer, and David Getsy. "Queer Formalisms: Jennifer Doyle and David Getsy in Conversation." *Art Journal Open* (blog). *Art Journal*, March 31, 2014. http://artjournal.collegeart.org/?p=4468.

Doyle, Laura. "The Flat, the Round, and Gertrude Stein: Race and the Shape of Modern(ist) History)." *Modernism/modernity* 7, no. 2 (April 2000): 274-71.

Dydo, Ulla E. *Gertrude Stein: The Language That Rises, 1923-1934*. Evanston, IL: Northwestern University Press, 2003.

Eagleton, Terry. *Walter Benjamin; or, Towards a Revolutionary Criticism*. New York: Verso, 2009.

Echeverría, Bolívar. *La modernidad de lo barroco*. Mexico City: Ediciones Era, 1998.

———. *Modernity and "Whiteness."* Translated by Rodrigo Ferreira. Cambridge: Polity, 2019.

Eco, Umberto. *The Open Work*. Translated by Anna Cancogni. Cambridge, MA: Harvard University Press, 1989.

Egginton, William. *How the World Became a Stage: Presence, Theatricality, and the Question of Modernity*. Albany: State University of New York Press, 2003.

———. *The Theater of Truth: The Ideology of (Neo)Baroque Aesthetics*. Stanford, CA: Stanford University Press, 2010.

Ehlers, Nadine. *Racial Imperatives: Discipline, Performativity, and Struggles against Subjection*. Bloomington: Indiana University Press, 2012.

"Eine barocke Party" (A baroque party). Kunsthalle Wien. Accessed February 3, 2020. http://kunsthallewien.at/social/en/exhibitions/baroque-party.

Eliot, T. S. *For Lancelot Andrewes: Essays on Style and Order*. Garden City, NY: Doubleday, 1929.

———. *The Sacred Wood: Essays on Poetry and Criticism*. New York: Barnes & Noble, 1928.

Elsner, Gary. *Nietzsche: A Philosophical Biography*. Lanham, MD: University Press of America, 1992.

Farfan, Penny. *Performing Queer Modernism*. Oxford: Oxford University Press, 2017.

Farrell, Joseph, and Paolo Puppa, eds. *A History of Italian Theatre*. Cambridge: Cambridge University Press, 2006.

Fateman, Johanna. "Jacolby Satterwhite." 4Columns. Accessed February 3, 2020. http://4columns.org/fateman-johanna/jacolby-satterwhite.

Fehér, Ferenc. "Lukács, Benjamin, Theatre." *Theatre Journal* 37, no. 4 (1985): 415-25. https://doi.org/10.2307/3207517.

Bibliography

Fenves, Peter David. *Arresting Language: From Leibniz to Benjamin*. Stanford, CA: Stanford University Press, 2001.

Féral, Josette. "Foreword." *SubStance* 31, nos. 2-3 (2002): 3-13.

——. "Performance and Theatricality: The Subject Demystified." *Modern Drama* 25, no. 1 (Spring 1982): 170-81.

Féral, Josette, and Ronald P. Bermingham, eds. "Theatricality: The Specificity of Theatrical Language." Special issue, *SubStance* 31, nos. 2-3 (2002): 94-108. https://doi.org/10.2307/3685480.

Fischer-Lichte, Erika. *The Show and the Gaze of Theatre: A European Perspective*. Translated by Jo Riley. Iowa City: University of Iowa Press, 1997.

——. *The Transformative Power of Performance: A New Aesthetics*. New York: Routledge, 2008.

——. "Theatricality: A Key Concept in Theatre and Cultural Studies." *Theatre Research International* 20, no. 2 (1995): 85-89. https://doi.org/10.1017/S030788330 0008294.

——. "Walter Benjamin's 'Allegory.'" *American Journal of Semiotics* 4, nos. 1-2 (2008): 151-68.

Fish, Stanley Eugene. *Self-Consuming Artifacts: The Experience of Seventeenth-Century Literature*. Berkeley: University of California Press, 1972.

Flatley, Jonathan. *Like Andy Warhol*. Chicago: University of Chicago Press, 2017.

Fleischmann, Benno. *Die Wiederentdeckung des Barocktheaters*. Vienna: Paul Neff, 1948.

Fletcher, Angus. *Allegory: The Theory of a Symbolic Mode*. Princeton, NJ: Princeton University Press, 2012.

——. "Allegory in Literary History." In *Dictionary of the History of Ideas*. University of Virginia Library. Accessed February 15, 2020. http://xtf.lib.virginia.edu/xtf/view ?docId=DicHist/uvaBook/tei/DicHist1.xml;brand=default;;query=allegory.

Focillon, Henri. *The Life of Forms in Art*. Translated by Charles Beecher Hogan and George Kubler. New York: Zone Books, 1989.

Foreman, Richard. *Unbalancing Acts: Foundations for a Theater*. Edited by Ken Jordan. New York: Theatre Communications Group, 1992.

Foucault, Michel. *Archaeology of Knowledge*. Translated by A. M. Sheridan Smith. London: Routledge, 2002.

——. *The Foucault Reader*. Edited by Paul Rabinow. New York: Pantheon, 1984.

——. *The History of Sexuality: An Introduction*. Translated by Robert Hurley. New York: Knopf Doubleday, 2012.

Language, Counter-memory, Practice: Selected Essays and Interviews. Edited by Donald Bouchard. Translated by Donald Bouchard and Sherry Simon. Ithaca, NY: Cornell University Press, 1980.

——. *The Order of Things*. New York: Routledge, 2005.

Frank, Manfred. "Style in Philosophy: Part I." *Metaphilosophy* 30, no. 3 (July 1999): 145.

Fredette, Nathalie. *Figures baroques de Jean Genet*. Paris: XYZ, 2001.

Freeman, Elizabeth. *Time Binds: Queer Temporalities, Queer Histories*. Durham, NC: Duke University Press, 2010.

Freeman, Michael, Elizabeth Fallaize, Jill Forbes, Toby Garfitt, and Roger Peterson, eds. *The Process of Art: Essays on Nineteenth-Century French Literature, Music, and Painting in Honor of Alain Riatt*. Oxford, UK: Clarendon, 1998.

Freud, Sigmund. *Civilization and Its Discontents*. Translated by James Strachey. New York: W. W. Norton, 2010.

——. *General Psychological Theory: Papers on Metapsychology*. Edited by Philip Rieff. New York: Simon & Schuster, 2008.

Fried, Michael. *Absorption and Theatricality: Painting and Beholder in the Age of Diderot*. Berkeley: University of California Press, 1980.

——. *Art and Objecthood: Essays and Reviews*. Chicago: University of Chicago Press, 1998.

——. *Courbet's Realism*. Chicago: University of Chicago Press, 1992.

——. *Manet's Modernism; or, the Face of Painting in the 1860s*. Chicago: University of Chicago Press, 1998.

——. *The Moment of Caravaggio*. Princeton, NJ: Princeton University Press, 2010.

Friedlander, Eli. "On the Musical Gathering of Echoes of the Voice." *Opera Quarterly* 21, no. 4 (2005): 631-46. https://doi.org/10.1093/oq/kbi097.

Fuchs, Elinor. *The Death of Character: Perspectives on Theater after Modernism*. Bloomington: Indiana University Press, 1996.

Fuchs, Elinor, and Una Chaudhuri, eds. *Land/Scape/Theater*. Ann Arbor: University of Michigan Press, 2002.

Fuchs, Georg. *Revolution in the Theatre: Conclusions concerning the Munich Artists' Theatre*. Translated by Constance Connor Kuhn. Ithaca, NY: Cornell University Press, 1959.

Fülöp-Miller, René. *The Power and Secret of the Jesuits*. London: Putnam and Sons, 1930. http://archive.org/details/in.ernet.dli.2015.217152.

Gaddis, Eugene R. *Magician of the Modern: Chick Austin and the Transformation of the Arts in America*. New York: Alfred A. Knopf, 2000.

Gaonkar, Dilip Parameshwar, ed. *Alternative Modernities*. Durham, NC: Duke University Press, 2001.

Garelick, Rhonda. *Rising Star: Dandyism, Gender, and Performance in the Fin de Siècle*. Princeton, NJ: Princeton University Press, 1998.

Gerould, Daniel, ed. *Doubles, Demons, and Dreamers: An International Collection of Symbolist Drama*. New York: PAJ, 1985.

Getsy, David. "Ten Queer Theses on Abstraction." Des Moines Art Center. Accessed January 13, 2020. https://www.desmoinesartcenter.org/webres/File/Getsy-Queer ThesesOnAbstraction-2019.pdf.

Bibliography

Giedion, Sigfried. *Space, Time, and Architecture: The Growth of a New Tradition*. Cambridge, MA: Harvard University Press, 1967.

Gillespie, Gerald. *German Theater before 1750: Sachs, Gryphius, Schlegel, and Others*. New York: Bloomsbury, 1992.

Girard, René. "Dionysus versus the Crucified." *MLN* 99, no. 4 (1984): 816-35. https://doi.org/10.2307/2905504.

Gobert, R. Darren. *The Mind-Body Stage: Passion and Interaction in the Cartesian Theater*. Stanford, CA: Stanford University Press, 2013.

Goldberg, RoseLee. *Performance Art: From Futurism to the Present*. London: Thames & Hudson, 2011.

Goldmann, Lucien. *The Hidden God: A Study of Tragic Vision in the Pensées of Pascal and the Tragedies of Racine*. Translated by Philip Thody. New York: Verso Books, 2016.

Golub, Spencer. *The Baroque Night*. Evanston, IL: Northwestern University Press, 2018.

Gordon, Mel, ed. *Expressionist Texts*. New York: PAJ, 1986.

Gordon, Rae Beth. *Ornament, Fantasy, and Desire in Nineteenth-Century French Literature*. Princeton, NJ: Princeton University Press, 1992.

Gould, Evlyn. *Virtual Theater from Diderot to Mallarmé*. Baltimore: Johns Hopkins University Press, 1989.

Gould, Stephen Jay. *Time's Arrow, Time's Cycle: Myth and Metaphor in the Discovery of Geological Time*. Cambridge, MA: Harvard University Press, 1987.

Greenblatt, Stephen, ed. *Allegory and Representation*. Baltimore: Johns Hopkins University Press, 1986.

Gregor-Dellin, Martin. *Richard Wagner: Sein Leben, Sein Werk, Sein Jahrhundert*. Munich: R. Piper, 1980.

Grossman, Jeffrey. "The Reception of Walter Benjamin in the Anglo-American Literary Institution." *German Quarterly* 65, no. 3 (Summer-Autumn, 1992): 414-28.

Gryphius, Andreas. *Catharina von Georgien: Trauerspiel*. Stuttgart: Reclam Verlag, 1975.

———. "Catharine of Georgia, or Proven Constancy." Translated by Janifer Stackhouse. Unpublished manuscript, Microsoft Word file, 2014.

———. *Leo Armenius: Trauerspiel*. Stuttgart: Reclam Verlag, 1971.

Habermas, Jürgen. *The Philosophical Discourse of Modernity: Twelve Lectures*. Translated by Frederick G. Lawrence. Cambridge, MA: MIT Press, 1990.

Halberstam, J. Jack. *In a Queer Time and Place: Transgender Bodies, Subcultural Lives*. New York: New York University Press, 2005.

Halpern, Richard. *Shakespeare among the Moderns*. Ithaca, NY: Cornell University Press, 1997.

———. "The King's Two Buckets: Kantorowicz, Richard II, and Fiscal Trauerspiel." *Representations* 106, no. 1 (2009): 67-76. https://doi.org/10.1525/rep.2009.106.1.67.

Hannah, Dorita. *Event-Space: Theatre Architecture and the Historical Avant-Garde*. New York: Routledge, 2018.

Hansen, Miriam Bratu. "Benjamin's Aura." *Critical Inquiry* 34, no. 2 (2008): 336-75. https://doi.org/10.1086/529060.

Harries, Martin. *Forgetting Lot's Wife: On Destructive Spectatorship*. New York: Fordham University Press, 2007.

Harris, David. "The Original 'Four Saints in Three Acts.'" *TDR: The Drama Review* 26, no. 1 (1982): 101-30. https://doi.org/10.2307/1145448.

Hartman, Saidiya. *Scenes of Subjection: Terror, Slavery, and Self-Making in Nineteenth-Century America*. Oxford: Oxford University Press, 1997.

Hassan, Ihab. *The Dismemberment of Orpheus: Toward a Postmodern Literature*. Madison: University of Wisconsin Press, 1982.

Hegel, Georg Wilhelm Friedrich. *Hegel on Tragedy*. Edited by Anne Paolucci and Henry Paolucci. Westport, CT: Greenwood Press, 1975.

——. *Introductory Lectures on Aesthetics*. 1835. Translated by Bernard Bosanquet, 1886. London: Penguin Classics, 2004.

Herring, Scott. *Queering the Underworld: Slumming, Literature, and the Undoing of Lesbian and Gay History*. Chicago: University of Chicago Press, 2009.

Higgins, Dick. *George Herbert's Pattern Poems: In Their Tradition*. West Glover, VT: Unpublished Editions, 1977.

Holmberg, Arthur. *The Theatre of Robert Wilson*. Cambridge: Cambridge University Press, 1996.

Honig, Edwin. *Dark Conceit: The Making of Allegory*. Evanston, IL: Northwestern University Press, 2018.

Horkheimer, Max, and Theodor W. Adorno. *Dialectic of Enlightenment*. Translated by John Cumming. London: Continuum, 1982.

Hoxby, Blair. *What Was Tragedy? Theory and the Early Modern Canon*. Oxford: Oxford University Press, 2015.

Innes, Christopher. "Modernism in Drama." In *The Cambridge Companion to Modernism*, 2nd ed., edited by Michael Levenson, 128-54. Cambridge: Cambridge University Press, 2011.

Innes, Christopher, and Maria Shevtsova, eds. *The Cambridge Introduction to Theatre Directing*. Cambridge: Cambridge University Press, 2013.

Isherwood, Christopher. *The World in the Evening*. New York: Macmillan, 1988.

Jack Smith and the Destruction of Atlantis. Directed by Mary Jordan. Arthouse Films, 2010.

Jakovljevic, Branislav. "Wooster Baroque." *TDR: The Drama Review* 54, no. 3 (August 24, 2010): 87-122.

James, William. *The Varieties of Religious Experience*. New York: Macmillan, 1961.

Jameson, Fredric. *Allegory and Ideology*. New York: Verso Books, 2019.

——. *Brecht and Method*. New York: Verso, 1998.

Bibliography 273

———. *The Modernist Papers*. New York: Verso, 2007.

———. *Postmodernism; or, the Cultural Logic of Late Capitalism*. 1991. Reprint, Durham, NC: Duke University Press, 2005.

Jarcho, Julia. *Writing and the Modern Stage: Theater beyond Drama*. Cambridge: Cambridge University Press, 2017.

Jennings, M., M. Bullock, H. Eiland, and G. Smith, eds. *Walter Benjamin: Selected Writings*. 4 vols. Cambridge, MA: Harvard University Press, 2003.

Johnson, Barbara. *The Critical Difference: Essays in the Contemporary Rhetoric of Reading*. Baltimore: Johns Hopkins University Press, 1981.

———. "Mallarmé Gets a Life." *London Review of Books*, August 18, 1994.

———. *A World of Difference*. Baltimore: Johns Hopkins University Press, 1987.

Johnson, Christopher. "On Borges's B/baroque." *Comparative Literature* 72, no. 4 (December 2020): 377-405.

Johnson, Samuel. *The Lives of the English Poets*. Vol. 1. 3 vols. Leipzig, Germany: Tauchnitz, 1858.Judd, Donald. "Specific Objects—Donald Judd." *Art Theory*. First published, 1965. Accessed February 11, 2020. http://theoria.art-zoo.com/specific -objects-donald-judd/.

Kaes, Anton, Martin Jay, and Edward Dimendberg, eds. *The Weimar Republic Sourcebook*. Berkeley: University of California Press, 1994.

Kahn, Victoria. *The Future of Illusion: Political Theology and Early Modern Texts*. Chicago: University of Chicago Press, 2014.

Kant, Marion, ed. *The Cambridge Companion to Ballet*. Cambridge: Cambridge University Press, 2007.

Kantorowicz, Ernst. *The King's Two Bodies: A Study in Medieval Political Theology*. Princeton, NJ: Princeton University Press, 2016.

Kantrowitz, Joanne Spencer. *Dramatic Allegory: Lindsay's Ane Satyre of the Thrie Estaitis*. Lincoln: University of Nebraska Press, 1975.

Kastleman, Rebecca. "An Acquaintance with Religion: Pluralizing Knowledge in Gertrude Stein's Doctor Faustus Lights the Lights." *Modern Drama* 62, no. 3 (August 27, 2019): 338-60.

Kinderman, William. *Wagner's Parsifal*. Oxford: Oxford University Press, 2018.

Kitson, Michael. *The Age of Baroque*. New York: McGraw Hill, 1966.

Kleist, Heinrich von. "On the Marionette Theatre." Translated by Thomas G. Neumiller. *TDR: The Drama Review* 16, no. 3 (1972): 22-26. https://doi.org/10.2307/114 4768.

Knowles, Ric, Joanne Tompkins, and W. B. Worthen, eds. *Modern Drama: Defining the Field*. Toronto: University of Toronto Press, 2003.

Köhler, Joachim. *Nietzsche and Wagner: A Lesson in Subjugation*. New Haven, CT: Yale University Press, 1999.

Kornhaber, David. *The Birth of Theater from the Spirit of Philosophy: Nietzsche and the Modern Drama*. Evanston, IL: Northwestern University Press, 2016.

Koselleck, Reinhart. *Futures Past: On the Semantics of Historical Time*. Translated by Keith Tribe. Revised edition. Cambridge: MIT Press, 2004.

Koss, Juliet. *Modernism after Wagner*. Minneapolis: University of Minnesota Press, 2010.

Kostka, Alexandre, and Irving Wohlfarth. *Nietzsche and "an Architecture of Our Minds."* Los Angeles: Getty Research Institute for the History of Art and the Humanities, 1999.

Kottman, Paul. *A Politics of the Scene*. Stanford, CA: Stanford University Press, 2007.

Kotzamani, Marina. "Red: An Exhibition of Theater Costumes from the Eighteenth to the Twenty-First Century." *Theater* 37, no. 2 (January 1, 2007): 102–9. https://doi.org/10.1215/01610775-2006-026.

Kracauer, Siegfried. *Theory of Film: The Redemption of Physical Reality*. Princeton, NJ: Princeton University Press, 1997.

Kramnick, Jonathan, and Anahid Nersessian. "Form and Explanation." *Critical Inquiry* 43, no. 3 (March 1, 2017): 650–69. https://doi.org/10.1086/691017.

Krauss, Rosalind E. *The Originality of the Avant-Garde and Other Modernist Myths*. Cambridge, MA: MIT Press, 1986.

Kushner, Tony. *Death and Taxes:* Hydriotaphia *and Other Plays*. New York: Theatre Communications Group, 2000.

Lacoue-Labarthe, Philippe. *Musica Ficta: Figures of Wagner*. Stanford, CA: Stanford University Press, 1994.

Lahiji, Nadir. *Adventures with the Theory of the Baroque and French Philosophy*. London: Bloomsbury Academic, 2018.

Lambert, Gregg. *On the (New) Baroque*. Aurora, CO: Davies Group, 2008.

———. *The Return of the Baroque in Modern Culture*. London: Bloomsbury Academic, 2004.

Lancaster, Lex Morgan. "Queer Abstraction." *ASAP Journal*, July 16, 2019. http://asapjournal.com/queer-abstraction-lex-morgan-lancaster/.

Langan, Janine. *Hegel and Mallarmé*. Lanham, MD: University Press of America, 1986.

Laplanche, Jean. *Essays on Otherness*. New York: Routledge, 2005.

Large, Duncan. "Nietzsche's Orientalism." *Nietzsche-Studien* 42, no. 1 (2013).

Latham, Sean, and Gayle Rogers. *Modernism: Evolution of an Idea*. London: Bloomsbury Academic, 2015.

Lavin, Irving. *Visible Spirit: The Art of Gianlorenzo Bernini*. Vol. 2. 3 vols. London: Pindar, 2007.

Lehmann, Hans-Thies. *Postdramatic Theatre*. Translated by Karen Jürs-Munby. London: Routledge, 2006.

———. *Tragedy and Dramatic Theatre*. Translated by Erik Butler. New York: Routledge, 2016.

Lemon, Lee T., and Marion J. Reis, trans. *Russian Formalist Criticism: Four Essays*. Lincoln: University of Nebraska Press, 1965.

Bibliography

Leslie, Christopher. "'Melanctha Was Too Many for Him': Gertrude Stein's Challenges to Essentialism in *Three Lives*." *Interdisciplinary Literary Studies* 22, no. 3 (2020) 262-307.

Levenson, Michael, ed. *The Cambridge Companion to Modernism*. Cambridge: Cambridge University Press, 2011.

Levin, David J., ed. *Opera through Other Eyes*. Stanford, CA: Stanford University Press, 1993.

Levin, Thomas Y. "Walter Benjamin and the Theory of Art History." *October* 47 (1988): 77-83. https://doi.org/10.2307/778982.

Levine, Caroline. *Forms: Whole, Rhythm, Hierarchy, Network*. Princeton, NJ: Princeton University Press, 2017.

Levinson, Marjorie. "What Is New Formalism?" *PMLA* 122, no. 2 (2007): 558-69.

Lewis, Pericles, ed. *The Cambridge Introduction to Modernism*. Cambridge: Cambridge University Press, 2007.

Lorenz, Martin. *Musik und Nihilismus: Zur Relation von Kunst und Erkennen in der Philosophie Nietzsches*. Würzburg, Germany: Königshausen & Neumann, 2008.

"L'Orfeo, from Claudio Monteverdi." Opera Guide. Accessed 7 February 2021. https://opera-guide.ch/en/operas/lorfeo.

Losurdo, Domenico. *Nietzsche, il ribelle aristocratico: biografia intellettuale e bilancio critico*. Torino, Italy: Bollati Boringhieri, 2004.

Ludlam, Charles. *Ridiculous Theater: Scourge of Human Folly*. Edited by Steven Samuels. New York: Theatre Communications Group, 1992.

Luis-Martínez, Zenón. "Shakespeare's Historical Drama as Trauerspiel: *Richard II*—and After." *ELH* 75, no. 3 (Fall 2008): 673-705.

Lukács, György. *History and Class Consciousness: Studies in Marxist Dialectics*. Translated by Rodney Livingstone. Cambridge, MA: MIT Press, 1972.

———. *The Theory of the Novel: A Historico-Philosophical Essay on the Forms of Great Epic Literature*. Translated by Anna Bostock. Cambridge, MA: MIT Press, 1971.

Lyons, John D., ed. *The Oxford Handbook of the Baroque*. Oxford: Oxford University Press, 2018.

Lyotard, Jean-François. *Discourse, Figure*. Translated by Antony Hudek and Mary Lydon. Minneapolis: University of Minnesota Press, 2011.

———. *The Inhuman: Reflections on Time*. Translated by Geoffrey Bennington and Rachel Bowlby. Cambridge, UK: Polity, 1991.

———. *The Postmodern Condition: A Report on Knowledge*. Translated by Geoffrey Bennington and Brian Massumi. Minneapolis: University of Minnesota Press, 1984.

MacDonald, Dwight. *Against the American Grain*. New York: Da Capo, 1962.

Machosky, Brenda. *Structures of Appearing: Allegory and the Work of Literature*. New York: Fordham University Press, 2012.

Maciunas, George. "*Fluxus Manifesto, 1963*." Museum of Modern Art. Accessed February 11, 2020. https://www.moma.org/collection/works/127947.

Macpherson, Sandra. "A Little Formalism." *ELH* 82, no. 2 (June 11, 2015): 385–405. https://doi.org/10.1353/elh.2015.0025.

Mallarmé, Stéphane. *The Book*. Translated & Introduction by Sylvia Gorelick. Cambridge, MA: Exact Change, 2018.

———. *Collected Poems: A Bilingual Edition*. Translated by H. Weinfield. Berkeley: University of California Press, 1994.

———. *Correspondance*. Edited by H. Mondor, J. Richard, and L. Austin. Paris: Gallimard, 1985.

———. *Divagations*. Translated by Barbara Johnson. Cambridge, MA: Harvard University Press, 2009.

———. *Le "Livre" de Mallarmé: premières recherches sur des documents inédits*. 2nd ed. Edited by Jacques Scherer. Paris: Gallimard, 1978.

———. *Mallarmé on Fashion : A Translation of the Fashion Magazine, La Dernière Mode, with Commentary*. Translated by P. N. Furbank and Alex Cain. New York: Berg, 2004.

———. *Oeuvres Complètes*. Edited by H. Mondor and G. Jean-Aubry. Paris: Gallimard, 1945.

———. *Selected Letters of Stéphane Mallarmé*. Translated by Rosemary Lloyd. Chicago: University of Chicago Press, 1988.

Mao, Douglas, and Rebecca L. Walkowitz, eds. *Bad Modernisms*. Durham, NC: Duke University Press, 2006.

———. "The New Modernist Studies." *PMLA* 123, no. 3 (May 2008): 737–48.

Maravall, José Antonio. *Culture of the Baroque: Analysis of a Historical Structure*. Translation by Terry Cochran. Minneapolis: University of Minnesota Press, 1986.

Marchi, Dudley M. "Participatory Aesthetics: Reading Mallarmé and Joyce." *Comparatist* 19 (May 1995): 76–96.

"Marina Abramović: Balkan Baroque, 1997." MoMA. Accessed February 3, 2020. https://www.moma.org/audio/playlist/243/3126.

Marranca, Bonnie. *Ecologies of Theater: Essays at the Century Turning*. Baltimore: Johns Hopkins University Press, 1996.

———. *Performance Histories*. New York: PAJ, 2008.

———. "Robert Wilson and the Idea of the Archive Dramaturgy as an Ecology." *Performing Arts Journal* 15, no. 1 (1993): 66–79. https://doi.org/10.2307/3245799.

———. *Theatrewritings*. New York: PAJ, 1984.

Masten, Jeffrey. *Queer Philologies: Sex, Language, and Affect in Shakespeare's Time*. Philadelphia: University of Pennsylvania Press, 2016.

Mauron, Charles. *Mallarmé l'obscur*. Paris: Éditions Denoël, 1941.

McCown, Donald, Diane K. Reibel, and Marc S. Micozzi. *Teaching Mindfulness: A Practical Guide for Clinicians and Educators*. New York: Springer, 2010.

McFarland, James. *Constellation: Friedrich Nietzsche and Walter Benjamin in the Now-Time of History*. New York: Fordham University Press, 2012.

Bibliography

McGann, Jerome J. *The Textual Condition*. Princeton, NJ: Princeton University Press, 1991.

McGillivray, Glen. "The Discursive Formation of Theatricality as a Critical Concept." *Metaphorik De.* 17 (2009): 101-14.

McGuinness, Patrick. *Maurice Maeterlinck and the Making of Modern Theatre*. Oxford: Oxford University Press, 2000.

McKenzie, Jon. *Perform or Else: From Discipline to Performance*. New York: Routledge, 2001.

Meillassoux, Quintin. *The Number and the Siren: A Decipherment of Mallarmé's Coup de Dés*. Translated by Robin Mackay. New York: Sequence Press, 2012.

Melville, Stephen. "Notes on the Reemergence of Allegory, the Forgetting of Modernism, the Necessity of Rhetoric, and the Conditions of Publicity in Art and Criticism." *October* 19 (Winter 1981): 55-92.

———. *Philosophy Beside Itself: On Deconstruction and Modernism*. Minneapolis: University of Minnesota Press, 1986.

Mendelsohn, Daniel Adam. *The Elusive Embrace: Desire and the Riddle of Identity*. New York: Alfred A. Knopf, 1999.

Merrow, Kathleen Marie. "Nietzsche and the Baroque: The Nietzschean Critique of Morality, Culture, and Politics in Nineteenth-Century Germany." Ph.D. dissertation, Cornell University, 1998. http://search.proquest.com.ezproxy.cul.columbia.edu/pqdtglobal/docview/304418541/abstract/E44FD137F2F84B9APQ/1.

Millington, Barry. *The Sorcerer of Bayreuth: Richard Wagner, His Work, and His World*. New York: Oxford University Press, 2012.

Minor, Vernon Hyde. *The Death of the Baroque and the Rhetoric of Good Taste*. Cambridge: Cambridge University Press, 2006.

Moffett, Charles. *The New Painting: Impressionism, 1874-1886*. Seattle: University of Washington Press, 1986.

Moretti, Franco. *Signs Taken for Wonders: Essays in the Sociology of Literary Forms*. London: Verso, 1988.

Moses, Harry. "'Background Notes and Data.' Press Release for New York Production of 'Four Saints in Three Acts,'" 1934. Box 26, Gertrude Stein and Alice B. Toklas Papers. Yale University Beinecke Rare Book and Manuscript Archive.

Moten, Fred. *Black and Blur*. Durham, NC: Duke University Press, 2017.

———. "'Black Optimism/Black Operation.'" Paper presented at Anxiety, Urgency, Outrage, Hope . . . A Conference on Political Feeling, University of Chicago, October 19-20, 2007. http://lucian.uchicago.edu/blogs/politicalfeeling/files/2007/12/moten-black-optimism.doc.

———. *The Universal Machine*. Durham, NC: Duke University Press, 2018.

Müller, Ulrich, and Peter Wapnewski, eds. *Wagner Handbook*. Cambridge, MA: Harvard University Press, 1992.

278   Bibliography

Muñoz, José Esteban. *Cruising Utopia: The Then and There of Queer Futurity*. New York: New York University Press, 2009.

Murji, Karim, and John Solomos, eds. *Theories of Race and Ethnicity: Contemporary Debates and Perspectives*. Cambridge: Cambridge University Press, 2015.

Murray, Timothy. *Digital Baroque: New Media Art and Cinematic Folds*. Minneapolis: University of Minnesota Press, 2008.

———, ed. *Mimesis, Masochism, and Mime: The Politics of Theatricality in Contemporary French Thought*. Ann Arbor: University of Michigan Press, 1997.

Nagel, Barbara Natalie. *Der Skandal des Literalen: Barocke Literalisierungen bei Gryphius, Kleist, Büchner*. Munich: Wilhelm Fink, 2012.

Ndalianis, Angela. *Neo-Baroque Aesthetics and Contemporary Entertainment*. Cambridge, MA: MIT Press, 2004.

Newman, Jane O. *Benjamin's Library: Modernity, Nation, and the Baroque*. Ithaca, NY: Cornell University Press, 2011.

Ngai, Sianne. *Ugly Feelings*. Cambridge, MA: Harvard University Press, 2009.

Nietzsche, Friedrich. *The Anti-Christ, Ecce Homo, Twilight of the Idols, and Other Writings*. Edited by Aaron Ridley and Judith Norman. Translated by Judith Norman. Cambridge: Cambridge University Press, 2010.

———. *Beyond Good and Evil*. Edited by Rolf-Peter Horstmann. Translated by Judith Norman. Cambridge: Cambridge University Press, 2002.

———. *The Birth of Tragedy and Other Writings*. Edited by Raymond Geuss and Ronald Speirs. Translated by Ronald Speirs. Cambridge: Cambridge University Press, 2002.

———. *Briefwechsel: Kritische Gesamtausgabe*. Edited by Giorgio Colli and Mazzino Montinari. 24 vols. Berlin: De Gruyter, 2005.

———. *Dithyrambs of Dionysus*. Translated by R. J. Hollingdale. London: Anvil Press Poetry, 1984.

———. *Friedrich Nietzsche on Rhetoric and Language*. Edited by Sander L. Gilman, Carole Blair, and David J. Parent. New York: Oxford University Press, 1989.

———. *The Gay Science*. Edited by Bernard Williams. Translated by Josefine Nauckhoff. Cambridge: Cambridge University Press, 2001.

———. *Gesammelte Werke*. 23 vols. Edited by Richard Oehler, Max Oehler, and Friedrich C. Würzbach. Munich: Musarion Verlag, 1920-29.

———. *The Greek Music-Drama*. Translated by Paul Bishop. New York: Contra Mundum Press, 2013.

———. *Human, All Too Human: A Book for Free Spirits*. Translated by R. J. Hollingdale. Cambridge: Cambridge University Press, 1996.

———. *Kritische Gesamtausgabe*. Edited by Giorgio Colli and Mazzino Montinari. 40 vols. Berlin: De Gruyter, 2005.

———. *On the Genealogy of Morality*. Edited by Keith Ansell-Pearson. Translated by Carol Diethe. Cambridge: Cambridge University Press, 2010.

Bibliography

———. *Philosophy in the Tragic Age of the Greeks*. Translated by Marianne Cowan. Washington, DC: Regnery, 1998.

———. *Selected Letters of Friedrich Nietzsche*. Chicago: University of Chicago Press, 1969.

———. *Thus Spoke Zarathustra: A Book for Everyone and Nobody*. Edited by Adrian Del Caro and Robert Pippin. Translated by Adrian Del Caro. Cambridge: Cambridge University Press, 2006.

———. *Thus Spoke Zarathustra*. Translated by Graham Parkes. Oxford: Oxford University Press, 2009.

———. *Untimely Meditations*. Edited by Daniel Breazeale and R. J. Hollingdale. Cambridge: Cambridge University Press, 2006.

———. *The Will to Power*. Edited by Walter Kaufmann. Translated by Walter Kaufmann and R. J. Hollingdale. New York: Vintage, 1968.

Niven, Penelope. *Thornton Wilder: A Life*. New York: Harper Perennial, 2013.

Noland, Carrie, and Sally Ann Ness, eds. *Migrations of Gesture*. Minneapolis: University of Minnesota Press, 2008.

Norman, Barnaby. *Mallarme's Sunset: Poetry at the End of Time*. London: Routledge, 2014.

North, Joseph. *Literary Criticism*. Cambridge, MA: Harvard University Press, 2017.

Nuttall, Anthony David. *Two Concepts of Allegory: A Study of Shakespeare's* The Tempest *and the Logic of Allegorical Expression*. New Haven, CT: Yale University Press, 2007.

"Gordon Matta-Clark: Office Baroque," January 1, 1977. Guggenheim. Accessed January 8, 2021. https://www.guggenheim.org/artwork/5209.

Nyong'o, Tavia. *Afro-Fabulations: The Queer Drama of Black Life*. New York: New York University Press, 2018.

Ophir, Adi. "Concept." Translated by Naveh Frumer. *Political Concepts* (Winter 2012). http://www.politicalconcepts.org/concept-adi-ophir/

Orgel, Stephen. *The Illusion of Power: Political Theater in the English Renaissance*. Berkeley: University of California Press, 1975.

Paik, Nam June. *Nam June Paik: Baroque Laser*. Ostfildern, Germany: Cantz, 1996.

Painter, Nell Irvin. *The History of White People*. New York: W. W. Norton, 2010.

Palisca, Claude. *Baroque Music*. Englewood Cliffs, NJ: Prentice Hall, 1961.

Panofsky, Erwin. *Three Essays on Style*. Irving Lavin, editor. Cambridge, MA: MIT Press, 1997.

Parker, Geoffrey. "Crisis and Catastrophe: The Global Crisis of the Seventeenth Century Reconsidered." *American Historical Review* 113, no. 4 (2008): 1053-79.

Parker, Geoffrey, and Lesley M. Smith. *The General Crisis of the Seventeenth Century*. New York: Routledge, 1978.

Parks, Suzan-Lori. *The America Play and Other Works*. New York: Theatre Communications Group, 2013.

Paster, Gail Kern, Katherine Rowe, and Mary Floyd-Wilson. *Reading the Early Modern Passions: Essays in the Cultural History of Emotion*. Philadelphia: University of Pennsylvania Press, 2004.

Payne, Alina. *From Ornament to Object: Genealogies of Architectural Modernism*. New Haven, CT: Yale University Press, 2012.

Paz, Octavio. *Sor Juana; or, The Traps of Faith*. Translated by Margaret Sayers Peden. Cambridge, MA: Harvard University Press, 1988.

Pearson, Roger. "'Les Chiffres et les Lettres': Mallarmé's 'Or' and the Gold Standard of Poetry." *Dix-Neuf* 2, no. 1 (2004): 44–60.

———. *Stéphane Mallarmé*. London: Reaktion Books, 2010.

Pérez-Simón, Andrés. *Baroque Lorca: An Archaist Playwright for the New Stage*. New York: Routledge, 2019.

Perloff, Marjorie. *Poetics in a New Key: Interviews and Essays*. Chicago: University of Chicago Press, 2015.

Perniola, Mario. *Enigmas: The Egyptian Moment in Art and Society*. Translated by Christopher Woodall. London: Verso, 1995.

Pernot, Laurent, and W. E. Higgins. *Rhetoric in Antiquity*. Washington, DC: CUA Press, 2005.

Perrone, Jeff. "Approaching the Decorative." *Artforum* 15, no. 4 (December 1976). https://www.artforum.com/print/197610/approaching-the-decorative-37972.

Peters, Julie Stone. *Theatre of the Book, 1480–1880: Print, Text, and Performance in Europe*. Oxford: Oxford University Press, 2003.

Petersson, Robert. *The Art of Ecstasy: Teresa, Bernini, and Crashaw*. London: Routledge, 1970.

Petersson, Robert T. *Bernini and the Excesses of Art*. New York: Fordham University Press, 2002.

Phan, Hai-Dang. "My Father's 'Norton Introduction to Literature,' Third Edition (1981)." *The Best American Poetry, 2016*. Edited by Edward Hirsch and David Lehman. New York: Scribner Poetry, 2016.

Phelan, Peggy. *Unmarked: The Politics of Performance*. New York: Routledge, 2003.

Phelan, Peggy, and Jill Lane, eds. *The Ends of Performance*. New York: New York University Press, 1998.

Pickard, Zachariah. *Elizabeth Bishop's Poetics of Description*. Montreal: McGill-Queen's University Press, 2009.

Plato. *Complete Works*. Edited by John M. Cooper and D. S. Hutchinson. Indianapolis: Hackett, 1997.

Platt, Peter G. *Reason Diminished: Shakespeare and the Marvelous*. Lincoln: University of Nebraska Press, 1997.

Ponzi, Mauro. *Nietzsche's Nihilism in Walter Benjamin*. London: Palgrave, 2017.

Praz, Mario. *The Romantic Agony*. Translated by Angus Davidson. Oxford: Oxford University Press, 1951.

Bibliography

Preciado, Paul B. "Baroque Technopatriarchy: Reproduction." *Artforum* 56, no. 5 (January 2018). https://artforum.com/print/201801/baroque-technopatriarchy-repro duction-73189.

"Proposed Executive Order to Mandate Neoclassical Style for Federal Buildings." *Artforum International*, February 5, 2020. Accessed February 11, 2020. https://www .artforum.com/news/proposed-executive-order-to-mandate-neoclassical-style -for-federal-buildings-82096.

Puchner, Martin. *The Drama of Ideas: Platonic Provocations in Theater and Philosophy*. Oxford: Oxford University Press, 2010.

——. "The Gestures of Modernism: Studies in Theatrical Reform and Literary Practice." PhD dissertation, Harvard University, 1998. http://search.proquest.com.ez proxy.cul.columbia.edu/pqdtglobal/docview/304434870/abstract/9FCC66DF2 EFA46B5PQ/2.

——. *Stage Fright: Modernism, Anti-theatricality, and Drama*. Baltimore: Johns Hopkins University Press, 2002.

Quilligan, Maureen. *The Language of Allegory: Defining the Genre*. Ithaca, NY: Cornell University Press, 1992.

Quintilian. *The Institutio Oratoria of Quintilian*. 4 vols. Loeb Classical Library. Cambridge, MA: Harvard University Press, 1922.

Rabkin, Gerald. *Richard Foreman*. Baltimore: Johns Hopkins University Press, 1999.

——. "Theatre of the Ridiculous: An Introduction." *Performing Arts Journal* 3, no. 1 (Summer 1978): 40–42.

Racine, Jean. *Phèdre*. 1677. Penguin Classics. London: Penguin, 1961.

Rainer, Yvonne. "*Trio A*." Museum of Modern Art. Accessed February 11, 2020. https:// www.moma.org/learn/moma_learning/yvonne-rainer-trio-a-1978/.

Rajan, Tilottama, and Arkady Plotnitsky, eds. *Idealism without Absolutes: Philosophy and Romantic Culture*. Albany: State University of New York Press, 2012.

Rancière, Jacques. *The Future of the Image*. Translated by Gregory Elliott. New York: Verso, 2009.

——. *Mallarmé: The Politics of the Siren*. Translated by Steven Corcoran. London: Continuum, 2011.

——. *Mute Speech: Literature, Critical Theory, and Politics*. Translated by James Swenson. New York: Columbia University Press, 1998.

——. *The Politics of Aesthetics*. Translated by Gabriel Rockhill. London: Bloomsbury, 2006.

——. "The Sublime from Lyotard to Schiller: Two Readings of Kant and Their Political Significance." *Radical Philosophy* 126 (2004): 8–15.

Reinelt, Janelle G. "The Politics of Discourse: Performativity Meets Theatricality." *SubStance* 31, nos. 2–3 (2002): 201–15. https://doi.org/10.2307/3685486.

Reinelt, Janelle G., and Joseph R. Roach, eds. *Critical Theory and Performance*. Ann Arbor: University of Michigan Press, 2007.

Reynolds, Dee. "Mallarmé and the Décor of Modern Life." *Forum for Modern Language Studies* 42, no. 3 (July 2006): 268-85.

Reynolds, Deirdre. "Mallarmé and Hegel: Speculation and the Poetics of Reflection." *French Cultural Studies* 2 (1991): 71-89.

Richard, Jean-Pierre. *L'univers Imaginaire de Mallarmé*. Paris: Éditions du Seuil, 1962.

Ridout, Nicholas. *Stage Fright, Animals, and Other Theatrical Problems*. Cambridge, UK: Cambridge University Press, 2006.

Richter, Gerhard. *Inheriting Walter Benjamin*. London: Bloomsbury, 2016.

———. *Walter Benjamin and the Corpus of Autobiography*. Detroit: Wayne State University Press, 2000.

Riegl, Alois. *The Origins of Baroque Art in Rome*. Translated by Andrew Hopkins and Arnold Alexander Witte. Los Angeles: Getty, 2010.

Roach, Joseph. *Cities of the Dead: Circum-Atlantic Performance*. New York: Columbia University Press, 1996.

———. *It*. Ann Arbor: University of Michigan Press, 2007.

———. "Performance: The Blunders of Orpheus." *PMLA* 125, no. 4 (October 2010): 1078-86.

———. *The Player's Passion: Studies in the Science of Acting*. Newark: University of Delaware Press, 1985.

Roberts, David. *The Total Work of Art*. Ithaca, NY: Cornell University Press, 2011.

Robillard, Monic. *Le Désir de la Vierge: Hérodiade chez Mallarmé*. Geneva: Droz, 1993.

Robinson, Marc. *The Other American Drama*. Baltimore: Johns Hopkins University Press, 1997.

Rokem, Freddie. *Philosophers and Thespians: Thinking Performance*. Stanford, CA: Stanford University Press, 2010.

———. "'Suddenly a stranger comes into the room': Interruptions in Benjamin, Brecht and Kafka." *Studies in Theatre and Performance* 36, no. 1 (December 2015): 21-26.

Rosenzweig, Franz. *The Star of Redemption*. Translated by Barbara E. Galli. Madison: University of Wisconsin Press, 2004.

Ross, Alex. "Stéphane Mallarmé: Prophet of Modernism." *New Yorker*, April 4, 2016. https://www.newyorker.com/magazine/2016/04/11/stephane-mallarme-prophet -of-modernism.

Ruddick, Lisa. *Reading Gertrude Stein: Body, Text, Gnosis*. Ithaca, NY: Cornell University Press, 1990.

Ruiz, Alan. "Radical Formalism." *Women & Performance*, February 17, 2017. https:// www.womenandperformance.org/ampersand/alanruiz.

Safranski, Rüdiger. *Nietzsche: A Philosophical Biography*. New York: W. W. Norton, 2002.

Said, Edward W. "The Problem of Textuality: Two Exemplary Positions." *Critical Inquiry* 4, no. 4 (1978): 673-714.

Bibliography

Sack, Daniel. *After Live: Possibility, Potentiality, and the Future of Performance.* Ann Arbor: University of Michigan Press, 2015.

"Salon #16: Designs for a Contemporary Baroque Stage." Wingspace Theatrical Design. Accessed February 3, 2020. http://wingspace.com/blog-1/2015/4/6/salon-16-designs-for-a-contemporary-baroque-stage?rq=%22salon%2016%22.

Salvato, Nick. *Uncloseting Drama: American Modernism and Queer Performance.* New Haven, CT: Yale University Press, 2010.

Schechner, Richard. "The Conservative Avant-Garde." *New Literary History* 41, no. 4 (2010): 895–913.

Scherer, Jacques. *L'Expression litteraire dans l'oeuvre de Mallarme.* Paris: Droz, 1947.

Schiller, Friedrich. *On the Aesthetic Education of Man.* 1795. Translated by Keith Tribe. Penguin Classics. London: Penguin, 2016.

Schmitt, Carl. *Hamlet or Hecuba: The Intrusion of the Time into the Play.* Candor, NY: Telos Press, 2009.

———. *Political Theology: Four Chapters on the Concept of Sovereignty.* Chicago: University of Chicago Press, 2010.

Schneider, Rebecca. *Performing Remains: Art and War in Times of Theatrical Reenactment.* New York: Routledge, 2011.

Scholz-Hänsel, Michael. *El Greco and Modernism.* Edited by Beat Wismer. Berlin: Hatje Cantz, 2012.

Schor, Mira. *Wet: On Painting, Feminism, and Art Culture.* Durham, NC: Duke University Press, 1997.

Schramm, Helmar, Ludger Schwarte, and Jan Lazardzig, eds. *Collection, Laboratory, Theater: Scenes of Knowledge in the 17th Century.* Berlin: De Gruyter, 2008.

Schrift, Alan D., ed. *Why Nietzsche Still? Reflections on Drama, Culture, and Politics.* Berkeley: University of California Press, 2000.

Sedgwick, Eve Kosofsky. *Epistemology of the Closet.* Berkeley: University of California Press, 1990.

Shaw, George Bernard. *The Perfect Wagnerite: A Commentary on the Niblung's Ring.* New York: Dover, 1967.

Shaw, Mary Lewis. *Performance in the Texts of Mallarmé: The Passage from Art to Ritual.* University Park: Pennsylvania State University Press, 1992.

Shepherd, Reginald. *Orpheus in the Bronx: Essays on Identity, Politics, and the Freedom of Poetry.* Ann Arbor: University of Michigan Press, 2007.

Simmons, William. "Notes on Queer Formalism." Radcliffe Institute for Advanced Study at Harvard University, December 18, 2013. https://www.radcliffe.harvard.edu/news/in-news/notes-queer-formalism.

Sloterdijk, Peter. *Nietzsche Apostle.* Cambridge, MA: Semiotext(e), 2013.

———. *Thinker on Stage: Nietzsche's Materialism.* Translated by Jamie Owen Daniel. Minneapolis: University of Minnesota Press, 1989.

284 Bibliography

Sloterdijk, Peter, and Harrison, Robert. "Peter Sloterdijk on Friedrich Nietzsche." *Entitled Opinions*. Podcast, December 15, 2016.

Smart, Mary Ann. *Mimomania: Music and Gesture in Nineteenth-Century Opera*. Berkeley: University of California Press, 2004.

Smith, Gary. *Benjamin: Philosophy, Aesthetics, History*. Chicago: University of Chicago Press, 1989.

Smith, Harold J. "The Mirror of Art: Mallarmé's 'Hérodiade' and Tennyson's 'The Lady of Shalott.'" *Romance Notes* 16, no. 1 (1974): 91–94.

Smith, Matthew Wilson. *The Total Work of Art: From Bayreuth to Cyberspace*. New York: Routledge, 2007.

Smith, Pamela. *The Business of Alchemy: Science and Culture in the Holy Roman Empire*. Princeton, NJ: Princeton University Press, 1997.

Snyder, Jon. *L'estetica del Barocco*. Bologna: Il Mulino, 2005.

Sokel, Walter H. "On the Dionysian in Nietzsche." *New Literary History* 36, no. 4 (2005): 501–20.

Sontag, Susan. *Against Interpretation and Other Essays*. New York: Macmillan, 1966.

———. "Artaud: An Essay." In *Antonin Artaud: Selected Writings*, edited by Susan Sontag. Berkeley: University of California Press, 1988.

———. "Syberberg's 'Hitler'" (1979). Syberberg.de. Accessed February 29, 2016. http://www.syberberg.de/Syberberg4_2010/Susan-Sontag-Syberbergs-Hitler -engl.html.

———. *Under the Sign of Saturn*. New York: Farrar, Straus & Giroux, 1980.

Sousa Santos, Boaventura de. "Stay Baroque: Boaventura de Sousa Santos on Postabyssal Thinking." *Artforum International*, Summer 2018. https://www.artforum .com/print/201806/boaventura-de-sousa-santos-on-postabyssal-thinking-75522.

Spadaccini, Nicholas, and Luis Martín-Estudillo, eds. *Hispanic Baroques : Reading Cultures in Context*. Nashville: Vanderbilt University Press, 2005.

Spencer, Stewart. *Wagner Remembered*. New York: Faber & Faber, 2000.

Spenser, Edmund. *The Faerie Queene*. 1609. Penguin Classics ed. London: Penguin, 1978.

Spivak, Gayatri Chakravorty. "Foreword: Cosmopolitanisms and the Cosmopolitical." *Cultural Dynamics* 24, nos. 2–3 (July 1, 2012): 107–14. https://doi.org/10.1177 /0921374013482350.

Spotts, Frederic. *Bayreuth: A History of the Wagner Festival*. New Haven, CT: Yale University Press, 1994.

Stein, Gertrude. *Four in America*. New Haven, CT: Yale University Press, 1947.

———. *Last Operas and Plays*. Edited by Carl Van Vechten. Baltimore: Johns Hopkins University Press, 1995.

———. *Lectures in America*. Boston: Beacon Press, 1935

———. *The Letters of Gertrude Stein and Thornton Wilder*. Edited by Edward Burns and Ulla E. Dydo. New Haven, CT: Yale University Press, 1996.

Bibliography

———. *The Letters of Gertrude Stein and Virgil Thomson: Composition as Conversation.* Edited by Susan Holbrook and Thomas Dilworth. Oxford: Oxford University Press, 2010.

———. *Writings, 1903-1932.* New York: Library of America, 1998.

Steiner, George. *After Babel: Aspects of Language and Translation.* Oxford: Oxford University Press, 1992.

———. "On Difficulty." *Journal of Aesthetics and Art Criticism* 36, no. 3 (Spring 1978): 263-76.

Stevenson, Jane. *Baroque between the Wars: Alternative Style in the Arts, 1918-1939.* Oxford: Oxford University Press, 2018.

Street, Anna, Julien Alliot, and Magnolia Pauker. *Inter Views in Performance Philosophy: Crossings and Conversations.* London: Palgrave Macmillan, 2017.

Symons, Arthur. *Studies in Seven Arts.* New York: E. P. Dutton and Co., 1907.

Szondi, Péter. *Das lyrische Drama des Fin de siècle.* Berlin: Suhrkamp Verlag, 1975.

———. *Theory of the Modern Drama: A Critical Edition.* Minneapolis: University of Minnesota Press, 1987.

Taussig, Michael. *Mimesis and Alterity: A Particular History of the Senses.* New York: Routledge, 1993.

Taylor, Diana. *The Archive and the Repertoire: Performing Cultural Memory in the Americas.* Durham, NC: Duke University Press, 2003.

Teskey, Gordon. *Allegory and Violence.* Ithaca, NY: Cornell University Press, 1996.

Thibaudet, Albert. *La poésie de Stéphane Mallarmé.* Paris: Éditions de la Nouvelle Revue Française, 1926.

Thomson, Virgil, and Gertrude Stein. *Four Saints in Three Acts.* Edited by H. Wiley Hitchcock and Charles Fussell. Middleton, WI: American Musicological Society, 2008.

Thorne, Christian. *The Dialectic of Counter-Enlightenment.* Cambridge, MA: Harvard University Press, 2010.

Turner, Henry S., ed. *Early Modern Theatricality.* Oxford: Oxford University Press, 2013.

Tuve, Rosemond. *Allegorical Imagery: Some Mediaeval Books and Their Posterity.* Princeton, NJ: Princeton University Press, 1966.

Underwood, Ted. *Why Literary Periods Mattered: Historical Contrast and the Prestige of English Studies.* Stanford, CA: Stanford University Press, 2013.

Untersteiner, Mario. *The Sophists.* Translated by Kathleen Freeman. Oxford: Philosophical Library, 1954.

Van Dyke, Carolynn. *The Fiction of Truth: Structures of Meaning in Narrative and Dramatic Allegory.* Ithaca, NY: Cornell University Press, 1985.

Van Vechten, Carl. "'How I Listen to Four Saints in Three Acts': Souvenir Program Notes from Four Saints in Three Acts Broadway Premiere." 44th Street Theatre, New York, NY, February 20, 1934. Box 26, Gertrude Stein and Alice B. Toklas Papers. Yale University Beinecke Rare Book and Manuscript Archive.

Vélez, Daniel Villegas. "Allegory, Noise, and History: The Arcades Project Looks Back at the Trauerspielbuch." *New Writing* 16, no. 4 (October 2, 2019): 429-32. https://doi.org/10.1080/14790726.2019.1567795.

Vogue Not. Edited by Trajal Harrell. Online program for *Twenty Looks, or Paris Is Burning at the Judson Church*. Centre national de la danse. Accessed 15 March 2021. https://www.cnd.fr/fr/file/file/80/inline/harell.pdf.

Von Der Luft, Eric. "Sources of Nietzsche's 'God Is Dead!' and Its Meaning for Heidegger." *Journal of the History of Ideas* 45, no. 2 (1984): 263-76. https://doi.org/10.2307/2709291.

Von Held, Phoebe. "Brecht's Anti-theatricality? Reflections on Brecht's Place in Michael Fried's Conceptual Framework." *Journal of Visual Culture* 16, no. 1 (April 1, 2017): 28-42. https://doi.org/10.1177/1470412917694514.

Wagner, Richard. *The Art-Work of the Future and Other Works*. Translated by William Ashton Ellis. Lincoln, NE: University of Nebraska Press, 1994

———. *Oper und Drama*. Edited by Klaus Kropfinger. Stuttgart: Reclam Verlag, 1994.

———. *Opera and Drama*. Translated by William Ashton Ellis. Lincoln: University of Nebraska Press, 1995.

———. *Parsifal*. English libretto translated by Stewart Robb. New York: Schirmer, 1962.

Waite, Geoff. *Nietzsche's Corps/e : Aesthetics, Politics, Prophecy; or, The Spectacular Technoculture of Everyday Life*. Durham, NC: Duke University Press, 1996.

Walker, Julia A., and Glenn Odom. "Comparative Modernist Performance Studies: A Not So Modest Proposal." *Journal of Dramatic Theory and Criticism* 31, no. 1 (2016): 129-53. https://doi.org/10.1353/dtc.2016.0025.

Walls, Peter, ed. *Baroque Music*. London: Routledge, 2011.

Warner, Sara. *Acts of Gaiety: LGBT Performance and the Politics of Pleasure*. Ann Arbor, MI: University of Michigan Press, 2012.

Warren, Austin. *Richard Crashaw: A Study in Baroque Sensibility*. Baton Rouge: Louisiana State University Press, 1939.

Watson, Steven. *Prepare for Saints: Gertrude Stein, Virgil Thomson, and the Mainstreaming of American Modernism*. New York: Random House, 1998.

Weber, Max. *The Protestant Ethic and the Spirit of Capitalism and Other Writings*. Translated by Peter Baehr and Gordon C. Wells. New York: Penguin Classics, 2002.

Weber, Samuel. *Benjamin's -abilities*. Cambridge, MA: Harvard University Press, 2008.

———. *Theatricality as Medium*. New York: Fordham University Press, 2004.

Weigel, Sigrid. *Body- and Image-Space: Re-reading Walter Benjamin*. Translated by Georgina Paul, Rachel McNicholl, and Jeremy Gaines. London: Routledge, 1996.

Weintraub, Alex. "Art History in Light of Mallarmé." *Journal of Art Historiography* 23, no. 23 (December 2020): 1-18.

Wellek, René. "The Concept of Baroque in Literary Scholarship." *Journal of Aesthetics and Art Criticism* 5, no. 2 (1946): 77-109. https://doi.org/10.2307/425797.

Bibliography

———. "The Early Literary Criticism of Walter Benjamin." *Rice University Studies* 57 (1971): 123-34.

Wetzler, Rachel. "Walter Benjamin: Writings after Death." *Los Angeles Review of Books*. Accessed January 23, 2020. https://lareviewofbooks.org/article/walter-benjamin-writings-death/.

Whenham, John, ed. *Claudio Monteverdi: Orfeo*. Cambridge: Cambridge University Press, 1986.

Wilder, Thornton. *American Characteristics and Other Essays*. New York: Harper & Row, 1979.

———. "The Barock; or, How to Recognize a Miracle in the Daily Life." *PMLA* 136, no. 2 (March 2021): 248-53.

———. *The Bridge of San Luis Rey and Other Novels, 1926-1948*. Edited by J. D. McClatchy. New York: Library of America, 2009.

———. *The Eighth Day, Theophilus North, Autobiographical Writings*. Edited by J. D. McClatchy. New York: Library of America, 2011.

———. *Thornton Wilder: Collected Plays and Writings on Theater*. Edited by J. D. McClatchy. New York: Library of America, 2007.

———. *Three Plays: Our Town, The Skin of Our Teeth, and The Matchmaker*. New York: Harper, 1998.

Williams, Raymond. *The Politics of Modernism: Against the New Conformists*. New York: Verso, 1989.

Williamson, George S. *The Longing for Myth in Germany: Religion and Aesthetic Culture from Romanticism to Nietzsche*. Chicago: University of Chicago Press, 2007.

Willoughby, Ian. "Architect Recalls Genesis of Dancing Building as Coffee Table Book Published." Radio Prague International. Accessed January 6, 2020. http://www.radio.cz/en/section/arts/architect-recalls-genesis-of-dancing-building-as-coffee-table-book-published.

Wilson, Robert. "Robert Wilson and Umberto Eco: A Conversation." *Performing Arts Journal* 15, no. 1 (January 1993): 87-96.

Witt, Mary Ann Frese. *Metatheater and Modernity: Baroque and Neobaroque*. Madison, NJ: Fairleigh Dickinson University Press, 2013.

———, ed. *Nietzsche and the Rebirth of the Tragic*. Madison, NJ: Fairleigh Dickinson University Press, 2007.

Wizisla, Erdmut. *Benjamin and Brecht: The Story of a Friendship*. Translated by Christine Shuttleworth. New York: Verso Books, 2016.

Wölfflin, Heinrich. *Principles of Art History*. Translated by M. D. Hottinger. Mineola, NY: Dover, 2012.

———. *Renaissance and Baroque*. Translated by Kathrin Simon. Ithaca, NY: Cornell University Press, 1966.

Wolfson, Susan J., and Marshall Brown, eds. *Reading for Form*. Seattle: University of Washington Press, 2015.

Worthen, W. B. "Disciplines of the Text/Sites of Performance." *TDR: The Drama Review (1988–)* 39, no. 1 (1995): 13-28. https://doi.org/10.2307/1146399.

Wu, Yi-Ping. "Stein's *Melanctha*." *Explicator* 66, no. 3 (2010): 178-80.

Young, Julian. *Friedrich Nietzsche: A Philosophical Biography*. New York: Cambridge University Press, 2010.

Young, Stark. "One Moment Alit." *New Republic* 78, no. 1005 (7 March 1934): 105-105.

——. "Reading Lesson." *Theater Arts Monthly* 18 (May 1934): 356-57.

Zacharasiewicz, Waldemar. *Transatlantic Networks and the Perception and Representation of Vienna and Austria between the 1920s and 1950s*. Vienna: Austrian Academy of Sciences Press, 2018.

Zamora, Lois Parkinson, and Wendy B. Faris, eds. *Magical Realism: Theory, History, Community*. Durham, NC: Duke University Press, 1995.

Zamora, Lois Parkinson, and Monika Kaup, eds. *Baroque New Worlds: Representation, Transculturation, Counterconquest*. Durham, NC: Duke University Press, 2010.

Index

Figures and illustrations are indicated by italic page numbers.

absorption: acting and, 137; allegory vs., 240n62; baroque theatricality vs., 104, 110, 124-26; Mallarmé and, 64, 89, 90; as project of modern art, 13-14, 49; reading and, 142-43; Wagner and, 49

acting: Brecht and, 136-37; gesture and, 9, 116, 136-37, 202n35; Mallarmé and, 73-74, 233n103, 250n41; rhetoric and, 34, 213n14

Adorno, Theodor, 16-17, 24, 43, 184, 220-21n71

Aercke, Kristiaan, 42

Agamben, Giorgio, 62, 236n22

Albright, Daniel, 176

aleatoric composition, 95-96

allegory: Baudelaire and, 130-33; Benjamin on baroque and, 62, 67, 70, 76, 102-5, 113, 118-34, 136-38, 240n57, 242n79, 243n91; Brecht and, 133-38, 243n85; commodification and, 92, 131-33, 141; *Four Saints* and, 148, 169, 171-72, 175; gesture and, 116-17, 128, 238n39; in *Hérodiade*, 83-84, 87, 89, 90, 92; language and, 109, 115, 121-22; Mallarmé and, 67, 70; mimetic representation vs., 17-19, 243n85; redemptive power of, 128-30, 136, 142, 186; spectatorship and, 48, 125-27; symbol and, 120-24, 126, 239n49; violence of, 78, 132, 228n50, 239n52; Wilson and, 186-87

Ambros, August Wilhelm, 47, 49, 212n2; *History of Music*, 7

Anaximander, 46

Andreas-Salomé, Lou, 46-47

Antoine, André, 43, 68, 90, 124

Aragon, Louis, 185-86, 258n14

Aristotle and Aristotelian theater, 17, 19, 33, 39, 54; Nietzsche on, 214n20; on rhetoric, 213n14; Trauerspiel theatricality compared to, 104-5, 110-11, 135. *See also* mimesis and mimetic representation

Artaud, Antonin, 23

Ashton, Frederick, 155-57, 164, 180, 248n28, 252n53

Auden, W. H.: *The Age of Anxiety*, 25

Austin, Arthur Everett "Chick," 149-50, 180, 247n14

Austin, J. L., 36, 70, 214n22

avant-gardism in performance, 4, 23, 26, 67, 72, 133, 146-47, 191, 233n104

Bach, Johann Sebastian, 42

Balakian, Anna, 227n42

ballet, 9, 125, 181, 202n35, 227nn32-33

Barg, Lisa, 255n87

Barish, Jonas, 44

baroque: as condition of modernity, 17; naming/terminology of, xxi-xxii, 7-10, 15, 17, 199n15, 202n29, 207n69; naturalization of, 25; political economies of, 106; queerness and, 8, 19-21, 149, 181, 191; redemptive power of, 106, 119, 123, 128-30, 136, 142, 186, 187. *See also* allegory; gesture; space and spatialization; theatricality

Barthes, Roland, 2, 19, 216n34
Baudelaire, Charles, 7; Benjamin on, 130-33, 140, 238-39n48, 240n56, 242n78
Baur-Heinhold, Margarete: *Theater des Barock*, 183
Bayreuth Festival and Festspielhaus, 2, 10, 27-28, *28*, 32, 42-43, 50, 233n97
Beckett, Samuel, 183
Bell, Richard, 220-21n71
Benjamin, Walter, 21, 22; Adorno and, 24; *Arcades Project*, 130-32, 140-41, 143; "The Author as Producer," 244nn93-94; on ballet, 227n33; Baudelaire and, 130-33, 140, 238-39n48, 240n56, 242n78; Brecht and, 102-6, 133-39, 142, 144, 226n31, 242n81, 243n90, 244nn96-97; "crisis of the aura," 31, 120, 127, 240n61; deconstruction and, 144-45; on hieroglyphic theater, 76, 239n50; on Kafka, 242n80, 244n96, 246n112; Marxism and, 130-32; Nietzsche and, 31, 139-45, 245nn104-5; *One-Way Street*, 130, 145; "On Some Motifs in Baudelaire," 126-27, 133; "On the Concept of History," 102, 137, 191, 241n68; *Origin of the German Trauerspiel*, 18, 22; on secularization, 68, 111-12, 120-21, 143, 236n19; Stein and, 147-49, 152, 159, 246-47n7, 246n6; theater theory of, 103-6, 133-34, 137, 139, 144-45, 236n17, 238n35; on total artwork, 42; on tradition, 187, 199n14, 243n90; "What is Epic Theatre?," 134. *See also Origin of the German Trauerspiel*; Trauerspiel
Berman, Marshall, 1, 6, 7, 201n21, 204-5n55
Bernhardt, Sarah, 164
Bernini, Gian Lorenzo, 203n44; baroque of, 15; defamiliarization and, 12-13; *Four Saints* and, 149; *Hérodiade* compared to works of, 89; Nietzsche on, 31, 41-42, 52, 219n55; propaganda and, 16; spectacle and, 11-12, 182, 203n42; *Teresa in Ecstasy*, 154, 169, 173; theatricality of, 10-13, 202-3n38
Bernstein, Charles, 64, 99
Bersani, Leo, 19, 69, 81, 82, 90, 229n56
Bibiena, Giuseppe Galli, 27
Blackmer, Corinne, 148, 254n68, 256n94
Blackness and *Four Saints*, 157-58, 181, 249n33, 249n37, 255n86

Blau, Herbert, 206n64
Bloom, Harold, 223n6
bodies and kinesthetic action: in *Hérodiade*, 81-82, 87, 89, 92; Mallarmé and, 70, 76, 99-100; Nietzsche and, 37; Trauerspiel and, 114-16. *See also* dance and choreography; gesture
Borges, Jorge Luis, 65, 98
Bourget, Paul, 52
Bowers, Jane Palatini, 251n51, 254n68
Brecht, Bertolt: allegory and, 133-38, 243n85; Benjamin and, 102-6, 133-39, 142, 144, 226n31, 242n81, 243n90, 244nn96-97; *Edward II*, 102; epic theater of, 23, 73, 133-35, 144, 242n83; *A Man's a Man*, 134-35; Nietzsche and, 62; *The Seven Deadly Sins of the Petty Bourgeoisie* (with Weill), 138-39; *The Threepenny Opera*, 133; Trauerspiel form and, 104, 134-39
Bredekamp, Horst, 10
Brown, Wendy, 58
Brückwald, Otto, 27
Buci-Glucksmann, Christine, 206n68, 213n17
Buck-Morss, Susan, 130, 207n68
Bulwer, John, 116
Burckhardt, Jacob, 29, 212n2
Butler, Judith, 36, 202n32, 211n103, 233-34n104, 244nn96-97, 250n41

Caccini, Giulio, 47
Cage, John, 22, 23, 178
Calderón de la Barca, Pedro, 11, 105, 129
Calloway, Stephen, 25
camp sensibility, 21, 24, 153-54, 157, 180-81, 183, 185, 189, 257n100
Caravaggio, 42, 93
Carney, Sean, 138, 139
catastrophe, 37, 114, 117, 121, 128, 130-42, 143, 145, 173
Catholicism and Catholic liturgy, 5, 15, 24, 42, 97, 149, 155-57, 220n71, 232n86. *See also* Counter-Reformation; Jesuit theater
Caygill, Howard, 245n105
Chauncey, George, 155-58
Chladni, Ernst, 239n53
choreography. *See* dance and choreography; gesture
classical-baroque binary, 32-35
Clements, Elicia, 252n54

Index

climate emergency, 182, 191

closet epistemologies and closet drama, 52, 67, 76

commodities and commodification: allegory and, 92, 131-33, 141; in *Hérodiade*, 92-93; Jack Smith on, 189-90

constellations in *Origin of the German Trauerspiel* (Benjamin), 107, 115, 143, 233n99, 235n8

Corneille, Pierre: *Le Cid*, 102

costumes: allegory and, 124; *Four Saints* and, 151-52, 155, 158; sovereignty and, 117, 158

Counter-Reformation: allegory and, 106, 119; baroque style and, 5, 15; Benjamin on, 31, 68, 114; Nietzsche on, 31, 41, 51, 55; Trauerspiel and, 111; tyranny and, 16, 151; Wilder on, 200n17

Crashaw, Richard, 149

Creuzer, Georg Friedrich, 120-21

crises of thought and belief: Berman on, 204-5n55; climate emergency and, 182, 191; Mallarmé and, 68-69; mimesis and, 243n85; Nietzsche on baroque forms and, 31-32, 63; Stein on, 160; theatricality in modernist art, 63, 216n30; Trauerspiel and, 109-14

Critchley, Simon, 37

Croll, Morris, 7, 256n93

dance and choreography: allegory and, 125; Benjamin's *Origin of Trauerspiel* and, 22-23, 105, 116; emblematic images of, 227n33; in *Four Saints*, 155-58, 164, 249n33; *Hérodiade* and, 77; Mallarmé and, 73, 90, 227n32

Danto, Arthur, 32

Debord, Guy, 16, 184, 258n8

deconstruction, 232n93; of Aristotelian systems, 205n55; baroque as precursor to, 18, 24-25; Mallarmé and, 66, 94; Nietzsche and, 45, 213n17; Said on, 245n110; Stein and, 181. *See also* Derrida, Jacques

defamiliarization: Benjamin and, 142-43; Bernini and, 12-13; Brecht and, 134, 136; of language, 35-36, 174, 178; in Mallarmé's writings, 64-65; ornament and, 117; seventeenth-century plays and, 139; spectatorship and, 127; Stein and, 162,

165, 174, 178; through baroque wonder, 61-63, 180

Deleuze, Gilles, 8, 20, 66, 76, 203-4n46, 209n86, 216n29, 230n68

de Man, Paul, 18, 36, 44, 45, 144, 216n33, 239n49

Derrida, Jacques, 36, 46, 66, 73-75, 79, 144, 208n75, 213n17, 223n6, 225n21, 225n27, 232n93, 245n110

de Saussure, Ferdinand, 36

desengaño of Spanish Golden Age literature, 15

Diaghilev, Sergei, 153

Diamond, Elin, 180, 256n96

Diderot, Denis, 48, 124, 165

Dionysus and Dionysian dithyramb, 33-34, 39-40, 44-45, 48-50, 54-60, 149

direct address (parabasis): Bernini and, 12; *Hamlet* and, 129-30; mimesis vs., 17; in Nietzsche's works, 30, 44-49, 219n54; spectatorship and, 127, 204n49; Trauerspiel and, 104, 123-24; in Wagner's works, 48-49, 60-61

Dolan, Jill, 255n86

Dorsey, Abner, 158

Doyle, Jennifer, 20

drag balls, 158-59

drama: Benjamin and, 103-4, 106, 113; Lehman and, 216n34; Mallarmé and, 67, 71-74, 224n12; Nietzsche and, 39-40, 46, 51-52

Dresden revolutions (1848), 32

Dydo, Ulla, 169, 172, 246n1, 252n58, 253n65

Echeverría, Bolívar, 16-17, 25, 199n8, 205n61, 211n99, 211n101

Eco, Umberto, 65, 259n15

écriture, 94, 170, 231n83, 245n110

Egginton, William, 17, 18, 202n37, 206n65, 252n54

El Greco, 156

Eliot, T. S., 5, 199n16, 251n45

elites and elitism, 57-58

Elsner, Gary, 215n24

emblems and emblem effects: allegory and, 119-20, 137, 141, 143; Benjamin on, 92, 102, 107, 112-13, 117-18, 123, 126, 128, 130, 142, 143; *Four Saints* and, 170-71; gesture and, 71, 116-17; in *Hérodiade*, 77,

emblems and emblem effects (*cont.*)
89; Mallarmé's miming and, 73–74; Trauerspiel and, 112–13; Wagner and, 49; Wilson and, 186
Enlightenment drama, 31, 43, 105, 151–52, 191, 207n68, 260n16
Epic Theater. *See* Brecht, Bertolt
erotics of art: in *Four Saints*, 157; in *Hérodiade*, 82–83, 89, 90; Mallarmé and, 65, 75
Eucharist, 5, 97, 120, 255n88. *See also* Catholicism and Catholic liturgy
Evelyn, John, 10
Expressionism. *See* German Expressionism

Fischer-Lichte, Erika, 216n30
Flatley, Jonathan, 20
Foreman, Richard, 205-6n61
Foucault, Michel, 260n16
Four Saints in Three Acts (Stein), 146–48, 246n1; afterlife of, 178–79; allegory and, 148, 169, 171–72, 175; baroque inheritance and, 147, 151, 156–57; Blackness and, 157–58, 181, 249n33, 249n37, 255n86; continuous present of, 162–63; costumes in, 151–52, 155, 158; dance in, 155–58, 164, 249n33; gesture in, 147, 155–59, 164, 165; historiography in, 147–48; music in, 176–78, 253n66; premiere and program of, 149–51, *150*, *154*, *177*; queerness and, 158–59, 175–76; repetition in, 168, 170, 174; space in, 148, 163–64
fourth wall, 43, 45, 61, 90, 124–25, 155
Francavilla, Pietro, 149
Franko, Mark, 200n16
Frege, Gottlob, 36
Fried, Michael, 13–15, 17, 40, 49, 63, 89, 184, 204n51, 209n86, 212n4
Fuchs, Elinor, 243n91
Fuchs, Georg, 75, 90, 216n30, 233n103
Fuller, Loie, 89, *91*

gaze: Benjamin on, 113, 126–28; as dialectical process, 126–27; Mallarmé and, 101; Trauerspiel and, 126, 128. *See also* spectators and spectatorship
Gehry, Frank, 4
George, Stefan, 108

German Expressionism, 108–10, 135, 185, 235n12
Gesamtkunstwerk, 42–44, 95, 98, 124, 153, 185, 216n40
gesture: Agamben on, 236n22; allegory and, 116–17, 128, 238n39; Benjamin on, 73, 105-6, 116–18, 128, 136, 164, 244n94; in Brecht's epic theater, 136–37; citation of, 157–59; in early modern theater, 48–50; in *Four Saints*, 147, 155–59, 164, 165; in *Hérodiade*, 84–85; interruption and, 110, 117, 142–43; leitmotiv as, 43; Mallarmé and, 67, 71–75, 96, 97, 100, 229n57; Nietzsche and, 30, 32–33, 37–39, 44–47, 50, 54–55, 60–61, 73; passion and, 238n37; Puchner on, 215n26; Stein and, 164–65; in Trauerspiel, 116–18, 123, 136–37
Getsy, David, 20, 209n84
Glissant, Édouard, 25, 252n60
Goethe, Johann Wolfgang von, 107, 111
Gordon, Mel, 235n12
Gorelick, Sylvia, 231-32n84
Gorgias, 35, 60
Gould, Evelyn, 227n42
Gould, Stephen Jay, 183
Greenblatt, Stephen, 18
Gris, Juan, 152
Grosser, Maurice, 151–52, 154, 155, 157, 168, 171–73, 180, 252n61, 255n88
Gryphius, Andreas, 23, 111, 112, 114–15, 134, 236n26
Guillemot, Maurice, 65

Hallmann, Johann Christian, 111
Hamlet (Shakespeare), 46, 116, 119, 128–30, 138, 237n34, 241n72
Hannah, Dorita, 242n82
Hansen, Miriam Bratu, 240n61, 240nn65–66
Harries, Karsten, 59
Harris, David, 155, 164, 172, 248n28, 252n53
Hassan, Ihab, 197-98n3
Hegel, Georg Wilhelm Friedrich, 68, 207n68, 224n14, 241n72
Held, Phoebe von, 15
Herbert, George, 228n49
Hérodiade (Mallarmé): allegory in, 83–84, 87, 89, 90, 92; dance in, 77; manuscript

Index

293

variants, 227n39; myths and, 77-78; ornament in, 83-89, 90; queerness and, 89; reconstruction and, 99; spectatorship and, 90, 93; theatricality and, 75-77, 81-82, 89, 90

hieroglyphs and hieroglyphic forms, 72, 76, 97, 119-21, 123, 127, 137, 165, 239n50

Higgins, Dick, 22, 228n49

Hines, Altonell, 158

Hofmannsthal, Hugo von, 24, 42, 108

Howard, Bruce, 158

identity and self-identity: drag theatricality and, 159; in *Four Saints*, 170; in *Hérodiade*, 82, 86; Mallarmé and, 99-101, 234n104; repetition and, 250-51n44, 251n45; Stein and, 160-62, 174, 181, 251n44; Wilder and, 200n17

Ignatius of Loyola, Saint, 42, 152-53

Ihering, Herbert, 109

Impressionist painting, 70-71, 77, 81

Isherwood, Christopher, 180-81

Jameson, Fredric, 74, 93, 99, 122, 233n99

James, William, 152

Jessye, Eva, 158, 249n36

Jesuit theater, 2, 3, 5, 42, 182, 236n20. *See also* Catholicism and Catholic liturgy

Johnson, Barbara, 227n34, 229n56, 229n60

Johnson, Samuel, 228n50

Jordan, Mary, 187, 190

Judd, Donald, 13, 184

Kafka, Franz, 16, 108, 242n80

Kantorowicz, Ernst, 237n33

Kornhaber, David, 63

Kraus, Karl, 24, 239n48

Krauss, Rosalind, 4

labyrinths and labyrinth figures, 59-61, 130

Lacis, Asja, 130

Lacoue-Labarthe, Philippe, 69-70, 224n11, 226-27n32, 227n33

La Farge, John, 156-57, 164, 165

landscape: Stein and, 148, 163-64, 172, 252n52, 256n96; Trauerspiel and, 105-6, 122-23, 237n29, 238n42; Wilson and, 186

Lang, Franciscus, 116, *117*

language: allegory and, 109, 115, 121-22; defamiliarization of, 35-36, 174, 178; in *Four Saints*, 170; in *Hérodiade*, 87-89, 95; Mallarmé's theory of, 69-70, 229n60; Nietzsche's theory of, 35-37, 44, 69, 213n19, 214n22, 215n24; Stein and, 165; in Trauerspiel, 108, 120, 121

Lavin, Irving, 11, 202-3n38

Lehmann, Hans-Thies, 19, 76, 104, 172, 207n71, 216n34, 225n27, 226n31, 236n19, 238n39, 258-59n15

Leibniz, Gottfried, 66, 169; *Monadology*, 8

little theaters, 6-7

Lohenstein, Daniel Caspar von, 111

Loos, Adolf, 27, 65

Lorenz, Martin, 58

Lotringer, Sylvère, 190

Ludlam, Charles, 185

Luis-Martínez, Zenón, 237n34

Lukács, György, 122, 130, 201n20

Lyons, Charles, 87-89, 90

Lyotard, Jean-François, 197n3, 207n70, 259-60n24

Macdonald, Dwight, 24

Machosky, Brenda, 207n68

Maciunas, George, 183

Maeterlinck, Maurice, 72

magical realism, 3-4

Mallarmé, Stéphane, 21, 22, 64-68, 224nn13-14, 229n53, 234n104; *Afternoon of a Faun*, 76; ballet and, 227nn32-33; Book/*Livre* of, 22, 67-68, 94-95, 97-101, 231-32n84, 232n85, 232n95, 233n97; "Crisis of Verse," 69; "Don du Poëme," 78-80; "The Ecclesiastic," 64; health and spiritual crisis of, 68-69; *Hérodiade*, 22, 67, 70, 71, 75-83; "The Impressionists and Édouard Manet," 70, 81, 82; linguistic theory of, 69-70, 229n60; "Mimique," 22, 71-74, 84, 97; new aesthetics/poetics of, 68-75, 94, 100-101; Nietzsche and, 31; on political economy, 99-101, 231n80; "Restricted Action," 99-100; theater theory of, 71-73, 99-100, 233n103; *A Throw of the Dice Will Never Abolish Chance*, 69, 94, 225n19; Wölfflin and, 71. *See also Hérodiade*

Manet, Édouard, 81, 82, 204n50
Mao, Douglas, 4, 199nn11-12
Maravall, José Antonio, 205n58
Margravial Opera House, 27, 28, 29
Margueritte, Paul, 71-72, 226n28
Marinetti, F. T., 22
Marranca, Bonnie, 147, 159, 178, 254nn78-79, 258n15
Marx, Karl (and Marxism), 62, 130-32, 137, 205n55
masque forms and traditions, 2, 73, 87, 97, 113, 124, 125, 219n51, 258n15
Mass. *See* Catholicism and Catholic liturgy
materialism: allegory and, 19, 103, 106, 116, 124; Brecht and, 135; *Four Saints and*, 157, 165; in *Hérodiade*, 22, 76, 82, 87, 90-91; instruments as baroque forms, 151-52; Mallarmé and, 75; mimetic drama vs., 104; Nietzsche and, 35-37
Matthews, Edward, 158
McGuinness, Patrick, 84
Meillassoux, Quentin, 98
Melville, Stephen, 7
metatheater, 9, 127-29, 134, 165
Michaels, Walter Benn, 231n80
Michelangelo, 40
mimes and pantomime, 72-75, 98-100, 165, 211n103, 227n34
mimesis and mimetic representation: allegory and, 17-19, 243n85; baroque style vs., 37, 39-40, 48, 61-62, 71, 106, 116, 123-24, 208n79; Benjamin and, 104, 106, 127; Brecht and, 104-5; *Four Saints* and, 147, 165; Mallarmé and, 67, 69-71, 73-74, 76-77, 85, 98-99; Nietzsche and, 30, 45, 56, 63, 216n33; Trauerspiel and, 125-26
minimalism, 4, 5, 13, 20, 183, 185, 209n84
montage effects, 107, 168, 186
Monteverdi, Claudio, 47, 49-50, 58-59, 220n68
Moreau, Gustave: *The Apparition*, 87, *88*
Moretti, Franco, 129, 241n73
Morris, Mark, 23, 178
Morris, Robert, 13
Morris, William, 189
mosaics, 87, 90, 107, 143, 145
Mozart, Wolfgang, 2

Muñoz, José Esteban, 189
myths: Benjamin and loss of, 111, 134; Debord and loss of, 184; *Four Saints* and, 151; *Hérodiade* and, 77-78; of progressive history, 62-63

Nagel, Barbara, 24
new formalism, 21
Ngai, Sianne, 221n83
Nietzsche, Friedrich, 213n9; on ascetic ideal, 215n27; *Assorted Opinions and Maxims*, 37-38, 44, 47, 49; baroque conceptualized by, 10, 21-22, 36-41, 53, 57-63, 141-43, 212n2, 213n17; Benjamin and, 31, 139-45, 245nn104-5; *The Birth of Tragedy*, 31-34, 44-45, 47-48, 55, 68, 139-40, 142, 186, 216n33; Brecht and, 62; *The Case of Wagner*, 51-58, 61; *Dithyrambs of Dionysus*, 50, 58-59; *Ecce Homo*, 45, 50, 52-53, 61; eternal recurrence and, 40, 58, 140-41, 212n6; on God's death, 19, 68; *Human, All Too Human*, 31-34, 41, 43-44, 48, 50, 52, 66; linguistic theories of, 36-37, 69, 213n19, 214n22, 215n24; *Nachlass*, 47; *Nietzsche contra Wagner*, 51-52, 55; "On Truth and Lying," 35, 215n25; on rhetoric, 32-36, 38-40, 46-47, 214n20, 214n22, 215n24, 215n28; Sophism and, 16; *Untimely Meditations* ("Richard Wagner in Bayreuth"), 28-29, 38-39, 62; on Wagner's baroque style, 28-29, 34, 40-42, 48-58, 61-62, 142, 221n79
Nijinsky, Vaslav, 90, 248n28
Norman, Barnaby, 230n66
Nyong'o, Tavia, 255n86

Olds, Marshall, 229n57
O'Neill, Eugene, 63, 146
Opitz, Martin, 108
Orgel, Stephen, 11, 97
Origin of the German Trauerspiel (Benjamin), 21-22, 235n15; on baroque allegory, 118-30, 133, 238n45, 252n52; on baroque spatialization, 106-18; *Birth of Tragedy* and, 139-40, 142; *Le Cid* as inspiration for, 102; on German Expressionism, 108-11; on *Hamlet*, 119; on language, 238n47; on "origin," 161, 200n19, 238n42; paratactic

Index

form of, 107-8, 143; philosophy of history in, 111-15, 118, 119, 137-38, 141; on spectatorship, 103, 109-10, 113, 126-28; Stein's theater theory compared to, 148-49; theatricality of, 106-8; as theory of modern theater, 103-6, 148

ornament, 207n74; allegory and, 124; Benjamin and, 143; Foreman on, 205-6n61; in *Hérodiade*, 83-89, 90; Mallarmé and, 65, 83; Racine and, 230n65; sovereignty and, 117-18

Orpheus and Orphic movement, 6, 10, 12, 26, 49, 94

Palfrey, Simon, 208n79

Palladio, Andrea, 130, *131*

Panama Canal construction scandal (1892), 90-92, 231n80

Panofsky, Erwin, 238n45

pantomime. *See* mimes and pantomime

parabasis. *See* direct address

Payne, Alina, 207n74, 218n43

Paz, Octavio, 65

performance studies and performance art, 96, 246n3, 250n41

Peri, Jacopo, 47

Phelan, Peggy, 250-51n44

Picasso, Pablo, 152, 247n14

Plato, 52, 135

political economy: Benjamin's baroque and, 130-32, 139-42; in *Hérodiade*, 90-93, 99; Mallarmé on, 99-101, 231n80; Jack Smith and, 189-91; Stein and, 180-81; in Trauerspiel, 118, 130

Pollack, Della, 170

ponderación misteriosa, 129, 136, 241n70

postdramatic theater, 19, 72, 76, 104, 144, 172, 184, 186, 225n27

postmodernism, 24, 53, 197n3, 207nn69-70, 246n3

poststructuralism, 66, 143-44

Pound, Ezra, 1

Preciado, Paul, 211n101

proscenium arch: allegory and, 123-24; Bernini and, 11, 13; in early modern theater, 9-10, 17; landscape painting and, 251n51; performance studies and, 250n41; Wagner and, 27-28, 43

Puchner, Martin, 14, 44, 84, 96, 204n53, 215n26, 228n49, 254n68

queerness and queer epistemologies: baroque style and, 8, 19-21, 149, 181, 191; camp sensibilities and, 180-81; *Four Saints* and, 158-59, 175-76; *Hérodiade* and, 89; historiography and, 209n87; Mallarmé and, 101; Nietzsche and, 32-33, 36, 52; Jack Smith and, 189-90; Stein and, 180-81; theatricality and, 211n103; Wagner and, 32-33, 52

Racine, Jean, 22, 67, 80, 84-86, 164-65, 207n71, 230n65, 234n5

Rainer, Yvonne, 183-84

Rancière, Jacques, 182, 259-60n24

Rang, Florens Christian, 245n104

realism and realistic theater: absorption in, 89, 90; *Four Saints* vs., 180; Fried on, 204n50; Stein on, 159-60; Wilder on, 3, 198n7. *See also* mimesis and mimetic representation

Regietheater (director's theater), 184

Reinhardt, Max, 2, 3, 153

religion of art, 50, 68, 87, 90, 98, 164-65, 175-76

repetition: in *Four Saints*, 168, 170, 174; as rudiment of baroque, 5, 8; in Stein's theater theory, 161-62, 250-51n44, 250nn42-43

rhetoric and rhetorical devices: Benjamin on, 108, 142-43; classical-baroque binary in, 32-38, 53-54; gesture as ornament in, 30, 37, 49, 60; in *Hérodiade*, 76-77, 229n56; Mallarmé and, 96; Nietzsche and, 32-36, 38-40, 45-47, 50, 52-53, 60, 96, 142-43, 214n20, 214n22, 215n24, 215n28

Richard, Jean-Pierre, 66

Richter, Gerhard, 199n14

Riegl, Alois, 7, 108

Rinuccini, Ottavio, 47

Ripa, Cesare, 126, 240n60

Ritter, Johann Wilhelm, 239n53

ritual in Mallarmé's *Livre*, 95-98, 100

Roach, Joseph, 20-21, 48-49, 200n19, 220n66, 238n37

Robinson, Marc, 251n50, 253n64

Romanticism, 120-21, 133-34, 136-37, 239n53
Rosen, Charles, 128
Roßmann, Karl, 16
Ruddick, Lisa, 152, 248n18
ruination, 7, 52, 92, 103, 112, 118, 122, 129, 145, 153, 162, 186

Said, Edward, 232n93, 245n110
Sarduy, Severo, 181
scenery, 9, 104, 124, 127, 153-54, 202n35, 249n32
Schiller, Friedrich, 190
Schmitt, Carl, 114
Schneider, Rebecca, 31, 161, 209n87, 210n91
Scholem, Gershom, 103
secularization: allegory and, 121-22; Benjamin on, 68, 111-12, 120-21, 143, 236n19; Brecht and, 135; Mallarmé and, 68-69, 87, 97, 225n19; Nietzsche and, 31, 56, 63; Stein and, 160, 175; Wilder on, 2-3
Sedgwick, Eve, 8, 36, 52, 201n28
Seeling, Heinrich, 242n82
Semper, Gottfried, 211-12n1
Shakespeare, William, 11, 80, 105, 115, 119, 128, 129
Shaw, George Bernard, 63, 220n71, 231-32n84
Shaw, Mary Lewis, 95, 232n95
Shepherd, Reginald, 6, 200n16
Slawinski, Maurice, 203n42
Sloterdijk, Peter, 215n28, 222n89
Smith, Jack, 187-91, *188*, 259n19
Smith, Matthew Wilson, 42, 220n71
Smith, Pamela, 10-11
Sontag, Susan, 23, 143, 180, 181, 183, 242n76, 257n100
Sophism, 16, 31-35, 37, 38, 69, 213n19, 216n29, 225n21
Sousa Santos, Boaventura de, 191
sovereignty and sovereigns: Benjamin on, 113-15, 117-18, 123, 237n33; Brecht and, 134; *Hamlet* and, 129-30; spectatorship and, 125, 127, 134
space and spatialization: allegory and, 121-24; Benjamin on Trauerspiel and, 111-13; Brecht and, 137; deconstruction and, 144; *Four Saints* and, 148, 163-64;

in *Hérodiade*, 76, 81-82; theatricality and, 206n65
spectacle: allegory and, 122-23; Benjamin on, 22-23, 145; Bernini and, 10-12, 182, 203n42; of commodities, 132; Mallarmé and, 66-68, 74; Nietzsche on, 39, 56-57; propaganda and, 182, 191; temporality and, 74; Trauerspiel and, 119, 123-24
spectators and spectatorship: allegory and, 48, 125-27; baroque's appeal to, 11-14, 37, 48-49, 60-61; Benjamin and, 103, 109-10, 113, 126-28; Brecht and, 102, 134, 136, 137; defamiliarization and, 127; *Hérodiade* and, 90, 93; Mallarmé and, 95-96, 99; Nietzsche's baroque and, 40, 60-61; Stein and, 160-61, 165; Symbolists and, 248n28; total artwork and, 42
Spenser, Edmund: *Faerie Queene*, 237n33
Spinoza, Baruch, 30, 220n65
Stackhouse, Janifer, 236n26
Stein, Gertrude, 21; baroque inspirations of, 152-53; Benjamin and, 147-49, 152, 159, 246-47n7, 246n6; collaboration model of, 153; *Doctor Faustus Lights the Lights*, 178; *Four Saints in Three Acts*, 23; influence of, 256n91; Jameson on, 74; landscape and, 148, 163-64, 172, 252n52, 256n96; Nietzsche and, 31; "Plays," 148, 159-60, 163-64, 246n6; *Sacred Emily*, 162; Saint Teresa of Avila and, 148, 150, 152, 222n89, 254n79; theater theory of, 148-49, 159-65, 250-51n44, 250nn42-43; Wagner and, 151, 153, 163, 255n88. *See also Four Saints in Three Acts*
Stettheimer, Florine, 153-56, *154*, 180, 249n32
Strauss, David, 28
Strindberg, August, 63, 108
Symbolists and Théâtre d'Art, 72, 75, 85, 185, 248n28
Szondi, Péter, 48, 203-4n46, 204n49, 235n8

tableau vivant, 125, 155, 169
Teatro Olimpico, 130, *131*
temporality: allegory and, 121, 159-65; of baroque conventions, 20-21, 182-83, 210n91; in *Four Saints*, 168, 171-72; gesture and, 116-17; in *Hérodiade*, 76;

Index

297

in Mallarmé's "Mimique," 74; queerness and, 209n87; Stein and, 74, 148, 159-61, 251n50; in Trauerspiel, 112

Teresa of Avila, Saint, 148, 150, 152, 222n89, 254n79. *See also* Bernini, Gian Lorenzo; *Four Saints in Three Acts*

text and performance: deconstruction and, 144; *Four Saints* and, 166-70, 172-73, 253n66; Mallarmé and, 72, 73, 95, 98, 226n31, 228n49; Trauerspiel form and, 104

Theater am Schiffbauerdamm, 133, 242n82

theatricality: baroque style and, 29, 30, 40, 63, 110, 126-27, 202n37, 212n4; Benjamin on, 103, 106, 109-10, 118-30, 142-44, 239n54; Bernini and, 10-13, 202-3n38; deconstruction and, 232n93; *Four Saints* and, 153-54, 159; *Hérodiade* and, 75-77, 81-82, 89, 90; in linguistic theories, 36-37; Mallarmé and, 64, 66-68, 73, 75, 97-99, 101, 224nn11-12, 227n34; Nietzsche and, 30-31, 38-40, 43-50, 53, 56, 58, 60-61, 142-43, 218n44; performativity and, 214n22; queerness and, 211n103; Stein and, 161, 163-64; Wagner and, 42-48, 51-53, 56; of writing, 142-44, 170

theatrum mundi: baroque spatialization and, 113, 123; Baudelaire and, 123, 130; Benjamin on, 113, 130; Debord on, 184; Mallarmé's Book and, 97-98, 101; Nietzsche and, 36, 61, 215n25

Thibaudet, Albert, 65, 87, 90

Thomson, Virgil, 138, 151-58, 166-68, 170, 172-73, 175-81, 247n14, 248n15, 249n37, 255nn86-87

Tieck, Ludwig, 127

Toklas, Alice B., 152, 256n96

total artwork. *See Gesamtkunstwerk*

Trauerspiel: Brecht's epic theater compared to, 104, 134-39; crisis of experience and, 109-14; English influences on, 236n20; gesture in, 116-18, 123, 136-37; landscape and, 105-6, 122-23, 237n29, 238n42; in later theater forms, 236n18; metatheater of, 128-29; Nietzsche and, 44; redemption in, 106, 119, 123, 128-29, 136, 142, 187; *Ring* cycle and, 221n80; Shakespeare's works as, 237n34; sovereignty in, 113-15,

136; spatial dramaturgy of, 104-6; spectacle and, 119, 123-24; Stein's works compared to, 165; temporality in, 112; theatricality of, 110. *See also Origin of the German Trauerspiel*

Turner, Henry, 208n79

tyranny: baroque style and, 16; Benjamin on, 103-4, 106, 114-15, 117-18; Nietzsche's criticisms of Wagner, 56-58

Untersteiner, Mario, 215-16n29

Van Vechten, Carl, 156, 158, 164

Wadsworth Atheneum, 149-50

Wagner, Richard, 21-22; Bayreuth Festspielhaus and Festival, 27-28, *28*, 32, 75, 211-12n1; *Der Ring des Nibelungen*, 32, 42, 221n80; direct address in works of, 48-49, 60-61; *Gesamtkunstwerk* and, 42-43, 98; gesture in works of, 60; Mallarmé and, 98-99; modernist vision of, 29; Nietzsche and, 28-29, 32-34, 39-44, 48-58, 61-62, 142, 213n13, 221n79; *Opera and Drama*, 219n61; *Parsifal*, 41, 42, 50-51, 55-56, 112, 220-21n71; Stein compared to, 151, 153, 163, 255n88; *Tristan und Isolde*, 49-50, 87, 218n48

Waite, Geoff, 221n82

Walkowitz, Rebecca, 4, 199nn11-12

Warburg, Aby, 238n45

Warhol, Andy, 190

Watson, Steven, 24, 158, 247n14, 249n36

Wayne, Beatrice Robinson, 158

Weber, Samuel, 55, 66, 75, 125-26, 144, 200n17, 221n80, 227n34, 239nn54-55, 251n49

Webster, Jamieson, 37

Weigel, Sigrid, 18

Weill, Kurt, 138

Weinfield, Henry, 68, 77, 79-80, 95, 228n43, 229n53

Wellek, René, 7-9, 65, 210n98

Werfel, Franz: *Trojan Women*, 108

whiteness, 25, 211n99

Wilder, Thornton: "The Barock, or how to recognize a miracle in the daily life," 1-7, 10, 14-15, 24, 179-80, 200n17, 256n93; *Our Town*, 1, 4, 5, 24, 201n24; on realistic

Wilder, Thornton (*cont.*)
  theater, 198n7; Stein and, 179–80; on total artwork, 42; on Wagner, 220n71
Williamson, George S., 220n71
Wilson, Robert, 23, 147, 178, 185–87, 258–59n15, 259n19
Witt, Mary Ann Frese, 203n44
Wizisla, Erdmut, 243n88
Wölfflin, Heinrich, 7–8, 29–30, 63, 71
wonder: Baudelaire and, 123; Benjamin on, 136, 244nn92–93; Bernini and, 15; early modern conceptions of, 203n41; in Nietzsche's baroque style, 60–61; Stein and, 170, 178, 180

Young, Stark, 157, 164, 249n32

Zinn, Jon Kabat, 251n48
Zola, Émile, 68
Zweig, Stefan, 24